BEOWULF
AND THE BEOWULF *MANUSCRIPT*

Frontispiece. Fol. 179, recto and verso, of the *Beowulf* MS is a palimpsest. The recto is here reproduced in color to highlight those features of the MS that are obscured in black and white facsimiles (see Plate 14a).

reopul ꝼt bɲade hɲer onhand ge
luge heold tela ꝼiꝼtiᵹ pintɲu þa
ꝼɲod cyninᵹ eald eþel peaɲd oððe
on onᵹan dsoɲcū nihtcū dɲaca
ɲede on hɩa hoɲd be pɲot
ꝼɲan bɩorᵹh scɩapue feɲᵹ undiɲ lī
eldū uncuð þaþ on innan ᵹionᵹ nē
nɩt sɩpe hæðnū lī
hond ꝛince ꝼac ne
ꝼyððan þ d ꝼ ꝼpiɲde
ꝛype hɩor es eɲapte þ si
ᵹ fole bɩoɲn þɩaᵹo
bolᵹɲ þas xxxɩɩ

N ealles peoldū þɲiu hoɲda
enᵹꝺeꝼet ꝛylꝼes piſſū ᵹede lū
ꝛeod ac ꝼoɲ hɲɩɩɲ nedlan þ
haɩeda bɩiomon hɩte spoɩᵹ
ꝼɩɩoh þɩa dūh innɩ pɩol
ꝛeᵹ ꝛyn sɩᵹ fona inꝛtaɲde þ
dū ᵹyſt bɲ ᵹ ſtoð hɩ
ꝛe piɩ

KEVIN S. KIERNAN

Beowulf
and the Beowulf Manuscript

RUTGERS UNIVERSITY PRESS
New Brunswick, New Jersey

Copyright © 1981 by Rutgers, The State University of New Jersey

All rights reserved

Manufactured in the United States of America

Library of Congress Cataloging in Publication Data

Kiernan, Kevin S   1945–
    Beowulf and the Beowulf manuscript.
    Bibliography: p.
    Includes index.
    1. Beowulf.   2. Beowulf—Manuscripts.   3. British
Museum. MSS. (Cottonian Vitellius A. XV)   4. Nowell,
codex.   5. Manuscripts, Anglo-Saxon.   I. Title.

    PR1585.K5   1981   829′.3   80–27635
                ISBN 0–8135–0925–4

FOR AÏDINE

Contents

Preface

It is perhaps inevitable that some readers will be incredulous of an argument that dates *Beowulf* in the 11th century, no less than of one that would date *Hamlet* in the 20th century. Yet literary history can routinely prove that *Hamlet* was indeed produced in the early 17th century, while no linguistic or historical fact compels us to believe that *Beowulf* was written before the time of the only extant MS. There are, to be sure, pressing linguistic, historical, and cultural reasons for wanting the poem to be early, the earlier the better, but they are founded on desire, not fact, and they must not cloud our judgments. We want to see the deep past for a variety of lofty and trivial motives, and we are inclined to resent anything that threatens to obstruct our view. Our predecessors resented the "monkish blockheads" who interpolated the Christian elements in *Beowulf;* but over the years the date of *Beowulf* has been inching its way out of the misty past, and scholars now assume that a Christian, probably a cleric, actually wrote the poem. When did he live? If we really want to know, we cannot allow unabashed passions to decide the question for us.

My answer evolved, unavoidably it seemed to me, from a study of the scribal proofreading in the *Beowulf* MS. In the course of my investigation of the scribes' corrections, it became increasingly apparent that the scribes did not copy the MS mechanically, and that they understood the poem far better than is usually assumed. Their proofreading was authoritative, showing consistent care, intelligence, and attentiveness. I was obliged accordingly to regard their MS with perhaps unprecedented interest, and then with mounting excitement, as it began to take on the aspect of an authorized text. Freed from the old assumption that the *Beowulf* MS was necessarily a late copy of an early poem, I began to find recurring clues that ultimately led me to believe that the MS was contemporary with the poem. There was undoubtedly a new case to pursue, and reason enough to be skeptical of the old assumptions prohibiting it. The linguistic and historical evidence that always seemed to rule out a late date for the poem was clearly susceptible to alternative interpretations. The MS evidence I have used to argue that *Beowulf* is an early 11th-century poem can and will be interpreted in other ways too, but I doubt that it can be shown that all of the MS evidence consistently supports the view that the *Beowulf* MS is a late copy of an early poem. It is remarkable that the MS evidence all coheres to a pattern suggesting that the poem was actually revised in the extant MS.

When I wrote this book the consensus in print was that *Beowulf* was an 8th-century poem preserved in a MS of the late 10th or early 11th century. I have since learned that many scholars, skeptical too of the traditional arguments for an early date, have been busy reconsidering all aspects of the evidence. On 28 March 1980, at the meeting of the Medieval Association of the Pacific, John D. Niles gave historical reasons for a much later dating in "The Danes and the Date of *Beowulf*." At the University of Toronto an organized investigation was well underway, which came to my attention in December 1979, when the Centre for Medieval Studies asked me to participate in an international symposium to reconsider the date of composition of *Beowulf*. The results of this conference, held in Toronto from 20–23 April 1980, will be published in a special volume, "Approaches to the Date of Composition of *Beowulf*." The dates proposed, and fervently defended, range from the 7th to the 11th century, but much new evidence was brought to light supporting a considerably later date than ever thought possible before. Though no consensus was reached by those implicitly or explicitly supporting a late date, the new evidence unquestionably enhances the possibility of a MS contemporary with the poem. In fact, once the arguments of the participants had been published, a reinvestigation of the MS in light of them would necessarily have followed as a matter of course. But since the reinvestigation of the MS came first, a brief acknowledgment of some of these contributions to the question can highlight the extent to which they independently corroborate mine.

The linguistic and metrical arguments for an early date have been effectively undermined. Ashley Crandell Amos, in *Linguistic Means of Determining the Dates of Old English Literary Texts* (forthcoming from the Monograph Series of the Medieval Academy of America), has shown that the old linguistic tests alone cannot rule out a contemporary MS of the poem. Furthermore, the editorial group of the *Dictionary of Old English,* led by Angus Cameron and including Ashley Amos, Gregory Waite, Sharon Butler, and Antonette Healey, has discovered in the course of extensive comparative research that the mixture of forms in *Beowulf* is not in fact unnatural, and may reflect copying conventions in some late 10th- and early 11th-century scriptoria. Thomas Cable compared the meter of *Beowulf* with the meter of the 11th-century Chronicle poem *The Death of Edward* (1065), and found that though there was a difference in style there was no difference in the metrical paradigm. Even contractions as a means of dating lost ground: Cable noticed that *bealuleas kyng* in line 15b of *The Death of Edward* was an ordinary Type A line if the contraction *kyng* was expanded to *kyning;* Eric Stanley pointed to the metrically required, but supposedly obsolete form, *heahan* (not *hean*), in the 11th-century poem *The Gloria I.* It appears, then, that 11th-century poets had available to them metrical options reflected in these contracted and uncontracted spellings, just as later poets had available "loved" or archaic "lovéd," as their meter or mood required. Thus conservative spellings like *hean* in *Beowulf* cannot rule out late, disyllabic pronunciations where they are metrically desirable.

The historical premise for an early date, mainly the negative assumption that *Beowulf* could not have been composed during the Viking Age of the 9th and 10th centuries, has lost its former hold too. There was widespread agreement among the participants that the elimination of the Viking Age, by political history alone, was insecurely based. None of the participants, however, had considered the reign of Cnut the Great (1016–1035) as a viable possibility, because the popular date of the MS, "circa 1000," seemed to preclude it. Actually, Neil Ker's authoritative paleographical dating places the script in the first quarter of the 11th century, which of course includes a good part of Cnut's reign. Perhaps it is just as well that his reign was excluded, though, for as a result, the new historical arguments were not fettered to a specific time, but only tried to show that *Beowulf,* on historical grounds, could well have been composed after the Danish settlement. They incidentally showed that Cnut's reign was an eminently suitable time within this broad frame. While I am inclined to agree that the Viking Age of the 9th and 10th centuries was too hastily dismissed by earlier scholars as a possible period for the composition of *Beowulf*, I am still convinced that the best historical period is the Age of Cnut.

Three historical contributions to the conference, Raymond I. Page's "The Audience of *Beowulf* and the Vikings," Alexander Murray's "*Beowulf*, the Danish Invasions, and Royal Genealogy," and Roberta Frank's "Skaldic Verse and the Date of *Beowulf*," most obviously support my convictions. Page convincingly argues that sophisticated Anglo-Saxons of the 9th and 10th centuries would have been able to distinguish between current Danish marauders and good Danes of the distant past, who at least under Hroðgar were no longer tied to a life of rapine. Murray shows beyond reasonable doubt that the incorporation of the Danish Scyld and Scef by the West Saxon genealogy was a late 9th-century innovation, designed to face the political reality of the Danish settlement; hence the opening of *Beowulf* is in part a genealogical allusion to the line of Alfred, and cannot very well predate Alfred. Frank assembles an impressive array of lexical, syntactic, thematic, and cultural parallels from late 10th- and early 11th-century skaldic verse, and concludes that the skald most like the *Beowulf* poet was Sighvat the Poet, King Olaf's skald. All three of these essays furnish extremely persuasive reasons for dating *Beowulf* after the Danish settlement, but they all implicitly support a narrower dating within the reign of Cnut. Thus, as the opening lines of *Beowulf* tell us, Hroðgar's reign comes at the end of a Viking Age, when a mighty dynasty of *Þeod-scyldingas* lost the need for raiding other lands and were honored internationally. The West Saxon genealogy was also Cnut's, and the one that begins *Beowulf* records the Danish Scylding line; the two separate branches, however, were ultimately united when Cnut married Æthelred's widow, Emma. Finally, a good deal of the skaldic connections derive from the early 11th century, when Sighvat himself composed verse for Cnut.

At any rate, these revolutionary interpretations of the language and the historical context of *Beowulf* open the way as never before for serious consideration of an equally revolutionary interpretation of the *Beowulf* MS. If the linguistic and historical evidence can fit a 9th- or 10th-century date, when Anglo-Danish relations were at least ambivalent, it certainly cannot exclude an early 11th-century one, when Anglo-Saxons, Anglo-Danes, and Danes were all united under a powerful Danish Scylding lord. If *Beowulf* was composed in the early 11th century, the single extant MS is contemporary with the poem and may well be the first formal copy of it ever made. The polemics that will naturally arise from this suggestion will run their best course if they are based on facts rather than desires. Some needless arguments can be avoided, too, if we remember that paleographical and codicological facts must ultimately be evaluated, as they can only have been gathered, by direct and prolonged access to the MS, not to the FSS, no matter how faithful or reliable they may seem.

Acknowledgments

I have accumulated many welcome debts in the course of writing this book. I shall always be grateful to the British Library, Department of Manuscripts, for giving me daily access to Cotton Vitellius A. xv., and permission to study it under high-intensity and ultraviolet lighting, throughout April 1977, and again in March 1979. As a result of this cooperation I can be confident in the accuracy of my descriptions. I must especially thank Dr. M. A. E. Nickson and Miss Janet Backhouse, assistant keepers of MSS, for patiently answering my questions and for helping me track down uncatalogued information on Cotton Vitellius A. xv. The Photographic Service of the British Library prepared the photographs, including the frontispiece, a color reproduction of the palimpsest, fol. 179 recto. All of the photographs were newly made for this book, with the exception of the first page of *Beowulf,* which was not rephotographed to avoid unnecessary wear to a page always on display.

Many busy scholars agreed to read the entire typescript at various stages in its life and made substantive suggestions for revision. I am accordingly very much obliged for the generosity and encouragement of Professors Whitney F. Bolton, David S. Durant, Donald K. Fry, Stephen Manning, Fred C. Robinson, Walter Scheps, and Robert D. Stevick. Their expert guidance changed the book in ways they will readily see. I must also thank Professors Joan Blythe and Rupert Pickens for reading portions of the typescript and making helpful suggestions; Dr. Ann Blues for checking some details for me in the *Beowulf* MS while she was in London in the spring of 1978; and Mr. Joe Nickell and Professor Roy F. Leslie for providing me with information on infrared photography and digital image processing.

I have been helped, too, by the National Endowment for the Humanities, which provided a research grant in the summer of 1975 to study paleography and codicology at first hand at the Pierpont Morgan Library in New York. My department and college at the University of Kentucky have provided consistent support: a sabbatical leave in 1976–1977, and numerous grants (including a subsidy for the color plate of fol. 179r) from the University of Kentucky

Research Foundation between 1976 and the present, gave me the time and the means for such an extensive and expensive project; Professor Joseph A. Bryant, chairman of the Department of English, was interested and encouraging from the start; and Miss Helen Farmer, our administrative assistant (now retired), planned my trips with care and efficiency. My parents, Mr. and Mrs. Terence Kiernan, and my wife's parents, Mr. and Mrs. Necdet Biyal, gave the abiding support only families can, as well as ideal places to stay near New England and New York libraries. Warm thanks go to Mrs. Venus Keen, too, of Pinner, Middlesex, for making me feel so welcome on my trips to London.

Acknowledgments are due the British Library Board for permission to quote from Cottonian MSS. Repairing and Binding Account 1839, Add. MS. 24,932, Harley MS. 7055, and Cotton MS. Vitellius A. XV.; D. C. Heath and Company for permission to quote from the third edition of F. Klaeber, *Beowulf and the Fight at Finnsburg* (Lexington, Mass.: D. C. Heath & Co., 1950); Columbia University Press for permission to quote from The Anglo-Saxon Poetic Records; the Council of the Early English Text Society for permission to quote from the Zupitza-Davis facsimile of *Beowulf* (vol. 245, 1959, reprint 1967); Oxford, Bodleian Library, for permission to quote from MS Add. D. 82 and MS Junius 105; Rosenkilde and Bagger for permission to quote from Kemp Malone's facsimile of *The Nowell Codex* (Early English Manuscripts in Facsimile, vol. 12); and Oxford University Press for permission to quote from Alistair Campbell's *Old English Grammar* (1959), Neil R. Ker's *Catalogue of Manuscripts Containing Anglo-Saxon* (1957), and Kenneth Sisam's *Studies in the History of Old English Literature* (1953). I was lucky to have an extremely efficient typist, Mrs. Nikki Swingle, and an equally efficient copyeditor, Ms. Barbara Westergaard. Finally, I would like to thank Mr. Herbert F. Mann, director of Rutgers University Press, and Ms. Leslie Mitchner, managing editor, for their enthusiasm and care in seeing the book through the press.

My greatest debt is to my wife, Aïdine, as my dedication tries vainly to express.

BEOWULF
AND THE BEOWULF *MANUSCRIPT*

Introduction

It may well be surprising that a study of *Beowulf* in conjunction with its unique MS represents a radical departure from all previous approaches to the poem. In fact, the *Beowulf* MS has scarcely been studied at all. It still holds a wealth of undiscovered paleographical and codicological evidence, which, under ordinary circumstances, textual scholars would have uncovered and weighed long ago, as a matter of course, for the purpose of founding a reliable text. This evidence has remained safely hidden away because most editors of the poem have relied on photographic FSS of the MS, and, often enough, modern transcriptions of the FSS, rather than on the MS itself. Their tacit justification for this decidedly unorthodox procedure is that the MS cannot possibly hold any relevant textual evidence that FSS would not show as well. For, however variegated and contentious *Beowulf* studies are in all other respects, there was until very recently complete unanimity in the view that *Beowulf* is an early Anglo-Saxon poem preserved in a late Anglo-Saxon MS. The chronological gulf between the poem and the MS is usually reckoned to be two to three centuries. Under these circumstances, we are lucky to have an extant MS at all, but still rather unlucky to have such a late one. Surely, the broad paleographical features of a MS that ends an untraceably ancient transmission of the archetype are not textually vital. *Beowulf and the Beowulf Manuscript* challenges the unproven premise that *Beowulf* is an early poem. It argues instead, ultimately on the basis of extraordinary paleographical and codicological evidence, that the poem is contemporary with the MS.

The argument of the book is presented in three main stages. The first stage reconsiders the historical and linguistic evidence that has seemed to justify the neglect of the MS, and concludes that, historically and linguistically, both the poem and the MS could have been created in the early 11th century. The second stage is an extensive physical description of Cotton Vitellius A. xv., the composite codex in which the *Beowulf* MS now resides. The immediate relevance of this description is that it affords a clear view of the construction of the *Beowulf* MS, in relation to the construction of contiguous texts, and leads to the conclusion that the poem could have been copied in the early 11th century as a separate codex. The third stage studies the *Beowulf* MS as a contemporary MS of the poem. A variety of paleographical and codicological evidence shows that the poem may have been still undergoing revision while the MS was being copied, and that it was again undergoing revision later in the 11th century. In short, the evidence suggests that the actual creation of *Beowulf,* as we now know it, is partially preserved in the MS that has come down to us.

This relatively straightforward argument is necessarily embedded in a long and complicated train of subsidiary arguments that can be fruitfully summarized here. Part 1, "The Poem's Eleventh-Century Provenance," argues that the paleographical dating of the MS, roughly between 975 and 1025, can be safely placed on historical grounds after 1016. Anglo-Saxon scriptoria during the reign of Æthelred Unræd (978–1016) would not have copied a poem that praised the Danish Scylding dynasty, while the latest Scyldings, led by Swein Forkbeard, plundered and murdered throughout the country. By 1016 the Danes had conquered England. Swein's son, Cnut the Great, soon made England the center of his dynasty, and by the way provided a suitable historical context for copying a poem like *Beowulf.* But Cnut's reign (1016–1035) also provided an excellent environment for the creation of the poem, and we must not neglect the exciting possibility that the poem is contemporary with the extant MS. Until now, the origin of the poem has nearly always been restricted to the 8th century or earlier on the rough historical grounds that a poem eliciting sympathy for the Danes could not have been composed by Anglo-Saxons during the Viking Age of the 9th and 10th centuries. Historically, at least, there is a better argument for an 11th-century, post-Viking origin of the poem, since an 8th-century poem would still have to be transmitted by Anglo-Saxons through the Viking Age.

The great problem of accepting an early 11th-century provenance of *Beowulf* is linguistic, not historical. On closer scrutiny, the linguistic arguments for an early date (or against a late date) are by no means decisive. The specific linguistic tests of the poem's antiquity are especially weak: the syntactical tests magnify the occurrence in *Beowulf* of some acknowledged archaisms found in unquestionably late verse; the phonetic-metrical tests are based on subjective interpretations of the meter that require sweeping, yet inconsistently selective emendations to unrecorded, early, linguistic forms; and the lonely phonetic-morphological-orthographical test is based on a MS "ghost." The most compelling linguistic evidence that *Beowulf* is an early poem that has endured a long and complex transmission is its rich mixture of linguistic forms. The language of the extant MS is basically Late West Saxon, but this base is permeated with apparent non–West Saxonisms and, more significantly, with earlier linguistic forms, all of which would seem to prove that the poem had passed through many dialect areas on the way to its present form. There are, however, other explanations for this mixture of forms that do not rule out an 11th-century provenance, and do not even require a linguistically diverse transmission of the text.

Late West Saxon was a standard literary dialect used throughout England in the early 11th century. Complete orthographical uniformity, however, even in West Saxon territory, cannot be expected in an age before printing and formal dictionaries, and all Late West Saxon texts exhibit a natural mixture of forms, including some early forms. If the *Beowulf* MS was copied in non–West Saxon territory, there would be good reason to expect the occasional intrusion of late, non–West Saxon spellings in the text, as indeed is the case. The mixture of forms in the poem is further complicated by the fact that Anglo-Saxon poets of all periods shunned the language of prose, and consciously employed an artificial, archaic, poetic diction, whose roots were in Anglian territory. This fact explains the persistent occurrence of certain early, non–West Saxon forms beside the basically Late West Saxon language of the MS as a whole. Finally, if the poet and his two scribes each spoke a slightly different dialect, a confusing mixture of occasional spellings in the MS might well have been inevitable. An 11th-century convergence of all of these factors in *Beowulf* explains the mixture of forms, and accordingly eliminates the need to presume a long and complicated transmission of the text. The 11th-century provenance of *Beowulf* is historically and linguistically possible.

Part 2, "The History and Construction of the Composite Codex," prepares the way for a close analysis of the *Beowulf* MS. The composite codex, known as British Library MS Cotton Vitellius A. XV., to which the *Beowulf* MS belongs, has never been fully described in English, and a full description is desperately needed. The only existing study (in German) is not only out of date and rather inaccessible; it is also demonstrably inaccurate in dating, foliation, and collation. Moreover, it is rendered practically worthless as a reference, because among its many other errors it mistakenly uses a foliation of the codex that was abandoned in 1884, thirty-five years before the description of the codex was published. But a complete description of Cotton Vitellius A. XV. is needed for another, even more urgent reason. What is now the official foliation of the *Beowulf* MS is inaccurate, and it cannot be corrected without discussing Cotton Vitellius A. XV. as a whole. A new description of the entire codex, then, has the practical advantage of facilitating references to the *Beowulf* MS.

At present, it is very difficult indeed to make clear references to folios in the *Beowulf* MS, because a single, acceptable foliation has not been established. Thus, one FS uses the official foliation, a second FS uses a foliation written on the MS leaves, and a third FS uses the same MS foliation, while acknowledging the technical rectitude of the official foliation. As a result, it is not possible simply to refer, for example, to fol. 133 of the *Beowulf* MS, for it will not be clear which foliation it belongs to: fol. 133 is the second leaf of the *Beowulf* MS in the official foliation, but the fourth leaf in the MS foliation. Even those scholars who accept the official foliation have not been able to ignore the MS foliation because of the FSS, and because the different numbers on the MS leaves always need to be explained. Consequently, those who accept the official foliation still use the MS foliation in tandem with it, so that fol. 133 is normally referred to as fol. 133(130). Obviously, a complicated system of reference like this vitiates the purpose of a foliation. What makes matters even worse is that the official foliation, in addition to perpetuating some of the errors of the MS foliation, has been pervasively wrong since a flyleaf that it counts was removed from the codex. All of these difficulties are easily resolved by abandoning the confusing official foliation and by correcting the MS foliation in the few places where it is wrong. Except for two numbers, the foliation written on the *Beowulf* MS is accurate. For convenience of reference it needs to be reinstated as the official foliation.

The inadequacy of the current official foliation is best explained by discussing the flyleaves of Cotton Vitellius A. xv., which account for the marked discrepancies between the official and the MS foliations. A description of these prefixed leaves is useful in itself, for they have not been fully or accurately represented before, but a knowledge of their contents helps justify a return to the MS foliation. In addition, one of the leaves contains a scrap of new information about the state of the *Beowulf* MS before the fire of 1731. This subject is further investigated in a separate section on the history of the multiple foliations of the composite codex. Until now, scholars have mistakenly thought that the composite codex was not foliated in its entirety until after the fire. The discovery of two distinct foliations before the fire provides startling proof that the *Beowulf* MS was missing a folio at the time. A study of the various foliations (six different ones are documented and dated) shows precisely how three different folios from *Beowulf* were shifted from place to place from the early 17th century to the late 18th century.

To an extent, then, it is necessary to study Cotton Vitellius A. xv. as a whole in order to establish a simple and accurate foliation for the *Beowulf* MS. The utter confusion in the current system of foliation, and the history of the many abortive efforts to provide a correct foliation, are good indications of the astonishing lack of interest scholars have shown in Cotton Vitellius A. xv. and the MSS that comprise it. The rest of Part 2 is devoted to describing the physical makeup of the various MSS, and to defining their relation to the codex as a unit. To begin with, in Cotton Vitellius A. xv. Sir Robert Cotton artificially combined two totally unrelated codices, a 12th-century collection known as the Southwick Codex, and an 11th-century collection (which includes *Beowulf*) known as the Nowell Codex. This basic construction of Cotton's codex is self-evident. What is far more interesting, but not at all self-evident, is the basic construction of the Southwick and Nowell codices. The evidence shows that both are themselves composite codices. The original construction of the Southwick and Nowell codices has remained somewhat obscure to scholars because the fire of 1731 destroyed the threads and folds of the gatherings, reducing books to a stack of separate leaves. To recreate the Anglo-Saxon genesis of the book in which *Beowulf* was actually written, it is necessary to deduce the most probable construction of the original gatherings.

The task is comparatively simple in the case of the Southwick Codex, though no one before has ever deduced from the evidence at hand that the Southwick Codex is a Middle English composite of two late Old English MSS, copied by the same scribe at different times in his life. The original gatherings of these two MSS can be confidently reconstructed on the basis of sheet and quire signatures that were made in late Middle English times when the new book was rebound from old MSS. But there are no sheet or quire signatures on the leaves of the Nowell Codex, and the job of reconstructing the original gatherings is considerably more complicated. Strangely, the most reliable method of reconstruction has been used to identify only one gathering. Each vellum sheet has, of course, a hair and a flesh side, and the difference in color and texture between them is noticeable. Gatherings can be identified, usually with virtual certitude, by collating the hair and flesh sides of separate folios, to see if two leaves that are presumed to be two halves of the same folded sheet are in fact conjugate. The method is not infallible, because the pattern of hair and flesh sides occasionally permits alternative gatherings, but usually there is other paleographical evidence that confirms one description over another. Moreover, the method can eliminate as impossible some established descriptions of the original gatherings; it can prove beyond doubt that some falsely paired folios are nonconjugate, and so could not once have been a single, folded sheet of vellum.

A close study of the original gatherings of the Nowell Codex leads to a revolutionary view of the *Beowulf* MS. The usual view is that *Beowulf* was copied as the fourth item in a basically prose codex. The traditional description of the gatherings seems to confirm this view by showing that the scribe began copying *Beowulf* within the last prose gathering, making the *Beowulf* MS an inextricable part of the prose codex. But a close analysis of the hair-and-flesh patterns throughout the Nowell Codex reveals that the scribe could have begun copying the *Beowulf* MS on a new gathering, while distinct differences in format and in execution indicate that the prose codex and the *Beowulf* MS were originally copied as separate books. It now seems that the Nowell Codex became a composite codex in two stages: first, the *Beowulf* MS was combined with the prose codex, probably soon after *Beowulf* was copied; then, undoubtedly, the *Judith* fragment was added on in early modern times at the end of this composite codex by ripping out a sheet from the *Beowulf* MS and using it as a cover for the late accretion.

The discovery that *Beowulf* was probably copied as a separate codex strengthens the argument that *Beowulf* is an 11th-century poem preserved in an 11th-century MS. Certainly, it suggests that *Beowulf* was important to the scriptorium in which it was copied, and that it had an 11th-century audience who understood it and appreciated its merits. Textual scholars have always assumed that the poem was mechanically copied by scribes who, since they were largely ignorant of its meaning, were consequently lazy and inattentive. Yet one of the most striking indications that *Beowulf* at first existed as a separate codex emerges from the scribes' manifest efforts to provide an accurate copy of the poem. The first scribe carefully proofread his part of *Beowulf*, but did not proofread the prose texts; the second scribe carefully proofread his own part of *Beowulf*, and the first scribe's part, but again not the prose texts. Thus, the scribal proofreading of *Beowulf* alone strongly implies that the *Beowulf* MS once existed as a separate codex. More important, it is eloquent testimony that the scribes were neither lazy nor inattentive in copying the poem; on the contrary, they understood and appreciated it enough to want an accurate copy. In any case, *Beowulf* was obviously a special poem in the early 11th century, and all the indications are that it was intelligently copied in our extant MS as a separate codex.

Part 3, "The *Beowulf* Codex and the Making of the Poem," studies the MS as a separate codex from the entirely new perspective that the MS and the remarkable poem it preserves share the same 11th-century origin. A belief in the absolute textual and paleographical authority of the MS has, to be sure, revolutionary implications for the study of the poem. Until now, it has been impossible to see the MS as anything other than a very late transcript of a very early poem, and this limited view has not only justified many scores of needless emendations, but has made the conscious neglect of paleographical and codicological evidence appear to be a sound editorial principle. By this view, the 11th-century scribes are so hopelessly distant from the archetype, and separated by so many intermediate copies, that they cannot have had any better knowledge of it than we do today. These assumptions are invalidated by postulating a contemporary MS. If *Beowulf* had no appreciable transmission at all, the degree of corruption reflected in all current editions must be challenged, for the causes of deep-seated corruption are gone. Moreover, the fresh conviction that the MS has a good chance of being right where it was always perceived to be wrong has a liberating effect

on the most intractable cruces. At the same time, a rigorous textual conservatism becomes an exciting means of discovering new and intriguing
variations in alliterative and metrical patterns, most of which have gone
unnoticed in *Beowulf* because of the doubtful assumption that an early
poet would adhere mechanically to standard patterns. Only by rejecting
those emendations and interpolations based solely on an arid application
of "rules" can the individual style of a late, traditional poet be studied.

The theoretical authority of the *Beowulf* MS is most effectively vindicated by the quality and extent of the scribal proofreading. There can
be no doubt whatever that the MS was subjected to thorough and intelligent scrutiny, by both scribes, while the copying was in progress and
after it was done. The nature of the proofreading firmly establishes the
authority of the MS. The two scribes' written corrections and erasures
unequivocally identify the kinds of errors each scribe was prone to
make, and frequently show, as well, how alert the scribe was in the act
of copying, for many corrections were made at the moment of the incipient error. The erasures (all of which were studied under ultraviolet
light) are particularly informative in this respect, because the erased
material can be used to recreate the causes of scribal error. All previous
studies of scribal error in *Beowulf* are founded on editorial emendations,
but this reasoning is circular, and hence untrustworthy. In most cases
a conjectural emendation is only presumptive evidence of an error, and
even when an error is certain, an emendation without the aid of another
text is at best only a good guess at what the correct reading might have
been. The scribes, on the other hand, have identified unquestionable
errors, and have presumably corrected them on the authority of the
exemplar.

The vast evidence of scribal proofreading clearly illustrates the
importance of a close paleographical investigation of the MS. Surely, no
valid assessment of the reliability of the scribes (or the authority of the
MS) can afford to ignore the scribes' written corrections and erasures,
and yet no editor has ever taken them into account. On the contrary,
there are several cases in all editions of the poem where a scribal correction has itself been subjected to a conjectural emendation. In such
cases we can be sure that the MS reading, however difficult it may be,
is right, and the emendation is wrong. Paleographical study of the
scribes' work also reveals that the second scribe's connection with the
MS was not limited to copying and proofreading. Apparently the MS

remained in the second scribe's possession, presumably as part of a monastic library, for this scribe continued to work with the MS long after he had originally copied it. He has restored readings that were later damaged through accident or by ordinary wear and tear, most notably on the last page of the MS, where he freshened up a badly faded text. But the most extraordinary instance of his later work is that he made a palimpsest of an entire folio, and copied on it a new text.

The palimpsest provides startling paleographical evidence that *Beowulf* was revised in the course of the 11th century, long after the original text was copied. It is certain that the entire folio, containing lines 2207–2252, was scraped and washed down after the binding of the MS, for the palimpsest is part of the outside sheet of a gathering, yet the vellum's surface contrasts sharply with its conjugate leaf. Scholars have long believed that all of the original text on the folio in question was freshened up by a later hand, but a recent study has shown that the handwriting is still in fact the second scribe's, in a later stage of development. In any event, there is no credible reason for the palimpsest other than revision. A full paleographical and codicological investigation supports this conclusion in various ways. An objective transcription of the new text on the folio discloses a number of anomalous linguistic forms, which can be interpreted as signs of later attrition in the standard literary dialect, a process that accelerated as the 11th century advanced. A closer look at the badly damaged condition of the text, particularly at the textual lacunas, shows that the revised text was shorter than the original text, that parts of the revised text were erased for some reason, and that a full restoration *of the revised text* was never carried out.

The incipient state of the text on the palimpsest, and the fact that it contains in any case a late revision, opens the possibility that the *Beowulf* MS is in effect an unfinished draft of the poem. As incredible as it may seem, there is considerable paleographical and codicological support for the view that the *Beowulf* MS actually preserves the last formative stages in the creation of the epic. Three lines of text thematically related to the new text on the palimpsest have been imperfectly, but deliberately, deleted on the next folio, verso. The erasing was never finished, though it seems likely that the vellum was being prepared for a new text, as well. Presumably, both folios are part of the same revision. An analysis of the construction of the *Beowulf* MS provides a possible explanation for the purpose of this revision. The palimpsest begins a self-contained unit of the MS. It is the first leaf of the last two gatherings. The number of sheets in these last two gatherings, the manner in which the sheets are arranged, and the number of rulings to the sheets, are unique in the *Beowulf* MS. It is possible, then, that this part of the MS formerly existed separately, and was artificially appended to the extant MS. If so, the revised text on the palimpsest may have been written to provide a smoother, more natural transition between the two, originally distinct, and perhaps even totally unrelated MSS.

The theory is based on paleographical and codicological grounds, and it is defended with other paleographical and codicological facts. But it is surprisingly corroborated as well by the three-part structure of the poem:

1. Beowulf's fights in Denmark with Grendel and Grendel's dam;
2. His homecoming, and report to Hygelac;
3. His fight with the dragon and his death in Geatland.

Indeed, many critics have argued that the first and last parts once existed as separate poems, or oral narratives, and that the homecoming was composed at a later stage to link the Danish and Geatish narratives. The paleographical and codicological evidence leads to precisely the same conclusion. The palimpsest is the first folio of the dragon episode. And there is paleographical and codicological proof that the gathering immediately preceding the palimpsest, which holds the text of Beowulf's homecoming, was copied by the second scribe *after* he had copied the last two gatherings of the MS. The obvious conclusion is that the Danish and Geatish exploits of Beowulf were first brought together in the extant MS by the second scribe. The aesthetic fusion of these parts does not reflect a dim, romantic view of a non-Anglo-Saxon past, but rather a vivid imaginative response to chilling contemporary events. The fall of a great and noble hero, and the imminent extinction of the race he ruled, was well understood by this 11th-century Anglo-Saxon who had recently seen the fall of Alfred's house and the subsumption of his homeland in the Danish empire. The second scribe begins to look like "the last survivor of a noble race," while the *Beowulf* MS, the treasure he continued to polish after the death of his old lord, no longer looks like a reproduction.

1

‿‿‿‿‿‿‿‿‿‿‿‿‿‿‿‿‿‿‿‿‿‿‿‿‿‿‿‿‿‿‿‿‿

The Poem's Eleventh-Century Provenance

Beowulf, we are told, was first written down sometime in the 7th or 8th century, in one of the Anglian parts of England; over the succeeding centuries it was transmitted through the major dialect areas, undergoing dialectal "translation" all the while, until it reached its present, Late West Saxon form in our single extant MS, Cotton Vitellius A. xv.[1] Paleographical dating places the MS at the end of the 10th century or the beginning of the 11th, or, roughly speaking, between the years 975 and 1025.[2] It is usually dated "for convenience," as Kemp Malone says,

---

1. A classic statement of this theory of transmission is in Jane Weightman, *The Language and Dialect of the Later Old English Poetry,* p. v. It is the underlying assumption of all previous discussions of the language of *Beowulf.*

2. These are loose limits, based on Neil R. Ker's dating of the script as "s. x/xi" in his *Catalogue of Manuscripts Containing Anglo-Saxon,* pp. xvii and 281. Within quarter-century limits, s. x/xi presumably means early 11th century: Ker says that his list of MSS (pp. xv–xix) "is in three parts, in order to show how many of these principal manuscripts were written (1) before, (2) in, and (3) after the eleventh century" (p. xv), and MSS dated s. x/xi are in part 2; moreover, he explicitly says that a date "at the beginning . . . of the half-century would be expressed as s. x/xi" (p. xx). Nonetheless, I have included the late 10th century in my reckoning because Ker also says, "All my dates are certainly not right within the limits of a quarter-century. I can only hope that not too many of them are wrong within the limits of a half-century" (p. xx). On some of the problems of dating the script, see Max Förster, "Das Alter der Schreiberhände," in *Die Beowulf-Handschrift,* pp. 36–46, who dates it between 980 and 1020. Förster's preference for the late 10th century, "oder um das Jahr 1000 herum" (p. 46), is based on an unacceptably restrictive dating of the first hand of *The Blickling Homilies,* which bears some resemblance to the second hand of *Beowulf.* Ker

"circa A.D. 1000,"[3] but historical considerations, to be discussed in a moment, make a date after 1016 most probable. A more precise dating of the MS does not, in itself, alter the main theory: the text of *Beowulf* is supposed to have endured the vicissitudes of three centuries or so of scribal transmission. There is good reason to believe, however, that *Beowulf* was created, not in the 7th or 8th century, but in the 11th century, and that our extant MS adequately preserves the original creation. A review of the linguistic evidence, mainly the infamous "mixture of forms" that "points plainly to a checkered history of the written text,"[4] shows that there is no reason to assume a complicated transmission for *Beowulf* at all. Taken together, the linguistic and historical evidence plainly point to an 11th-century provenance for the poem, as well as for the MS.

The arguments against a long and complicated transmission of *Beowulf* are, unfortunately, long and complicated. For clarity and ease of reference they are presented under four main headings: The Historical Context of the Extant Manuscript, The Linguistic Tests for an Early Date, The Late Literary and the Early Poetic Dialects, and The Mixture of Forms in *Beowulf.*

---

dates the script of the *Homilies* s. x/xi, and Rudolph Willard, the editor of the FS of the *Homilies,* dates the MS in the early 11th century, following Ker (*The Blickling Homilies,* p. 13). Paleographical dating is not, of course, an exact science. After the middle of the 10th century, the dated charters become the chief guides for dating script (Ker, *Catalogue,* p. xx), and this guide can be precarious since the charters are likely to come from main centers where handwriting, under the strong influence of the Benedictine Reform, changed more rapidly than in backwater scriptoria. The danger is well illustrated in the *Beowulf* MS itself, where the second scribe writes a more old-fashioned script than the first by resisting the change toward caroline minuscule. Evidently the *Beowulf* scriptorium was not unduly influenced by the Reform, perhaps because it was a provincial ecclesiastical center, rather than a monastic center.

3. Ed., *The Nowell Codex, British Museum Cotton Vitellius A. XV., Second MS,* p. 11. Ker warns us that approximate year numbers like "*c.* 1000" are "not satisfactory dates for manuscripts datable only by their script and decoration unless we remember how approximate they must be" (p. xx). There has been a tendency among *Beowulf* scholars to interpret circa 1000 as a *terminus ad quem* for the MS, eliminating without foundation the early 11th century.

4. Frederick Klaeber, ed., *Beowulf and the Fight at Finnsburg,* p. lxxxviii. *Beowulf* citations are from this edition unless otherwise noted.

The Historical Context of the Extant Manuscript

Assuming that the paleographers are right in their estimates, it is virtually certain that the poem was copied sometime after 1016. It is, at least, highly unlikely that a poem so obviously sympathetic to the Danes, and indeed extolling them for their peaceful foreign policy, could have been copied in Late West Saxon during the calamitous reign of Æthelred Unræd, from 978 to 1016. Danish-English relations were never more hostile. The Anglo-Saxon Chronicle for the years of Æthelred's rule is little more than a grim record of Danish invasions and English defeats.[5] In the 980s, with sudden raids all along the English coast, Danish Vikings sacked and murdered and plundered at will. In the 990s the Viking incursions escalated, the raiders beginning to take on, as F. M. Stenton observes, "the character of an organized army."[6] At the start of the decade Byrhtnoð fell in the proud defeat at Maldon, and a new phase in Viking-English relations commenced when "it was determined that tribute should first be paid to the Danish men because of the great terror they were causing along the coast" (A.D. 991).

The tribute did not halt the terror for long. There was fighting and pillaging almost immediately afterward, and in 994 Olaf Tryggvason of Norway and Swein Forkbeard of Denmark descended with a combined force of ninety-four warships. It was, says Stenton, "the most formidable invasion which England had experienced for half a century, and it was made more dangerous by the fact that some English nobles despairing, it would seem, of Æthelred's government, were prepared to accept Swein as king" (*Anglo-Saxon England*, p. 378). Swein, who like Hroðgar, traced his descent back to the legendary Scyld, would have to wait another eighteen years before "all the nation regarded him as full

---

5. Chronicle references are by year, from Dorothy Whitelock et al., eds., *The Anglo-Saxon Chronicle*. For two recent accounts of the Viking invasions of England and their aftermath, see H. R. Loyn, "The Course of the Scandinavian Invasions in England *c*. 954–*c*. 1100," in *The Vikings in Britain*, pp. 81–101; and Gwyn Jones, "Svein Forkbeard, Saint Olaf, Knut the Great," in *A History of the Vikings*, pp. 354–386.

6. *Anglo-Saxon England*, p. 376.

king" (A.D. 1013). And it is safe to say that in the intervening years there were very few Englishmen who would have been able to read or hear with equanimity of the founding of the Danish Scylding dynasty in the proem of *Beowulf* (lines 1–52).[7] It is unimaginable that an English monastic or ecclesiastical establishment from any area would have engaged scribes to copy such politically untimely, if not topically repugnant, material. After an unsuccessful siege of London, Swein and his army, as the Chronicle laments, "went away from there, and did the greatest damage that ever any army could do, by burning, ravaging, and slaying, everywhere along the coast, and in Essex, Kent, Sussex, and Hampshire; and finally they seized horses and rode as widely as they wished, and continued to do indescribable damage" (A.D. 994). The damage was again halted by another enormous tribute, but again it was only a short time before the Vikings were back in England for more booty. The last decade of the 10th century ended in a series of devastating raids along the Wessex coastline. These were not years for Englishmen, least of all Anglo-Danes, to be openly betraying Danish sympathies in splendid epic poems.[8]

Presumably it was to punish the expression of Danish sympathies in the Norse settlements in the kingdom of Strathclyde and the Isle of Man

7. If the genealogy led to English, instead of Danish kings, it would be a different matter, for there is a tradition that includes Scyld in the line of West Saxon kings; but Healfdene and Hroðgar, needless to say, are not part of the line. See the Chronicle, A.D. 855, and especially Alistair Campbell, ed., *The Chronicle of Æthelweard*, pp. 32–33, where the genealogy ends with Beo, Scyld, and Scef, and the story of Scyld's arrival by ship at Skaney is applied instead to Scef. The Norse line of the Scylding dynasty, from Scyld to Swein Forkbeard's son, Cnut the Great, is traced in Arngrim Jónsson's Latin abstract of the *Skiǫldunga saga*. See *Rerum Danicarum Fragmenta* in Jakob Benediktsson, ed., *Arngrimi Jonae Opera Latine Conscripta*, pp. 333–386. On the coincidence of the Anglo-Saxon and Norse genealogies see H. M. Chadwick, *The Origin of the English Nation*, esp. pp. 137 ff., and 252 ff.

8. It should not be presumed that the Anglo-Danes were disloyal English subjects: they hated Viking raiders as much as their Anglo-Saxon countrymen did, and it was the Danelaw that provided Edmund Ironside's main force in his last stand against the Danish conquest. As Stenton says, the Anglo-Danes in the wars of the 11th century "were ready to fight at any time for their ancestral liberties, but they continued to regard themselves as members of a united English state." "The Scandinavian Colonies in England and Normandy," p. 11.

that Æthelred ravaged these areas in the year 1000, while the Viking host was in Normandy.[9] The traditional year 1000 thus seems a particularly inauspicious time for Englishmen to be copying the *Beowulf* MS. The Danes were back harrying England in the following year, and peace was finally bought with £24,000 in A.D. 1002; but later in the year Æthelred himself broke the peace with a stupidly brutal royal order that accounts in large measure for his derogatory epithet. The Chronicle simply states that "the king ordered to be slain all the Danish men who were in England—this was done on St. Brice's day—because the king had been informed that they would treacherously deprive him, and then all his councillors, of life, and possess this kingdom afterwards." The St. Brice's Day massacre doubtless made Æthelred's fears prophetic: "According to a well-recorded tradition," Stenton writes, "the victims included Gunnhild, sister of King Swein of Denmark, then living as a hostage in England. It is highly probable that the wish to avenge her was a principal motive for his invasion of England in the following year" (*Anglo-Saxon England,* p. 380). At any rate there was no letup in the Danish assaults on the English kingdom for ten long years. They were years in which the Vikings grew rich on English pillage and tribute. In 1011 Æthelred was ready to pay for peace again, and the Chronicle takes grim stock of the vast extent of the Danish ravaging for that year alone:

They had then overrun: (i) East Anglia, (ii) Essex, (iii) Middlesex, (iv) Oxfordshire, (v) Cambridgeshire, (vi) Hertfordshire, (vii) Buckinghamshire, (viii) Bedfordshire, (ix) halfHuntingdonshire, (x) much of Northamptonshire; and south of the Thames all Kent, Sussex, Hastings, Surrey, Berkshire, Hampshire, and much of Wiltshire.

Later in the year Ælfheah, archbishop of Canterbury, was captured; his martyrdom in the following year during a drunken orgy, when his Viking captors pelted him to death with bones from their meal, so disgusted many of the Danes that forty-five ships switched allegiance, and

---

9. In addition to the Chronicle, see L. M. Larson, *Canute the Great,* pp. 37–38, and Stenton, *Anglo-Saxon England,* p. 379.

under the leadership of Thorkel the Tall, promised Æthelred to defend his country as mercenaries.[10]

But even the atrocity of Ælfheah's murder and the defection of a major part of the Danish fleet could not check the momentum of the Danish conquest of England. The Chronicle says that in the next year, 1013, "King Swein came with his fleet to Sandwich, and then went very quickly round East Anglia into the mouth of the Humber, and so up along the Trent until he reached Gainsborough. And then at once Earl Uhtred and all the Northumbrians submitted to him, as did all the people of Lindsey, and then all the people belonging to the district of the Five Boroughs, and quickly afterwards all the Danish settlers north of Watling Street." When Swein went south of Watling Street only London resisted him, and London too submitted as soon as Æthelred fled to Normandy. Thus England was conquered, the Chronicle tells us, "until the happy event of Swein's death" on 3 February 1014, when the English councillors recalled Æthelred and solemnly, but shortsightedly, "proclaimed every Danish king an outlaw from England for ever." Within two years Swein's son, Cnut the Great, began his long and peaceful reign (1016–1035), which freed his subjects, for the first time in two centuries, from the constant threat of Viking raids. In view of the calm admiration for Hroðgar and his Victory-Scyldings in *Beowulf,* it is safe to say that if the *Beowulf* MS was indeed copied in the late 10th or early 11th century, a date after 1016 is most likely.

One can well understand how *Beowulf* would have gained popularity in the early 11th century, during the reign of Cnut. In *Beowulf* the Danes are spoken of as a dynasty of unparalleled sovereignty and influence, a true representation of the Danish realm in Cnut's time. The poem speaks of North Danes, South Danes, East Danes, and West Danes; Bright-Danes, Spear-Danes, and Ring-Danes; and Scyldings (Cnut's patronymic), Honor-Scyldings, Army-Scyldings, People-Scyldings, and Victory-Scyldings. Hroðgar, like King Cnut, ruled Danes who were above petty raiding and pirating. Compared to the Danes, Beowulf's people are like Vikings—Weather-Geats, War-Geats, Sea-

---

10. Stenton, *Anglo-Saxon England,* p. 384. There is a contemporary account of Thorkel's attempt to save Ælfheah in the *Chronicle of Thietmar of Merseberg,* printed as an excerpt in Dorothy Whitelock, ed., *English Historical Documents, I, c. 500–1042,* p. 321.

Geats. Higelac dies on a Viking-type raid in which Beowulf valiantly participates. To be sure, the Northern stories in *Beowulf* find their analogues in the scaldic poetry that flourished during Cnut's reign. Larson notes, for example, that "before the onslaught at Stiklestead [1030] one of Saint Olaf's scalds recited the ancient Bjarkamál, the Old Norse version of Beowulf's last fight." As Larson says, "The four decades that the Norns allotted to Canute (995?–1035) are a notable period in the history of Northern literature: it was the grand age of Old Norse poetry. . . . Just when each individual tale was cast into the form that has come down to us is impossible to say; the probabilities are, however, that a considerable number of the heroic lays were composed in the age of Canute" (pp. 292–293). Famous scalds, the Northern counterparts of the Anglo-Saxon *scops,* often visited Cnut's court to recite songs in praise of Cnut,[11] and no doubt also to recite ancient Scandinavian lays and sagas of heroes and dragons, of great families like the Volsungs, and of great nations like the Danish Scyldings. One can be sure that the English courts in the reign of Cnut would have known and appreciated the allusions to Northern stories in *Beowulf* far better than they would have in the reign of Æthelred, or for that matter in the reigns of any of the English kings preceding him.[12]

Historically, both the creation of *Beowulf* and the copying of it become not only credible activities during the reign of Cnut, but desirable and officially approbated efforts. The poem is permeated with Scandinavian interests. Antiquarians may prefer a poem deriving from the earliest periods of Anglo-Saxon life, but historically, and, as we shall see, linguistically, there is nothing that prohibits an early 11th-century origin, while there is much in its favor. An 11th-century poet would have had available to him the heathen Norse stories and the rich reli-

11. See Sighvat the Poet's "Tog-drápa," Othere the Black's "Knútz-drápa," and Thorarinn Praisetongue's "Tog-drápa" and "Höfuð-lausn," in Gudbrand Vigfusson and F. York Powell, eds., *Corpus Poeticum Boreale,* vol. 2, pp. 135–136, 155–156, 159–162.

12. R. W. Chambers uses the Northern allusions as indications of an early date in *Beowulf, An Introduction,* p. 487. The poem suggests otherwise: in the first two lines the poet says, "We have *learned by asking about* the glory of the Spear-Danes in days gone by." Bosworth-Toller and the Toller supplement gloss *gefrignan,* "to learn by asking," while Klaeber has "learn (orig. 'by inquiry')." The sources in Cnut's day were Cnut's court poets, traveling scalds, and Danish settlers.

gious tradition of Anglo-Saxon poetic style and method which come together so remarkably in *Beowulf*. The cultural milieu of early 11th-century England is clearly suitable for the creation of a poem like *Beowulf*, and the cultural milieu of early 11th-century Denmark would have helped provide its setting. It is, in fact, the predominance of Danish interests in the poem that has led scholars to rule out a 9th- or 10th-century provenance. Only two scholars have dated the poem so late. Levin Schücking's arguments for placing the poem in a Danelaw court around the year 900 recognize the undeniable Anglo-Danish character of the poem, but the government of the Danelaw was too recent and precarious, and too near Alfred's death, for an English poet, under commission, to be able to acquiesce so superbly. The language of the petty Danelaw courts, at any rate, was Norse, and if, as Schücking suggests, the poem was made for the instruction of young Danish princes, one would expect fewer *hapax legomena* and less eccentric poetic language, in general.[13]

It is notable, however, that no direct linguistic evidence has been used to undermine Schücking's thesis. If there were such evidence, Schücking's dating the poem nearly two centuries beyond the traditional date would have been promptly discredited. Instead, his dating is merely countered by a rather fuzzy historical argument, which actually substantiates an 11th-century provenance. As Dorothy Whitelock puts the case, "So late a date [as Schücking's] seems highly unlikely. The poem is surely pre-Viking Age."[14] Whitelock rightly doubts whether "the high terms of praise and respect with which the poet speaks of the Danes and their rulers" and the poet's "stress on the might and splendour of the [Danish] court" would have been possible "during the Viking Age, or whether his audience would have given him a patient hearing if he had. It is not how men like to hear the people described who are burning their homes, pillaging their churches, ravaging their cattle, killing their

13. See "Wann entstand der Beowulf? Glossen, Zweifel, und Fragen"; and "Die Beowulfdatierung: Eine Replik." Of special interest in the latter is the discussion of words that suggest a much later date than the 8th century. Schücking's date, for less cogent reasons, has recently been advanced again by Norman F. Blake, in an impressionistic revision in "The Dating of Old English Poetry," p. 26. See also Nicholas Jacobs, "Anglo-Danish Relations, Poetic Archaism and the Date of *Beowulf*: A Reconsideration of the Evidence," whose arguments appeared too late for me to use.

14. *The Audience of Beowulf*, p. 24.

countrymen or carrying them off into slavery" (*Audience,* pp. 24–25).
However, what Whitelock overlooks in her otherwise cogent argument
is the question of the transmission of *Beowulf.* Those who propose a
7th- or 8th-century provenance for the poem neglect to discuss how it
passed through all of the Anglo-Saxon kingdoms, including Alfred's,
during the Viking Age of the 9th and 10th centuries. The current
explanation for the mixture of linguistic forms in *Beowulf* requires that
it first be composed in the 7th or 8th century, and then go through all
of the major dialect areas in the following two or more centuries before
reaching its Late West Saxon form. The same arguments against a 9th-
or 10th-century origin work equally well against a 9th- or 10th-century
transmission. If it is hard to conceive of an Anglo-Saxon poet in these
centuries who would have composed *Beowulf,* it is just as hard to conceive of scriptoria throughout these centuries that would repeatedly
engage scribes to copy a poem praising the people who were ravaging
their country. It is even harder to imagine receptive audiences in Northumbria, Mercia, Wessex, or Kent, but these are the dialect areas that
supposedly contributed the mixture of forms in the course of the poem's
transmission.

Thus, the historical evidence suggests a post-Viking date for the
poem, as well as for the copy of it that has come down to us. Consider,
for example, the following passage from *Beowulf,* in which the poet
praises the Danes for the same qualities that made the Anglo-Saxons of
the 9th and 10th centuries hate and fear them:

> Wæs þeaw hyra,
> þæt hie oft wæron   an wig gearwe,
> ge æt ham ge on herge,   ge gehwæþer þara
> efne swylce mæla,   swylce hira mandryhtne
> þearf gesælde;   wæs seo þeod tilu. (1246b–1250)

As Bosworth-Toller notes, the *here* (d. s. *herge*) "is the word which in
the Chronicle is always used of the Danish force in England, while the
English troops are always the *fyrd,* hence the word is used for *devas-
tation* and *robbery*" (p. 532). It is inconceivable that this passage could
have survived an Anglo-Saxon transmission through Northumbria,
Mercia, Wessex, and Kent during the Viking Age. The Danish readi-
ness for war, at home and in the *here,* became a virtue to the Anglo-

Saxons, and the Danes themselves became a *þeod tilu,* during the reign
of Cnut, and surely not in the 9th and 10th centuries. The great improbability of a text of this nature being transmitted through the centuries
of the Viking Age renders a 7th- or 8th-century origin equally unlikely.
And, as Whitelock says, "if the poem is later than the time when Viking
invasions began in earnest, about 835, it can hardly be placed before the
tenth century, and even then it would have to be put, as Schücking puts
it, in the court of an Anglo-Danish king in the Danelaw" (*Audience,*
p. 25). The simplest solution, that both the poem and the MS belong to
the reign of Cnut the Great, has never been considered before, perhaps
because it was not recognized that the paleographical dating of the MS
placed it within Cnut's reign. Whitelock, for instance, believed that
Cnut's reign was excluded: "It could hardly be located in English
England until the reign of Cnut, and that is later than our surviving
manuscript."[15] Since Cnut's reign is not, in fact, later than the surviving
MS, it is imperative to study the possibility that the poem was composed
then, too.

Like *Beowulf,* Cnut brought together Danish and Anglo-Saxon culture the way no petty king of the Danelaw ever could have done. As his
first official act as king of England he accepted the laws of King Edgar
and promised to enforce them; he later issued laws of his own that were
based on Anglo-Saxon legal traditions;[16] from the start he honored the
Anglo-Saxon church and its saints, many of whom had been martyred

15. Ibid., p. 25; Whitelock wrote this before Ker placed the script s. x/xi. She
perhaps relied on Wolfgang Keller's dating in the last decades of the 10th century
(*Angelsächsische Palaeographie,* p. 37), though Förster showed that Keller's reasons
were paleographically untenable (*Die Beowulf-Handschrift,* pp. 41-42). Or she may
have been following the popular "convenient" date, 1000. There is no ready explanation for Blake's exclusion of Cnut's reign, when he limits the *Beowulf* MS, and the
other poetic codices, to the end of the 10th century ("Dating," p. 20). This inaccurate
limitation affects his dating of the poetry.

16. See A. J. Robertson, ed., *The Laws of the Kings of England from Edmund to
Henry I,* pp. 137-219. The laws that Cnut himself enacted are based on those of his
predecessors, and there is even frequent dependence on those of his old enemy,
Æthelred. Whitelock has convincingly argued that Wulfstan, the author of the *Sermo
ad Anglos,* wrote Cnut's laws, and as she says, "our estimate of Cnut's character is
greatly affected if it can be established that he was so much influenced by the veteran
archbishop who had loyally supported Ethelred and striven against the disorder of the
reign." "Wulfstan and the Laws of Cnut," p. 451.

by his Viking countrymen;[17] he outlawed all forms of heathenism in a law that would surely affect his Danish subjects more than his English ones;[18] he made every effort to show his Anglo-Saxon subjects that he regarded himself as a legitimate Anglo-Saxon king, not as a foreign usurper; he even married Æthelred's widow, Emma, who may have been twice his age, to create a symbolic union between Danes and Englishmen.[19] He was a strong, internationally honored Christian king, and the first king of England who was able to bring an end to the constant threat from Viking raiders. Even those Anglo-Saxons who would have lamented, and resented, the fall of Alfred's house would have been happy with the stability that followed the disaster. Cnut's reign was no doubt a pleasant surprise for most Anglo-Saxons, and it can be for us, too, if its mighty cultural legacy was *Beowulf.*

The Linguistic Tests for an Early Date

Though detailed historical arguments still need to be made for an 11th-century provenance of the poem, as the matter now stands the general arguments for a pre-Viking date are no better than they would be for a post-Viking date. The difficulty of transmission through the Viking Age, however, tips the balance toward the Age of Cnut, and away from the Age of Bede. The linguistic, and pseudolinguistic, arguments for an early date seem far more formidable, because it seems, at first glance, that they are less open to doubts. By far the most persuasive case for an early date rests in the bewildering variety of linguistic forms, of uncertain date and dialect, embedded in the essentially Late West Saxon dialect of the preserved text. It is this conglomeration of forms that gives

17. Notably St. Edmund and St. Ælfheah; see Larson's chapter, "Canute and the English Church," *Canute the Great,* pp. 162–179.

18. Dorothy Bethurum points to the parallel between Wulfstan VI, 85–87, and *Beowulf,* lines 175–178, for the reversion to heathen practices (*The Homilies of Wulfstan,* p. 296); elsewhere she notes the similarity between þeodþreaum at line 178 of this passage from *Beowulf* and Wulfstan's "characteristic compounds in which the first member is used with intensifying force, such as þeod- in þeodsceaða (p. 90 and n. 2). She might have added the use of þeodsceaða in *Beowulf,* lines 2278 and 2688.

19. The marriage of Havelok and Goldboru in *Havelok the Dane* is perhaps based on the historical marriage of Cnut and Emma.

scholars concrete evidence that *Beowulf* has endured a long and complicated transmission through all the main dialect areas. This broad
mixture of forms, together with an explanation for early and late cross-
dialectal forms in an 11th-century text, will be considered fully in the
following sections. Here, a word must be said about the considerably
less compelling linguistic tests that have helped keep the poem rooted in
the 7th or 8th century. As Klaeber says, "Investigations have been carried on with a view to ascertaining the relative dates of Old English
poems by means of syntactical and phonetic-metrical tests" (p. cviii).
The first test has validity only for those scholars who assume from the
start that *Beowulf* is an early poem; the second is probably valid in its
metrical assumptions, but these assumptions do not lead inevitably to an
early date for *Beowulf*.

The syntactical test, as condensed by Klaeber, is this: "A study of the
gradual increase in the use of the definite article (originally demonstra-
tive pronoun), the decrease of the combination of weak adjective and
noun *(wisa fengel)*, the increase of the combination of article and weak
adjective and noun *(se grimma gæst)*" (p. cviii). Most scholars, including Klaeber (see pp. cviii–cix and xcii), have realized that this test
proves nothing. Long ago, Tupper astutely remarked on the use of the
weak adjective without the article that "the survival of an archaic form
in a poetical text is surely no proof of antiquity," and he noted the usage
in the 10th-century poem, *The Battle of Brunanburh*.[20] Even Chambers,
who felt that the relatively high proportion of this syntactical construction in *Beowulf* pointed to its relative antiquity, admitted that "certain
late texts show how fallible this criterion is. Anyone dating Maldon,"
he added, "solely by [this test] would assuredly place it much earlier
than 991" (p. 106). The high incidence of the usage in *Beowulf* may be
simply due to the poet's wish to be more archaic in a poem about *gear-
dagum* than he would in a poem about contemporary affairs (like *Brunanburh* and *Maldon*) or about religious subjects. Obviously, the test is
not a test of dating but of chosen style.

The phonetic-metrical test, despite its more compelling claims, is also
inconclusive as a test for date. It attempts to show the relative antiquity
of *Beowulf* by deducing primitive sound changes from what appears to

---

20. Frederick Tupper, Jr., ed., *The Riddles of the Exeter Book*, p. lxxvii and note.

be faulty meter.[21] The argument is, chiefly, that some half-lines containing historical contractions can be metrically "restored" by introducing hypothetical decontracted forms in place of the contractions. For example, line 25b reads *man geþeon,* which has only three syllables rather than four; the meter is restored by deducing the presumptive archetype, **geþihan,* normally marked in the editions with a circumflex over the MS contraction: *man geþeôn.*[22] The phonetic-metrical analysis seems quite sound, but the chronological inference, the so-called test, is not only implausible but inconsistent with the general principles metrists have formulated for scanning the lines of the poem. It is highly unlikely that the Anglo-Saxons transmitted *Beowulf* over several centuries without realizing that linguistic change had ruined the meter. It is more plausible to assume that they understood the meter of their poetry and that, in a Type A line like *man geþeôn,* they naturally pronounced *-þeon* with two syllables rather than one. The first advantage of this explanation is that it accords so well with the similar metrical principles of syncopating medial vowels or of suppressing vocalic consonants whenever such pronunciations are metrically desirable. Thus, in recitation if not in spelling, syncopation and dissyllabic pronunciation produce identical Type C lines from apparent metrical aberrations: *Ne seah ic elþeodige* (336b) and *þa git on sund reôn* (512b). If the metrical rule holds for *elþeodige* it also holds for *reon.* No doubt a trained Anglo-Saxon reader could readily detect when to pronounce a normally monosyllabic form like *reon* dissyllabically, for (with one exception) all of the forms in question occur in Type A or Type C lines, in contexts where dissyllabic forms (an arsis and thesis) are expected, and presumably required.

---

21. For the seminal studies see Eduard Sievers, "Zur Rhythmik des germanischen Alliterationsverses: Erster Abschnitt, Die Metrik des Beowulf"; and *Altgermanische Metrik,* pp. 120–149. Yet as A. J. Bliss says of these *causa metri* changes, "The question is a singularly difficult one, since the necessity for emendation may seem at first sight to discredit the rule on which the emendation is based." *The Metre of 'Beowulf,'* p. 4.

22. Wrenn printed the hypothetical decontracted forms in his edition, but Bolton restored them to MS forms (without the circumflex) in the revised edition. Bolton's exemplary trust in the MS is remarkably shown by "a return to MS. forms where the sole or principal exception to them has been on metrical grounds." C. L. Wrenn, ed., *Beowulf with the Finnesburg Fragment,* 3rd ed., rev. W. F. Bolton, pp. 6 and 56.

A look at the evidence will illustrate how a knowledgeable reader is almost obliged to give the proper metrical pronunciation of the contracted forms. In Type A lines containing only three syllables one instinctively gives the natural metrical pronunciation, just as one instinctively pronounces final *e* in Chaucer when the meter requires it: *man geþéon* (25b), *feorhseoc fléon* (820a), *mandream fléon* (1264b), *deaþwic séon* (1275b), *héan huses* (116a), *néan bidan* (528b), *age[n]d-fréan* (1883a). Metrical pronunciations are equally natural in the remaining Type A lines as well: *metodsceaft séon* (1180a), *morþorbed stréd* (2436b), *beorh þone héan* (3097b), *feorran ond néan* (839b), *éam his nefan* (881a), *egesan ðéon* (2736a), and *Deniga fréan* (271a, 359a, 1680b). Some of these contractions may still have been formally pronounced with two syllables. It is likely, for instance, that speakers of Old English recognized *hean* and *nean* as contractions, which would enhance metrical pronunciation, since the nominative forms *heah* and *neah* retain the final *h* lost in oblique cases and in derivatives. The Type C lines are even more conducive to metrical pronunciation than the Type A lines considered above. All of the Type C lines are off-verses,[23] with the stave immediately preceding the contractions, so that dissyllabic pronunciations of them are virtually unavoidable: *on flet téon* (1036), *þæt he me ongean sléa* (681), *þa git on sund réon* (512), *þa wit on sund réon* (539), *ond órcnéas* (112), *him þæs Liffréa* (16), *nefne sinfréa* (1934), *þeah ðe he rof síe* (682), *þeah ðe he geong sý* (1831), *þenden hyt sý* (2649), *þær wæs Hondscio* (2076a), *æt Wealhþéon* (629), and *swa hy næfre man lýhð* (1048). In most of these cases the two vowels of the contracted form are an aid to the metrical pronunciation (*sy* and *lyhð* have the variant spellings *sie* and *liehð*). Perhaps in a class by themselves are the Type C off-verses with the contracted forms *don/ deð* and *gan/gæð*. But speakers of Old English would certainly realize (by analogy) that these forms were contractions, and the Middle English evidence suggests that, despite the spellings, they were pronounced dissyllabically in some Old English dialects. In any case, the persistent occurrence of these contractions in the off-verse, right after

---

23. An apparent exception occurs in the on-verse, *þær wæs Hondscio* (2076), but there is no reason to assume that in the personal name *-scio* was pronounced monosyllabically. The on-verse *to befleonne* (1003) is usually interpreted, by decontraction, as Type C, but it is more naturally read, with or without decontraction, as Type A.

the alliterative stress, more or less forces an informed reader to make the proper metrical pronunciation: *hat ín gân* (386), *on flet(t) gǽð* (2034, 2054), *ond on bǽl dôn* (1116), *swa sceal m̄an* (or *m̄æg) dôn* (1172, 1534, 2166), *swa (he) nu gít (gyt* or *gen) dêð* (1058, 1134, 2859). The on-verse *Ða com in gan* (1644) is exceptional, but can be read as Type A, with stress on the adverbs and monosyllabic pronunciation (as in 1163a) of *gan*.

As an aid to scansion, editors would perhaps be wise to continue to use a circumflex over the relevant contracted forms, just as some use pointing to mark metrically syncopated or suppressed sounds. These diacritical marks, however, need not imply editorial emendation of the MS, for there is no compelling reason to believe that the forms themselves have any bearing on the date of *Beowulf*. The contractions would be naturally pronounced dissyllabically in Type A and C lines, even in an 11th-century poem, to maintain the prevailing rhythm. The one exceptional Type D line, *oferfleôn fotes trem* (2525a), well illustrates how unreliable and insubstantial the phonetic-metrical test is as a criterion of date: the same Type D line, without the anacrusis, occurs in the *Battle of Maldon* (*fleôn fotes trym,* 247a), composed sometime after the battle was fought in the late 10th century.[24] We may safely conclude that the line in *Beowulf*, like the rest of the lines containing contractions, need not have come about as the result of three centuries or so of sound changes and of consistently inept scribal transmission.

In fact, the logistics of the supposedly long and complicated transmission of *Beowulf* have never been worked out, and some of the most problematic aspects of this standard theory of transmission need to be scrutinized. All of the linguistic tests for an early date necessarily begin with the long and complicated transmission as a premise. As an additional linguistic test, for instance, Klaeber gingerly suggests that two forms may have survived the long transmission relatively intact—that is, without substantive modernization by redactors or scribes. "There is a possibility," according to Klaeber, "that in our only extant MS. a few

---

24. For an early review of the pitfalls of the phonetic-metrical test, see Aldo Ricci, "The Chronology of Anglo-Saxon Poetry." In recent years metrical tests of date have steadily lost ground. As Blake says, "It has so far proved impossible for modern scholars to achieve a consensus of opinion on the problem of metre; we must disregard it as any guide to dating." "Dating," p. 16. Cf. Wrenn, *Beowulf,* rev. Bolton, p. 57; and Samuel Jay Keyser, "Old English Prosody," p. 347.

forms are preserved which would seem to indicate a date anterior to about 750 A.D., viz. *wundini* 1382 and *unigmetes* 1792" (p. cix). Actually, *unigmetes* is a very late form, showing, as Klaeber explains elsewhere, "a late transition of *ge-* to *i-* . . . and analogical spelling *ig* (which is rather frequent in that portion of the MS.)" (p. lxxxii). He adds in a note, "That this *ig* should stand, by mistake, for an old or dialectal *gi-* . . . is a far less plausible hypothesis." So much for *unigmetes* as a relic from the 7th or 8th century. The infamous form *wundini* will be discussed at length in a moment. The standard theory of transmission ought to be clarified first.

The theory as it is applied to *Beowulf* can best be seen in Klaeber's discussion of the language of the poem (pp. lxxxviii–lxxxix). Klaeber confidently states that "the origin of the poem on Anglian soil [is] to be postulated on general principles," but admits that "a decision in favor of either Northumbria or Mercia as the original home cannot be made on the basis of the language." He goes on to say, then, that "before receiving its broad, general LWS. complexion, the MS.—at any rate, part of it—passed through EWS. and Kentish hands." We are thus left with "this mixture of forms, early and late, West Saxon, Northumbrian, Mercian, Kentish, Saxon patois," which Klaeber felt "points plainly to a checkered history of the written text as the chief factor in bringing about the unnatural medley of spellings." It is a reasonable deduction and, at first sight, the only possible one. Many of the spellings in *Beowulf* simply could not have developed from standard Early West Saxon phonological forms, while they could have developed from standard Northumbrian, or Mercian, or in some cases, Kentish forms. So it was natural to assume that the mixture of forms was brought about in the course of a long and very complicated transmission, which must have included, in addition to a recension or two, modernization of forms and dialectal transliteration.

This theory of the scribal transmission of *Beowulf,* which all editors of the poem share, necessitates some remarkably consistent and sophisticated blundering from the generations of scribes involved. If we take Klaeber's lists of linguistic forms seriously, we must assume that, for him, there was both a Northumbrian and Mercian version, though he says that the language cannot determine which version would have represented the original. In either case, Klaeber believed that the poem passed through the two Anglian dialects, then through an Early West

Saxon version, and then through a Kentish version, before coming down to us in the Late West Saxon version of the preserved text. Taking into account only the first and last stages of the transmission, it is evident that *Beowulf*'s textual history must have been very complicated indeed: it is enough to say that the early 11th-century scribes have recorded a nearly complete, normalized translation from the original Anglian dialect to the present Late West Saxon dialect. But it is the evidence of the textual history itself that makes the theory so improbable, for how would Northumbrian or Mercian forms (whichever came first) survive the modernization of forms and the general dialectal translation over the three hundred years or more of scribal transmission? The theory presupposes a translating transmission of the text, in which, at each new stage of translation some forms from the previous stage were retained; in fact, it presupposes that the *same* forms from the first stage were for some reason retained as the poem passed through the dialects and through the centuries.

It is worth stressing what the theory requires one to accept. Let us assume, for the sake of the argument, that *Beowulf* was originally composed in the 8th century in the Northumbrian dialect. Whenever it was "translated" into the Mercian dialect, the Mercian version retained some Northumbrian forms; whenever it was translated into Early West Saxon, this version continued to retain at least some of the same Northumbrian forms as well as some Mercian forms; when it was translated into Kentish, the Kentish version once again retained some of the same Northumbrian forms that had been retained by both the Mercian and Early West Saxon versions, as well as some Mercian forms that had been retained by the Early West Saxon version, and some forms from the Early West Saxon version. Finally, after about three hundred years, the Late West Saxon version, apparently for no other reason than to preserve the "checkered history of the written text" for modern editors, retained some of the Northumbrian forms also retained by the Mercian, Early West Saxon, and Kentish versions; some of the Mercianisms also retained by the Early West Saxon and Kentish versions; some of the Early West Saxon forms also retained by the Kentish version; as well as some Kentish features.

It is virtually impossible to imagine how such a process of transmission could have been sustained from dialect to dialect, from generation to generation, from scribe to scribe. Surely one good recension along the way would have wiped out a century or two of the linguistic evidence from the history of transmission, as indeed has happened in the case of the MSS of *Cædmon's Hymn* and *Bede's Death Song*. If we did not know the history of these poems we could not possibly deduce an early Northumbrian archetype from the Late West Saxon MSS.[25] But it is clear that the editors of *Beowulf* never closely consider the *process* of transmission, only the putative results of the process. These editors are not bothered by the fact that the text supposedly retains phonological evidence of its textual history, but preserves no ancient orthographical forms. For example, the *hapax* word *wiðer-ræhtes*, "opposite" (3039), should be in normal Late West Saxon spelling *wiðer-rihtes* or *-ryhtes*. Klaeber explains the case as an instance of Anglian smoothing of *eo* to *e (æ)*, an explanation that itself is complicated by orthographical variation of *æ* and *e*. He cites two examples of *ræht-* from the *Lindisfarne Gospel* glosses, a 10th-century text (p. lxxv). What is so unsatisfying about this explanation is that it means that heterogeneous scribes from heterogeneous dialect areas transmitted accurately the phonological characteristics of a Northumbrian word to the extent that it appears in a Late West Saxon text in exactly the form in which it would appear in a Late Northumbrian text. Yet the early Northumbrian form would have been something like *uuidir-reoctaes*, or *-rectaes* after smoothing. Later, non-Anglian scribes would have to understand, at least vaguely, the meaning of the word to modernize the spelling to *wiðer-ræhtes*. But if a Late West Saxon scribe understood the meaning of the word (and it is not a difficult word to interpret, despite its apparent rarity), why would he give it a non–West Saxon spelling? The answer that it developed over the centuries, in non-Anglian territory, the same way that it developed over the centuries in Anglian territory is not compelling. Among other possibilities a simpler answer would be that the word had no Late West Saxon spelling, because it was a (late) Anglian loanword.

It should be indisputable that sporadic indications of possibly late Northumbrian phonology cannot be used to prove an early Northumbrian provenance of the poem. Only evidence of early phonology, in the form of early spellings, can prove early provenance, but the practice of modernizing forms in the course of transmission obviously obliterates

25. See E. V. K. Dobbie, *The Manuscripts of Cædmon's Hymn and Bede's Death Song.*

the evidence. The one scrap of evidence of this kind that has not been obliterated, according to Klaeber's last linguistic test, is *wundini*. Most editors of *Beowulf* realize the importance of this kind of evidence, as their resorting to the reading *wundini* illustrates. However, this form can be used to show how weak the linguistic argument is for a 7th- or 8th-century origin of *Beowulf*. Basically, the argument is that *wundini* is a very early (ante c. 750) instrumental form, and as such is the single, surviving, orthographical vestige from the 7th- or 8th-century phono-logical-morphological archetype. The issue is an extremely important one as far as dating the poem in the early 8th century or the early 11th century is concerned, and must be considered in some detail. The con-servative editors, Chambers, Wrenn, Wrenn-Bolton, and von Schau-bert,[26] all print *wundini;* less conservative editors, like Klaeber, emend to *wundnum,* but even Klaeber conceded in his second supplement that "it may, after all, be advisable to give *wundini* (instead of *wundnum*) as an archaic instrumental form a place in the text" (p. 467). So, of all modern editors, only E. V. K. Dobbie rejects *wundini* as a legitimate MS reading, commenting to the point that if *wundini* is correct, "it is odd that we have no other early endings of this sort in the poem. The emendation to *wundnum* puts less of a strain on probability."[27]

The critical consequences of accepting the reading *wundini* are nowhere more apparent than in Wrenn's edition, where the form is used as the chief linguistic evidence for dating the poem. Indeed, Wrenn's opening sentence broadly states that "archaic spellings and forms in the MS., such as *wundini golde* (1382), may imply that there was already a written form of *Beowulf* in the eighth century." And while this remark suggests that *wundini* is only one of many archaic spellings and forms implying an 8th-century provenance, Wrenn elsewhere admits that *wundini* is in fact "the only certain evidence for dating *Beowulf* before *circa* 750 on purely linguistic grounds" (*Beowulf*, p. 21, n. 2). Wrenn uses the evidence repeatedly throughout his introduction, and at one point even refers to it as "the much-discussed phrase" (p. 36). Wrenn is shaken by at least one major objection to the reading, for he freely admits "the improbability of such a fossilized form being pre-served through the two and a half or so centuries that must have passed

---

26. Else von Schaubert, ed., *Heyne-Schückings Beowulf,* pt. 1.
27. *Beowulf and Judith,* p. 193n.

between its first appearance in the original Northumbrian (or Mercian) *Beowulf* and the making of the extant Classical Anglo-Saxon copy."[28] Nonetheless, the form remained for him "at least strong as a piece of evidence" for dating the poem around 750 (p. 35), and it is made to bear the main weight of Wrenn's entire linguistic argument.[29]

Chambers makes the conservative case for printing *wundini* more strongly than most other editors, because when he was writing most other editors were printing the emendation *wundnum*. His defense exemplifies the habit of editors of accentuating the results of scribal transmission while submerging the actual process. "It is strange," he complains, "that whilst recent editors frequently restore into the text ancient forms which the later scribes refused to admit, yet here, when the scribe, by a curious oversight, seems to have copied the early 8th century form *wundini*, 'with twisted gold,' most editors refuse to accept it, and modernize to *wundnum*." It was impossible, of course, for the scribe of the preserved MS to make this "curious oversight" using an 8th-century exemplar, and the only alternative is that a series of scribes, who wrote in different dialects, committed the same curious oversight again and again in the course of three or more centuries of transmission. Chambers's comment that the last scribe "would hardly have copied the old form except through momentary inadvertence" is quite true, but it applies as well to the scribes of the 9th and 10th centuries, who are supposed to have preceded him. The sheer incredibility of this process of transmission did not occur to Chambers, for *wundini* in the preserved MS proved, to him, that "*Beowulf* must have been already written down in the 8th century and our MS. must be derived *(no doubt with many intermediate stages)* from this early MS." (pp. 69–70n, my italics).

---

28. *Beowulf*, pp. 34–35; Kenneth Sisam points out that "it is doubtful whether a form *wundini* ever existed: in the recorded -*numini,* all the examples of which go back to a single late-seventh-century gloss, the stem is short." *Studies in the History of Old English Literature*, p. 36n.

29. Bolton, in his revision of Wrenn's *Beowulf,* removes *wundini* from prominence in the first sentence of the introduction, yet the word haplessly comes to bear nearly *all* the weight of the linguistic argument, since Bolton also deletes Wrenn's obsolete metrical arguments (cf. Wrenn, *Beowulf,* p. 17 and Wrenn, *Beowulf,* rev. Bolton, p. 16). Without Wrenn's *causa metri* emendations "showing" early origin, *wundini* stands alone. On the other hand, Bolton (p. 27) deletes Wrenn's doubts (pp. 34–35) over the likelihood of *wundini* surviving a long transmission. See Fred Robinson's review of Wrenn-Bolton.

The long battle between conservative and conjectural critics on behalf of *wundini* and *wundnum* was really fought for nothing, for *wundini* is a MS ghost: it is not in the MS, as anyone who looks there carefully may see.[30] The first three minims after the *d* are ligatured at the top; the last minim is unligatured. The MS reads *wundmi*. The reading *wundini* was invented by Thorkelin, who knew enough Old English to know that *wundmi* could not possibly make sense (compare his writing *inwatide* for MS *mwatide* at line 2226b).[31] Ever since, Thorkelin has been used as the authority for this reading, instead of the MS itself. The reason for this is that Julius Zupitza admitted Thorkelin's spurious reading into his FS transliteration,[32] and nearly all editors, in turn, have founded their texts on Zupitza's FS, rather than on the MS.[33] But Zupitza was nervous about the reading, as his note indicates: "*dini* or *dmi* MS. (cf. *run-dmi* A, *wund-dini* B), the *d* entirely covered (certainly not *dum*)." His nervousness was warranted.

For a number of reasons it is certain that Wrenn used the FS instead of the MS in this case. In the first place, he never asserts that he himself read *wundini* in the MS, but only that it is "authenticated in the MS. by Thorkelin B as well as by Zupitza" (*Beowulf*, p. 34). In the second place, Wrenn says in his note to the line (p. 130) that the MS "has lost *d* of its *wun[d]ini* at beginning of line, but *ini* seem clear." The reference to the lost *d* arises from the fact that in Zupitza's old FS, as Zupitza duly noted, the *d* was "entirely covered" by the edge of the paper mounting, and so could appear to be lost to the observer of the FS. If he had consulted the MS, Wrenn would not have made the error.[34] In his

30. As Plate 1 and the Zupitza-Davis FS testify, the reading is perfectly clear in the FS, too. Donald K. Fry, who studied the MS in 1968, has written to me agreeing that *wundmi* is unmistakable in the MS.

31. Kemp Malone, ed., *The Thorkelin Transcripts of Beowulf*, p. 101a. Thorkelin is markedly untrustworthy for the reading at 1382, which in his copy appears as *wund/dini goldi* (thus, in addition to a spurious *d*, there is an attempt to legitimize the inflection on *wundini* by matching it on *goldi*). His scribe (Thorkelin A) knew no Old English and confuses insular *wynn* and *r* (which are similar), but he is accurate otherwise in his reading, *run/dmi golde* (pp. 64a and 42).

32. Julius Zupitza, ed., *Beowulf, Reproduced in Facsimile*.

33. A notable exception is W. J. Sedgefield, ed., *Beowulf,* but as a conjectural editor the return to the MS was of less use to him than it might have been to a conservative editor.

34. The error is unfortunately repeated in G. L. Brook's discussion of the form, *wun[d]ini* (*sic*), in "The Textual and Linguistic Study of Old English," pp. 289–290.

...eald git ne const frecne stowe
þær þu findan miht felasinnigne secg
sec gif þu dyrre ic þe þa fæhðe feo leanige
ge ealdgestreonum swa ic ær dyde wundnum golde gyf þu on weg cymest

BEOWVLF maþelode bearn ecgþeo
wes ne sorga snotor guma selre bið
æghwæm þæt he his freond wrece þonne
he fela murne ure æghwylc sceal ende
gebidan worolde lifes wyrce se þe mote
domes ær deaþe þæt bið drihtguman unlif
gendum æfter selest aris rices weard uton
hraþe feran grendles magan gang sceawi-
gan ic hit þe gehate no he on helm losaþ
ne on foldan fæþm ne on fyrgen holt ne
on gyfenes grund ga þær he wille ðys dogor
þu geþyld hafa weana gehwylces swa ic þe
wene to ahleop ða se gomela gode þan-
code mihtigan drihtne þæs se man ge-

"Preliminary Notice" Zupitza informs his reader that "the binder could not help covering some letters or portions of letters in every back page with the edge of the paper which now surrounds every parchment leaf. I grudged no pains in trying to decipher as much of what is covered as possible. When, in my notes, I simply state that something is covered, I always mean to say that, by holding the leaf to the light, I was able to read it nevertheless" (p. xix). In the new FS, edited by Davis, the edge of the paper covering the *d* has been cut away, and the *d* is now in plain view in both FS and MS. The point is not that Wrenn and most other editors have relied on the FS instead of the MS. It is that editors, beginning with Zupitza, have allowed Thorkelin to remain an authority for a *crucial* reading, a linguistic test used to date the text, that is not only disputed, but is flatly contradicted by the MS itself. As such *wundini* is a conjectural reading, not a conservative one.

A problem, of course, remains. What is one to make of MS *wundmi?* It will not do to lose an improbable, or even an impossible, reading like *wundini* only to gain a nonsensical reading like *wundmi.* The string of minims must be reinterpreted, but before doing so it is necessary to keep in mind that the false ligaturing and nonligaturing of minims is a common occurrence in insular MSS. Scribes used pen and ink, and human hands, not type fonts, to achieve their letters, and minor slips of this nature are to be expected, and indeed are ubiquitous in all MSS. For example, in the last line of the same folio on which *wundmi* occurs, the MS "reads" *inihtigan* (see Plate 1), yet the word in question is without a doubt *mihtigan* (line 1398a). Here the scribe has failed to ligature the first two minims, yet no transcriber has ever been confused about the actual reading. It should also be clear, however, that *wundmi* cannot be reinterpreted as *wundini*, for there is no parallel form in this or any other MS of the period. Indeed, one must go back several centuries before any kind of parallel can be found. A case could be made for *wundini* only as long as it was considered the MS reading. On the other hand, it can be reinterpreted as *wundnum*, as has been done by those editors who reject *wundini*, since this interprets the four minims as *nu*, and emends to *num* on the assumption that the scribe failed to make the mark of abbreviation over the *u*. Thus, this conjectural emendation is

---

Plate 1. Fol. 160v: *wun/dmi*, lines 4 and 5; *inihtigan*, line 20.

a conservative attempt to establish an acceptable reading out of the combination of four closely adjacent minims.

An acceptable reading can be obtained, however, without resorting to emendation if the four minims are construed as *un* rather than *nu*.[35] The form *wundun* is a leveled form (or back spelling) of *wunden*. *Wundun* is recorded in the Bosworth-Toller as a leveled form of *wundon*. Moreover, leveling is well attested in the *Beowulf* MS, as it is in the four great Old English poetic codices in general, which are all dated at roughly the same time (end of the 10th century, beginning of the 11th). Kemp Malone lists hundreds of leveled forms from these codices in his article "When Did Middle English Begin?"[36] He lists thirty-two examples from *Beowulf* alone. An example of *un* for *en* occurs in the *Exeter Book, Christ* (line 527), where *befengun* is written for *befongen*. Besides avoiding an emendation (for a strong adjectival participle is not always inflected in oblique cases), there is sufficient reason to prefer *wundun* even to the plausible emendation, *wundnum*. It seems likely that *wunden-gold*, "twisted gold," was used as a compound by the *Beowulf* poet (cf. lines 1193 and 3134, as well). Certainly, *wunden-* is never used elsewhere in *Beowulf* except in compound nouns: *wunden-feax*, *wunden-hals*, *wunden-mæl*, *wunden-stefna*. There can be no metrical objection to *wundun-golde* in line 1382a, for it is prosodically identical to *wunden-stefna* in line 220a. Moreover, (-)*gold* is consistently used in *Beowulf* as a "mass" noun in the singular. Thus *fættan golde* ("with plated gold") is a variation of *manegum maðmum* ("with many treasures") in lines 2102–2103, just as *wundun-golde* ("with twisted gold") is a variation of *ealdgestreonum* ("with ancient treasures") in lines 1381–1382. The compound mass noun *fæt-gold* ("plated gold," line 1921), furnishes a pertinent parallel to the possible compound *wunden-gold*, for *fæt-gold* ultimately derives from a combination of the weak adjectival participle *fæted* with *gold;* the loss of the participial suffix *-ed* is comparable to the weakening of the participial suffix *-en* in *wundun-*. The occasional spelling is yet another reason for dating the MS, if

---

35. *Wundun* for MS *wundmi* is no more an emendation than *mihtigan* is for MS *inihtigan* at 1398 (fol. 160v20).

36. Cf. Albert H. Marckwardt, "Verb Inflections in Late Old English"; and David Armborst, "Evidence for Phonetic Weakening in Inflectional Syllables in *Beowulf*."

not the poem, in the early 11th century.[37] It cannot be argued, of course, that the scribe intended to write an occasional spelling. But it can be argued that he was confused by an occasional spelling in his exemplar, and so miscopied it, minim for minim, as *wundmi*.

The linguistic tests of an early date for *Beowulf,* then, do not after all prohibit an 11th-century provenance. The syntactical test uses an admitted archaism that is found in unquestionably late poems as if it were not an archaism at all. Statistics recording the frequency of archaisms in individual poems may be interesting and enlightening, but they have no essential bearing on relative chronology. The phonetic-metrical test is based on a subjective interpretation of the meter, and recent studies, also subjective but far more respectful of the MS, have undermined the authority of the phonetic-metrical test as a means for dating the poem. The single phonetic-morphological-orthographical test falls on *wundini, a figment of Thorkelin's imagination. What still needs to be explained is the "mixture of forms, early and late, West Saxon, Northumbrian, Mercian, Kentish, Saxon patois," which according to Klaeber and the standard theory of transmission, "points plainly to a checkered history of the written text as the chief factor in bringing about the unnatural medley of spellings." As we shall see, these linguistic data do not rule out an 11th-century provenance for the poem either.

The Late Literary and the Early Poetic Dialects

The literary language in which *Beowulf* is written is, basically, standard Late Old English, or what Randolph Quirk and C. L. Wrenn

---

37. Karl Luick, in *Historische Grammatik der englischen Sprache,* vol. 1, pt.1, pp. 489–490, assigned this type of leveling to the early 11th century; Malone used the examples from the poetic codices to show that leveling had already begun in the late 10th century, but he ignored the chance that these codices might belong to the early 11th century. The Junius MS, for instance, like the *Beowulf* MS, is dated by Old English scholars "at about the year 1000" (G. P. Krapp, ed., *The Junius Manuscript,* p. x); yet art historians give good reasons why it, too, should be dated in the reign of Cnut (Francis Klingender, *Animals in Art and Thought to the End of the Middle Ages,* pp. 187–188). It should be noted that Ker dates the script of the main hand s. x/xi (pp. xviii and 406), which as we have seen is misleadingly interpreted as "about the year 1000," and surely includes the early 11th century.

refer to as the "classical OE *koiné*" of the time of Ælfric and Wulf-stan.[38] The mixture of linguistic forms in the poem, notably the older, cross-dialectal forms, arises from a variety of natural causes, which have no essential connection with the original date of the poem. Three causes, in particular, need to be specified and explained before we proceed to a detailed consideration of the forms themselves. In the first place, the spoken dialects in the early 11th century, or for that matter throughout the Old English period, were never completely homogeneous.[39] All spoken dialects were mixed to some degree, and in an age before printing and formal dictionaries, this linguistic heterogeneity naturally induced occasional orthographical confusion in all written records, regardless of date or dialect. Second, Late Old English, in its literary manifestation, was essentially Late West Saxon, but this in itself has no geographical significance, for Late West Saxon was the literary language used throughout England in the early 11th century. Wherever it was used, but especially in non–West Saxon centers, it contained a mixture of forms, both early and late, from other dialects, just as our own literary dialect is highly eclectic and contains many archaic forms.[40] The third cause for the mixture of forms in *Beowulf* accounts for most of the non–West Saxon archaisms: Old English poets from all periods and all dialect areas drew many of their synonyms, compounds, formulas, spellings, and syntactic constructions from an archaic poetic dialect of ultimately Anglian origin. This source contributed enough forms to Old English poems to give them all an archaic Anglian flavor, regardless of their real dates or dialects. Taken all together, an 11th-century convergence in *Beowulf* of the standard literary dialect, the archaic poetic dialect, and the individual spoken dialect of the poet and his scribes, eliminates the need for a long and complicated transmission of the poem.

The dialects of Old English are conventionally delineated as Northumbrian and Mercian (or the Anglian dialects), and West Saxon and Kentish. Linguists and the standard grammars recognize, however, that the spoken dialects of Old English were eclectic, or to put it differently, that there were far more than four spoken dialects in Old English times.

38. Randolph Quirk and C. L. Wrenn, eds., *An Old English Grammar*, pp. 4–7.

39. See, for example, G. L. Brook, *English Dialects*, p. 40.

40. The main difference is that in the Old English standard literary dialect the mixture of forms was not yet crystallized, and varied from center to center.

For this reason Alistair Campbell, for example, explains in the introduction to his *Old English Grammar* that "it is not possible to draw a dialect map of England in the Old English period" (p. 10). All of the preserved records, particularly the late ones, point to linguistic diffusion rather than dialectal purity. David DeCamp has illustrated the inadequacy of seeing the traditional dialects "as mere extensions of the dialects of the continental Germanic tribes before their migration to Britain." He stresses instead postmigration developments, on the assumption that "linguistic features can move from one area to another without mass migration of the speakers, through imitation of the speech of one area by speakers from another."[41] And in discussing the four conventional Old English dialects, G. L. Brook gives the pertinent warning that "there were very few linguistic features of Old English that were to be found exclusively in any one dialect, since dialectal forms were freely borrowed from one dialect into another" (*English Dialects,* p. 42). Accordingly, Northumbrian, Mercian, West Saxon, and Kentish are somewhat misleading terms, and as such have been used, misleadingly, to plot the supposed dialectal course of *Beowulf*'s transmission.

Unfortunately, we have no trustworthy records of Old English spoken dialects, since all of our records are written. The general unreliability of late Old English written records as a reflection of late speech is well illustrated by the retention of traditional spellings long after the weakening of unstressed inflections.[42] Still, perhaps it needs to be emphasized that it is a literary language, not a spoken one, that we must assess in *Beowulf.* As R. M. Wilson has observed, "much of the difficulty [of dating and assigning dialects] appears to be due to the unwillingness of scholars to admit how little we do know of the different Old English dialects. They tend to ignore the possibility that some of the variations which hitherto have been treated as phonetic and dialectal may in fact be merely scribal, and they tend to ignore too the inevitable influence of one dialect upon another resulting in mixed dialects."[43] These tendencies are no doubt encouraged by traditional grammars,

41. "The Genesis of the Old English Dialects: A New Hypothesis," pp. 355–356.

42. For a pertinent warning against equating orthography and phonology, see C. L. Wrenn, "The Value of Spelling as Evidence," p. 17.

43. "The Provenance of the Vespasian Psalter Gloss: The Linguistic Evidence," p. 294.

which quite naturally emphasize phonology and morphology, and
dialectal distinctions in phonology and morphology, rather than the con-
fluence of dialectal features, or simple orthographical variation, in the
written records. The standard grammars do recognize, of course, the
fact of mixed dialects and of literary dialects. Campbell says of the late
literary dialect of the late 10th and early 11th centuries: "Even when
West-Saxon had become a well-established literary dialect, and was
used as something of a standard written language, many manuscripts
display a considerable non-West-Saxon element in their orthography
and inflexions" (*Old English Grammar*, p. 9). But it is not the aim of
traditional grammars to describe mixed and artificial dialects, and literary dialects cannot be studied in them.

In fact, a comprehensive investigation of the late Old English literary
dialect, with all of its local and scribal permutations, has yet to be written, but R. Vleeskruyer's pioneer work on the Mercian, or early Old
English, literary dialect suggests some of the difficulties awaiting the
investigator. He says that, "like any other 'standard' written language,
it contained, no doubt, a variety of imported elements. The influence of
Latin syntax and vocabulary is always in evidence in its records; but
quite possibly Northumbrian and other English dialectal influence
served further to modify it and to increase its stock of words and constructions. Even phonology and inflections may have been incidentally
affected by such borrowing."[44] The old theories of transmission will only
be an impediment to the study of the natural mixture of forms in literary dialects, early and late, for the study will have to be founded on
the mixture of forms in individual MSS. Vleeskruyer emphasizes that a
mixture of forms played a necessary part in fashioning a flexible written
language: "The West-Saxonisms in the early *Martyrology* manuscripts
and the Mercianisms in Alfred's West Saxon are, after all, essentially
the early symptoms of a process of extensive linguistic 'acculturation'
that continued into the early Middle English period" (p. 62). And it is
nearly impossible to distinguish regional characteristics in late texts,
since Late Old English "and Transitional sound-changes that affected
this West Mercian dialect were shared by the South-West; inversely,

44. "The Mercian Literary Dialect," *The Life of St. Chad: An Old English Homily*, pp. 39–62. Vleeskruyer ascribes the three prose texts preceding *Beowulf* in the
Nowell Codex to the Mercian literary dialect (p. 55).

the LWS. religious vocabulary had incorporated many West Mercian terms" (ibid.). This linguistic acculturation was well advanced in the early 11th century and is part of the gradual transition from Old to Middle English.

Scholars do not doubt that the foundation of the Late Old English literary dialect was Late West Saxon, no matter where it was written. As Kenneth Sisam says, "The early 11th century was the period in which West Saxon was recognized all over England as the official and literary language. The York surveys of about 1030 supply a good instance in local documents from the North. The prayers to St. Dunstan and St. Ælfheah in MS. Arundel 155 give an equally striking example from Kent, for though they were certainly copied at Christ Church, Canterbury, into an official service-book, and were presumably composed and Englished at Canterbury, yet they are normal West Saxon. Dialect does break through, the more frequently as the eleventh century advances; but good West Saxon may be written anywhere in its first half" (*Studies*, p. 153). The intrusion of non–West Saxonisms can be illustrated by the language of the Worcester scriptorium in the late 10th and early 11th centuries. In discussing the MSS of Wulfstan's homilies "written at Worcester by the scribe Wulfgeat," Dorothy Bethurum says that "the forms of these five [MSS] confirm the opinion of most scholars that Wulfstan wrote conventional late West Saxon. There are a few dialectal features, but it is hard to determine whether they represent Wulfstan's own speech or the language of the Worcester scriptorium." Bethurum goes on to remark that "the scriptorium at Worcester, as Keller remarked, developed a literary *patois* containing a few Mercian, Anglian, or Kentish features which it imposed on all its texts."[45] If the 11th-century language of the Worcester scriptorium in Mercian territory was basic West Saxon with an admixture of Mercian, Anglian, and Kentish features, a comparable mixture of forms in *Beowulf* cannot be

---

45. *The Homilies of Wulfstan,* p. 50 (and n. 2, for corroborating views). See also Robert J. Menner, "Anglian and Saxon Elements in Wulfstan's Vocabulary." Elsewhere, Menner points out that Ælfric, "whose works were once assumed to represent Late West Saxon in its purest form, borrowed copiously . . . from the Anglian vocabulary." "The Vocabulary of the Old English Poems on Judgment Day," p. 584. For the rise of Late West Saxon as the foundation of the standard literary dialect see Helmut Gneuss, "The Origin of Standard Old English and Æthelwold's School at Winchester."

rightly used to prove that the poem was transmitted through several dialect areas over several centuries.

So far, it is possible to argue that three, slightly different, mixed, spoken dialects of the poet and his scribes came together with the mixed literary dialect in the early 11th century when *Beowulf* was composed. At this point the possibilities of their interrelationships seem infinite, but let us suppose, for example, that the poet came from a border area between English and Danish Mercia, his first scribe from Wessex, and his second scribe from Kent. The literary language of the monastic community in Mercia to which all three belonged was, as is to be expected, standard Late West Saxon. The poet's literary borrowing would have been mainly from the Mercian sources in his monastic library, at least some of which (like the three prose texts that precede *Beowulf* in the Nowell Codex) would have been in the early Mercian literary dialect. Poetic texts in the library, like the poems by the earlier Mercian poet Cynewulf, would have helped school the poet in the traditional poetic dialect. Certainly this hypothetical situation would not be impossible, or even unlikely, in early 11th-century Mercia, and it would explain not only the mixture of Danish folklore and English verse technique, but the mixture of forms, early and late, Anglian, Kentish, and standard Late West Saxon. The crucial problem is to explain the archaisms, for only early forms, surely not a mixture, suggest a long transmission. It should be remembered that the standard literary dialect was itself manifestly archaic in its inflections, and it was in phonology, as well, as its continued use of digraphs after monophthongization shows. Wrenn points out in his classic essay "'Standard' Old English" that "the blending of older and younger forms . . . is not—as I have shown—entirely absent from the accepted 'Standard' O. E. of our orthodox grammarians: it is, to some extent, a factor in the natural writing of any scribe before the time of printing" (p. 87). The preponderance of archaic forms in *Beowulf*, however, is caused by the use of an archaic poetic dialect that all poets, early and late, employed to some extent.

Beowulf, like most Old English poems, draws heavily upon a purely artificial language, usually referred to as the "poetic dialect," for many of its words and formulas. It is remarkable that most of the dialectal forms in *Beowulf* are poetic words, found exclusively in poetry, or only very rarely, and then very exceptionally, in prose. Klaeber's glossary conveniently employs a dagger to designate poetic words, a double dag-

ger to identify *hapax legomena,* and various other symbols for other
rare or unusual words. It is now generally admitted that non–West
Saxon forms like *heaðo-, alwalda, beado-* and *mece,* for example, cannot
be used for dialect tests (though some editors still use them) since they
were all incorporated into a common, cross-dialectal, poetic word-hoard
that could be used as well in Wessex as in Anglia, and as well in the
11th century as in the 7th or 8th. There are many other traditional
words in this word-hoard that are misleadingly used in dialect tests of
Beowulf's transmission. A poetic dialect for all Old English poetry was
recognized from the earliest days of Anglo-Saxon studies,[46] but the concept has never been applied with any rigor in attempts to establish the
original dialects for most Old English poems, and certainly not for *Beowulf.* Although no editor has yet denied the use of archaic poetic words,
formulas, and syntactic constructions in *Beowulf* that are common to all
the poetry, no editor has yet admitted that the use of what amounts to
an archaic poetic dialect radically weakens, if it does not eliminate, the
need for a complicated, and an ancient, transmission of the poem.

The concept of an Old English poetic dialect has recently come under
fire from Hans Schabram, as part of the conclusions reached in an
impressive study of word geography based on prose documents.[47] Schabram's attack needs to be discussed at this point in order to reaffirm the
validity of a common, archaic, poetic dialect for all eras and areas of
Anglo-Saxon England. Schabram learned from studying word groups
used to render the idea of *superbia,* "pride," that Anglian prose invariably used the word group *oferhygd-,* while West Saxon (and Kentish)
prose used the word groups *ofermod-, modig-,* and *prut-.* But he applied
his discovery rather recklessly to poetic texts in a separate section entitled "Das *Superbia* Wortgut in der Poesie" (pp. 123–129). The dangers
of this procedure had already been well summarized by Robert J. Menner: "The best studies of the differences between the Anglian and Saxon
vocabularies have been deliberately based on prose texts and have

46. Wrenn notes that George Hickes "discusses 'Dano-Saxon' . . . and the 'Dialec-
tus poetica' quite naturally." "'Standard' Old English," pp. 66–67. A clear expression
of the concept of a poetic dialect is in some editions of Otto Jespersen, *Growth and
Structure of the English Language,* for example, the ninth, pp. 50–51. More recent
views are cited below.

47. *Superbia: Studien zum altenglischen Wortschatz,* vol. 1, *Die dialektale und
zeitliche Verbreitung des Wortguts.*

adduced the poetic vocabulary only in confirmation of the results obtained from an examination of the prose. . . . As a consequence, with the materials readily available one can test the vocabulary of poetry for dialect only by the words it shares with prose, and the Old English poets' avoidance of prosaic words and cultivation of a distinct poetic vocabulary make this inconvenient."[48] Menner goes on to discuss the "archaic and traditional character of Old English poetic diction," stressing the fact that the avoidance of prosaic expressions and the search for unusual words and compounds enhanced cross-dialectal borrowing. The circumstances make word geography an extremely uncertain criterion when applied to poetry. Menner adds the relevant point that "the Saxon poet, steeped in the poetic tradition, must sometimes have borrowed words from Anglian poetry that were not poeticisms at all, words that were used in Anglian prose but not in West Saxon prose" ("Vocabulary," p. 585). Yet, according to Schabram, the appearance of *ofer-hygd-* in a West Saxon poem would be certain evidence of its Anglian origin, or of its contamination by an Anglian scribe, or some sort of aberration.

Without question, the evidence from the four word groups is far more complicated in the poetry than it is in the prose. Schabram oversimplifies the evidence when he says that only *oferhygd-* and *ofermod-* play a role in the poetry. It is not surprising, of course, that *prut-* is totally absent in Old English poems, regardless of their date and dialect. It was a loanword of the latter part of the 10th century, and Anglo-Saxon poets were always, as Schabram admits, anything but "fremdwortfreundlich" (p. 123). So the word *prut-* helps highlight the sharp distinction between the vocabulary of prose and poetry. The case is different with the native word group *modig-*. *Modig* (and its derivatives) appears with great frequency in the poetry, yet with a different meaning than it has in the prose. In poetry it generally means "high-spirited, courageous, brave"—that is, "proud" in the honorific sense. In prose it means "proud" in the deadly sense of the sin, *superbia*. Schabram demonstrates the distinction by citing examples from prose where Lucifer and the fallen angels are *modig,* and from verse, where God and the chosen are given the epithet (pp. 123–124, n. 2). But the evidence is not as unequivocal as Schabram suggests. In *Judith,* for instance, the poem

48. "The Vocabulary of the Old English Poems on Judgment Day," pp. 583–584.

that follows *Beowulf* in the Nowell Codex, *modig* is used in the prosaic sense to describe Holofernes (lines 26 and 52), while it is used in the poetic sense to describe Judith (line 334).[49] This case would seem to be a good example of an Anglian poet borrowing a word meaning that was used in West Saxon prose, but not in Anglian prose. One thing the distinct meanings for *modig-* show is that the old Anglian poetic meaning was part of an enduring "poetic dialect" that was intelligibly used by Late West Saxon poets (as *Maldon* testifies), even though the newer meaning was being used exclusively in West Saxon prose at the same time.

Schabram's reasons for doubting the validity of a common poetic dialect of ultimately Anglian origin do not stand up under scrutiny. Using only the two word groups *oferhygd-* and *ofermod-* in his investigation of the poetic texts, Schabram showed that Anglian poems invariably used *oferhygd-*, while Southern poems seemed to use *ofermod-*. He concluded that "dieses Resultat steht eindeutig im Widerspruch zu der gerade in neuerer Zeit oft geäusserten Vermutung, dass die ae. Dichtersprache hinsichtlich ihres Wortschatzes im grossen und ganzen ein supradialektales Gebilde auf anglishcher Basis sei, eine Art poetischer Kunstsprache, die ihre ursprüngliche lokale Eigenart im Laufe der Zeit weitgehend abgelegt habe" (p. 129). The nature of Schabram's evidence for the use of *ofermod-* in West Saxon poetry cannot support this vast conclusion, which totally ignores the scores of words (including *modig-*), compounds, formulas, and archaic forms and constructions, that are common to Old English poetry in general, from the earliest Anglian to the latest West Saxon poetry. Schabram's evidence that West Saxon poets invariably used *ofermod-* instead of *oferhygd-* is based on only three poetic texts: *The Meters of Boethius, Genesis B,* and *The Battle of Maldon.* The evidence is weak.

The Meters of Boethius and *Genesis B* cannot be used as representative West Saxon poems. Words from the *ofermod-* group appear in the *Meters* seven times, but these verses are a fairly faithful translation of an earlier *prose* translation of the Latin source.[50] Furthermore, the versifier, who may have been King Alfred, was in any case an amateur

---

49. B. J. Timmer, ed., *Judith.*
50. See G. P. Krapp, ed., *The Paris Psalter and the Meters of Boethius,* pp. xlv–xlviii.

poet, whose uneven use of the older "poetic dialect" was permeated, as Sisam has shown, by "a strong blend of contemporary West Saxon prose which is alien to the earlier poetry" (*Studies*, p. 297). Words from the prosaic *ofermod-* family in the *Meters* can be safely regarded as part of this blend. *Genesis B,* on the other hand, is not a good example of West Saxon poetry, because it is a faithful translation of an Old Saxon poem.[51] Like the *Meters,* it too uses words from the *ofermod-* group seven times, but it also uses *oferhygd* once. Schabram accounts for the appearance of *oferhygd* in this "West Saxon" poem by describing the word as a direct translation from Old Saxon: "Bedenkt man nämlich, dass der *Heliand* im *superbia*-Bereich als Adjektiv zwar *oƀarmod* und *oƀarmodig,* als Substantiv dagegen *oƀarhugd* verwendet, so ist der Schluss berechtigt, dass die Vorlage der *Genesis B* in Vers 328 *oƀarhugd* bot" (p. 128). Notably, Schabram's explanation also accounts for the occurrence of *ofermod-* words in *Genesis B.* Surely a verse translation of an Anglo-Saxon prose text by an amateur poet, or a faithful translation of an old Saxon poem, cannot be fairly used to typify West Saxon poetic usage.

With this evidence gone, Schabram's case against a common poetic dialect of ultimately Anglian origin rests on an isolated occurrence of *ofermode* in *The Battle of Maldon.* The context explains its usage here:

> Ða se eorl ongan   for his ofermode
> alyfan landes to fela   laþere ðeode.[52]

The West Saxon poet used the strongest word in his vocabulary for the pride that led Byrhtnoð to his defeat and death at Maldon. In this case the use of a prosaic West Saxon word is fully justified, and does not in the least undermine the wealth of evidence attesting a "poetic dialect" (used pervasively in *Maldon*) as part of a verse tradition that began early in the Anglian parts of England.

The best accounts of the archaic poetic dialect are encountered in studies of the poetry itself, but the concept is not alien even to the tra-

---

51. As Krapp says, "The Anglo-Saxon translation follows the Old Saxon so closely that all thought of accidental similarity or mere imitation is excluded." *The Junius Manuscript,* pp. xxv–xxvi.

52. E. V. K. Dobbie, ed., *The Anglo-Saxon Minor Poems,* lines 89–90.

ditional grammars.[53] Campbell's *Old English Grammar* provides an especially good summary:

> A lack of dialectal uniformity also characterizes the bulk of the extant Old English verse. This verse is mostly preserved in copies dating from *c.* 1000, and while these are predominantly late West-Saxon they are extremely rich in dialectal forms of various kinds. Although most of these non-West-Saxon forms can be classified as phonologically or morphologically proper to one dialect or another, it is seldom possible to declare with confidence that a given poem was originally in a particular dialect, or even that it was non-West-Saxon. For example, the two poems on the victories of Æthelstan and Eadmund in 937 and 942 can hardly be regarded as non-West-Saxon in origin, but all the extant copies are rich in non-West-Saxon forms. There seems to have been, in fact, a "general OE poetic dialect," mixed in vocabulary, phonology, and inflexion, and an originally dialectally pure poem, which achieved general popularity, would in transmission become approximated to this poetic dialect, while new poems would be written down from the beginning with considerable indifference to dialectal consistency. (pp. 9–10)

Theoretically, then, a poet using an archaic poetic dialect could have created *Beowulf* during the reign of Cnut the Great.[54]

The theory is well illustrated in Wrenn's comments on *The Battle of Brunanburh.* The superior achievement of the *Beowulf* poet in the use of the common traditions should be viewed aesthetically, not chronologically. Wrenn says of *The Battle of Brunanburh,* a Chronicle poem that commemorates an English victory over Scandinavian raiders in 937: "The poem abounds in phrases and formulaic expressions from the

---

53. Especially Sisam in "Dialect Origins of the Earlier Old English Verse" and "The Authorship of the Verse Translation of Boethius's Metra," *Studies,* pp. 119–139 and 293–297. Cf. the introduction to Wrenn's edition as well as *A Study of Old English Literature,* pp. 35–37, 48 ff., 185–187; and especially Robert Menner's "The Vocabulary of the Old English Poems on Judgment Day," pp. 583–585.

54. The aims of standard grammars, to describe the phonology and morphology of spoken Old English, preclude any systematic description of the poetic dialect, or for that matter, of the standard Late West Saxon literary dialect, the vagaries of which are primarily orthographical. Since purely orthographical variations are ignored in the standard grammars, the grammars are of rather limited use for explaining the mixture of forms in *Beowulf.*

traditional earlier heroic poetry, in the use of the stylistic device of parallel variation, and in forms which were by the tenth century archaic or dialectal, but which were felt to be proper to a deliberate revival of the ancient ways of heroic verse, where such forms were probably part of a traditional poetic vocabulary. Of the 146 half-lines in *The Battle of Brunanburh* one-seventh had already occurred in earlier verse."[55] As Wrenn says, "For the literary historian . . . it is important as a reminder that the ancient ways of verse were effectively revived and cultivated at so late a period. But in fact this kind of courtly verse continued to be produced parallel with the free popular verse right up to the Norman Conquest, as the relative correctness of the *Chronicle* poem on the *Death of Edward the Confessor* clearly demonstrates" (*Study*, p. 183). Since the Anglo-Saxon Chronicles were presumably well known in monastic centers throughout England, 11th-century poets must have known *Brunanburh,* and other poems like it, and if they were better poets they would have produced better poems. *Beowulf* cannot be dated before *Brunanburh* solely on the assumption that early heroic poems were better heroic poems. Great poets have lived in unlikely times.

The mixture of forms in *Beowulf* should no longer preclude the possibility at least of dating the poem late. Klaeber had answered his own question, "How can this mixture of forms, early and late, West Saxon, Northumbrian, Mercian, Kentish, Saxon patois be accounted for?" with the old, unquestioned assumption of a very early date and of a long, complicated transmission. But, as we have seen, the question can be answered otherwise. The common literary language of the early 11th century known as Late West Saxon, or better as Late Old English, was itself a mixture of forms, early and late, with numerous cross-dialectal features, determined in large measure only by the idiosyncracies of its user and his scribes. And the acknowledged use of an archaic poetic dialect of ultimately Anglian origin, in tandem with the common literary language of the early 11th century, is all that is necessary to answer Klaeber's question in a simpler and more credible way.

Klaeber himself makes, in passing, all of the concessions that are needed to vitiate his own theory of transmission: he admits that there was "an artificial, conventional standard, a sort of compromise dialect [that] had come into use as the acknowledged medium for the compo-

55. *Study* pp. 182–183.

sition of Anglo-Saxon poetry," though he accepts it "only in regard to the continued employment of ancient forms (archaisms) and of certain Anglian elements firmly embedded in the vocabulary of early Anglian poetry" (p. lxxxviii). This concession alone, which constitutes a good definition of the poetic dialect, would account for most of the mixture of forms in *Beowulf*. But Klaeber also concedes that there was "occasional fluctuation between traditional and phonetic spelling"; a "pronounced Anglo-Saxon delight in variation" (orthographical variation is cited); "the mingling of dialects in monastic communities" (p. lxxxix, n. 2); that there are archaisms in the poem, forms like *mece, beadu-,* and *heaþu-,* which, despite their dialectal origins, were "uniformly adhered to even in Southern texts" (p. lxxxviii); and that the individual scribes were undoubtedly responsible for many characteristic forms (pp. lxxxix–xci). A complicated transmission is simply not needed for an early 11th-century poem, written in an eclectic, standard literary dialect, that itself admits archaisms and orthographical variations, and was thoroughly permeated by an archaic, poetic dialect that was also eclectic.

There is sufficient reason for placing the poet's homeland, as suggested earlier, somewhere in Mercian territory. The language of *Beowulf* is literary Late West Saxon mainly, but the frequent intrusions of Mercianisms and the self-assured and skillful use of the Anglian poetic dialect argue strongly in favor of a Mercian provenance. If the poem is to be dated late, the persistent Mercianisms, and what appears to be a vestigial influence of the Old Mercian literary dialect (as defined by Vleeskruyer), stem from the poet and his reading. If he was an 11th-century Mercian, the literary tradition of his region and, indeed, the contents of his monastic library were to a large extent in the Mercian literary dialect, even though it had been superseded by the Late West Saxon literary dialect. The older MSS were not discarded, it is safe to say. Vleeskruyer reasonably guesses that the Mercian literary dialect most likely grew "from the local speech of Tamworth and Lichfield, the administrative and ecclesiastical centres of the Mercian kingdom, which were within ten miles of each other" (p. 62). If the *Beowulf* poet came from this general area, too, in the heart of Mercian territory, there would be good reason for the conservative retention of some of the salient characteristics of the old literary dialect. Moreover, since both towns fall on or near the Danelaw boundary of Watling Street, Danish traditions would have had well over a century to ripen in English minds.

Surely many Danish stories were part of Anglo-Saxon folklore by the time of Cnut, and it is precisely in such areas as these that English receptiveness to Cnut's reign would have been quickest to develop. It is significant that when Swein made his great march south in the conquest of 1013, "it was not until he had crossed Watling Street into English Mercia that he allowed his men to harry the countryside" (Stenton, *Anglo-Saxon England*, p. 385). In all likelihood the Danish materials in *Beowulf* had matured in Danish Mercia and in the border areas between English and Danish Mercia long before Swein or Cnut arrived.[56]

The Mixture of Forms in *Beowulf*

Still the most compelling argument against the historical evidence for an 11th-century provenance of *Beowulf* appears implicitly in Klaeber's seemingly endless lists of "Non–West Saxon Elements" (pp. lxxiv–lxxxi). This mixture of forms must now be accounted for explicitly, in order to show, using the actual evidence, that *Beowulf* could have been produced in the early 11th century. The following explanations for non-standard forms are not meant to be dogmatic or exclusive, but they are meant to be acceptable. A close examination of the amorphous mass of linguistic data assembled by Klaeber shows that the forms are actually indigenous to the Late West Saxon literary dialect or to the archaic poetic word-hoard, and that the residue should be seen as sporadic Mercian intrusions to be expected in a poem of Mercian origin. In other words, a literate, 11th-century Mercian poet alone could have brought about the particular mixture of forms in *Beowulf.* Klaeber's formidable lists under non–West Saxon "Vowels of Accented Syllables" are confusing to work with, because he makes no attempt to distinguish exclusively between dialects. There are many problems that his method tends to obscure. Many of the forms are palpably orthographical, not phonological, and these forms need especially to be carefully distinguished. Others, such as personal names and emendations, cannot be used for dialect tests. Still others, as Klaeber freely admits, are Late West Saxon

---

56. See C. E. Wright, *The Cultivation of Saga in Anglo-Saxon England*, esp. p. 136.

features. But the most befuddling aspect of the method is that it becomes nearly impossible to keep track of the various "dialect colorings" in the poem: one wants to know how much of a general Anglian coloring there is, how much of a Northumbrian, Mercian, Early West Saxon, and Kentish, and how much is early and how much is late. For this reason it will be well to found an analysis of the linguistic forms on P. G. Thomas's "Notes on the Language of *Beowulf*," which Klaeber justly calls a "convenient summary of dialectal forms" (p. clxv). However, any significant additions by Klaeber to Thomas's data will also be discussed in passing.

Thomas organizes his linguistic material under the West Saxon element and the non–West Saxon element, and breaks down the latter under Anglian, Mercian, and Kentish subsections. He lists some heterogeneous non–West Saxon elements first, without attempting to label them under any particular non–West Saxon dialect. The personal names from the so-called Northumbrian lists prove nothing about the linguistic origin of the poem. It is interesting, perhaps, to know from the 9th-century *Liber Vitæ ecclesiæ Dunelmensis* that among the donors to the Durham church of St. Cuthbert were men named Biu[u]ulf, Wiglaf, Hyglac, Ingild, Heardred, Hama, Offa, and Herebald, though where the donors all came from in England is anyone's guess.[57] Equally inconclusive are the names in the 9th-century "Northumbrian" *Genealogies,* which are in fact lists of bishops from throughout the country, and royal genealogies for Mercia and Kent, as well as Northumbria. In any event, scholars now know that the text is Mercian, and Sisam has argued for a Lichfield provenance.[58] Thomas cites only the names Finn,

---

57. As A. Campbell says, "In using names for linguistic purposes it should always be remembered that in them archaic and dialectal forms tend to be crystallized, so that they do not reflect the dialect of the writers of the texts in which they are preserved." *Old English Grammar,* p. 5. The lists of names do show, however, the irrelevance of the forms of the personal names in *Beowulf* as a criterion of date. Chambers made much of the fact that the names in *Beowulf* are "in the correct English forms which we should expect, according to English sound laws, if the names had been brought over in the sixth century, and handed down traditionally." *Beowulf,* p. 323. The argument does not affect the 11th-century origin of the poem, for the names were transmitted by people, from generation to generation, not necessarily by poems.

58. Sisam argues that "the bishops of Lichfield alone have been brought up to date, once between 828 and 836, and again at the end of the twelfth century." *Studies,* pp. 5–6. Vleeskruyer adds that the handwriting is Mercian. (*Life of St. Chad,* p. 51).

Hroðmund, and Iurmenric (Eormenric) from the *Genealogies;* he might have added Wærmund (Garmund) Hunfrið (Hunferð),[59] Ecglaf, Heardred, Hengest, and Offa Rex.[60] But, despite the Lichfield connection, there is no reason whatever to reach any conclusions regarding dialect origins on the basis of personal names.

The few cases Thomas cites of non–West Saxon grammatical forms are either weak evidence or no evidence at all. Thomas himself notes that examples of genitive singular in -*as,* instead of -*es,* occur in Late West Saxon; surely they are to be counted among the many leveled forms in the poem. The verbal forms *hafu, hafo, ful-læstu, hafast,* and *hafað,* are poetic archaisms (Klaeber, p. lxxxvii), though an Anglian poet might be most likely to use them. Yet *hafað* and *nafað* occur occasionally in Ælfric, too. The forms *eaweð* and *ge-eawed* are, Thomas says, "probably" non–West Saxon, while Klaeber says they are "practically" non–West Saxon (p. lxxiii). Campbell points out that "a mark of Class III [verbs] is the appearance side by side of forms with and without . . . *i*-umlaut of the root vowel," and he gives *iewan/eawan* as an example (*Old English Grammar,* pp. 339–340). With one exception this is the extent of Thomas's evidence of non–West Saxon grammatical forms, and not a single example was unquestionably non–West Saxon. Thomas is more certain of the exception, and says, "In the imperative 'wæs' (407) we have a Northumbrian form"; but Klaeber is more accurate when he says that *æ* for West Saxon *e* is "not infrequent in several Angl. texts, but sporadically found also elsewhere" (p. lxxiv). Frequent confusion between the graphs *æ* and *e* is characteristic of Late Old English spelling—it is salient, for instance, in the works of Ælfric— and is part of the transition from Old to Middle English spelling.[61]

59. M. F. Vaughan, "A Reconsideration of 'Unferð,'" shows with good onomastic, paleographical, and phonological reasons that Hunferð (as the name always appears in the MS) should be given back his real name.

60. Henry Sweet, ed., *The Oldest English Texts,* p. 168, lines 11, 21, and 29 (twice), p. 170, line 93, and p. 171, lines 110, 114, 120, and 123.

61. Late Old English spelling, and scribal spelling habits, are fully presented in Willy Schlemilch, *Beiträge zur Sprache und Orthographie spätaltengl. Sprachdenkmäler der Übergangszeit (1000–1150).* Klaeber (in *Beowulf*) cites Schlemilch for the interchange of *æ* and *e* on p. lxxvii, and elsewhere (for example, p. lxxv) admits its purely orthographical nature. DeCamp notes that *æ* for *e* "became a shibboleth of the standard West Saxon dialect, and so was more widely imitated than were other West Saxon features." "Genesis," p. 366.

Thomas lists the remainder of his general "Non–W.S. Element" under the following phonological headings: narrowing of $\bar{æ}$ to $\bar{e}$; absence of breaking; non–West Saxon breaking; absence of palatalization; non–West Saxon *u*- or *a*-umlaut. The bulk of the examples may well be orthographical, not phonological. Thus, narrowing of *æ* to *e* may again be Late Old English confusion between the two letters, at a time when they had become almost equivalent graphs. This is also characteristic of the Mercian literary dialect, and the phenomenon is perhaps ultimately to be ascribed to the mingling of dialects. Linguistic diffusion (not phonology) is certainly the explanation for the spelling *mece* in West Saxon texts, for as Klaeber says, "This, the invariable form in OE., had become stereotyped through its use in Anglian poetry" (p. lxxvii, n. 4). That the second scribe was aware of the spelling variation between *æ* and *e* is indicated by his use of a hooklike mark beneath the *e*'s of *bel* (2126, *bæl* elsewhere), *reced* (1981, first *e*), and *fæðmie* (2652), and beneath the *æ* of *sæcce* (1989). Klaeber describes the interchange of *secce* (600) and *sæcce* as characteristic of Saxon patois (p. lxxv), an old theoretical subdialect that is now recognized as Mercian.[62] G. I. Needham says of *æ/e* variation in his edition of *Ælfric: Lives of Three English Saints*, "These spellings are probably better regarded as due to the late date of the MSS [mostly 11th-century], than as dialectal features" (p. 7). The same caveat applies to the 11th-century MS of *Beowulf*. In any case, purely orthographical variations between *æ* and *e* are undoubted features of the Mercian literary dialect and of standard Late Old English.

The four other phonological headings are equally misleading. Thomas can cite only one example under "absence of breaking," where he describes the disputed word *hard-fyrde* (that is, *-fyrdne*, 2245), as an example of unbroken *a* before *r* + consonant. Zupitza's transcript of the MS reads *hard-wyrðne*. The MS is badly damaged on this folio, and the letters in question are so faded that *f* may indeed be *w*, and *d* may be *ð*, as Zupitza says. If Zupitza is right, *hard*- must be emended to *hord*-, as all current editors have done. Consequently, Klaeber's only example of absence of breaking does not even exist in the MS and

---

62. Vleeskruyer refers to Saxon patois as "an unhappy relic of the older confusion between Kentish and Mercian." *Life of St. Chad,* p. 54. See J. J. Campbell, "The Harley Glossary and 'Saxon Patois.'"

depends on a tortuous, and totally unneeded, emendation: "Original unbroken *a* before *r* + *consonant* is possibly hidden behind the MS. spelling *brand* in 1020, i. e. *barn [*sic*]"[63] Thomas and Klaeber's lonely example of non–West Saxon breaking of *e* before *l* + consonant occurs in *seolfa* (3067), which may be considered a distinctly Anglian form; yet Vleeskruyer notes that "Crawford (p. 10) regards *seolf* as late West Saxon, which is true in so far as it occurs in Westernized late MSS" (p. 111, n. 4). Similarly, Thomas and Klaeber can cite only one word, (-)*gæst*, as an example of non–West Saxon absence of palatalization, and this example is surely a ghost: in each case the meanings "spirit, sprite, demon" (that is, *gast, gæst*) fit the context as well as, if not better than, "stranger, visitor" (*gist*).[64] Klaeber admits the ambiguity in his glossary (p. 338), and the confusion is nicely illustrated when one contrasts Thomas's examples (lines 102, 1331, 1800, 1995, 2073, 2312, 2670, 2699) with Klaeber's (1800, 1893, 2312, 2670, 2699). There is more evidence of *u*- or *a*-mutation of *e* to *eo* and *i* to *io(eo)*, but it is not clear to what extent the evidence is non–West Saxon. Vleeskruyer, following Luick, states that these mutations are common to all Old English dialects when the vowel is followed by *r, l,* or *f* (pp. 112 and 113), and this exception disposes of much of the evidence. The remaining mutations of *e* to *eo* occur before dentals, which is "mainly non–West Saxon" (Vleeskruyer, p. 113), but probably "mainly" Mercian poeticisms (such as *eodor,* "protector, prince," *eoten,* "giant," and *eotenisc,* "made by giants"; and the poetic compounds, *eoten-weard,* "watch against a giant," *meodo-benc, -heal, -setl, -scenc, -wong,* and *meotod-sceaft,* "decree of fate"). It would have been natural for an 11th-

63. The MS reading *brand* has been ably defended by Sherman M. Kuhn, "The Sword of Healfdene"; and by Hertha Marquardt, "Fürstenund Kriegerkenning im *Beowulf.*" The MS reading is given in the editions of Wrenn-Bolton and von Schaubert.

64. The only exception is a conjectural restoration at line 1893. Thorkelin A wrote *gæs* . . . , but the reading was not confirmed by Thorkelin B, which tells us that the upper corner had broken off by the time B made his transcript (see Zupitza's FS). A's reading here (on the verso, fol. 171) is suspicious, for both A's and B's readings for the upper corner on the recto suggest that the corner was already gone when A made his transcript (*seodð* A, *seodda* B—not *seoððan*). If the corner was gone when A transcribed fol. 171v, he may have metathesized *sæg* . . . , by mistake, from *sægeatas* in the upper corner of 170v. In any case, a phonological argument cannot rest on a conjectural restoration.

century Mercian poet using a poetic dialect to contribute such forms to the poem. The cases of back mutation of *i* to *io (eo)* before dentals (and nasals) are not necessarily non–West Saxon, and examples are often found in late Old English MSS, as Vleeskruyer points out (p. 113). This is the extent of Thomas's broad delineation of non–West Saxon elements. It is obvious that, so far, there is no linguistic basis for assuming a complicated transmission of the text. So far, it can still be claimed that the poem was written by an 11th-century Mercian poet in standard Late Old English, with poetic and a few distinctively Anglian forms mixed in.

Under the somewhat more specific "Anglian Element" (pp. 205–206), Thomas lists six dialectal traits found in *Beowulf:* unbroken *a* before *l* + consonant; *i*-mutation of *ea* as *e*; *i*-mutation of *ea* before *r* + consonant and before *l* + consonant; *i*-mutation of *iu*; smoothing of *eu* to *e* before *rh* and before *h*; and smoothing of *œo* to *œ* before *h* and before *rg*. In all, Thomas lists ninety-two forms that according to him belong to the Anglian dialects (that is, Northumbrian *or* Mercian). Nearly half (forty-two forms) are examples of unbroken *a* before *l* + consonant. Frederick Tupper has rightly called this spelling the weakest of all weak arguments for Anglian provenance;[65] it is certain that this feature cannot fairly be used in dialect tests, for it is found in all dialects, and is especially frequent in Southern poems. The words in *Beowulf* are mostly poetic. B. J. Timmer has pointed out that the cases in *Judith* (*waldend, alwalda,* and *aldor* and its derivatives) "should be seen as traditional words, appearing in WSax from the early Anglian poetry."[66] The same three words in *Beowulf* account for thirty-six of the forty-two cases cited by Thomas. Schlemilch shows that the variation between broken and unbroken forms exists in Late West Saxon texts (p. 27),

---

65. "The Philological Legend of Cynewulf," p. 248. For a full discussion of this problem, see E. G. Stanley, "Spellings of the *Waldend* Group."

66. Timmer assigns the mixture of forms in *Judith* to the language of the Worcester scriptorium (*Judith,* pp. 4–6). Sisam has complained, with some justice, that "Worcester tends to become a limbo for texts that show both Anglian and West Saxon forms"; Sisam was right to object that no one has yet "specified the mixture of dialect which is supposed to distinguish books produced at Worcester from those produced at other places near the old border between Mercia and Wessex." "Canterbury, Lichfield, and the Vespasian Psalter," p. 123, n. 2. Timmer speaks of the language of the Worcester scriptorium as if it were the standard literary dialect of England.

while Vleeskruyer marks the same variation as a characteristic of the Mercian literary dialect, and notes that its use in Early West Saxon "would seem to bespeak divergence of spelling practices rather than of phonology" (pp. 98–100). Spelling practice is undoubtedly behind the sporadic uses of unbroken forms in Wulfstan MSS (for example, *waldend* beside *wealdend,* as in *Beowulf*). The rich mixture of broken and unbroken forms from the "*waldend* group" in a late Old English poem suggests, as Stanley has shown, an Anglian poet, mixing Anglian phonology with hypercorrect West Saxon spelling—but the forms themselves had become nondialectal.

The same is generally true of the other "Anglianisms" Thomas isolates. He gives twelve examples of *i*-mutation of *ea* as *e*. Two examples are emendations and must be dismissed. Of the ten remaining cases, there are six word elements involved: *eg-, eð(e)-, -gesene, -hedige, leg-,* and *-nedlan*. Vleeskruyer, citing Luick and Napier, states that *eg-* is "not distinctively Anglian, and may be late West Saxon" (p. 93). The next two word elements appear, alternately, in the same word: *eð-gesyne* (1110) and *yð-gesene* (1244). The reversal of the mixture of forms here is more likely to occur from conscious variation, or laxity in the spelling tradition, than from remarkably coincidental scribal slips in the course of transmission. An orthographical explanation can also be given for *leg-,* which occurs in *leg-draca* (3040) along with the normal Late West Saxon form, *lig-draca* (2333); *leg-* is the usual spelling in the poetry, even in Late West Saxon poems (see *Maldon,* line 276). The two remaining cases are in poetic compounds (*þrea-nedlan,* "sore distress," and *nið-hedige,* "hostile," a *hapax* word), and may be reasonably ascribed to the Mercian poet.

An occasional interchange between *e* and *y* also occurs in some words that Thomas assigns to Anglian *i*-umlaut of *ea* before *r* + consonant, though he acknowledges that a "similar phenomenon" is found in common Late Old English. The cases of mutation before *l* + consonant in *eldo* and *eldum,* as well as in *wælm,* all appear in the second part of the MS, after line 1939; these are possibly Kentish features, but the interchange of *e (æ)* and *y (i)* in these cases is characteristic of texts written in the Mercian literary dialect, and may be equally attributed to the Mercian poet (Vleeskruyer, pp. 72–73). The one certain case that Thomas cites of *i*-mutation of *iu* (*eorres,* 1447), and the few additional cases cited by Klaeber (p. lxxix) constitute another feature of the Mercian literary dialect, but as Vleeskruyer mentions, "This *eo* is sometimes found in late copies of West Saxon texts" (p. 112). The thirteen uncertain cases are common Late Old English, as Thomas remarks. The few supposed cases of Anglian smoothing perhaps show the poet's dialect creeping in, but *ferh* (305, 2706, instead of the usual *feorh*) may simply be by analogy to the invariable poetic word *ferhð,* or a late phonetic spelling reflecting general monophthongization of a diphthong; similarly, *gecehtlan* (369) and *gecehted* (1885), where *ce* appears instead of *ea,* may only reflect Late Old English orthography after monophthongization. Thus, the "Anglian" forms surveyed by Thomas do not undermine the thesis that *Beowulf* is a late poem by a Mercian poet, who wrote in the standard Late West Saxon literary dialect. The Anglianisms, in the few cases where they seem clearly distinct from common Late Old English, can all be assigned to the Mercian subdialect. There is no reason to assume that a Northumbrian version ever existed.

The question of a Mercian origin is another matter. The confident attribution of the prose texts of the Nowell Codex to the Mercian literary dialect, and Sisam's inference that all the texts "were assembled into a collection . . . someplace in Mercia where West Saxon influences were strong in the later tenth century" (*Studies,* pp. 94 ff.), at least imply a sound Mercian connection for the poem. And the broad non–West Saxon and Anglian elements, when not in fact common Late Old English, point toward Mercia rather than Northumbria. Obviously the Mercian element itself can only add more support to the thesis of a Mercian poet, but it must be emphasized that the distinctively Mercian forms in the poem, like the general Anglian forms (which may also be Mercian), do not markedly alter the pervasive, common Late West Saxon character of the language in its literary form. Thomas's Mercian element, that is to say, displays precisely the same kind of linguistic relation to standard Late Old English as do the non–West Saxon and Anglian elements. Many of the forms are nondialectal, in the sense that they are found in standard Late Old English, or are shared by other dialects, or are part of the cross-dialectal poetic word-hoard.

Thomas lists seventy-three forms that he assigns to the Mercian dialect. The evidence is not overwhelming. As he says, "the most characteristic feature of Mercian" is the back mutation of *a* to *ea.* But the feature is still not a very reliable test of dialect, since a large number of poetic terms (notably *heaþu-,* which never occurs *in any dialect* without

back mutation) belong to the cross-dialectal poetic word-hoard.[67] Three
of these poetic terms—*heaþu-, eafora,* and *eafoð*—account for no fewer
than sixty of the seventy-three Mercian forms listed by Thomas. Klaeber adds about forty back-mutated forms, but with the same result: he
counts one more case each for *heaþu-, eafora,* and *eafoð,* and adds two
more poetic terms, *beadu-* (used sixteen times) and *cearu-* (eight times).
He also lists *ealu-* (seven times) and draws attention to the significant
fact that the Mercian spelling had passed into West Saxon as well
(p. lxxviii). There were doubtless other Mercian words incorporated
into West Saxon, and variant spellings for those that did not make a
complete transition. Aside from back mutation, Thomas lists three
forms as exhibiting Mercian (or Kentish) narrowing of *æ* to *e,* and one
word, twice used in poetic compounds, as exhibiting Mercian (or Kentish) *i*-mutation of *ea* (or *æ*). With a Mercian poet these words raise no
problems, though it is possible to assign both phonological features,
especially the ubiquitous *æ/e* variation, to Late Old English spelling.

If the Mercian evidence appears to be somewhat scanty for a poem
supposedly written by an 11th-century Mercian poet, it should be
remembered that the non–West Saxon and Anglian evidence was also
possibly Mercian. As a matter of fact the Mercian evidence can be reasonably used to argue that the Anglian poetic archaisms are all of Mercian origin. Since the largest group, by far, of dialectally distinct poetic
terms (the back mutations) is of unquestionably Mercian origin, one
can confidently assign the other poetic terms, which are Anglian anyway, to a Mercian origin as well. This process of deduction would
incorporate such words as *mece, alwalda, anwalda, b(e)aldor, beorn,
aldre, waldend, ferhð, h(e)afola, me(o)tod,* and all the dialectally neu-
tral synonyms and poetic compounds, into the Mercian poetic word-
hoard, along with the Mercian back mutations *beadu, cearu, eafora,
eafoð,* and *heaþu.* In this way the Mercian underpinning of the poem
can begin to emerge from the rubble of non–West Saxon and Anglian
elements. Mercian can incorporate all of the Anglian poetic vocabulary,
while Northumbrian, because of the back-mutated forms, cannot. A
Mercian poet becomes a distinct probability, and the need for a complicated transmission of the poem dissolves.

67. A. Campbell, *Old English Grammar,* pp. 5 and 86–87.

Thomas ends his survey on the language of *Beowulf* with a few brief comments on the Kentish element. He says that "the Kentish forms are all doubtful" and that "most of the supposed Kentish forms may be either Anglian, Mercian, or L. W. S." (p. 207). Since Anglian includes Mercian, further reduction to Mercian and standard Late Old English is possible. Yet a word should be said about what many scholars have taken for a persistent Kentish element in the second scribe's part of the MS. The old transmission theory presumed a Kentish exemplar, which was more accurately preserved by the second scribe than by the first.[68] The theory is based on the high incidence of *io* forms (rather than *eo*) in the second part of the MS, compared to the relative lack of *io* forms in the first part. Thomas presents the facts: "It is remarkable that up to the point where the first hand ceases to appear in the MS. (l. 1939), there are but 11 examples of *io* as against 786 of *eo*. From this point to the end of the poem there are 117 examples of *io* as against 482 of *eo*. The total number of *eo* forms in *Beowulf* is thus 1268, of *io* 128" (p. 203). The *io* forms, as Thomas says, are not necessarily non–West Saxon, but the proportions of their usage are still in some way significant. The simplest explanation is that, when he copied *Beowulf*, *io/eo* variation was an orthographical peculiarity of the second scribe, perhaps because he was Kentish, or, equally plausibly, Anglian.[69]

The only real objection that can be made to this explanation is that the *Judith* fragment, which was also copied by the second scribe, contains no *io* spellings at all. However, since *Judith* originally belonged to a different codex,[70] the objection loses its force: after copying *Beowulf* the scribe could well have standardized his spelling to conform to the

---

68. Bernhard ten Brink, *Beowulf: Untersuchungen, Quellen und Forschungen zur Sprach- und Kulturgeschichte der germanischen Völker*, p. 239.

69. As Menner points out, *io* forms may be Anglian in a late poem. *The Poetical Dialogues of Solomon and Saturn*, p. 18.

70. Ker observes that a pattern of wormholes running through the last ten folios of *Beowulf*, but not through *Judith*, and the bad condition of the last page of *Beowulf*, "show that Beowulf was once at the end of the manuscript and not followed, as it now is, by Judith." He concludes that *Judith* must have been at one time in a different position in the codex (*Catalogue*, p. 282), but Malone makes the more acceptable conjecture that it was added on at a later time (*Nowell Codex*, p. 17). The differences in the rulings and in the style of the capital initials confirm Malone's guess.

practice at the Mercian scriptorium.[71] Moreover, the textual evidence
that the *io/eo* variation was the second scribe's orthographical peculiarity is hard to refute. Sisam noticed that the first scribe's eleven *io*
forms are uniformly derived from historical *iu* forms, while the second
scribe freely substitutes *io* for historical *eu*, as well as *iu,* forms. Obviously, as Sisam concluded, "the first scribe cannot have eliminated *io*
spellings from his part of *Beowulf,* for even if the evidence that he usually copied mechanically is set aside . . . he could hardly distinguish the
few examples of historical *io* which remain in his part of *Beowulf*"
(*Studies,* p. 93). That the free, unhistorical *io/eo* variation is purely
orthographical is shown, as well, in the scores of instances where both
io and *eo* are found in a single line or in two consecutive lines (Rypins,
p. xxv). It is highly unlikely that the phonological history of the poem
would have been inadvertently preserved in this way: the scribe could
not have been so capriciously dim-witted. The clearest sign that the *io/*
eo variation is orthographical rather than phonological can be seen in
the name *Beowulf,* which the second scribe spells *Biowulf* fourteen of
seventeen times. It would be hard to argue, and hard to accept, that the
scribe could not decide whether the hero's name should be Beowulf or
Biowulf, yet on a single folio he writes *Beowulf* once and *Biowulf* twice
(1971, 1987, 1999). The same variation occurs in the name of Beowulf's
father, Ecgþeow (versus Ecgþiow). Surely spelling tradition, not faulty
transmission is behind a line like *Biowulf maþelade, bearn Ecgþeowes*
(2425). And since the spelling tradition in this respect so markedly differs from that in the first part of the MS, it should most naturally be
charged to the scribe, not to his exemplar. On the other hand, the Mercian poet himself might have introduced the *io* spellings late in the text,
as a pseudoarchaism, or merely as a spelling variant. There is simply
no reason to believe that the free variation between *io* and *eo* is more
phonologically significant than the free variation between *i* and *y* (as in
drihten/dryhten) or between *a* and *o* before nasals (as in *man/mon*).

71. Stanley Rypins, citing Skeat, makes the interesting observation that "at Chap.
xx, verse 23 of the Lindisfarne *St. John,* the scribe begins, oddly enough, to write *gi*
in place of the prefix *ge* which previously he had been consistently using—a phenomenon which in large measure parallels the interchange of *io* and *eo* in *Beowulf.*" *Three
Old English Prose Texts in* MS *Cotton Vitellius A.* XV, p. xiv.

A mixed orthography was natural to the Late West Saxon literary dialect.

So the mixture of forms Klaeber speaks of—"early and late, West Saxon, Northumbrian, Mercian, Kentish, Saxon patois"— does not so plainly point "to a checkered history of the written text," as he so confidently asserted, and as the other editors of *Beowulf* confidently believed. This revaluation of the mixture of forms points more plainly, it seems, to a comparatively straightforward history of the written text: an 11th-century MS; an 11th-century Mercian poet using an archaic poetic dialect; an 11th-century standard literary dialect that contained early and late, cross-dialectal forms, and admitted many spelling variations; and (perhaps) two 11th-century scribes following slightly different spelling practices. With this theory in hand one can approach with more courage Klaeber's frightening mound of forms, where non–West Saxon elements are supposed to lurk in the vowels of accented syllables (pp. lxxiv–lxxxi). One can pass quickly from vowel to vowel, sweeping away the many forms that Klaeber admits can be Late West Saxon, then the emendations and the personal names, the archaic poetic diction that is found even in unquestionably late poems, and the virtually certain cases (*œ/e* and *io/eo*) of orthographical variation. And when one reaches the chimera * īo*, at the end of the lists, the mixture of phonological forms, and the complicated transmission it created, will be gone.

Conclusion

That the *Beowulf* MS was copied in the early 11th century, during the reign of Cnut the Great, strikes me as beyond reasonable doubt. The thesis should not be very controversial, since paleographers agree that it was copied in the late 10th or early 11th century, and history shows that it was probably copied after 1016. What really matters, of course, is the possible 11th-century provenance of *Beowulf* itself, and the consequences of accepting this thesis are wide-ranging. Indeed, many issues relating to the poem are turned upside down. Three centuries or so of turbulent history make a big difference. *Beowulf,* by losing some of its age, may lose some of its interest for antiquarians; but it becomes a poem that was itself largely the product of antiquarian interests. Instead of a pre-Viking poem, it becomes a post-Viking poem. It tells us more of an 11th-century Anglo-Saxon's notions about Denmark, and its pre-history, than it does of the Age of Bede and a 7th- or 8th-century Anglo-Saxon's notions about his ancestors' homeland.[72]

But the difference is advantageous. The Chronicles (even Æthel-weard's); the Viking invasions; Anglo-Saxon religious verse from Cædmon to Cynewulf and beyond; Anglo-Saxon prose, like Blickling Homily XVII, which in all probability gave the poet his description of Grendel's *mere;* Ælfric and Wulfstan; scaldic verse and Scandinavian sagas; untold works in Latin from rhetorics to histories, and through the whole vast corpus of Anglo-Latin literature; Anglo-Saxon writs and charters; the recorded genealogies, both Anglo-Saxon and Norse; Cnut's court and the new Anglo-Danish society—in fact, literary, folkloristic, and historical resources of all kinds at once become possible influences on, or keys to, the poem. By searching 11th-century Mercia, perhaps along the old Danelaw boundary, or in Danish Mercia itself, rather than in the misty moors of the 7th and 8th centuries, a better notion of the poet and his cultural milieu can yet be unearthed. A better notion of the poem is the ultimate advantage.

Finally, but now of the first importance, the belief in an 11th-century provenance for *Beowulf* requires a complete reconsideration of the so-called *textus receptus.* If we have a contemporary MS, there are far too many emendations of it in all current editions. The old transmission theory radically impugned the credibility of the MS, for as Sisam prop-erly argues, if the poem was indeed subjected to "the vicissitudes of three centuries," there is no need to accord "extraordinary authority" to a late, unique MS (*Studies,* p. 51). It must now be recognized that no edition of the poem has ever granted extraordinary authority to the MS. Even the ultraconservative German edition, presently edited by Else von Schaubert, contains over 220 emendations (counting interpolations), or an average of about one emendation every fourteen lines. The rate is much higher in all other conservative editions. Klaeber, for instance, averages about one emendation every ten lines, not counting decon-tracted forms. Yet conservative editors who believe in a 7th- or 8th-cen-

---

72. In this respect the title of the poem in its first edition takes on new significance: Grímur Jónsson Thorkelin, ed., *De Danorum Rebus Gestis Secul. III & IV. Poëma Danicum Dialecto Anglosaxonica.*

tury archetype, in an Anglian dialect, are in the impossible position of conserving an inarguably corrupted text, by defending and printing the predominantly Late West Saxon forms of the MS. These editors might well do better to resurrect the old attempts at reconstructing an early Anglian text. But if *Beowulf* is the chief Anglo-Saxon cultural legacy from the reign of Cnut the Great, we now have the exciting prospect of restudying it in a truly conservative edition that resists emendations of any kind, and in all ways respects and preserves the text of a contemporary MS.

2

~~~~~~

The History and Construction
of the Composite Codex

The *Beowulf* MS is today preserved at the British Museum in a thick, quarto-sized volume with an aging, brown calf binding. Tourists to the museum see the volume in its display case, and relatively few scholars have hindered the tourists by asking to study the codex at first hand. The curious neglect of the *Beowulf* MS, and of the composite codex that contains it, is directly attributable to the ancient prejudice of Old English scholars that *Beowulf* was originally composed in the 7th or 8th century. As we shall see, a thorough study of the composite codex that includes *Beowulf* is not irrelevant to a thorough study of the poem itself. In any case, a full description of the composite codex, known as Cotton Vitellius A. XV., is long overdue. The only other description of it is Max Förster's *Die Beowulf-Handschrift,* which very erroneously represents, among other things, matters of dating, foliation, and collation.[1] Kemp Malone has published a FS of the second half of Cotton Vitellius A. XV., but under the confusing new name of the Nowell Codex.[2] The truth is that many scholars have little idea what Cotton Vitellius A. XV. is, and

1. The main shortcomings of Förster's report on the codex are discussed in the following pages. Förster's investigation of the MS was finished in 1913 (*Die Beowulf-Handschrift,* p. 66), but the outbreak of World War I delayed its publication until 1919. In fairness, many of Förster's errors may be due to the hiatus, and to his inability to recheck the MS during the war years. There are, of course, brief catalogue descriptions of Cotton Vitellius A. XV., and fuller descriptions of parts of the codex, the most important of which are cited below.

2. The reason, he says, was to "avoid confusion." *Nowell Codex,* p. 12, n. 3. The full title of Malone's FS is *The Nowell Codex (British Museum Cotton Vitellius A. XV. Second MS),* but as the ensuing analysis will show, there were more than two original MSS combined in Cotton's composite codex.

[65]

most have no idea what the Nowell Codex is, much less what its relation to Cotton Vitellius A. xv. might be. A basic value of studying in depth the construction of Cotton Vitellius A. xv. is that it necessarily clarifies the relation of parts of the codex to the whole. The most important result of the investigation is that it indicates that one part of the codex, *Beowulf,* was originally copied as a separate codex.

Cotton Vitellius A. xv.

The present binding is a 19th-century copy of the original, bearing on the front and back covers a gold impression of the Cotton family arms. On the spine is the following description, imprinted in gold capitals:

ANGLO-SAXON
VERSIONS AND POEMS:

FLORES SOLILOQUIORUM
S. AUGUSTINI,
NICODEMI EVANGELIUM,
ETC.,

BEOWULF, AND
JUDITH AND HOLOFERNES.

BRIT. MUS.
COTTON MS.
VITELLIUS A. XV.

The name Cotton Vitellius A. xv. dates from the 17th century, when the composite codex was assembled, and derives, as is well known, from the system of cataloguing used when the book belonged to the vast MS holdings of Sir Robert Bruce Cotton (1571–1631). The press in which the book was kept was surmounted by a bust of the Roman Emperor Aulus Vitellius; the book itself was kept on the first shelf (A), in the fifteenth position (xv). The Cotton collection became the principal MS collection of the British Museum, when the museum was founded by an Act of Parliament in 1753 (36 Geo. II, c. 22).

The history of the codex in the first third of the 18th century explains its unusual physical appearance and the need to replace Cotton's orig-

inal binding with a 19th-century one.[3] The Cotton collection was presented to the British people in 1700 (12 & 13 William III, c. 7) by Sir
Robert's grandson, Sir John Cotton. A committee of the House of Commons became the trustees of the library, with the speaker, Robert Harley, as the chief trustee. The trustees appointed a commission in 1703
to report on the state of the library, and Humfrey Wanley, whom Harley later chose to collect and preside over his own splendid library, was
providentially chosen as a member of the commission.[4] Wanley's unparalleled expertise and thoroughness have preserved for us a trustworthy
record of the original collection,[5] which sadly was about to be greatly
diminished. Cotton House was then dilapidated, and Wanley reported
that "in yᵉ Room above the Library . . . there are not only a good quantity of printed Books, but some Manuscripts; very many Originall
Charters of different Ages, as high as yᵉ Conqueror's time, and a very
great Number of Originall Letters & Writings of value which have
already suffered great hurt, & will be utterly spoiled if care be not taken
of them" (Bodleian MS Add. D. 82, fol. iii). A new building to house
the collection was planned and endorsed by an Act of Parliament in
1706 (6 Anne, c. 30), yet nothing was done. By 1722, Cotton House
was in such bad shape that the collection had to be removed to Essex
House, Strand, where it remained for the duration of a seven-year lease,
which was not renewed because Essex House was considered a firetrap.
So Cotton's library was moved to another interim home, and another
firetrap, ominously named Ashburnham House, in Little Dean's Yard,
Westminster. A contemporary account bleakly records the disastrous
result of this last move:

3. My account of the early history of the Cotton collection is based in part on
Arundell Esdaile, *The British Museum: A Short History and Survey*, pp. 17–37 and
228–229; and on BL Add. MS 24,932, *A Report from the Committee Appointed to
View the Cottonian Library*, pp. 7–15.

4. Wanley's report on behalf of this commission was prefixed to Robert Harley's
copy of Thomas Smith's *Catalogus Librorum Manuscriptorum Bibliothecæ Cottonianæ* and is dated 22. June. 1703. The book belongs to the Bodleian Library, Oxford,
and is catalogued as MS Add. D. 82. Drafts of Wanley's report are in BL MS Harley
7055.

5. Mainly in his own catalogue, published in 1705, but also in the report from the
commission of 1703, which was restricted in its scope primarily to corrections of foliations erroneously recorded in Smith's catalogue.

On *Saturday* Morning *October* 23, 1731. about two o'Clock, a great Smoak was perceived by Dr. *Bentley,* and the rest of the Family at *Ashburnham-House,* which soon after broke out into a Flame: It began from a wooden Mantle-Tree's taking Fire, which lay across a Stove-Chimney, that was under the Room, where the MSS. of the Royal and *Cottonian* Libraries were lodged, and was communicated to that Room by the Wainscot, and by pieces of Timber, that stood perpendicularly upon each end of the Mantle-Tree. They were in hopes at first to have put a Stop to the Fire by throwing Water upon the Pieces of Timber and Wainscot, where it first broke out, and therefore did not begin to remove the Books so soon as they otherwise would have done. But the Fire prevailing, notwithstanding the Means used to extinguish it, Mr. *Casley* the Deputy-Librarian took Care in the first Place to remove the famous *Alexandrian* MS. and the Books under the Head of *Augustus* in the *Cottonian* Library, as being esteemed the most valuable amongst the Collection. Several entire Presses with the Books in them were also removed; but the Fire increasing still, and the Engines sent for not coming so soon as could be wished, and several of the Backs of the Presses being already on Fire, they were obliged to be broke open, and the Books, as many as could be, were thrown out of the Windows.[6]

The *Beowulf* MS was presumably saved for us by being thrown from the window, for the present condition of Cotton Vitellius A. XV. shows that the Vitellius press was one of those that caught fire from the back. The fire left Cotton Vitellius A. XV. basically intact, but badly burned along its outer edges, and so in need of a new binding.

The codex stayed in its ruined binding until near the middle of the 19th century, when the British Museum began systematic repairs of the damaged Cotton books. Thus, the charred and brittle outer edges of Cotton Vitellius A. XV. were left unprotected for over a century, and many letters and words continued to crumble off from the time of the first transcripts in the late 18th century until the 19th-century binding prevented all further losses. The new binding is a remarkable piece of craftsmanship, as well as of preservation, even though the threads and folds of the original gatherings had to be sacrificed—if indeed they had not already been destroyed by the fire. In the present binding, each folio

6. Quoted from "A NARRATIVE of the Fire which happened at *Ashburnham-House,* Oct. 23, 1731. and of the Methods used for preserving and recovering the Manuscripts of the Royal and *Cottonian* Libraries" (BL MS 24,932, p. 11).

is inlaid in a heavy paper frame to protect the brittle margins of the vellum. These paper frames, which less impressively preserve *three* variously inaccurate foliations of the codex, are not reproduced in any of the FSS, and it is hard to appreciate the binder's methods from the FSS previously published (but see Plate 7). The binder first made pencil tracings of the separate folio leaves on sheets of heavy construction paper. These tracings are usually quite visible in the MS, and occasionally, if one is looking for them, even in the FSS. After the tracings were made, the binder then cut out the center part of the paper, following the outline, but leaving from 1 to 2 mm. of paper within the traced line, so that the frame would be slightly smaller than the vellum leaf it was designed to hold. Paste was then applied to this marginal retaining space, and the folio was pressed into place. Finally, transparent paper strips were pasted on like Scotch tape along the edge of the vellum on the recto, thus to secure the mounted leaf from both sides. Uncatalogued archival records in the Department of Manuscripts of the British Library reveal that a man named Gough inlaid the separate folios and rebound Cotton Vitellius A. xv. in August 1845.[7]

In addition to protecting the edges of the vellum from further deterioration, the heavy paper frames also obviate the need to handle the vellum at all while reading the MS. The advantages of this method of rebinding far outweigh its shortcomings. The main drawback is that the retaining edges of the paper frames, which hold the folios in place on the versos, also cover letters and parts of letters, especially along the left margins. When the ink is dark enough, these covered letters can be read with certainty by holding the page up against strong light, but in many cases the ink is too faded, or the condition of the vellum too impaired

7. Sir Frederic Madden kept a meticulous record of the restorations of the Cotton collection in a slender (13 x 4 cm.) ledger book titled *Cottonian MSS., Repairing and Binding Account.* The first flyleaf reads, "List of the *Cottonian MSS.* with the progress made in repairing, binding and inlaying of the Collection, from the year 1839." Beside Vitellius A. xv. Madden has written, "G inlaid and rebound Augt. 1845." I am grateful to Assistant Keeper Dr. M. A. E. Nickson for locating this uncatalogued record for me, and to Assistant Keeper Janet Backhouse for identifying "G" as Gough from other uncatalogued records kept by Madden. Heretofore the binding was erroneously dated between 1860 and 1871, and the binder was unknown (see Förster, *Die Beowulf-Handschrift,* pp. 6–7, 10–11, and Malone, *Nowell Codex,* p. 11). The official binder of the British Museum from 1825 to 1865 was Charles Tuckett, who restored most of the damaged Cotton MSS.

through shrinkage and scorching, to determine what the hidden letters are with absolute certainty. Still, there is something left to try to decipher; without the paper frames many of these uncertain letters would now be gone. A second shortcoming is that the threads and folds of the original gatherings, or what was left of them after the fire, had to be totally sacrificed to mount the folios individually. The absence of threads and folds greatly complicates the normally simple process of collation, but the probable composition of the original gatherings can be deduced by other means, which can also eliminate as impossible some overly mechanical guesswork by previous scholars.

As it now stands, Cotton Vitellius A. xv. is a composite codex assembled in the first half of the 17th century. It consists of two main Old English codices. The first, now called the Southwick Codex,[8] has four items:

1. *The Soliloquia of St. Augustine,* ascribed to King Alfred in the fragmentary colophon;
2. *The Gospel of Nicodemus* (acephalous);
3. *The Debate of Solomon and Saturn;*
4. Eleven lines of a *St. Quintin Homily* (the ending is lost).

The second codex is the one known as the Nowell Codex, and it consists of five articles, including *Beowulf:*

1. *The Life of St. Christopher* (the beginning is lost);
2. *The Wonders of the East* (illustrated);
3. *Alexander's Letter to Aristotle;*
4. *Beowulf;*
5. *Judith* (the beginning is lost, and the closing lines are copied in a rough imitation of insular script by an early modern hand).

What has not been fully recognized is that the Southwick and Nowell codices are, themselves, composite books. As far as I know, no one has ever noted the fact that the Southwick Codex is almost certainly made up of two originally separate and distinct books; and there are equally good reasons to believe that the Nowell Codex originally comprised

8. Malone was the first person to use this name to distinguish the group of 12th-century MSS, at the beginning of Cotton Vitellius A. xv., from the second group, which he called the Nowell Codex.

three books, rather than one or two. While some scholars realize that *Judith,* in all probability, was a late addition to the Nowell Codex, the effect its addition had on the physical construction of the *Beowulf* MS, and the subsequent damage it caused to the *Beowulf* MS, have gone entirely unnoticed. Moreover, and most important of all, there is evidence that the *Beowulf* MS itself was in the earliest stages of its history a separate codex. The full implications of this must be discussed later, but it is worth suggesting now that if the *Beowulf* MS was at the start of its history a separate codex, it enjoyed a particular popularity at the time that it was copied. It indicates, surely, that *Beowulf* was understood and appreciated in the early 11th century and enhances the theory that *Beowulf* may be an 11th-century poem. The usual view is that *Beowulf* was copied carelessly and mindlessly, by scribes largely ignorant of the poem's meaning, as the fourth item in a basically prose codex. The new view tremendously enhances, as well, the textual authority of the *Beowulf* MS. In any case, a good understanding of the construction of Cotton Vitellius A. XV. must include a good understanding of the construction of the original codices that now constitute it. Much of the lost history of the Southwick and Nowell codices can be deduced from the physical evidence left to us in these MSS.

The Prefixed Leaves

The present "official" foliation of Cotton Vitellius A. XV. is inaccurate. Even in June 1884, when it was introduced,[9] this foliation was not entirely accurate, for it failed to renumber in proper sequence the folios in two transposed quires from *Alexander's Letter* in the Nowell

---

9. On a paper endleaf facing the last page of the *Judith* fragment a note in pencil reads, "209 Fols FW. June 1884 / Ex.[d] S.S. / f. 1 removed Jan. 1913 (see note at beginning)." According to Dr. Backhouse "FW" was probably a minor clerk, charged with writing the foliation, and "S.S." an unidentified superior who subsequently examined the accuracy of the foliation. Malone erroneously identified "FW" as "G. F. Warner, i. e. George Frederic Warner, then an assistant in the Department of MSS; he was later made Keeper of MSS and still later was knighted." *Nowell Codex,* p. 13. Neither the initials nor the handwriting (specimens of which may be seen in BL MSS Add. 43,472, fol. iii, 43, 473, fol. i, and 44,875, fol. iii) is Warner's.

Codex.[10] Today, in addition to this error, the 1884 foliation is inaccurate throughout the codex, for it counts in the foliation of the two Old English codices three prefixed leaves, the first of which was removed from the codex in 1913. The foliation used throughout this book is a corrected version of an older foliation written on the vellum leaves of the Old English MSS. This older foliation, which will be referred to throughout as the MS foliation, can still be clearly seen in the MS and in the FSS in the vicinity of the upper right corners, recto, of each leaf. When it was introduced, late in the 18th century, several leaves were out of place, but these errors are easily enough corrected without abandoning this basically true, and historically informative, foliation. For instance, the foliation 1–90 of the Southwick Codex is perfectly in order. The 1884 foliation, by counting the three prefixed leaves, throws this count off by three, yet in reality, because one of the prefixed leaves is now gone, the difference is two.

The (quondam) first prefixed leaf was a mutilated page from a 14th-century Latin *Psalterium*. It was removed from Cotton Vitellius A. xv., permanently confounding the ill-advised foliation of 1884, when the British Museum reconstructed the original *Psalterium* (now Royal MS 13 D. I*) from bits and pieces gathered together from various MSS, many of which once belonged to Cotton. Apparently, Cotton's book-binder used pages, or rather parts of pages, from this *Psalterium* for scrap paper: from the looks of many of the fragmentary pages in Royal MS 13 D. I*, the MS was a regular source for pastedowns, flyleaves, and binding strips. In this case, the bottom third of a page, preserving parts of verses 28–32 and 42–45 of Psalm 104 (fol. 37 in the patchwork reconstruction of the *Psalterium*), was used as a flyleaf to Cotton Vitellius A. xv. The fire damage shows that it was placed in the codex sideways, with the verso on the outside, and with its left margin at the top (a 17th-century hand has written in this space, "Vitellius A. XV"). When the leaf was removed in 1913, the keeper of MSS, Julius P. Gilson, noted on the paper flyleaf that preceded it in the new binding: "a flyleaf (f. 1) taken out to be bound with Royal MS. 13 D. I*, the psalter

10. Notations on the paper frames of the new binding alert the reader of the MS to the dislocation of the gatherings. On the first folio of the first misplaced gathering a note reads, "Ff. 110–117 should follow f. 125"; and on this last folio a corresponding note reads, "ff. 110–117 should follow here." Since the 1884 foliation numbers are used, the notes must have been written in 1884 or later.

to which it originally belonged. / Jan. 1913. / J. P. G." There was never any justification for counting this leaf as the first folio of a codex comprising Old English texts. Now that it is gone from the codex, the 1884 foliation that it lamentably inspired should be abandoned.

The second prefixed vellum leaf, fol. 2 of the 1884 foliation, has been the first prefixed vellum leaf since 1913. On the recto, it preserves an odd, and an oddly flawed, table of contents, which may well reflect the unsettled state of the codex in the 17th century, prior to binding. The list is entitled *Elenchus contentorum in hoc codice,* and is in the handwriting of Richard James, who was Cotton's librarian from c. 1628 to 1638.[11] In the following transcript expanded abbreviations are in italics, and later additions to the *Elenchus,* all in pencil, are in brackets:

1 Flores soliloquiorum Augustini Saxonicè Ælfredo interprete vt apparet ex pag. 56.

2 Summa expensarum et militum quibus vsus est Edwardus [f.2.b.] 3 in expugnatione Caleti . in secundà facie primæ pag.

3 Fragmentum Saxonicum quod forte continet aliquam partem historiæ sive legendæ Thomæ Apostoli. pag. primà. habetur ibi mentio de Bocland. et cotagijs.   [f.1]

[+]4 Dialogi de Christo et christianitate vbi interloquntur Pilatus et alij . sicut melius visum est Legendario. Sax.   [f.57]

5 Dialogus inter Saturnum et Salomonem. Saxon. cum Legendis Sancti Christoferi.

6 Defloratio siue translatio Epistolarum Alexandri ad Aristotelem cum picturis prodigiosorum. Saxonicè.

[7 Beowulf]

8 Fragmentum Saxon: de Iuditha et Holoferne. [f.199]

[+ Fragmentum est de Nicodemi Evangelio?]

James wrote numbers 1–6 and 8, leaving a gap between numbers 6 and 8 to indicate that he had failed to describe a text that appeared at this

11. According to the *DNB,* James probably became Cotton's librarian after 1628, after helping Selden with *Marmora Arundeliana* (p. 655). A contemporary account states that James "had so screwed himself into the good opinion of Sir Robert Cotton, as whereas at first he had only permitted him in the use of some of his books, at last, some two or three years before his decease [d. 1631], he bestowed the custody of his whole library on him." James Orchard Halliwell, ed., *The Autobiography and Correspondence of Sir Simonds d'Ewes,* pp. 39–40. Why Förster (*Die Beowulf-Handschrift,* p. 67) and Malone (*Nowell Codex,* p. 11) say that James became librarian c. 1635 is never explained by either.

point. Either James had no idea how to describe *Beowulf* or the poem was temporarily out of the codex. The 7 and Beowulf were added in pencil in fairly recent times.[12] James's *Elenchus* is interesting both for what it includes and for what it excludes. In order to cite fol. 56 as the page containing the Alfredian colophon (number 1), James must have begun counting folios, or a foliation already on the MS must have begun, on the first folio of *The Soliloquia of St. Augustine*. Yet, according to the item James listed next (number 2), the *Summa expensarum* began on the verso of the *first* page. If James had really counted this leaf as the first folio of the codex, the Alfredian colophon would be on fol. 57, not fol. 56. It is also strange that what James describes as the first folio of the codex, the *Summa expensarum,* is in fact *listed* second. These difficulties can be resolved by assuming that the *Summa expensarum* is listed second because James found it after the *Soliloquia* when he first began describing the codex. Perhaps, then, he moved it to the beginning and noted its new position in the *Elenchus,* because it was not a Saxon text. At any rate, the *Summa expensarum* (transcribed below) is now the second prefixed leaf of the MS foliation, or fol. 3 of the erroneous 1884 foliation.

Number 3 in the *Elenchus,* the fragmentary *Legend of St. Thomas,* is no longer part of the codex. But it is hard to believe that James invented such an elaborate description for an imaginary text. At the time, James must have found the fragmentary *Legend* between the *Soliloquia* and the *Nicodemus* fragment, and so described it. The quire signatures of the Southwick Codex show that it was not a legitimate part of the Southwick Codex, but loose leaves often found their way in and out of Cotton's books.[13] James's comment, *pag. primâ. habetur ibi*

---

12. Evidently after 1913, for Förster does not mention them, but only says, "Hier sind vier Zeilen freigelassen." *Die Beowulf-Handschrift,* p. 67. There are two errors in Förster's transcript of the *Elenchus:* in item 3 he has *habitur* for *habetur* and in item 8 he has *Holoferno* for *Holoferne.*

13. Whitelock notes, for instance, that an 8th-century charter now in BL MS Cotton Augustus II. 3. "was at one time bound up with the Vespasian Psalter, and was taken out of it by the orders of Sir Robert Cotton." *English Historical Documents,* p. 453. Ker says that "Cotton was a chief offender in this kind of activity," noting that "leaves of manuscripts which he owned were taken out of the volumes to which they properly belonged and were bound up elsewhere." *Catalogue,* p. lxii.

Plate 2. Richard James's *Elenchus contentorum in hoc codice* is now the first prefixed leaf of BL MS Cotton Vitellius A. xv.

Elenchus Contentor.
in hoc codice

*

1. Flores Soliloquiorum Augustini Saxonicè Ælfredo interprete, ut apparet a pag. 56.

2. Summa expensaru et militum quibus usus est Edwardus 3 in expugnatione Caleti, in secunda facie primae pag.

3. Fragmentum Saxonicu quod forte continet aliquam partem historiae sive legendae Thomae Apli, pag. primo, habetur ibi mentio de Bocland et cotagiis.

4. Dialogi de Xpo et Xpianitate ubi inter loquuntur pilatus et alij sicut melius visum est Legendario Sax.

5. Dialogus inter Saturnum et Salomonem, Saxon, cum Legendis Sti Xpoferi.

6. Defloratio sive translatio Eptarum Alexandri ad Arlem cum picturis prodigiosorum. Saxonicè

7. Beowulf

8. Fragmentum Saxon: de Iuditha et Holoferne

mentio de Bocland. et cotagijs, may explain why the fragment was removed before Cotton Vitellius A. xv. was bound: it may have belonged more properly among Cotton's vast holdings of Anglo-Saxon charters. Or, the rest of the *Passio de Sancti Thomœ Apostoli* may have been located in another Cotton codex. The fact that f. 1 is written in pencil in the right margin indicates that, for a time, the fragmentary *Legend of St. Thomas* was the first prefixed leaf of the codex. Hence the *Summa expensarum* became the second prefixed leaf, as the folio number f. 2.b. in the margin would seem to confirm. It might be mentioned in passing that these folio numbers are not part of a true foliation, for whoever wrote them in the margin did not count the next fifty-six folios. Instead, he relied on James's statement that the Alfredian colophon was on fol. 56, and wrote 57 in the margin for the next item. If he had been counting folios he would have written fol. 59.

Beside number 4, *Dialogi de Christo et christianitate,* a later hand has made a cross-mark in pencil, and has noted at the foot of the page, *Fragmentum est de Nicodemi Evangelio?.* The last two words are blurred and faded, but the entire note can be read with certainty by holding the page up against strong light. The note and the folio numbers in pencil probably derive from the late 17th century, for the item had been identified as *The Gospel of Nicodemus* in time for Wanley's catalogue (1705), by which time the fragment from the *Legend of St. Thomas* was no longer part of the codex. The description in number 5 is a conflation of *The Debate of Solomon and Saturn,* from the Southwick Codex, and the *St. Christopher* fragment, from the Nowell Codex. Between them, James overlooked the eleven-line *St. Quintin* fragment, which ends the Southwick Codex. He had originally overlooked the *St. Christopher* fragment, too, but later, with a different pen and ink, he tacked on *cum Legendis Sancti Christoferi* after his description of the *Debate.* Thus Förster is misleading when he ascribes this phrase to "eine spätere Hand" (p. 67). There can be no doubt that the handwriting, which is very distinctive, is James's. Moreover, the phrase was inserted very soon after the *Elenchus* was made, for it is part of the description in the *Catalogue of the Cotton MSS. Circa 1635* (BL Add. MS. 36,789). Number 6 is an ingenuously combined description of *The*

Plate 3. An inverted palimpsest of a 14th-century Latin text is now the second prefixed leaf, recto, of Cotton Vitellius A. xv.

... en Englande par Charleres 65011

... 52004

... bataille stood 11 ... 60215

... de Bylbeon sont en flandres ... 1383

... ensamble comencoort desths sont 26 juny ... henry
... 1483

Le nombre de toutes ... de le Roy Edward le Roy y ...
il congues ... fut 4892 ... de toute ...
... 12 july ... de son ... le ...
... 26 may ... 50000 ...
... le ... Edward comencoort ...
3 ... de septembre ... 1586 ... et le gaigne
le 3 ... d ... ensuant

Wonders of the East (cum picturis prodigiosorum) and *Alexander's Letter to Aristotle.* James thought that *The Wonders of the East* was part of *Alexander's Letter.* As noted above, a gap after this composite description shows that *Beowulf* was certainly part of the codex when James made his description, but that he was unable to describe it. Number 8 shows that *Judith* was already a fragment before Cotton Vitellius A. xv. was bound.[14] Despite the importance of this page as a document that preserves some of the early modern history of Cotton Vitellius A. xv., there is no reason why it should be foliated with the Old English texts. It should, of course, be included in all descriptions of the codex, perhaps as roman numeral i, but it should only be *counted* as—what it is—a prefixed vellum leaf.

Fol. 3 of the 1884 foliation, now the second prefixed leaf of the MS foliation, holds on the verso the *Summa expensarum* mentioned second in James's *Elenchus.* The recto has not been accurately described by Förster, who says; "zeigt auf dem unteren Seitenviertel ein paar Schriftzeichen (Federproben) des 14. (?) Jahrhunderts—auf dem Kopfe stehend" (p. 73). As Förster says, the page is upside down, but the marks on the page, which are mostly unreadable, were not made solely to test a new pen. The page is a palimpsest, and whoever erased the original text simply failed to obliterate all of the writing. Some of the erased material appears as rows of stains, sharply accentuated under ultraviolet light. With the page right side up the words *auxiliam/et,* several letters (notably *d* and *h*), and indistinctive strings of minims, can be read on the second line. About one-third of the way down the page on the left there is a blurry ink mass, the remains of what was once a historiated initial. Flecks of what appear to be gold show up in this area under strong light.

14. This may well seem obvious, yet Dobbie strangely casts doubt on it, suggesting that the loss at the beginning of the *Judith* fragment "before the fire is highly probable but cannot be proved." *Beowulf and Judith,* p. xiv. There is no doubt at all that the poem was in its present fragmentary state in the 17th century, for Franciscus Junius made a transcript of it sometime before 1651 (Bodleian MS Junius 105). As Dobbie himself says elsewhere, "Dating from at least eighty years before the fire of 1731, Junius's transcript shows the text of the poem in its undamaged state (except for the loss of folios at the beginning) . . ." *Beowulf and Judith,* pp. xxii–xxiii.

Plate 4. The second prefixed leaf, verso, contains some statistics in English and notes relating to the Hundred Years War in Anglo-Norman.

James's overly simple description of the text on the verso of this leaf, *Summa expensarum et militum quibus vsus est Edwardus 3 in expugnatione Caleti,* has been little refined by subsequent scholars. Wanley is a bit more explicit but somewhat inaccurate when he says, *Nota de numero Parochiarum, villarum, feodorum & Militum in Anglia, & de expugnatione Caleti per Edwardum III.* Förster adds linguistic and paleographical details to Wanley's description, and an inaccurate date for Edward's victory at Calais: "Kurze Notizen von einer kleinen Hand des 16. Jahrhunderts in englischer und französischer Sprache, statistischen und historischen Inhalts. Erstere (engl.) behandeln die Zahl de Gemeindekirchen, der Zollerhebungsstellen und der Ritterlehen in England; letztere (franz.) die Eroberung Calais' durch Eduard III. (1383) u. a. m." (p. 74). Edward III died in 1377; his victory at Calais was in 1347. The general lack of interest in the contents of this page from James to the present is no doubt owing to the general dilution of the ink and to the sloppy Gothic scrawl and eccentric Anglo-Norman of the writer. The following transcript (with expanded abbreviations in italics) is given for its possible historical interest:

> Cherche in yngland parish churches   65011
> Subdued[?] _____   52004
>   knight Hood //_____   60214
>   Evesq*ue* de Norwich fuit in Flanders in l'an 1383
> (Se)ige q*ue* Taylbault comducdoit d'estre fait 29 Juny a*nn*o 31 Henrici
>   Sexti 1453.
>   le numbre de toutz q*ue* vaont ove le Roy Edward le terce qua[n]d
>   il conquer*oit* Calis fut 48392. Su*mmum* de toute charge
>   environ*ment* ceo del 12 July l'an de son regnie le 12
>   tamq*ue* 26. may l'an de son regne 14—330007£/104
>   96.3d. [*sic*] le roy Edward comducdout son seige le
>   3. iour de septembre. a*nn*o 1346. Il le gaigna
>   le 3. iour d'august ensuant.

The abrupt transition after line 3 from English to unrefined Anglo-Norman makes a late 15th-century date for these notes possible. The events mentioned all fall within the broadest limits (1337–1453) of the Hundred Years' War. I read (with some misgivings) "Subdued" in line 2 for Wanley's *villarum, feodorum* and Förster's "Zollerhebungsstellen." Line 4 refers to the "crusade" in Flanders of Henry Dispenser, bishop of Norwich. Lines 5 and 6 refer to a siege that John Talbot, commander of the English forces, ordered to be made on 29 June 1453. Talbot fell at Castillon, the last battle of the Hundred Years' War, less than three weeks later.[15] The remaining seven lines record the number of troops that gathered with Edward III when he conquered Calais, the cost of his campaign on the continent from 12 July 1338 to 26 May 1340,[16] the duration of his siege of Calais (eleven months), and his final victory on 3 August 1347.

None of these three prefixed leaves should ever have been counted in the foliation of the Old English MSS that constitute Cotton Vitellius A. XV. Their incorporation into the foliation of 1884 has caused many unnecessary problems. Because the present official foliation conflicts with the MS foliation written on the vellum leaves, scholars need to cite both foliations simultaneously, if their citations are to be unambiguous. Yet, as suggested above, there is little point in renumbering the leaves of the Southwick Codex for the sake of three prefixed leaves, one of which is no longer in the codex. The leaves of the Southwick Codex are numbered unerringly from 1 to 90 in the MS. The continuation of this MS foliation in the Nowell Codex is not entirely accurate, however, for the first ten folios of the codex and two folios from *Beowulf* were out of order, and two quires from *Alexander's Letter* were transposed, when it was written on the vellum leaves. These disorders are easily rectified without abandoning the MS foliation, by renumbering only the twelve folios and the transposed quires that need renumbering. The great advantage of adhering to the MS foliation is that only those folios that are out of order will need double citations: for example, the first ten folios of the Nowell Codex will have to be cited as, 91(93), 92(94), 93(91), 94(92), 95(97), 96(98), 97(99), 98(100), 99(95), 100(96).[17]

15. See Desmond Seward, *The Hundred Years War: The English in France, 1337–1453*, pp. 259–262.

16. The figures are apparently accurate; George Holmes mentions that Edward III's debts in 1339 were estimated at £300,000, "several times his annual income." *The Later Middle Ages: 1272–1485*, p. 120.

17. Even with the consistent use of the 1884 foliation there has been lack of consistency and full confusion in representing the disorder of these first ten folios of the Nowell Codex. Rypins very sensibly presented in parallel columns the correspondences between the 1884 foliation in the right order, and the MS foliation in the consequent disorder (*Three Texts,* p. xi). Malone, on the other hand, puts the 1884 foliation into disorder, which means that the MS foliation was in the right order (*Nowell*

Then, with the exception of the folios in the transposed quires and of the two folios from *Beowulf,* all other numbers from the MS foliation, throughout Cotton Vitellius A. XV., are right. The double citations, where they are needed, highlight the places where the Nowell Codex was formerly disordered.

The disadvantages of continuing to follow the 1884 foliation are manifold. The crowning annoyance is that the MS foliation must be used in tandem with it anyway, if one is to understand, however fuzzily, the pervasive discrepancy between the 1884 foliation and the foliation on the vellum leaves. The discrepancy is pointless, and it disappears with the rejection of the 1884 foliation and the reinstatement of the MS foliation. The salutary effect this will have on the foliation of *Beowulf* will illustrate the point. The two folios from the poem that were out of place when the MS foliation was written on the vellum leaves were numbered, according to their misplacement, 131 and 197. Folio 131 should have come after folio 146, and folio 197 after folio 188. If these two folios are renumbered as fol. 147A(131) and fol. 189A(197), the foliation numbers written on the *Beowulf* MS will be completely accurate. Moreover, the two new numbers will simultaneously provide the present locations of the two folios, and the former, erroneous locations which are properly left as gaps between folios 130 and 132, and 196 and 198. The total count of folios in the MS is unaffected, since the double citations for the formerly misplaced folios still use the MS numbers in parentheses.

The alternative provided by the 1884 foliation should be quite resistible. Its adoption requires a befuddling table of foliations to explain the numbers on the vellum leaves.[18] The table provided by Norman Davis

---

Codex, p. 15). It is surely strange that the editor of the FS edition of the Nowell Codex would choose to present the facts in a manner that is visually reversed in the FS. Dobbie, not realizing that the folios are in the right order when the number sequence of the MS foliation is in disorder, translates the disordered MS numbers to disordered 1884 numbers. The result is an entirely new disorder (of twelve, rather than ten folios), for if one retranslates Dobbie's sequence to the truly corresponding numbers of the MS foliation, the sequence reads, 91, 92, 93, 94, *99, 100,* 95, 96, 97, 98, *101, 102* (*Beowulf and Judith,* p. xv, and n. 19, where Dobbie ingenuously explains his blunder). The use of the MS numbers in the right order in tandem with the same numbers in disorder eliminates all of these obfuscations.

18. Malone's table of four distinct foliations (and there are at least two additional foliations, overlooked by Malone) occupies the better part of a large folio page (*Nowell Codex,* p. 14).

(pp. xvi-xvii) in the second edition of Zupitza's FS of *Beowulf* helps demonstrate the awkwardness of all such tables:

Old [MS]	*New*
129, 130	132, 133
132 to 146	134 to 148
131	149
147 to 188	150 to 191
197	192
189 to 196	193 to 200
198	201

These "correspondences," as Davis calls them, would be more tolerable, or at least more memorable, if the new numbers merely advanced the MS foliation numbers by three, as they do to the MS numbers in the Southwick Codex. Here in *Beowulf,* though, they advance the first two folios by three, the next fifteen folios by two, the first misplaced folio (131) by eighteen, the next forty-two folios by three again; the second misplaced folio (197) is itself five in advance of the new number, after which the new numbers advance the MS by four for eight folios, and finally by three for the last folio. No one using the 1884 foliation could be expected to remember which two folios had been originally misplaced in the *Beowulf* MS, or to have any clear conception of the reasons behind the wild discrepancies between the MS and the 1884 foliations.

A formal return to the use of the MS foliation is easily accomplished, mainly because it was never fully abandoned. Through ignorance of the 1884 foliation, most scholars still use the MS foliation. Zupitza used it, of course, in his FS edition, two years before the official foliation of 1884 was concocted. And since most editors used Zupitza, rather than the MS, to found their texts, the editors of the poem, even after 1884, follow the MS foliation. Whenever folios are mentioned in Holthausen, Wyatt, Chambers, Sedgefield, Klaeber, Wrenn, and Wrenn-Bolton,[19] the MS foliation numbers, alone, are used. Von Schaubert uses the 1884 foliation, but with the MS numbers in parentheses, and Dobbie, who in gen-

---

19. The comment in Wrenn-Bolton that the name Laurence Nouell appears "on folio 93r" (Wrenn, *Beowulf,* rev. Bolton, p. 9) is true according to the disordered MS foliation. A clearer citation, however, would use the double reference, fol. 91(93)r. The folio is the ninety-first in the codex, but was misplaced as the ninety-third sometime after Nowell wrote his name on it, and sometime before the MS foliation was made.

eral follows the 1884 foliation, still frequently uses double references (for example, *Beowulf and Judith,* p. xiv), and gives a full table of correspondences (pp. lxvi–lxx). Since Zupitza's transliteration was reproduced by photolithography in Norman Davis's second edition, the MS numbers at the top of each page are reproduced as well. Rypins uses double references in his edition of the prose texts of the Nowell Codex, and Cook uses the MS numbers alone in his editions of *Judith.* Even Malone uses the MS numbers in his FS edition of the Thorkelin transcripts, and while he adopts the 1884 numbers in his FS of the Nowell Codex, the numbers on the FS itself furnish double references, and Malone is obliged to furnish a table of foliations as well (*Nowell Codex,* p. 14). Unfortunately, Ker conforms to the 1884 foliation in his *Catalogue,* though this foliation clearly violates his own system of showing flyleaves and postmedieval insertions by roman numerals (p. xxii). For the reasons outlined above, the foliation adopted in this book is the MS foliation written on the vellum leaves of Cotton Vitellius A. xv. It differs from the foliation on the MS only where it needs to correct errors. When the late 18th-century foliation was written on the MS, twelve folios in the Nowell Codex were out of place, and two quires were transposed. In these relatively few cases a new number is assigned, giving the proper numerical position of the folio, but the old, erroneous number is also given in parentheses. Double citations in these relatively few cases are useful, because they highlight the precise places where the Nowell Codex was formerly disordered. For purposes of reference, the Old English contents of Cotton Vitellius A. xv. may now be identified following this MS foliation, so corrected:

I. The Southwick Codex
  1. Folio 1:   *The Soliloquia of St Augustine;*
  2. Folio 57: The *Nicodemus* fragment;
  3. Folio 83v: *The Debate of Solomon and Saturn;*
  4. Folio 90v: The *St. Quintin* fragment.
II. The Nowell Codex
  1. Folio 91(93): The *St. Christopher* fragment;
  2. Folio 95(97)v: *The Wonders of the East;*
  3. Folio 104:   *Alexander's Letter to Aristotle;*
  4. Folio 129:   *Beowulf;*
  5. Folio 199:   The *Judith* fragment.

The use of the MS numbers unquestionably simplifies references to the MS or the FSS, and ease of reference is the only good reason for having a foliation at all. But it should be well understood that the foliation of 1884 is not only complicated, but wrong, and for the sake of clarity and accuracy it must be abandoned at once. The three prefixed leaves that it counts have been reduced to two, and neither is an Old English text.

History of the Multiple Foliations

A long monograph could easily be written on the history of the various foliations. Scholars have tried, at least since the early 18th century, to unscramble the errors of previous foliations of Cotton Vitellius A. xv., and yet it is an astonishing fact that the codex has never been accurately foliated in its entirety. The various foliations used for Cotton Vitellius A. xv. since the early 17th century need to be discussed in some detail to clear up some persistent misunderstandings. Scholars currently believe, quite mistakenly, that the Nowell Codex was unfoliated before the fire of 1731, and they recognize only three, or sometimes four, distinct foliations. In reality, there are at least six distinct foliations for Cotton Vitellius A. xv. There were two complete foliations made before the fire, the second of which tried, futilely, to correct the errors of the first. Scholars have not realized that these two foliations extended through the Nowell Codex before the fire, and that they furnish our only information about the *Beowulf* MS before it was damaged and rebound.

The first foliation, which is still partly extant in the Southwick Codex but was lost to the Nowell Codex in the fire damage to the upper right corners, was made in the first half of the 17th century, probably under the orders of Richard James, between 1628 and 1638. The second foliation was made in 1703 by a committee whose job was to correct the foliations of the Cotton MSS. The third is the restoration made after the fire, the "MS foliation" that can be seen on the vellum leaves of the Nowell Codex today; it was made after the Thorkelin transcripts by Joseph Planta, sometime between 1793 and 1801. The fourth foliation was probably made in August 1845, when Frederic Madden was keeper and the MS leaves had been placed in the paper frames of the new binding; it corrects some errors of the third foliation, and it can be seen in the upper right-hand corners of the paper frames. The fifth foliation was made sometime in the early 1870s, and it can be seen in the lower right-hand corners of the paper frames. The sixth foliation, like the fourth, is recorded in the upper right-hand corners of the paper frames: this is the so-called official foliation of 1884. These are the multiple foliations of Cotton Vitellius A. xv. There may have been other distinct foliations, and indeed there is some evidence that there were. It is a rather complicated story.

Only Förster has really considered the complications of the various foliations independently. Johannes Hoops's "Die Foliierung der *Beowulf*-Handschrift" is in large measure an attempt to correct the many flaws in Förster's account.[20] Malone and Dobbie rather uncritically accept Hoops as definitive, yet ignore his most valuable contribution, an astute defense of the MS foliation as preferable to the hopelessly inaccurate and obfuscating foliation of 1884.[21] Hoops's main error, an error promptly and ubiquitously received as fact, was his belief that the Nowell Codex was not foliated until after the fire. As Malone put Hoops's case, "We have reason to think that the leaves of the Nowell codex were not given numbers until after the great fire of 1731; certainly this codex shows no traces of an earlier numbering." But the reasons for believing that the Nowell Codex was unnumbered before the fire cannot be sustained. "For want of such a foliation," Malone continues, "Cotton's bookbinder made serious mistakes in ordering the sheets of the codex and Wanley's count of folios here is repeatedly inaccurate" (*Nowell Codex*, p. 12). Of course, one would not expect the Southwick and Nowell codices to be numbered continuously, from 1 to 206, until after they had been bound together as a single book, and so Cotton's bookbinder is hardly a relevant factor. On the other hand, one would expect Wanley's count of folios to be accurate, for he was a meticulous paleographer. And his count is not only accurate, it corrects errors in the foliation that preceded it. Leaves in the Nowell Codex were out of place when

20. Rypins had given a fairly good account of the problems four years earlier, in his edition of the prose texts of the Nowell Codex (*Three Texts*, pp. ix–xi), though he recognized only a "threefold foliation."

21. Marjorie Daunt, who did not comprehend the range of difficulties involved, characterizes Hoops's defense of the MS foliation as an insult to the British Library: "The 1884 numbering is regarded as the official pagination, and it would surely be a simple matter for future editors to accept the arrangement of the Keeper of MSS." "Old English Studies," p. 75. The editors have shown that it is not a simple matter at all. It might be added that the MS foliation is the work of another keeper of MSS, though the real issue is accuracy and convenience of reference.

Wanley made his foliation, but the former arrangement of the leaves has no bearing on the accuracy of his count.

The reason the two earliest foliations of the Nowell Codex have not been recognized is that the fire destroyed all physical evidence of them in the MS. The upper right corner of the Nowell Codex suffered the most fire damage, and since this is where the earliest foliation was recorded, there is naturally no vestige of it left. The upper right corners of the Southwick Codex are comparatively well preserved, and so there is evidence in the MS of an early, if not the earliest, foliation. Förster claims (pp. 4–5) that the "ältesten Blattzahlen" derive from a hand of the late 16th or early 17th century, but in fact the forms of the numbers are not distinctive, and could have been used anytime between the late 16th century and the present. These numbers undoubtedly predate the fire, but Förster's implication that they predate the Cotton codex (1628–1638) is extremely misleading, for the numbers themselves simply cannot be dated. The only argument that can be used in favor of this position is James's reference to fol. 56 in his *Elenchus contentorum*. The reference to a folio number before Cotton Vitellius A. XV. was bound (the *Elenchus* was bound with it) would seem to suggest that *The Soliloquia of St. Augustine,* at any rate, was already numbered. On the other hand, James says that the next item in the codex was a fragment from a *Legend of St. Thomas the Apostle,* and if James is right, the codex could not have been numbered beyond the *Soliloquia* (and could not have been bound) until after the *St. Thomas* fragment was removed. If anything, the conflicting evidence argues against the view that the Southwick Codex was foliated before it was added to the Nowell Codex. After all, James might have simply counted the folios of the *Soliloquia* to mark the location of the Alfredian colophon, which must have been the most exciting feature of Vitellius A. XV. to Cotton.[22]

At any rate, we cannot be sure that the Southwick Codex was foliated in its entirety before it was combined with the Nowell Codex for Cotton's book, Vitellius A. XV., and so the oldest extant numbers in the Southwick Codex may well have continued through the Nowell Codex before the fire of 1731. Förster only distinguishes two extant sets of folio numbers on the vellum leaves of the Southwick Codex: the "ältesten

---

22. James does not date the codex, and his description could leave the impression that the MS was contemporary with Alfred.

Blattzahlen," which he ascribes to the end of the 16th or the beginning of the 17th century; and the restoration of the "ältesten Blattzahlen," wherever it was needed, which he dates "wohl bald nach dem Brande von 1731" (pp. 5–6). The evidence is much more complicated than this. There are two main hands that account for most of the foliation numbers, and Förster is right that one hand, in the Southwick Codex, wrote in numbers sometime before the fire, and the other hand restored numbers lost by the fire both in the Southwick Codex and throughout the Nowell Codex. The restorer's numbers are usually quite distinguishable from the numbers that survived the fire in the Southwick Codex, both by form and by difference in ink. But the distinction is sometimes virtually lost by fading or blurring, and by the restorer's apparently freshening up some of the old numbers, producing hybrid forms. Other hands have written in numbers, too, which of course adds to the complications.

Some notion of the problems involved in distinguishing number forms (the difference in ink, reddish brown versus black, is normally unequivocal) can be indicated here, before moving on to the central issue of identifying distinct foliations. According to Förster the following numbers are all that remain of the "ältesten Zahlen" (p. 5), which were written in reddish brown ink: 3, 6, 7, 8, 12, 13, 14, 15, 23, 24, 26, 27, 28, 29, 31, 32, 33, 37, 38, 39, 40, 41, 47, 50, 52 (Förster supplies the 2, though it is perfectly clear in the MS), 54, 56, 67, 73, and 77. Förster inexplicably overlooks the following "ältesten Zahlen": 9, 10, 11, 16, 17, 34, 36 (freshened up), 42, 57, 58 (beneath the tape), 65 (very faint), 70 (at the end of line 1), 80 (?), and perhaps 90 (freshened up). By this count nearly half of the original numbers in the Southwick Codex are still extant. The others were presumably destroyed in the fire along with the old foliation of the Nowell Codex. The restored numbers in the Southwick Codex are not as uniform as they normally are in the Nowell Codex. The first two folios of the Southwick Codex, for instance, seem to have been numbered or restored by a different hand entirely. Other notable idiosyncrasies in the restoration of the old foliation numbers in the Southwick Codex will be mentioned in passing.

Restored numbers (in black ink, unless otherwise noted) can be seen

---

Plate 5. Fol. 3r of the Southwick Codex preserves both the old foliation number in reddish brown ink (barely visible in the charred corner) and a superfluous restoration number in heavy black ink.

Augustinus þa answarode me sumding
ic nat hwæt hweðer þe ic sylf þeneað ⁊
þing ne þ nat hwæðer hit wæf. Innan
me ðe utanbutan wæf ic soðlicost þene
þat hit min ðeadwifhef were ⁊ þa cwæð
heo to me gif ðu enigne godne heorde
hæbbe þe welcunne healdan þ þ ðlige
streone ⁊ him be fæfte sceapa hine me
gif þu þonne nan ne spageradne ceh
be fec hine oðþu hine finde forþam
þu ne meht ægðer ge ealne weig ofon
þam fittan ðe þu ge ftrineð hæft ⁊he
aldan ge eac maren ftrinan. Ða cwæð
ic hwam wille ic ællef be fieftan þ ic ællef
ge ftrine butan minum ge minde þa
cwæð heo if þin ge mind fwa mihtig
þ hit mage eall ge healden þ þu ge
ðengft ⁊him be beoreft to healdenne.

on fols. 1, 2, 3 (even though the original 3 is extant), 4, 5, 6 (original 6 extant on the brittle edge), 18–22, 25 (beneath the tape), 30, 32 (the original is extant, and the superfluous restoration, in pencil at the end of line 3 is not in the hand of the main restorer), 33 (same as 32), 35, 38 (another superfluous restoration in pencil, at the end of line 7), 43–46, 48, 49, 51 (in pencil at the end of line 4), 53, 59, 60, 61–65, 66 (written very large, in pencil, in the center of the top margin, and then again at the end of line 2), 68 (like 66: moreover, the number 62, in yet another hand, is written in pencil at the end of lines 3–4), 69 and 71 (like 66 and 68, though possibly in another hand, and though the corners are intact no original numbers can be seen), 72 (over the original?), 74, 75 (written twice—in two different hands—once at the beginning and once at the end of line 1), 76, 77 (though the original is extant), 78–87, 88 (corner intact, but no original number visible), 89, and 90 (over the original?). It is clear that we have more to deal with here than the "ältesten Zahlen" and a restoration made soon after the fire. I would say that the penciled numbers 32, 38, 51, and 62 (on fol. 68), are by the same hand, and I would hypothesize that these numbers were made after the fire (because of their locations, away from the corners), but before the main restoration (because the number 62 is an error that was corrected before the main restoration was made). Thus, the possibility of a seventh distinct foliation, before the main restoration was written on the vellum leaves, cannot be ruled out.

Six different foliations of Cotton Vitellius A. xv. as a whole, including two before the fire which have never been recognized, can be definitely documented. The first foliation to include the Nowell Codex was made in the first half of the 17th century, most likely by the order of Richard James, between 1628 and 1638. The earliest extant reference to the first foliation of the Nowell Codex was made by Franciscus Junius, who made a transcription of the *Judith* fragment sometime between 1628 and 1650. At the head of the first page of this transcript (now Bodleian MS Junius 105), Junius noted the folio on which the fragment began:

Fragmentum historiæ Judith, descriptum ex Cottonianæ bibliothecæ MS⁰ codice, qui inscribitur VITELLIVS A. 15. *paginâ 199.*

The note tells us that when Junius made his copy, the *Judith* fragment was already in Cotton's possession as a fragment, the Southwick and

Nowell codices had already been bound together as Vitellius A. xv., and, most notably, the two codices had already been foliated consecutively.

Junius's transcript, and by extension the first complete foliation of Cotton Vitellius A. xv., can be dated with confidence between 1628 and 1650. Junius lived in England from 1620 to 1650, but since the contents of the composite codex had not been settled until Richard James became librarian for Cotton, the *terminus a quo* must be moved up to 1628. Junius returned to England as an octogenarian in 1674, and died at Oxford in 1677, but the handwriting of the transcript is that of a young man.[23] Moreover, there is proof that Junius had worked extensively with Cotton Vitellius A. xv. during his first stay in England: in his edition of the Gothic and Anglo-Saxon Gospels, which he published in Amsterdam in 1665, he mentions his transcript of *The Soliloquia of St. Augustine* (Bodleian MS Junius 70) and his collation of *The Gospel of Nicodemus* (Bodleian MS Junius 74).[24] In all, then, it seems safe to conclude that, since Junius refers to it between 1628 and 1650, the first complete foliation of Cotton Vitellius A. xv. was made between 1628 and 1638, when Richard James was Cotton's librarian, and after the contents of the composite codex had been settled.[25]

The next reference to this first complete foliation of the codex was made in the year 1703 as part of the report on the state of the Cottonian

23. The argument is Dobbie's, *Beowulf and Judith*, pp. xxii–xxiii, n. 7.

24. See Junius's address to the reader (n. pag.) in *Quatuor D. N. Jesu Christi* EVANGELIORUM *versiones perantiquae duae, Gothica scil. et Anglo-Saxonica*. According-ing to his first biographer, however, Junius expressly returned to England in 1674 to work with Anglo-Saxon MSS at the Cottonian Library; it is obvious that Junius, even as an octogenarian, had enormous energy, and the possibility that he transcribed the *Judith* fragment after 1674, though remote, should not be ruled out altogether. See Johannes Georgius Graevius, "Vita Francisci F. F. Junii."

25. As Förster points out (*Die Beowulf-Handschrift*, p. 6), the foliation was not written by James himself, but it is not to be supposed that James foliated all of Cotton's books by himself. The *Catalogue of the Cotton MSS. Circa 1635* (BL Add. MS. 36,789), done during James's tenure but not by James, contains a rough copy of the *Elenchus contentorum*, combining items 3 and 4 and leaving no space for *Beowulf* between items 6 and 8 (fol. 29v). The earliest Cotton catalogue, *Catalogus Librorum Manuscriptorum in Bibliotheca Roberti Cottoni, 1621* (BL Harley MS 6018), does not mention Vitellius A. xv., though, as C. E. Wright suggests, it "may be concealed under the word 'Saxon.'" "The Elizabethan Society of Antiquaries and the Formation of the Cottonian Library," p. 199.

Library. In that year, the trustees of the library commissioned the antiquaries Matthew Hutton, John Anstis, and Humfrey Wanley, along
with the Cotton librarian, Thomas Smith, to inspect the contents of the
library, and to correct Smith's *Catalogus Librorum Manuscriptorum
Bibliothecæ Cottonianæ* (1696). A primary duty of this commission was
to correct foliations and to provide them where they were lacking. Wanley, of course, wanted to do much more, but the draft of his letter "To
Mr Speaker" (that is, Robert Harley, the chief trustee), dated 29 May
1703, and preserved in BL MS Harley 7055, clarifies the main duty:

> If the Books in the Library were only to have their Leaves Number'd
> and to be Compar'd with Dr Smith's Catalogue, (as some of the Inspec-
> tors do Apprehend) the work will be at an end, as soon as they can find
> all things in their Places, which the Doctor ha's specified. But I under-
> stand your Honors Commands otherwise. . . . Sir, I am fearful that there
> may arise some differences in Opinion among the Inspectors, as to what
> is *Wanting* in Dr Smith's Catalogue. The Act of Parliament ha's most
> judiciously observed one thing, viz. *the not Numbering the Leaves of
> Every Book.* (fol. 25)

Wanley was soon to discover that his more elaborate conception of his
job was not going to be encouraged by the beleaguered librarian and
cataloguer, Thomas Smith. A note in Wanley's hand, dated May 31, on
fol. 21 of BL MS Harley 7055, reads:

> We attended on D^r. Smith in Obedience to the Commands of the Trus-
> tees for his Assistance at the Cottonian Library in order to the Inspection
> of the Books, &c. contained therein: The D^r said that he could not go
> along with us now, but would be there next Saturday by 10 a clock: at
> which time he would Agree that we should Inspect the Books: that is,
> compare the Numbers inscribed in them, with his Printed Catalogue; but
> would not then permit us to Examine the Books, as to the Tracts they
> comprehend, or allow any access to the Charters at all, saying that the
> former would take up more time than his hea[l]th would permit, & that
> the Latter ought not to be done 'till a Library-keeper be appointed.

Smith had no intention of helping Wanley humiliate him. The final
report on the state of the library (Bodleian MS. Add. D. 82) shows that
both Wanley and Smith had to bend a little. The "Books, Charters,

Coins, & other Rarities contained in the said Library" (fol. i) were all duly inspected, despite Smith, but the other inspectors managed to rein Wanley's more elaborate plans for perfecting Smith's catalogue. Wanley had to report, on behalf of the group, that the inspectors did not

> conceive it to be required by your Honors That we should compare all these Tracts with D^r. Smith's Catalogue to Correct such Mistakes in it as might occur, or to Insert the Titles of such Tracts as are omitted; because this seems to be a Work of time: But only to observe ye Volume each Book is written in; the Number of Leaves it contains; and whether the Book be of paper or Parchment, or both.

Fortunately, Wanley himself rectified these shortcomings in his own catalogue, published two years later.

The study of the first foliation of Cotton Vitellius A. XV. was not made by Wanley, however. Apparently, Matthew Hutton was in charge of checking the foliations of the Vitellius MSS, for there is a list of these MSS on fol. 87 of BL MS Harley 7055 that is not in Wanley's hand. A note by Frederic Madden in the upper left margin of this folio reads, "This is in D^r. Matthew Hutton's handwriting. FM." For Cotton Vitellius A. XV. Hutton makes the following notations:

A. 15. fol. 205. preter 1 fol. in indic.   male numerat.
pergam.
fol. 154 bis numeratus

Hutton's comments tell us that Cotton Vitellius A. XV. was a parchment codex containing 205 folios and a table of contents (that is, James's *Elenchus contentorum*); that the first foliation was inaccurate *(male numeratus)*; and that fol. 154 (in *Beowulf*) had been numbered twice. The most astonishing comment is that, by Hutton's count, the codex contained 205 folios, rather than 206. Surprisingly, the first foliation numbered 206 leaves, and the *Judith* fragment began on fol. 199 because fol. 154 had been numbered twice. In other words, a folio was missing from the codex when Hutton checked the accuracy of the first foliation. As we shall see, Hutton was right.

The second foliation is implied in Hutton's corrections of the first, which give the important information that a folio was missing in the

17th century. However, since the corrections of Smith's catalogue had been limited to observing "ye Volume each Book is written in; the Number of Leaves it contains; and whether the Book be of paper or Parchment," the second foliation numbers were not subsequently recorded in Smith's corrected catalogue. Only the number of leaves (205) was noted.[26] The first real application of the second foliation numbers came two years later, in Humfrey Wanley's mighty *Antiquœ Literaturœ Septentrionalis Liber Alter, seu Humphredi Wanleii Librorum Vett. Septentrionalium, qui in Angliœ Bibliothecis extant, nec non multorum Vett. Codd. Septentrionalium alibi extantium Catalogus Historico-Criticus, cum totius Thesauri Linguarum Septentrionalium sex Indicibus.*[27] For obvious reasons, this important book is better known as Wanley's Catalogue. As N. R. Ker says in the opening paragraph of his own catalogue, Wanley's "catalogue of Anglo-Saxon manuscripts is a book which scholars will continue to use, or neglect at their own peril. His opinion on any given matter will always be worth knowing" (*Catalogue,* p. xiii).

Nonetheless, scholars have persistently neglected the foliation numbers Wanley gives for the Nowell Codex. Their reason for doing so was the assumption (which we now know was wrong) that the Nowell Codex was unfoliated before the fire, and that Wanley was somehow incapable of counting the folios correctly himself. Malone, for instance, uses Wanley's seemingly inaccurate foliation as evidence that the Nowell Codex was unfoliated before the fire: "For want of such a foliation, Cotton's bookbinder made serious mistakes in ordering the sheets of the codex and Wanley's count of folios here is repeatedly inaccurate. The 90 leaves of the Southwick Codex, however, were early numbered. . . . By virtue of this foliation, Cotton's bookbinder made no mistakes in ordering the sheets of the Southwick codex and Wanley's count of folios here is uniformly accurate" (*Nowell Codex,* p. 12; cf. Hoops, p. 4). As a matter of fact, Wanley's count of folios was accurate when it was made, and this first full record of the second foliation provides some

26. The notation, in Wanley's hand, is made on p. 83 of Harley's copy of Smith's catalogue: it reads, *Cod. membr. in 4to constans folijs 205.* Since the descriptive phrase, *in 4to,* does not depend on Hutton, Wanley's count of folios may also be independent.

27. It was published as volume two of George Hickes, *Linguarum Vett. Septentrionalium Thesaurus Grammatico-Criticus et Archaeologicus.* Both volumes were reissued in 1970 in the FS series *English Linguistics: 1500–1800.*

valuable information about the state of the codex before the fire. Wanley's use of the second foliation in his catalogue confirms that there were only 205 folios in the codex at the time; indicates that there was a blank leaf between the Southwick and Nowell codices before the fire, which was replaced by a blank paper sheet when the new binding was made; proves that the first 10 folios of the Nowell Codex were already out of order before the fire; and shows that the missing folio came from *Beowulf.*

Wanley says that the *St. Christopher* fragment began on fol. 92 and that the *Judith* fragment began on fol. 199, while the MS foliation numbers the same section, from the beginning of the *St. Christopher* fragment to the beginning of the *Judith* fragment, 91 through 199. This discrepancy confirms Hutton's count of 205 folios, rather than 206, and shows that the missing folio came from the Nowell Codex, but before the *Judith* fragment. The first step in understanding the relation between the second foliation, used by Wanley, and the MS foliation is the realization that Wanley must have counted a blank leaf after the Southwick Codex: he says for the last page of the Southwick Codex, *fol. 90ᵇ. Fragmentum de SS. Jesu Christi martyribus* (that is, the eleven-line *St. Quintin* fragment); but then, for the first page of the Nowell Codex, he says *fol. 92. Legenda de S. Christophoro Martyre.* One cannot seriously argue that Wanley miscounted a folio here, for if there was not a blank vellum leaf separating the two codices, the last page of the Southwick Codex and the first page of the Nowell Codex would be facing pages. Wanley would not have written 90ᵇ for the left facing page and 92 for the right facing page.

It is admittedly uncharacteristic for Wanley to have counted a blank leaf in his foliation. He says in his report on the state of the Cottonian Library in 1703 that many of the erroneous foliations "seem to be occasioned . . . by their numbring Blank Leaves having nothing at all written upon them (which we conceive to be done amiss, since such leaves are of no use or value)" (Bodleian MS Add. D. 82). But Wanley had a good reason for counting the blank leaf at the start of the Nowell Codex. The discovery by Hutton that fol. 154 had been numbered twice in the first foliation meant that Junius's reference to fol. 199 as the first page of the *Judith* fragment was wrong by one. Junius had left all of his MSS and transcripts, including his transcript of the *Judith* fragment, to the Bodleian Library, Oxford, where Wanley had been assistant librarian until December 1700. As a librarian, Wanley would have recognized the value of maintaining the start of the *Judith* fragment at fol. 199. Edward Thwaites, who had published the first edition of *Judith* in 1698, and who was in charge of printing Wanley's catalogue,[28] may have provided other incentives. It is certain that Wanley had these two considerations in mind, at any rate, when he described Cotton Vitellius A. XV., for to his description of *Judith* he adds, *Quod descripsit cl. Junius, è cujus Apographo illus typis edidit Edwardus Thwaitesius, in libro suo supra laudat.*

After one realizes that Wanley counted a blank leaf, for whatever reason, between the Southwick and Nowell codices, his strange foliation of the Nowell Codex makes sense. The first ten folios of the Nowell Codex were out of order, one must remember, when the MS foliation was made in the late 18th century, and Wanley's foliation shows that these folios were already out of order before the fire, when the second foliation was made. To illustrate the accuracy of Wanley's foliation the following table shows how Wanley's numbers (fol. 92 and fol. 98v) for the beginnings of the *St. Christopher* fragment and *The Wonders of the East* reflect the former disorder of the first ten folios of the Nowell Codex:

Wanley	*MS*	*Textual references*	
fol. 92	91	*Christopher,*	pp. 5–6
—	92	″	pp. 7–8
—	93	″	pp. 1–2
—	94	″	pp. 3–4
—	95	*Wonders,*	pp. 8–9
—	96	″	pp. 10–11
fol. 98v	97v	*Christopher,*	p. 9; *Wonders,* p. 1 (on the verso)
—	98	*Wonders,*	pp. 2–3
—	99	″	pp. 4–5
—	100	″	pp. 6–7

Like the uncorrected MS foliation, Wanley's second foliation indicates that there were six and one-half folios in the *Christopher* fragment,

---

28. See J. A. W. Bennett, "Hickes's 'Thesaurus': A Study in Oxford Book-Production." Thwaites's first edition of *Judith*, in his *Heptateuchus, Liber Job, et Evangelium Nicodemi: Anglo-Saxonice. Historiae Judith Fragmentum; Dano-Saxonice,* was based on Junius's transcript, rather than on the MS. Note that Thwaites calls the language of *Judith* "Dano-Saxon."

rather than four and one-half, as there should have been. The two extra folios were the two (95 and 96 of the uncorrected MS foliation) misplaced from *The Wonders of the East*. But since Wanley began on fol. 92, he was right that *The Wonders of the East* began on fol. 98v. Wanley's numbers are one in advance of the corresponding MS numbers (91 and 97v) because he counted the blank leaf preceding the *St. Christopher* fragment. For the same reason, he says that *Beowulf* begins on fol. 130, rather than 129. He does not give a folio number for the beginning of *Alexander's Letter*, but the count of folios between the start of *The Wonders of the East* and the start of *Beowulf* is the same as the count in the MS foliation: in other words, two folios are missing between 98v and 130, which correspond to the two extra folios between 92 and 98v. Obviously, up to and including the start of *Beowulf*, Wanley's second foliation and the uncorrected MS foliation correspond, once an allowance of one folio is made for the blank leaf that must have separated the Southwick and Nowell codices when Wanley made his description.

What is most interesting, and most important, about Wanley's second foliation is what it implicitly tells us about the state of the *Beowulf* MS prior to the fire. The missing folio, first reflected in Hutton's count of folios for Cotton Vitellius A. XV., must have come from *Beowulf*, since Wanley records that *Beowulf* began on fol. 130, and that the *Judith* fragment began on fol. 199. Unless a folio was missing from *Beowulf*, the *Judith* fragment should have begun by Wanley's foliation on fol. 200, or one folio in advance of the MS foliation. By Wanley's second foliation, then, *Beowulf* before the fire consisted of only sixty-nine folios, rather than seventy.[29] This remarkable feature of Wanley's foliation has always been ignored in the past, because all of his foliation appeared to be inaccurate. Now that we know, from Hutton, that Cotton Vitellius A. XV. was lacking a folio before the fire, and that Wanley's apparently inaccurate foliation accurately reflects the disorder of the Nowell Codex before the fire, we know also that the missing folio came from *Beowulf*. Two facts may be immediately deduced regarding the whereabouts of this missing *Beowulf* folio. The first is that it must have been included

29. Thorkelin, who saw the MS after the fire and before the MS foliation was made, comes up with the same number (*foliis LXIX constante*) on the page prefacing his transcript (*Thorkelin Transcripts,* p. C). Evidently it was Thorkelin who discovered the missing folio, since his transcription is complete.

somewhere in the bound codex, since none of the seventy *Beowulf* folios
has escaped the general fire damage along the top and right sides that
was sustained by *all* folios in the codex. The second fact is more revealing: the missing folio must have been with the *Judith* fragment, since
Wanley, by his folio numbers, accounts for all of the folios prior to the
Judith fragment.

With this help, the mystery of the missing *Beowulf* folio can be
solved. The folio from *Beowulf* was not inserted in the *Judith* fragment,
or Junius, presumably, would have transcribed it by mistake, and certainly Hutton would have counted it, and come up with 206 folios for
Cotton Vitellius A. xv. instead of 205. The only place for it, then, is at
the end of the codex, after the *Judith* fragment, where Hutton could
regard it as a flyleaf, not to be counted in the foliation. Hutton does not
count the flyleaves (that is, the three prefixed leaves) at the beginning
of the codex either. The folio from *Beowulf* that served as the ending
flyleaf of Vitellius A. xv. in Cotton's original binding can be identified
by means of the fire damage it incurred in its position at the end of the
codex in 1731. The last page of the *Judith* fragment is scorched and
burned, and the only page from *Beowulf* that is more scorched and
burned is the last page, or fol. 198v of the MS foliation. Further proof
that the last folio of *Beowulf* followed the last folio of the *Judith* fragment at the time of the fire will be considered later, and will include an
explanation of how and even why the *Beowulf* folio was deliberately
misplaced. But to put off any possible skepticism now, it may be noted
in passing that the small hole burned through line 17 on fol. 206v of the
Judith fragment corresponds to the larger hole burned through the same
area on fol. 198v of *Beowulf.* There can be no doubt that fol. 198 was
at the end of the codex at the time of the fire, as Wanley's second foliation allows one to deduce.

The third foliation is the MS foliation in the Nowell Codex, the restoration of the old foliation (still partly extant) in the Southwick Codex.
The common belief[30] that this foliation was written on the MS leaves
soon after the fire is wrong. It was not done until sometime after 1787,
because fol. 147A(131), from *Beowulf*, was not misplaced until 1787,
when the Thorkelin transcripts were being made. The folio was in its

30. See Förster, *Die Beowulf-Handschrift,* p. 6; Hoops, "Die Foliierung," p. 5;
and Malone, *Nowell Codex,* p. 12.

proper place for the first transcript, but was out of place for the second. Hence the MS foliation must be dated after the second Thorkelin transcript. It is interesting to note, however, that the last folio of *Beowulf* was no longer a flyleaf at the end of the codex by 1787. It seems safe to assume that it was Thorkelin himself who discovered the misplacement of the last *Beowulf* folio and restored it to its proper place, for as far as we know he was the first person after Wanley to read *Beowulf* with any comprehension. The third or MS foliation can be dated with some confidence between 1793 and 1801. This foliation was first officially used in 1802 by Joseph Planta, then the principal librarian of the British Museum, in *A Catalogue of the Manuscripts in the Cottonian Library, Deposited in the British Museum*. Planta tells us in his preface that the curators of the museum directed him, in 1793, to begin work on the catalogue, and that his "first care . . . was to cause all of the volumes to be regularly paged" (p. xiv).

Planta's description of Cotton Vitellius A. xv. (pp. 380–381) was hastily dismissed by Förster as a servile copy of Wanley's description (p. 72). It is true that Planta bases his description on Wanley's, and he is somewhat misleading about his dependence on Wanley. His description of *Beowulf*, for instance, is drawn verbatim from Wanley, yet Planta deliberately hides his debt by saying, *Hunc Cl. Wanleius 'Poeseos Anglo-Saxonicæ egregium exemplum,' nuncupavit*. Still, Förster overlooks the fact that Planta makes new observations of his own and, more important, that Planta changed Wanley's foliation numbers. Planta was following the new MS foliation. Here is Planta's description, with the new folio numbers in the right margin:

Vitellius, A. XV.
Codex membran. in 4to. foliis constans 206.
1. Notulæ de numero parochiarum, villarum, feodorumque militum in Anglia; et de expugnatione Caleti per R. Edwardum III. Folio rejectanes verso.
2. Flores ex libro soliloquiorum D. Augustini Hipponensis Episc. selecti, et Saxonice versi, per Ælfredum regem. Tractatus iste

---

Plates 6a and 6b. The corresponding holes burned through fol. 198v17 of *Beowulf* and fol. 206v17 of the *Judith* fragment show that fol. 198 was misplaced at the end of Cotton Vitellius A. xv. at the time of the fire, 1731.

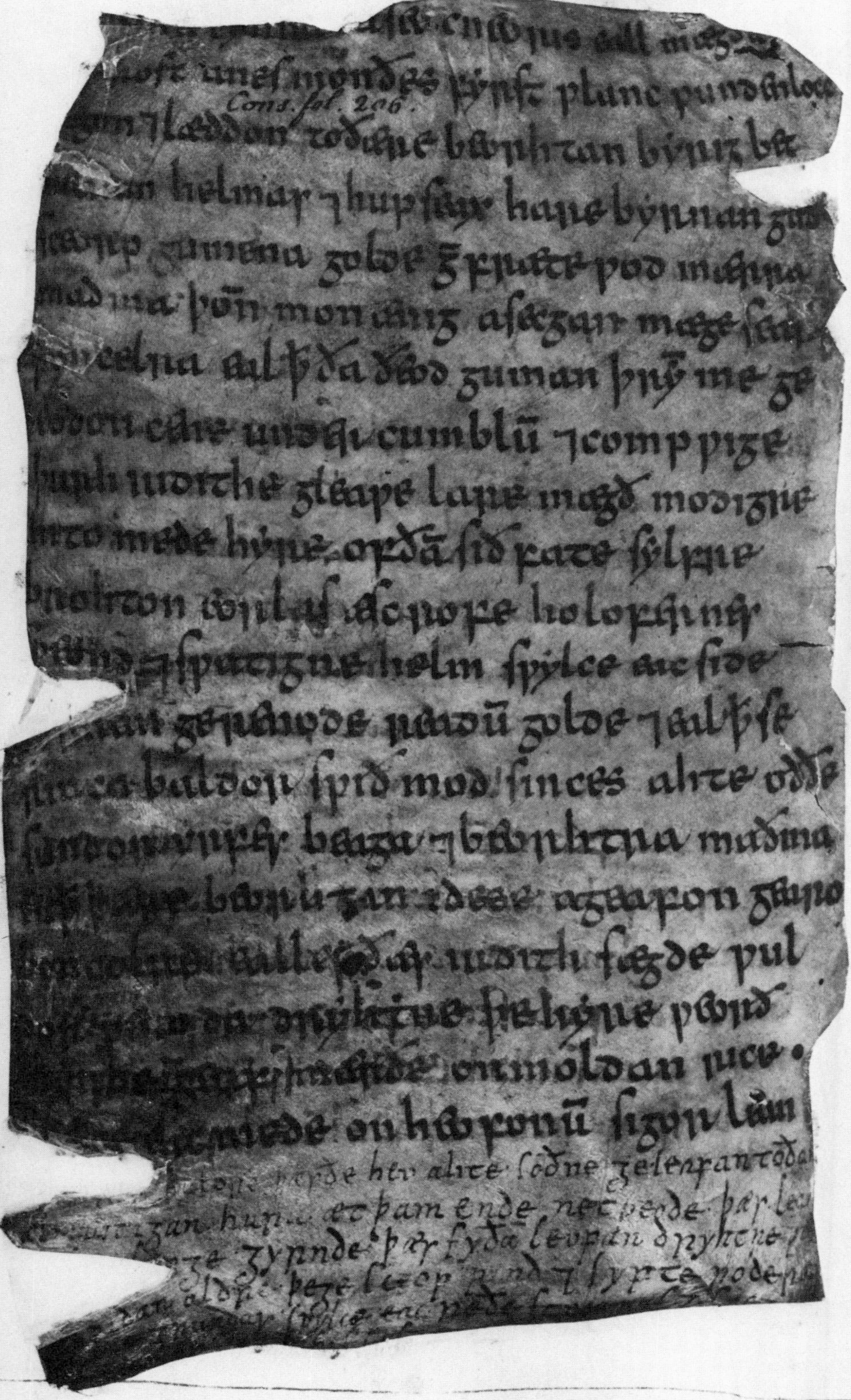

Cons. fol. 206.

quondam fuit ecclesiæ B. Mariæ de Suwika, ut patet ex fol. 2.
literis Normanno-Saxonicis, post conquæstum scriptus.   1.

3. Pseudo-Evangelium Nicodemi, Saxonice, capite, mutilum; cujus
exemplaris variantes lectiones apographo suo, ex codice Canta-
brigiensi descripto, attexuit Cl. Junius, ut videre est pag. 96 —
Extat ad calcem Heptateuchi a Thwaitesio editi.   57.

4. Dialogus inter Saturnum et Salomonem; Saxonice.   83b.

5. Fragmentum de SS. Jesu Christi martyribus; Saxonice.   90b.

6. Legenda de S. Christophoro martyre; Saxonice; capite et calce
mutila.   91.

7. Descriptio fabulosa Orientis, et monstrorum quæ ibi nascuntur;
cum figuris male delineatis; capite et calce mutila; haud diversa
ab illa (Latinis exceptis quæ in hoc codice desunt) quam exhibit
codex qui inscribitur. Tib. B. V. 51.   95.

8. Alexandri ad Aristotelem de situ Indiæ, &c epistola; Saxonice.   104.

9. Tractatus poeticus, quo descripta videntur bella quæ Beowulfus
quidam Danus, ex regia Scyldingorum stirpe ortus, gessit contra
Sueciæ regulos. — Hunc Cl. Wanleius "Poeseos Anglo-Saxonicæ
egregium exemplum," nuncupavit.   129.

10. Fragmentum poeticum historiæ Judithæ et Holofernis, Dano-
Saxonice, ante conquæstum scriptum: quod descripsit Cl. Junius;
e cujus apographo illud typis edidit Edw. Twaitesius ad calcem
Heptateuchi.   199.

This description is unquestionably based on an independent study of
the MS, despite the heavy reliance on Wanley. The new foliation of the
last five articles, that is, of the Nowell Codex, is enough to prove this.
In his preface, Planta says of the method in his catalogue, "The folio of
each article has been entered; and the number of folios in each volume
has been noted, both in the catalogue and at the end of the volume, in
hopes thereby to prevent all future mutilation, or at least to lay it open
to detection" (p. xv). These remarks make it possible to ascribe the MS
foliation to Planta: the total number of folios in Cotton Vitellius A. xv.
is duly noted, both in his catalogue *(foliis constans 206)* and at the end
of the MS, on the last page of the *Judith* fragment *(Cons. fol. 206)*. The
number 206 is written by the same hand that wrote the MS foliation in
the Nowell Codex, and since *Beowulf* fol. 147A(131) was not misplaced
until 1787, the foliation must be associated with Planta.

What is remarkable about the foliation, as it appears in the catalogue, is that at first glance it suggests that the first ten folios of the

Nowell Codex had been put in their right order: according to Planta, *The Wonders of the East* begins on fol. 95, rather than 97, as the uncorrected MS foliation says. The following table can elucidate this misleading feature of Planta's catalogue.

Planta's catalogue	MS	Textual references (with folios out of order)
fol. 91	91	*Christopher*, pp. 5–6
—	92	" pp. 7–8
—	93	" pp. 1–2
—	94	" pp. 3–4
fol. 95	95	*Wonders*, pp. 8–9
—	96	" pp. 10–11
—	97	*Christopher*, p. 9; *Wonders*, p. 1
—	98	*Wonders*, pp. 2–3
—	99	" pp. 4–5
—	100	" pp. 6–7

Obviously, Planta did not realize when he wrote the MS foliation that the first ten folios of the Nowell Codex were out of order. With the first two and the next two folios of the *St. Christopher* fragment transposed, and with the last page lost in the middle of *The Wonders of the East,* Planta's claim that the *St. Christopher* fragment had lost its beginning *and ending (capite et calce mutila)* makes sense. Similarly, with the two folios from *The Wonders of the East* misplaced, this text would seem to begin as a fragment *(capite . . . mutila)* on fol. 95.

The last three foliations of Cotton Vitellius A. xv.—the fourth, fifth, and sixth—are all recorded on the paper frames of the 19th-century binding. The fourth foliation is written in pencil in the upper right corners, recto, of the frames; it corrects most of the errors of the third, Planta's MS foliation.[31] It renumbers the first ten folios of the Nowell Codex from 91–100, but with the folios in their right order: for clarity, the third and fourth foliations should be used in tandem, with the MS numbers in parentheses, when citing these ten folios. The double references, 91(93), 92(94), 93(91), 94(92), 95(97), 96(98), 97(99), 98(100), 99(95), 100(96), will provide the proper sequence of these

---

31. As Daunt points out in her review of Hoops, "In the extreme right-hand top of the page, in some cases a number appears half cut away by the trimming of the page—where it can be seen . . . it appears to be the same as the pencilled numbering just described." "Old English Studies," p. 75.

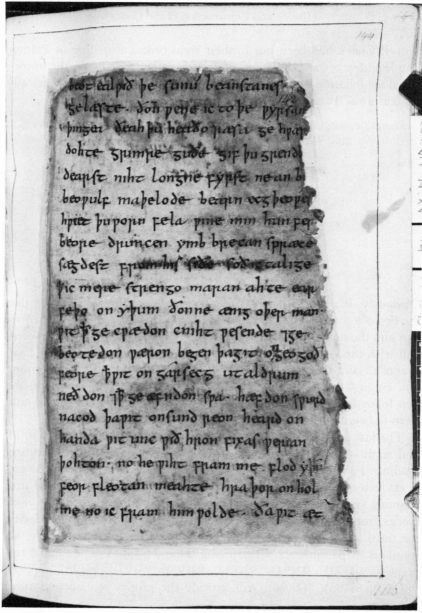

Plate 7. MS fol. 142r reduced. The protective paper frames of Gough's 1845 binding record the fourth foliation, crossed out in the extreme upper right corner; the fifth foliation in the lower right corner; and the sixth foliation, inside the ruled border of the upper right corner.

folios, preserve the fact of their former disorder, and simultaneously explain the erroneous MS foliation. The two misplaced folios from *Beowulf,* 131 and 197, were back in their proper places for the fourth foliation, but the fourth foliation does not renumber them, no doubt to prevent having to refoliate *Beowulf* from fol. 130 onward. The double references, 147A(131) and 189A(197), achieve the same result, but have the advantage of simultaneously indicating the present, correct locations and the former, incorrect locations. The fourth foliation does not correct the transposition of the two gatherings from *Alexander's Letter.*

The discovery of the proper order for the first ten folios of the Nowell Codex was made in two stages sometime in the interval between the writing of the third foliation on the MS and the writing of the fourth foliation on the paper frames of the new binding. Before the MS leaves were set in the paper frames, two different hands wrote catchwords in the lower right corners, verso, of folios 92(94) and 98(100). Malone, as far as I know, is the only scholar to have interpreted the purpose of these catchwords at all, and he is certainly wrong about them. He says of the catchword on fol. 92(94)v: "Lower margin: At the extreme right, some interpolator wrote *forðon* in a modern imitation of the insular hand; after it he set a point and the figure 96, but the 6 has been crossed out and a 1 set over it. The next folio in the MS as it now stands is 91, old foliation, but 96, official foliation. This folio begins with *forðon.* The interpolation was obviously made after the adoption, in 1884, of the present foliation of the MS" (*Nowell Codex,* pp. 33–34). Malone's explanation does not bear scrutiny. No one at the British Museum would be writing on the vellum leaves of the MS as late as 1884. The leaves had long been mounted in the paper frames by then, and if the catchwords were written as late as Malone maintains, they would have been written on the paper frames, not on the vellum. Malone did not realize that the *purpose* of the catchword was to identify the folio that should, but did not, follow fol. 92(94) when the catchword was written. That folio was the first misplaced folio of the MS foliation, fol. 93(91). Thus the catchword predates the 1845 rebinding, and indeed made it possible to rebind the folio in its proper place in 1845. The correction

---

Plates 8a and 8b. The catchwords in the bottom right corners of fols. 92(94)v and 98(100)v identified the proper sequence of the first ten folios of the Nowell Codex.

...sæza sinnum godum þdu onspa mane
...um nefor weorde spade ze zeaт
...yng Sehalza him and spawode ȝcpæd
...ine ȝoda iclaðec ze ꝫhim teonando
...ꝥon heminne ȝelæafan icuupenme ȝeheald
...feic onfulpihte onfeng
...mmȝe byðꝗ þahec bpunȝan ummæcꝥeꝛ
...elnesse ꝗicop þpæs epi heuh þæs halȝan
...lenȝo ꝫhe hit hec aseczan beꝛoꝛan
...heulle ꝫhyne hec þaꝛi onȝe pæsꝛman
...bend þðiꝛ cempan hyne scote don mid hyꝛa
...lum að ꝫheꝛaꝛe acpeild ꝥa cempan hyne
...ze don fram haꝛiꝛe æꝛiesтan тide þæꝛdaȝes
...ꝛor sceymmȝe þapeide þeulle þascꝛælaꝛ
...lichaman ȝeꝥast node ꝛaꝛoui aene pꝛꝛhon
...biꝛ lichaman ᴛieȝe hꝛian æ ȝodes mæȝen paꝛ
...dam pinde hanȝiȝende æc þæꝛ halȝan man
...ꝛ spyðꝛan heulfe ꝫse cymnȝo þacæꝛᴛeꝛ sun
...ieel ȝurȝe hesende ᴛodam cempum ꝫhe bend
...iꝛ spaȝe bundenne ȝeopnlice heol don
fondonȝi

cayhyſſum beoð acende þa miclan mẏcneʒo
olþen da
æt beoð cende men
hy beoð fiftyne
eota lange ⁊hy hab
bað hpit lic ⁊tpa
neb on anum heaſde
⁊cneopu ſpyðe

pcade ⁊lange noſa ⁊ſtẏenʒe feax · þonne hy
cennan pillað þonne faẏuað hy onſcipum to
indeum · ⁊þen hyʒu ʒecynda inpoplð bʒinʒað
icomu inʒallia hatte
ſtade þeyi beoð men a
cende on djuſ heoyeſ
hyu þæyðu beoð ʒe
monu ſpa leona heaf
du ⁊hi beoð · xx · fota
lange ⁊hy habbað

miceline muð ſpæ foy · ʒuſ hpylcne mon
nan onþæm landu onʒitað oððe ʒeſeoþ

oðte l...
fol...

was made in two stages, as the difference in ink shows. One interpolator, mistakenly thinking that the folio should precede fol. 96 of the MS foliation, wrote 96 in the lower right corner. The number seems to be in the same hand as the MS foliation itself. A second interpolator, still using the MS foliation, corrected 96 to 91, and wrote in *forðon* before the number to indicate that this page had to be placed before fol. 93(91) to correct the order of the folios.

Yet another interpolator (compare the handwriting with *forðon*) performed the same service for the other misplaced folios in the sequence. Malone says of the catchwords on fol. 98(100)v: "The catch-words in the right-hand corner anticipate the first words of the next page. . . . I read /odðe him h[w]i[lc]/ for the first line, /folgia*n*/ for the second" (*Nowell Codex,* p. 36). His reading, however, is incorrect. Some of the letters are badly faded, but they can still be made out with confidence. The interpolator incorrectly copied *odðe him hwilc man folgiende* as *odðe him man folgiande,* his major error being the omission of *hwilc.* His other two errors are spelling mistakes, the first of which (*odðe* for *oððe*) is supported by the way the Old English scribe crossed his *d*'s with a single stroke. These catchwords were demonstrably written before 1845, when the vellum leaves were inlaid in the paper frames, for the *n* in *man* and the *g* of *folgiande* are partly covered by the paper frame. Although the catchwords on folios 92(94)v and 98(100)v were written by two different people, they were obviously written before the fourth foliation, since the fourth foliation benefits from them by ordering and numbering the first ten folios of the Nowell Codex correctly. The catchwords showed that fol. 93(91) should follow fol. 92(94), and that fol. 99(95) should follow fol. 98(100). With these as guides, it was possible for Gough to put the first ten folios of the Nowell Codex in their proper order when he inlaid and rebound Cotton Vitellius A. xv. in August 1845.

The fifth foliation is written in pencil in the lower right corners, recto, of the paper frames. It is quite likely that the fifth foliation was never intended by the archivist who made it to supersede the fourth foliation. It seems strange, at any rate, that it would have been written in the lower right corners if it was meant to be considered the official foliation at any time. Possibly, the fifth foliation stems from an archivist's desire to keep an *additional* record of the leaves in Cotton Vitellius A. xv., which included the three prefixed leaves as well as the two blank paper leaves that were placed in the codex when the MS was rebound in the 19th century. As we have seen, the second blank paper leaf, after fol. 90, may well have replaced a blank vellum leaf from Cotton's original binding, for Wanley apparently counted a vellum leaf here in his foliation. If the first paper leaf, after fol. 56, also replaced an original vellum leaf, there would be a good explanation for the purpose of the fifth foliation. Hoops (p. 7) and Malone (*Nowell Codex,* p. 12) believed that the blank paper leaves were inserted in the codex at the time of the new binding to emphasize that sections of the original MSS were missing at these points. This explanation, however, fails to account for the lack of a paper leaf before the *Judith* fragment. It also fails to explain why an archivist then counted a blank leaf, representing an indeterminate number of lost folios, as a single folio.

If, on the other hand, the blank paper leaves replaced blank vellum leaves, there would be a reason why no blank paper leaf was inserted before the *Judith* fragment (there was no blank vellum leaf to replace), and there would be a reason for numbering the blank leaves as single folios in the fifth foliation (to represent the former existence of blank vellum leaves). Nor is it hard to explain how two blank paper leaves could have come to replace two blank vellum leaves when the codex was rebound in the 19th century. After the fire, when each leaf of the MS was mounted in the paper frames, the mounter substituted paper leaves for the vellum leaves because he did not see the need to mount empty vellum, especially since the MS foliation did not count them anyway. This interpretation of the origin of the two blank paper leaves also explains the origin of the fifth foliation, which, by counting five folios that had never been counted before, and were not Old English texts, would seem only to be creating problems where no problems existed. The officials at the British Museum wanted to record, as precisely as possible, the state of the codex before the new binding: the count in the lower right corners achieved this purpose without directly supplanting the MS foliation of the Old English texts. Surely, the officials who made the count knew the significance of the blank paper leaves, or they would not have been counted as single folios. These officials, whoever they were, were not amateurs, and it is unreasonable to believe that they would have counted modern paper leaves in the fifth foliation if these leaves merely represented an indeterminate number of lost folios.

If the fifth foliation was indeed only meant to supplement the MS foliation, it nevertheless came to have full status as a "neue foliierung" or "neue zählung" in Alfred Holder's paper on the collation he made in 1876 of *The Wonders of the East* and *Alexander's Letter*. It was abandoned in 1884, but not before it had caused some major confusion among scholars. Somehow, Förster managed to confuse it with the 1884 foliation. He says that this "Blätterzählung, die auf der unteren rechten Ecke des Papierrahmens angebracht ist, wurde erst nach 1884 einge-führt" (p. 10). Thus Förster considered the fifth foliation the last, and because he distinguishes only three distinct foliations, he refers to it as the third foliation, instead of the second. Since Förster's description of Cotton Vitellius A. xv. is the only full description of the MS there is, the various foliations of it have been very poorly understood indeed.

The sixth foliation has already been discussed in some detail in the section on the prefixed leaves. Like the fifth foliation it counts the three prefixed leaves, and like the fifth foliation it has been pervasively inaccurate since the first prefixed leaf was removed from the codex in 1913. Unlike the fifth foliation it does not count the two blank paper leaves, but if these leaves replace blank vellum leaves, as the evidence suggests, the sixth foliation only shares the inaccuracy of the fifth foliation. The sixth, then, tells us nothing about the codex that cannot be told in more efficient ways, and it hides important facts about the history of the codex that only the MS foliation clearly reveals to any extent. A return to the Old English MSS can now be facilitated by a return to the MS foliation preserved on them.

The Southwick Codex

The Southwick Codex takes its name from a decidedly threatening notice of ownership, written in a late 13th- or early 14th-century hand, on fol. 2r of *The Soliloquia of St. Augustine*. Part of the notice appears to have been destroyed along the bottom right margin, which is scorched, shrunken, creased, and covered by tape; but in fact the passage can be read in its entirety by holding the leaf up against strong light.

Plate 9. The notice of ownership for the Southwick Codex is in the bottom margin of fol. 2r.

halgan feoderaſ ſie ſpa. 2

Ne þearf nan þundor þeala me iſ þ
on timber ge pyrce ⁊ eac on þa
lade eac on þere bytlinge ac æſlene
man lyſt ſiddan he æniʒ cot lyſ on hiſ
hlafordeſ læne myd hiſ fultume ge
timbred hæfð þ he hine mote hpilum
þar on ge reſtan. ⁊ huntigan ⁊ fuʒlian.
⁊ fiſcian. ⁊ hiſ on ge hpilce piſan to þæ
re lænan tilian æʒ þær ge on ſe ge on
lande oð oð þone firſt þe he boeland
⁊ ece yfe þurh hiſ hlafordeſ miltſe
ge earniʒe ſpa ge do ſe pile ʒa ſið fola
ſeðe egðer pill ge þiſſa lænena ſtocli
ſe ſe þara ecena heona . Seðe egþer
ge ſcop. ⁊ egðereſ pilt; for gifeme þine
tpægdrum on haʒʒe ge her mit pyrðe
to beon   ne geſtruþider to cumane þ

Pholubey eſt æcclie beatæ æþlʒe de Sutona. Quem qui ab ea
abſtulerit. bel titulum iſtum doloſe deleuit. ſi eadem æcclie ...
ſatiſfecerit. Oxo anathema ʒeþolaðe. fiat. fiat. ... dñi. ...

The notice, for the first time transcribed in its entirety, stoutly proclaims:

Hic liber est Ecclesie beate Marie de Suwika. Quem qui ab eadem ab-
stulerit. vel Titulum istum dolose deleuerit nisi eidem Ecclesie condigne
satisfecerit? Sit Anathema. Maranatha. Fiat. Fiat? Amen? Amen.[32]

The curse makes it perfectly clear that *The Soliloquia of St. Augustine,*
at any rate, belonged at the time to the Augustinian priory of St. Mary
in Southwick, Hampshire. Since the other three texts (the *Nicodemus*
fragment, *The Debate of Solomon and Saturn,* and the *St. Quintin* fragment) were all copied by the same scribe, it is reasonable to assume that
all four texts belonged to St. Mary's Priory, and to refer to this part of
Cotton Vitellius A. xv. as the Southwick Codex. Moreover, there are
rust marks from a previous binding on the first and last pages of this
codex, which indicate that these four texts were bound together as a
separate book before Cotton had them rebound at the beginning of
Vitellius A. xv. But there are still other indications that the *Soliloquia*
and the other three texts were, at an earlier stage, parts of two distinct
codices.

Förster (p. 38) and Ker (*Catalogue,* p. 279) both date the script of
the Southwick Codex in the mid-12th century, but they disagree over
the number of scribes who copied the texts. Förster (pp. 24–25) maintained that one scribe copied the *Soliloquia,* and that a second scribe,
with a remarkably similar script,[33] copied the other texts. Ker, while
acknowledging that the script in the last three texts "has sometimes a
more irregular appearance" than it has in the *Soliloquia,* categorically
states that "there is no change of hand" (*Catalogue,* p. 208). Both positions are defensible, and, it seems to me, they share the truth. Förster

32. My transcript differs from those of Ker and Förster, who differ in some minor
respects from each other, in pointing and in capitalization. Moreover, *condigne* and
eadem are not conjectural restorations; they can be read with certainty along the
burned and taped edge by holding the page up to the light. Förster read *cond::::,* and
remarkably suggested *condigne* in his note (*Die Beowulf-Handschrift,* p. 54, n. 1).
Ker read *tandem,* confusing *co* and *ta* (but this scribe uniformly draws a large loop
over his *a*'s).

33. "einen so einheitlichen Eindruck im Schriftduktus und in den Buchstabenform-
en, dass man zunächst nur einen Schreiber annehmen möchte."

perhaps overplays the significance of slight variations in certain letter-forms, and Ker underplays their significance by ignoring them and stressing the similarities of other letterforms. Both agree on the relative uniformity of the script in the *Soliloquia* as compared to the relative variety of letterforms in the following texts. Förster explains this differ-ence as a difference in age between the two texts: "Hierzu stimmt auch die Beobachtung, dass die Schrift von [the first scribe] gleichmässiger und einheitlicher ist, wie das bei einem geübten Kopisten zu erwarten steht, während der jüngere Schreiber . . . mehrfach seine Buchstaben-formen variiert, weil sie ihm noch nicht so fest in der Feder sitzen" (p. 25). The conflict between Ker's and Förster's views may be easily reconciled by assuming that the same scribe copied all of the texts of the Southwick Codex, but at two different times in his life. If Förster's deductions are acceptable, we may conclude that the scribe copied the *Nicodemus* fragment, *The Debate of Solomon and Saturn,* and the *St. Quintin* fragment, for one codex as a young man, and that he copied the *Soliloquia* for another codex as an older man, after his script had become more established and uniform.

The bad physical condition of the first page of the *Nicodemus* frag-ment supports this conclusion. The page is so thoroughly soiled and worn that it must have served as an outside cover for some time before the Southwick Codex, as it now exists, was assembled. Pages, or even gatherings, could have fallen out of the codex between the *Soliloquia* and the *Nicodemus* fragment, of course, but this would not explain how the first page of the *Nicodemus* fragment could come to be exposed to so much wear and tear. Besides, there is proof that the Southwick Codex was put together in a fragmentary state, for the rust marks at the end of the codex show that the *St. Quintin Homily* was already an eleven-line fragment at the time of the earlier binding. The fact that the codex was assembled and bound in a fragmentary state suggests that there was an intermediate owner of the texts between the Southwick priory and Sir Robert Cotton. However, evidence from medieval sheet signatures shows that the codex was already in its present, fragmented state, during the 13th century. There are also quire signatures, made in roman numerals, that corroborate the evidence from the sheet signatures.

The sheet and quire signatures make it possible to identify with rel-ative certainty what is left of the original gatherings. Both series of sig-natures have been erroneously dated by Förster, who held that the quire

signatures were probably contemporary with the MS (second quarter of
the 12th century), and that the sheet signatures could be dated about a
quarter of a century later (pp. 12 and 19). The quire signatures appear
as roman numerals centered in the lower margins of the first folio of
each quire. They were drawn with a rudimentary pencil, varying in
color from reddish brown to almost black. The following table provides
an account of the gatherings based on these signatures.

Quire	Folios	Number of sheets	Comments
I	1–8	4	Signature, below and to the right of the taped tear, overlooked by Förster.
II	9–16	4	Overlooked by Förster.
III	17–24	4	
IIII	25–32	4	
V	33–40	4	The first side of V is elongated, and starts with an awkward loop, but it is not an arabic 5, *pace* Förster.
VI	41–48	4	First side of V elongated, but no loop.
VII	49–56	4	Note V, with both loop and long side.
VIII	57–64	4	Same V as V and VII.
Ix	65–74	5	Overlooked by Förster (long I, short x).
[X]	75–82	4	No signature now visible.
xI	83–90	4	Overlooked by Förster (short x, long I).

The quire signatures themselves prove that *The Gospel of Nicodemus*
was already a fragment when the quires were numbered, and thus the
quire signatures cannot possibly be contemporary with the MS, as Förster maintains. *The Soliloquia of St. Augustine* now comprises the first
seven gatherings. The Alfredian colophon on what is now the last page
of the *Soliloquia* (fol. 56v) reads, [*H*]*ær endiað þa cwidas þe ælfred
kining alæs of þære bec þe we hatað on,* but the sentence breaks off at
the end of the folio. Something like *læden Soliloquiorum Augustini* is
needed to complete the sentence, and surely the sentence was finished
on a folio that once followed fol. 56. But it does not make sense to
assume that a medieval binder folded on an extra leaf at the end of the
seventh quire for the sake of a few words. If another quire did not originally follow the *Soliloquia,* the scribe would have simply ruled an extra
line at the bottom of fol. 56v to complete the colophon. Thus, at least a
gathering is lost after the *Soliloquia.*

Förster did not realize that anything was missing after the *Soliloquia*, apparently because he did not realize that the colophon was a fragment. He did know, of course, that *The Gospel of Nicodemus* was a fragment, which makes it all the more surprising that he considered the quire signatures contemporary with the MS. According to the signatures, there is nothing lost between the last quire of the *Soliloquia* (VII) and the first quire of the *Nicodemus* fragment (VIII). Thus it seems clear that the quire signatures were made after material was lost between what are now quires VII and VIII. Förster unaccountably resists this conclusion, and argues instead that a single, folded-on leaf, containing the beginning of *The Gospel of Nicodemus,* was lost. Perhaps the best argument against this unreasonable conclusion is that a medieval bookbinder would not ordinarily begin a quire with a folded-on leaf. Halfsheets are frequently used in medieval MSS, but they are stitched into the middle of quires, usually in pairs between the second and third, or third and fourth sheets, to prevent them from falling out easily. Binders naturally avoided the most vulnerable places, the centers of quires and between quires, whenever they stitched in half-sheets. We may safely conclude that the quire signatures were made after the texts were copied, and after material had been lost both at the end of the *Soliloquia* and at the beginning of *The Gospel of Nicodemus.* The reason the quire signatures were made after the texts were copied seems obvious. A later medieval binder was arranging loose gatherings for a new binding, and probably for a newly constituted codex as well, one that for the first time combined the *Soliloquia* with the *Nicodemus* fragment, *The Debate of Solomon and Saturn,* and the *St. Quintin* fragment.

The sporadic use of sheet signatures in some of the quires should be associated with this new, medieval binding, too, for the same pencil that was used for the quire signatures was also used for the sheet signatures. The roman numerals I, V, and X of the quire signatures cannot be dated paleographically, but the medieval arabic numerals used for the sheet signatures can be dated with some degree of accuracy, because of the development of the forms in the course of the Middle Ages. Sheet signatures can be found, in whole or in part, in quires II, III, IIII, V, VI, VIII, and X. Their forms and their positions vary somewhat from quire to quire. In general, the sheets are signed alphabetically, *a* through *d,* and numerically, according to the number of the quire, in the lower left margins of the first four folios of the quires. Thus, fols.

9r, 10r, 11r, and 12r of the second quire are signed, respectively, *a7, b7, c7,* and *d7.* The figure 7 was the standard form of the arabic number 2 in the 13th century. In III, the sheet signatures were written in the lower *right* margins: *b3* on fol. 18r, *c3* on fol. 19r, and *d3* on fol. 20r; *a3* is missing on fol. 17r because the corner of the vellum has broken off. The medieval arabic 4, prevalent throughout the Middle English period, resembles an 8 with its bottom loop open—ᵹ. The sheet signatures for IIII are in the lower left margin, with the arabic 4 placed beneath, rather than beside, the letters: *a*/ᵹ (fol. 25r), *b,* with only the tip of the ᵹ still extant beneath it (fol. 26r), *c*/ᵹ (fol. 27r), and *d*/ᵹ (fol. 28r). For quire V there are vestiges of *a* in the lower right corner of fol. 33r, and of *b* at the edge of the tape on fol. 34r; fol. 35r is signed clearly with a *c,* and fol. 36r with a *d,* also in the lower right corners without accompanying numbers. Quire VI is fully signed by letter and number, after the manner of II, *a6-d6* on fols. 41r–44r.

There are no sheet signatures in quire VII, though Förster thought he saw *a, b,* and *d,* in the lower right margins of fols. 49r, 50r, and 52r (the bottom margin of fol. 51, where *c* might have been, is cut away). In VIII there are no visible sheet signatures on the first two folios; but in the bottom left margin of fol. 59r there is a *c,* and on fol. 60r a *d.* Since there are no arabic numbers whatever, I am mystified by Förster's claim that "bei keiner andern Lage ist die Signierung so gut erhalten wie hier; denn wir haben sowohl auf fol. [57r] die ältere Lagenbezeichnung mit der römischen VIII unten auf der Mitte des Randes wie die wohl jüngere Bezeichnung mit *a8, b8, c8* und *d8* auf den Blättern [57r, 58r, 59r, and 60r]."[34] The two systems of signatures are preserved together much more clearly in quires II and VI. There are no sheet signatures in quires IX and XI. Quire X has no quire signature or sheet signature visible on the first folio, but the next three folios, 66r–68r, are fairly clearly marked *b∅, c∅,* and *d∅.* The figure ∅ was the common

---

34. To avoid further confusion from the use of multiple foliations, the MS foliation is used, here and elsewhere, in place of the one Förster adhered to; whenever this change is made, the numbers will be bracketed.

Plate 10. Both the sheet (a6) and the quire (VI) signatures of the Southwick Codex are well preserved in the bottom margin of fol. 41r.

me ꝼ f guttel þu þille · þa cƿæð heo · deſ
ne cꝛeſt ⁊ ſecge me eft ſittan þu þiſ aſina
ead helibe þæpeꞇ þe þiſſeſ licie · ⁊ gif he·
be engum þiſſa þinga apiht · ⁊ þeægte þonne
ſecge þu me þæt · · ·

ef endudᵹ þa bloſtman þere forman
bocum ·

ef ongᵹnd ſeo gadoꞃung þere bloſtme
na þeþe efteꞃm bec · · ·

a cꝛeð ic · eal ꞃlange þeꞃon þiht nu eunᵹ
tᵹe ſ þᵹ ne ſþyꞃedon efteꞃ dam þe þuine
ei ge hete · þa cƿeð heo · uton ge becan þᵹt
uton ſon on adᵹe þoc foreþende · þa cꝛeð ic·
uton þæſ · þa cꝛeð heo · uton ge lyꞃſan þ gol
ſi on uncꞃum fultume · · þa cꝛeð ic georn
ne polde ic · þ þᵹt hyꞃge lyꞃſdun · gyf ic
ge þeald habte · ac me þincð þ ſe ge leaꞇa
ne ſi on uncꞃum on pealde · þe me þe þþe

sign for the arabic numeral 10 throughout most of the Middle English period.

Förster dates the sheet signatures in the third quarter of the 12th century, but he is probably about a century too early. Förster based his dating on the forms of the arabic numbers 2, 6, 8, and 10, which according to him were "die charakteristischen Formen des 12. Jahrhunderts" (p. 19). He based his conclusion on G. F. Hill's tables of facsimiles in "On the Early Use of Arabic Numerals in Europe,"[35] but Hill's tables do not, in fact, support Förster. First of all, a 12th-century date for the sheet signatures can be doubted on general principles. As Hill points out in his introduction, "The numerals are first found in MSS. of the tenth century, but they cannot be said to have been at all well known until the beginning of the thirteenth. During all this early period there is, perhaps naturally, considerable uncertainty in the forms, as a glance at Tables II and III will show" (p. 11). Förster's contention that the forms of the 2, 6, 8, and 10 were characteristic forms of the 12th century is simply not true. Hill's Table II lists 12th- and 13th-century forms. There is not a single example of the 7-like 2, and this absence alone is enough to dismiss Förster's dating of the sheet signatures. The 7-like 2 is truly characteristic of the 13th century, as Hill's Table III, numbers 1–12 (p. 30), will amply illustrate. The forms 6, 8, and 10 are also characteristic of the 13th century, as the same table makes clear. The facsimiles in this table show that the arabic numerals used for the sheet signatures in the Southwick Codex were the standard forms for these numbers throughout the 13th century. It is significant that all of the facsimiles from this table are taken from English MSS. Hill's Table V (p. 32) mainly relies on English examples from the 13th and 14th centuries. Number 6 of this table lists forms for 2, 3, 4, 6, 8, and 10—that is, all of the numbers used in the sheet signatures—that are virtually identical to the forms in the Southwick Codex. In other words, the sheet signatures can be safely dated, on the basis of the arabic numbers, in the late 13th century, or even in the early 14th century.[36] The medieval

35. Hill later expanded the study, as *The Development of Arabic Numerals in Europe, Exhibited in Sixty-Four Tables.*

36. See also the early MS forms under the date 1275 (row c), in David Eugene Smith and Louis Charles Karpinski, "The Spread of the Numerals in Europe," *The Hindu-Arabic Numerals*, p. 143. None of the letterforms (*a-d*, and *e* on fol. 13r, by mistake) is specifically 12th century, and even if the letters were distinctive forms, they

signature of ownership, on fol. 2r of the *Soliloquia,* is also dated in the late 13th or early 14th century; it now seems certain that the sheet signatures, the quire signatures, and the signature of ownership can all be dated at the same time—late in the 13th or early in the 14th century, when two 12th-century, fragmented codices were being bound together in a new composite codex, now known as the Southwick Codex. The front page of the *Nicodemus* fragment was in bad shape because this codex had lost its initial gathering(s) at some point in the intervening century between the date of the MS and the date of the rebinding and was exposed to unusual wear and tear. The *Soliloquia* was naturally placed first in the new codex, because the Southwick priory was an Augustinian house. The late-medieval binder made the sheet signatures first, so that all loose sheets would be properly placed within the separate quires, and these were usually numbered by quire, as well. After the order of the sheets was determined, the order of the quires was established, and the quire signatures were made, by roman numerals, in the proper sequence on the first folios of each quire. After the book was bound, a signature of ownership was written on fol. 2r of the new codex.

A few minor details relating to the scribe of the Southwick Codex may be mentioned before moving on to the Nowell Codex, and the central topic of this book, the *Beowulf* MS. The name *petrus* (with a *wynn*-like *þ*), is written at the foot of fol. 12r. The name was written with a very sharp pen point, considerably sharper than the pen used to copy the text, but the handwriting appears to be the scribe's caroline script (the *r* has no descender, but the scribe frequently writes his *r* in this manner). Perhaps the scribe who copied the two parts of the Southwick Codex at different times in his life was named Peter. We can see a bit of his personality at the foot of fol. 16v, where he doodles while he waits for a new quire. He treated his copy of the *Soliloquia* specially, highlighting on the first twenty-one folios parts of the text (most frequently the abbreviations for *ond* and *þæt,* and the letters *i, ð,* and *þ*) in bright red ink, and carefully tracing over *petrus* and his doodle in red, as well.

---

could not outweigh the much stronger evidence from the arabic numerals. They may, or may not, be feeble attempts to copy the letterforms of the MS, but in any case they do not provide any compelling paleographical information, despite Förster's dating of them in the third quarter of the 12th century (*Die Beowulf-Handschrift,* p. 19).

The Nowell Codex

The second main codex of Cotton Vitellius A. xv. is known as the Nowell Codex, after its earliest known owner, Laurence Nowell (1520–1576), the 16th-century "Saxonist" who compiled the first Anglo-Saxon dictionary.[37] Nowell has written his name and the date, 1563, at the top of the first folio of the Nowell Codex. The codex, as we have seen, consists of five Old English texts, two of which, the first and the last, are fragments: the *St. Christopher* fragment; *The Wonders of the East; Alexander's Letter to Aristotle; Beowulf;* and the *Judith* fragment. The first three texts are in prose, and the last two are, of course, poems. The Nowell Codex, as a whole, has been extensively described by Förster, Malone, and Sisam, and, in much less detail, by Rypins, Dobbie, and Ker.[38] All of these descriptions have overlooked, underestimated, or misrepresented important features of the codex that have crucial bearing on the original, as opposed to the present, construction of the codex. The attempt to rectify these shortcomings is not, in this case, simply an academic duty, for the results intimately involve one's understanding of the *Beowulf* MS, and ultimately, of *Beowulf* itself.

Scholars are not yet in accord over the original construction of the Nowell Codex. Förster, Dobbie, Ker, and Malone each give different accounts of the original gatherings, and all but Malone fail to realize that the *Judith* fragment was a late addition to the codex. The confusion can no doubt be traced to the fact that all five texts were copied by two scribes. The first scribe copied the three prose texts and *Beowulf,* up to line 1939; the second scribe copied the rest of *Beowulf* and *Judith.* This fact, taken alone, suggests that all five texts were copied together for a single codex. The fact that the hands change in the middle of the fourth text, *Beowulf,* suggests that the copying of the texts was continuous, another reason for assuming that the five texts, or at least the first four, were inseparable parts of the same codex. Moreover, the two hands are contemporary, and so there is no reason to assume that there was a hiatus after the first scribe stopped copying. As a matter of fact, the second scribe's handwriting is distinctly more archaic than the first

---

37. Preserved as Bodleian MS Selden supra 63; it has been edited by Albert H. Marckwardt, *Laurence Nowell's Vocabularium Saxonicum.*

38. Sisam's essays "The Beowulf Manuscript" and "The Compilation of the Beowulf Manuscript" are reprinted in *Studies,* pp. 61–96.

scribe's, which weakens any case there might have been for presuming that a hiatus in copying had occurred after line 1939 of *Beowulf.*

The 11th-century provenance of *Beowulf,* of course, tremendously enhances the importance of the 11th-century MS. A careful study of the physical makeup of the Nowell Codex shows that the *Beowulf* part of the codex may have been originally a separate book. Indeed, there is compelling physical evidence, which will be considered in detail in Part 3, that the unique MS of *Beowulf* was still undergoing revision in the 11th century, and consequently that the MS, or at any rate part of it, may represent something very close to an autograph. As we shall see, the extant MS may be the first MS in which *Beowulf,* as we now know it, was put together as a single poem from two originally distinct stories. The copy of the poem was proofread by both scribes, and the text was certainly altered after the copy was made. These momentous issues cannot be well discussed without a clear conception of the physical construction of the Nowell Codex as a whole.

It is far more difficult to determine the original gatherings of the Nowell Codex than it was for the Southwick Codex, because the Nowell Codex has no sheet or quire signatures. However, it is important to know how the Nowell Codex, and particularly how the *Beowulf* MS, was originally put together, for a knowledge of the actual construction of the MSS furnishes some revolutionary insights into the composition of *Beowulf* itself. The presumptive gatherings of the Nowell Codex have never been sufficiently described, and in fact there are major disagreements over their construction among Ker, Förster, Dobbie, and Malone. The reason for such wide divergence of opinion is twofold: in the first place, since all pages of the codex have been remounted in paper frames, the threads and margins are all modern, and so a collation cannot be achieved simply by examining the folds of the vellum sheets, which by virtue of the modern frames no longer exist; in the second place, the scholars mentioned above, particularly Förster and Dobbie, have not used all available resources in their attempts to determine the original gatherings. Absolute certainty in this matter cannot be expected, but some guesswork, which was never verified, can certainly be eliminated, and strong probabilities are always preferable to weak possibilities and impossibilities.

Despite the destruction of the original threads and margins (whether by the fire or by the modern bookbinder is uncertain), "the collation can be ascertained," as Ker says, "from the ruling, the arrangement of hair and flesh sides, the dislocation of quire 4 before quire 3, and the variation in the number of lines in different quires" (*Catalogue,* p. 282). Yet the usefulness and reliability of these methods of collation vary. The ruling, for instance, is of very little value in the case of the Nowell Codex. The normal insular practice was to rule an entire gathering in one simple process: the gathering (usually a quire of four sheets) was punctured along the outer margins, through all four sheets at once, at the required intervals for text lines and bounding lines; the rulings were then made using the prick marks for guides.[39] The particular shape, the angle of entry, and the linear configuration of prick marks can be enormously useful in determining original quires, since all leaves of a particular quire will share the same features, but the prick marks of the Nowell Codex were destroyed along with the outer margins in the fire of 1731. The rulings themselves are far less trustworthy, partly because the fire damage caused shrinkage at the edges of the vellum, and the measurements of the rulings are affected. The rulings in the Nowell Codex are unreliable for other reasons, too. Anglo-Saxon scribes sometimes ruled through two or more sheets at a time. Since they made rulings with a hard-point instrument, the indentations on the outside sheet could carry through to the inside sheets. Thus, if only one ruling was made for all four sheets, the outermost sheet would have the heaviest ruling, while the innermost sheet would have the lightest. The scribes of the Nowell Codex, however, invariably made more than one ruling for each quire, or else renewed particularly light inner rulings. In either case, the result affects the strict correlation of the rulings within a quire. Without the prick marks, we have no way of knowing the cause of various discrepancies. For example, if the awl was pushed through the vellum sheets on a slight angle, as often happened in MSS with surviving prick marks, the rulings of inner sheets when separately ruled would of course differ from the rulings of the outside sheets. Even in the highly improbable event that the prick marks were exactly identical from sheet to sheet, the rulings would not be, nor should one expect them to be: the scribe, who was not a machine after all, would naturally place his ruler sometimes slightly above, or below, or on top of, the prick marks, and these minor divergencies would vary from one side of a sheet to the

39. For a general discussion see Ker, *Catalogue,* pp. xxii–xxv; for a detailed study of the methods of ruling see Leslie Webber Jones, "Pricking Manuscripts: The Instruments and Their Significance." Ruling as a method of collation is interestingly applied by Dorothy K. Coveney, "The Ruling of the *Exeter Book.*"

other. As a result, the measurements for one side of a sheet often vary slightly from those on the other side. Discrepancies of this nature within uncontested quires of the Nowell Codex unfortunately vitiate the rulings, in the absence of prick marks, as definitive evidence of the original gatherings.

A related method for determining the original gatherings, the variation in the number of lines in separate gatherings, can also be risky. Eight leaves in the midst of *Beowulf* (fols. 163–170) are ruled for twenty-two lines per page, while on either side the folios are ruled for twenty lines per page. It is reasonable to assume from the unique ruling that fols. 163–170 constitute an original gathering, but it should be remembered that consecutive leaves, not necessarily constituting a quire, could be ruled for extra lines after binding. Indeed, extra lines have been added elsewhere in the Nowell Codex, in this way, after the original rulings were made. There is even a quire in *Beowulf* that was originally ruled for twenty lines of text to the page that has four consecutive pages (fols. 174v–176r) with twenty-one lines of text. Not too much reliance should be placed on a criterion so susceptible to alteration. In any case, only one quire (fols. 163–170) can be tentatively identified from the unique number of twenty-two rulings per page, while no quires at all can be firmly identified from ruling alone, since all the prick marks are gone.

The other two criteria mentioned by Ker for determining the original gatherings in the absence of the original threads and margins are quite reliable, yet one method, the dislocation of quires, can only be used to identify two quires. The second test, as we shall see, can be applied pervasively, yet for some reason has only been applied to one quire. This test checks the arrangement of hair and flesh sides of the vellum leaves, to see if pairs of leaves, which are presumed to be two halves of an original sheet, are in fact conjugate. For anyone unfamiliar with vellum MSS, checking the arrangement of hair and flesh sides of the vellum leaves is the least obvious method for determining the original gatherings. A brief explanation of the method will perhaps be useful. Each sheet of vellum has a hair and a flesh side. It is usually quite easy to distinguish between them, at least when the vellum is of the rather thick variety used in the Nowell Codex. A hair side generally has a yellowish tinge and is smoother and shinier than a flesh side, which has a whitish tinge and a rougher texture. The heat from the Cotton fire has often made the color distinction between hair and flesh more brown and gray than yellow and white, but the distinction remains evident in most cases. Moreover, the distinction is often aided by the appearance of groups of "hair dots" on the hair sides, showing that the hide has been shaved on these sides. This aid must be used cautiously, however, for on particularly thin parchments, these dots will sometimes show on both sides, and in such cases it is very difficult to distinguish hair side from flesh.[40] But with the exception of a group of deeply soiled folios at the beginning, which is almost surely a gathering, it is relatively easy to distinguish hair from flesh throughout the Nowell Codex.

Because of the frequently marked difference in color and texture between hair and flesh sides, scribes tended to arrange the sheets of quires, and then the quires themselves, so that a hair side would face a hair side and a flesh side would face a flesh side. This procedure has the satisfying aesthetic effect of obscuring the contrast in color and texture of the hair and flesh sides, for no matter where a reader opens a book arranged in this way, the facing pages are always of the same general color and texture. Fortunately, neither of the scribes of the Nowell Codex followed this procedure, for if they had, the arrangement of hair and flesh sides would be worthless as evidence of where one quire ended and another began. The second scribe's way of arranging the sheets of a quire is especially informative: he always places the sheets with the hair side facing outward, so that within the quire hair faces flesh, except in the center, where the two flesh sides of the center sheet face one another. Hair faces hair only *between* the second scribe's quires. Because of this characteristic arrangement, the last three quires of the Nowell Codex are very easy to establish. The first scribe's methods are less transparent. He is evidently more concerned with achieving uniformity between facing pages, but there is usually enough minor variation within quires to make the collation of hair and flesh sides a valuable tool for understanding the original construction of his quires, and consequently of the Nowell Codex as a whole.

The value of this test can be illustrated by applying it to two groups of leaves in the first scribe's section of the MS that are already firmly established as quires. There has never been any doubt that folios

40. The same problem occurs occasionally in the *Exeter Book*. According to Coveney, "it is very difficult to decide in one or two instances whether . . . the surface of the parchment is flesh or hair. The oiliness and transparency of the skin alluded to above causes the hair dots to show on both sides of some leaves, and both have the appearance of showing the hair dots." "The Ruling of the *Exeter Book*," p. 55.

107(115)–114(122) and 115(107)–122(114) from *Alexander's Letter to Aristotle* are two original quires, because the two sets of folios (as the double references signalize) were bound in the wrong order, and in fact are still in the wrong order in the MS today. As all commentators have recognized, these two groups of folios must have been original quires to have been transposed in this way. What is interesting is the way these two quires were originally constructed. The arrangement of hair and flesh sides in both quires is identical. It shows that both were originally constructed as three-sheet gatherings, with two half-sheets folded on between the second and third sheets. This is evident because only three pairs of leaves in each quire—the first and eighth, the second and seventh, and the fourth and fifth—are conjugate. It is certain that the third and sixth leaves in both quires were half-sheets when the gatherings were stitched together, for in both quires the third and sixth leaves are nonconjugate. The following diagram illustrates the construction of these two expanded gatherings, based on the arrangement of hair (H) and flesh (F) sides.

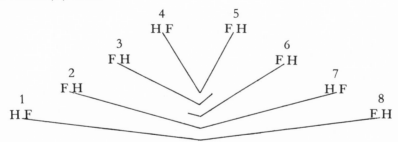

There is nothing unusual about expanding a gathering in this manner. In fact, Ker says that "the use of a pair of half-sheets in place of one sheet is common. The half-sheets are usually the third and sixth or the second and seventh leaves in the quire, rarely the first and eighth or the fourth and fifth leaves, which would be more likely to fall out" (*Catalogue,* p. xxiv).

The arrangement of the whole sheets follows the normal insular practice, whereby a hair side is placed on the outside of the quire, and within flesh faces flesh, and hair faces hair. The inserted half-sheets throw this arrangement off, so that hair faces flesh between the second and third and fifth and sixth leaves. This would seem to suggest that these two quires were originally constructed as three-sheet gatherings, and were expanded afterward, when it became clear how much parchment was needed to finish copying *Alexander's Letter*. A precise understanding of the construction of these two quires leads directly to a much more important understanding of the construction of contiguous gatherings. Förster, Dobbie, and Malone, for reasons that will be discussed in a moment, describe the immediately preceding group of folios (101–106) as an anomalous three-sheet gathering, and my examination of the arrangement of hair and flesh sides confirms their guess. The six leaves form three conjugate pairs. Yet a three-sheet gathering is no longer, strictly speaking, an anomaly in view of the original construction of the two transposed quires. This throws the presumptive construction of the prose section of the Nowell Codex into an entirely new light. Scholars have always assumed that the gathering following the transposed quires was a four-sheet quire, which makes *Beowulf* an inseparable part of the prose codex that precedes it, since *Beowulf* begins on the seventh leaf of this four-sheet quire. Now there is no reason to make this assumption. On the contrary, there is good reason to believe that the last gathering of the prose codex was another three-sheet gathering, which was all that was needed to finish *Alexander's Letter*. The exciting corollary of this conclusion is that the *Beowulf* part of the Nowell Codex once existed as a separate codex.

The following table of quires provides at a glance the most probable construction of these three distinct parts of the Nowell Codex.

	Quire	Number of sheets	Folios
Prose:	1 st	5	91(93)–100(96)
	2 d	3	101–106
	3rd	3 (+2 lvs.)	115–122 (117 + 120 folded on)
	4th	3 (+2 lvs.)	107–114 (109 + 112 folded on)
	5th	3	123–128
Beowulf:	6th	4 (+2 lvs.)	129–139 (133 + 136 folded on)
	7th	4	140–147A(131)
	8th	4	147–154
	9th	4	155–162
	10th	4	163–170
	11th	4	171–178
	12th	5	179–188
	13th	5	189A(197)–198
Judith:	14th	4	199–206

An exhaustive study of the arrangement of hair and flesh sides through-out the Nowell Codex justifies this description of the original quires.[41] The arrangement of hair and flesh sides in the fifth and sixth quires also permits them to be described as two four-sheet gatherings, but the particular arrangement favors one three-sheet and one five-sheet gath-ering. If the fifth quire is described as a four-sheet gathering, the arrangement of hair and flesh shows that it was originally a natural quire, which, as we have seen, is unprecedented in the prose part of the Nowell Codex. On the other hand, if the sixth quire is so described, the hair-flesh correspondence shows that it was originally a three-sheet gathering, which was expanded to a quire by the insertion of two leaves, which is unparalleled in the *Beowulf* part of the codex. If the Anglo-Saxon binder was at all consistent, the fifth quire was a three-sheet gathering that ended the prose codex, and the sixth was a quire expanded to a five-sheet gathering that began the poetic codex, *Beowulf.* The two originally separate codices were combined early in their his-tory, most likely in the scriptorium in which they were copied, but per-haps by Laurence Nowell or a previous owner in the 16th century.

Other corroborating indications that *Beowulf* once existed as a sep-arate codex, and thus was not mechanically copied along with three unrelated and undistinguished prose texts, will be discussed in due course. For now it is enough to note that the particular hair-flesh pat-tern of the sheets in the fifth and sixth gatherings supports the conten-tion that *Beowulf* begins with a new gathering. It is lamentable, of course, that the hair-flesh pattern is ambiguous at this one crucial point, but the corroborating evidence helps resolve the ambiguity by strongly supporting the view that the *Beowulf* MS was once a separate codex. In most other cases, the arrangement of the hair and flesh sides is not at all ambiguous, and the criterion can be used with confidence to elimi-nate some improbable and impossible guesswork regarding the original quires. For this reason it is surprising that scholars have not used the test, or, in the case of one quire, have used it where it is not even needed. Only Ker and Malone indicate that they have checked into the matter at all, but it is evident that neither thoroughly examined the hair and

41. Note that the two transposed quires from *Alexander's Letter,* the third and fourth, are here put in their proper order. To correct the MS foliation, consequently, double references are necessary: that is, 107(115)–114(122) and 115(107)–122(114).

flesh patterns to see if their accounts of the original gatherings were sustained by the pairings of the leaves.

While Ker rightly asserts that, in part, "the collation can be ascertained from . . . the arrangement of hair and flesh sides," he applies the method only to the solitary *Judith* quire: "Hair outside all sheets in quire 14" (*Catalogue,* p. 282). The implication would seem to be that this arrangement of the sheets was unique in the codex, yet the two preceding gatherings (the last two gatherings in *Beowulf*) are also arranged in this way. It would have made more sense for Ker to identify the fourteenth quire by means of the ruling (which is unique in the codex in distance from top line to bottom), or by means of the variation in the line numbers between this quire (which has twenty lines to the page) and the preceding quire (which has twenty-one lines to the page). But, really, there is no need to make any special argument for the eight leaves of the *Judith* fragment: one assumes that they constitute a natural quire of four sheets. If Ker had checked the hair and flesh patterns throughout the Nowell Codex, he would have realized that his account of the gatherings was wrong in at least two places. Malone gives the impression that he has investigated the sheet arrangement more carefully than Ker, for he says, quite rightly, that "the sheets of the codex do not show a consistent pattern in the arrangement of hair and flesh sides." Yet the results of Malone's investigation are no more enlightening than Ker's, for Malone merely quotes Ker: "As Ker points out (p. 282), all sheets of the fourteenth gathering have the hair side out. . . . But this sequence is varied more or less in the other gatherings" (*Nowell Codex,* p. 16). It is odd indeed that Malone uses the same example as Ker, especially since Malone correctly believed that the *Judith* fragment was a modern addition to the Nowell Codex (ibid., p. 119).

At any rate, the real impact of determining the hair-flesh patterns does not come by confirming the single-quire construction of the *Judith* fragment, about which no one ever had any doubts anyway. The impact comes when the test can be used to invalidate established descriptions of the gatherings, and confirm alternative descriptions. For example, Förster (and Dobbie, who followed his suggestion) explained the former misplacement of the two *Beowulf* folios—147A(131) and 189A(197)— by assuming that they had been single leaves that were folded on to four-sheet quires.[42] As single leaves, they could have fallen out of the codex and been misplaced by Cotton's bookbinder. The explanation is perfectly reasonable, but the arrangement of the hair and flesh sides in the putative gatherings in question proves that it is wrong. According to Förster, the seventh gathering consisted of fols. 140–147, with fol. 147A(131) folded on between the last two folios of the quire. It is obvious that Förster did not check the hair-flesh correspondences, for if he had he would have seen that fols. 140 and 147, the "outside sheet" of this supposed quire, are not conjugate. Similarly, Förster says that the twelfth quire consisted of fols. 182–189, with fol. 189A(197), the second misplaced folio from *Beowulf*, folded on between the last two folios. In this case three of the four "sheets" (the outside, the third, and the center sheet) are not conjugate pairs of folios, and so could not have been sheets at all. Many other supposed gatherings in Förster's table (for example, his eighth, ninth, tenth, and eleventh) are invalidated on the same grounds.

The test can be put to more positive use, as well. Förster (and Dobbie and Malone, who followed his suggestion) explained the former disorder in the first ten folios of the Nowell Codex by assuming that they constituted an original five-sheet gathering. As in the case of the two misplaced *Beowulf* folios, the disorder of the first ten folios of the Nowell Codex was permanently recorded by the old foliation written on the vellum leaves of the MS. Today, with the folios back in the right order, this foliation reads: 93, 94, 91, 92, 97, 98, 99, 100, 95, 96. Förster's idea was that "diese falsche Blätterzahlung erklärt sich am einfachsten so, wenn wir annehmen, dass die ebengenannten 10 Blätter . . . eine Lage zu 5 Bogen bildeten, deren 4 erste Bogen zur Zeit der Renaissance-

---

42. Dobbie (*Beowulf and Judith*, p. xv, n. 21) is a bit misleading about his dependence on Förster's account of the gatherings. The principal difference between them is that Dobbie curiously numbers the lost gatherings, though he has no way of knowing for sure how many gatherings were lost. Even in this difference, however, Dobbie is following Förster's conjectures (*Die Beowulf-Handschrift*, pp. 22–23). Dobbie says that "the principal point of difference" is that he describes the first two extant gatherings as five- and three-sheet gatherings, while Förster describes them as two four-sheet quires. In fact, Förster originated the theory that the first extant gathering was comprised of five sheets to explain the misplacement of the first ten folios reflected in the MS foliation (see Förster, *Die Beowulf-Handschrift*, pp. 7–8).

Paginierung in falscher Reihenfolge lagen, nämlich als *c. d. a. b.,* und deren 5. Bogen *e,* statt in der Mitte, zwischen die beiden letzten Blätter der Lage geraten war" (pp. 7–8). Förster was unhappy with this explanation, though, for he provides another unlikely "Erklärungsmöglichkeit" in a footnote (p. 8, n. 1), and then disregards both explanations in his discussion and table of gatherings, where he describes the first two gatherings of the Nowell Codex as normal four-sheet quires (pp. 21, 22–23). One can only surmise that Förster ultimately rejected his explanation for the misplaced folios because it left him with what he viewed as an anomalous three-sheet gathering for the second quire. Yet as the table of gatherings on p. 126 illustrates, a three-sheet gathering in the prose texts need not be considered anomalous. If Förster had made a collation of hair and flesh sides, he would have discovered that the second gathering could not have been a four-sheet quire, for only the center sheet of this proposed quire has conjugate pairs of folios.[43] The second gathering (fols. 101–106) is in fact a three-sheet gathering: the two outer sheets (101 and 106, and 102 and 105) have the hair sides out, while the center sheet (103 and 104) has the flesh side out, so that hair faces hair in the center of the gathering.

This roundabout way of confirming the five-sheet construction of the first gathering of the Nowell Codex is to some extent necessary. All ten folios of this presumptive first gathering are unusually dirty, and the sixth, seventh, and eighth folios are not only dirty, but napped on both sides, making collation very uncertain indeed. However, the two outside sheets (leaves 1 and 10, and 2 and 9) definitely have the hair side out, which strongly supports the deduction that the ten isolated folios must constitute a five-sheet gathering. The third, fourth, and fifth leaves (or folios) also definitely have the hair side out, and while they cannot be collated with certainty with the soiled and napped surfaces of the sixth, seventh, and eighth leaves, the best guess is obviously that the first ten folios of the codex constituted a five-sheet gathering, with hair facing out for all five sheets. In any case, the hair-flesh test rules out the possibility that the first two gatherings were four-sheet quires, shows that

---

43. Ker also describes the first two gatherings of the Nowell Codex as four-sheet quires (*Catalogue,* p. 282), while Malone correctly describes them as five- and three-sheet gatherings. Ker's summary description is cited in Zupitza (*Beowulf,* p. xvii).

the second gathering was comprised of three sheets, and provides strong evidence that the first gathering was comprised of five sheets.

Förster's insight, that the disorder of the first ten folios could best be explained by a separate gathering whose sheets had been jumbled, was staunchly championed by Malone after Förster himself had abandoned it. According to Malone, the disorder of the folios "is hardly explicable unless the first gathering had ten leaves" (*Nowell Codex*, p. 15n). However, Förster's and Malone's explanation of how the sheets were jumbled to produce the disorder is unnecessarily complicated and improbable. As Malone argues the case (ibid., p. 15), Cotton's bookbinder found the five sheets in disorder and mistakenly rearranged them in the following way: he made sheet 4 the outside sheet; next to it, he placed sheet 3, and then sheets 1 and 2; but instead of placing sheet 5 in the center of the gathering, after sheet 2, he instead slipped it in immediately before the last two folios of the gathering. This theory indeed explains the disorder of the folios, but at the expense of Cotton's bookbinder, who is obliged to behave as though he were not a bookbinder at all. Professional bookbinders do not make stitching problems for themselves by slipping in a folded sheet out of alignment with the other folds of a gathering. If all the sheets were still whole, a bookbinder would naturally place them properly, for a bookbinder, one inside the other. He might well mix up the order of the sheets, so that sheets 3 and 4 would precede sheets 1 and 2, but he would not randomly slip in sheet 5 outside the main fold of the gathering.

Fortunately, there is no need to make Cotton's bookbinder behave as an amateur to explain the disorder of the first ten folios, or to maintain the view that the ten folios constituted a gathering. The outside folds of gatherings in an unbound codex are exposed to wear and tear, while the inside folds are relatively protected. Before Cotton had the Nowell Codex bound with the Southwick Codex as Vitellius A. xv., the first gathering of the Nowell Codex would have been particularly vulnerable to wear and tear. Note the worn condition of the first folio, 91(93) of the *St. Christopher* fragment. If the folds of the first two sheets of this gathering broke, the first two and the last two folios of the gathering would become loose leaves. If this is what happened, Cotton's bookbinder wisely placed the four loose folios together within the gathering from which they came. The original gathering, thus disordered, subsequently was numbered by Joseph Planta from 91–100 on the vellum leaves, in the late 18th century. When the misplaced folios were put back in their proper places in the 19th century, the resulting disorder in the number sequence on the vellum leaves revealed where the book-binder had placed the four loose folios:

93, 94, 91, 92, ( ), 97, 98, 99, 100, 95, 96

The most important result of determining the sheet arrangement of the original gatherings of the prose texts is, of course, that it opens the possibility that *Beowulf* once existed as a separate codex. It shows that three-sheet gatherings were the norm, not the exception, in the prose texts, and that even if one disregards the original three-sheet makeup of the expanded third and fourth quires, the second gathering is a precedent for describing the fifth as another three-sheet gathering. Though the first gathering, of five sheets, is now anomalous in the prose section of the Nowell Codex, it may not have been unique before the *St. Christopher* fragment lost its beginning. Förster observes that the length of the Latin source, the *Passio S. Christophori,* indicates that about ten folios, or five sheets, have been lost at the beginning of the Old English translation (pp. 76–77). We may thus conclude, with Förster, that a five-sheet gathering has been lost at the beginning of the prose codex. We may also conclude that the three prose texts were inseparable parts of the same codex. Unlike *Beowulf,* neither of the two complete prose texts could have begun new quires. The *St. Christopher* fragment ends on the recto, and *The Wonders of the East* begins on the verso of fol. 95 (97); and though *Alexander's Letter* starts a new folio (104r), it starts only three leaves before the transposed quires, which proves that it begins within a gathering. But the *Beowulf* codex *can* be separated from the prose texts that precede it, and the advantage of doing so should be obvious. Suddenly the poem is no longer the fourth item in an otherwise undistinguished Anglo-Saxon anthology, which Sisam calls a "Liber de diversis monstris, anglice" (*Studies*, p. 96). It becomes instead a poem that 11th-century Anglo-Saxons appreciated enough to copy as an individual book.

The *Beowulf* Codex

There are many reasons for assuming that *Beowulf* originally existed as a separate codex. Humfrey Wanley, who discovered *Beowulf* in the early 18th century, and who published the first description of it in his monumental *Catalogus Historico-Criticus,* speaks of the poem as if it were a separate book.[44] His testimony is of special value because he was an expert paleographer, and because he studied the codex before the fire of 1731, when the original gatherings were still intact. Wanley realized that Cotton Vitellius A. xv. was comprised of more than two Old English codices, as his prefatory remark, *Cod. membran. ex diversis simul compactis constans,* clearly reveals. Moreover, he limits the Nowell Codex to the prose texts, when he says at the end of his description of *Alexander's Letter, Hoc autem exemplar cum 3 superioribus, veteri manu scriptum, fuit peculium doctiss. viri Laurentii Nowelli. a. d. 1563.* Finally, he begins his description of *Beowulf* itself with the phrase *In hoc libro.* There does not seem to have been any doubt in Wanley's mind that *Beowulf* began a new codex. When one looks for confirmation of this, it is not hard to find. No one has yet noted that at the bottom of fol. 129r, the first page of *Beowulf,* was written the name of the composite codex, *Vi(tellius) A 15.* The *-tellius* is entirely rubbed off, but *Vi-* and *A 15* are still quite readable, even in the FSS. The signature tells us that *Beowulf* was separable, if indeed it does not tell us that the poem was actually separate from the codex before it was bound, for there would be no point in writing the name of the composite codex in

---

44. Wanley took a special interest in *Beowulf,* and he discovered it long before he was appointed, in 1703, to the commission that was to report on the state of the Cotton MSS. Sisam points out that "he tells Hickes as soon as he lights on the Beowulf manuscript, for Hickes replies (20 August 1700) 'I can find nothing yet of Beowulph.'" *Studies,* p. 276. In fact, Wanley did some research on the poem. C. E. Wright recounts that Wanley wrote to Eric Benzelius, a Swedish scholar, on the discovery of *Beowulf:* "Lastly, Wanley comes to the story of his discovery of a 'Tract in the Cottonian Library (omitted in Dr. Smith's Catalogue) written in Dano-Saxon Poetry, and describing some Wars between Beowulf a King of the Danes of yᵉ Family of the Scyldingi, and of some of your Swedish Princes'. 'Pray, Dear Sir', adds Wanley, 'have you any Histories about such a King, & such Wars?'" "Humfrey Wanley: Saxonist and Library-Keeper," p. 109.

the middle of a gathering. We may surmise that *Vitellius A. 15* was written on the first page of *Beowulf* as instructions to Cotton's binder to include the poem in the composite codex.

The first page of *Beowulf* has left other telltale marks of its former existence as an outside cover. The bottom right-hand corner is especially soiled, and many letters have been lost—and where they are not lost, the ink is badly diluted—in this area of the page. Apparently the damage was caused by sweat and friction, from gripping the MS by the corner; the area of the damage is restricted to the space that a thumb would occupy. The damage was not done by modern users of the MS, for both Thorkelin transcripts confirm that readings in this area of the page were already illegible in 1787. The ruling of the folio also suggests that it was an outside cover. If *Beowulf* really began in the midst of a four-sheet quire, as all previous scholars maintain, fol. 129 would have been the second half of the second sheet of a quire consisting of fols. 123–130. But when the outside sheet (fols. 123r and 130v) of this quire was ruled, the indentations would have carried through to the second sheet, leaving secondary rulings on fols. 124r and 129v. There can be no doubt whatever, though, that primary rulings were made on the recto, not on the verso of fol. 129. The rulings are unusually clear, as one might expect them to be on the outside sheet of a gathering: they were drawn with an awl onto the recto face so firmly, in fact, that the awl cut through the vellum along the right vertical bounding line. The split in the vellum can be clearly seen in the FSS.[45] In the absence of compelling evidence to the contrary, there is no reason to doubt that fol. 129r began a new gathering.

One conceivable objection to this conclusion can be found in Malone's explanation for the misplacement of fol. 147A(131), which depends on the view that *Beowulf* was an inseparable part of the prose codex. It

---

45. Malone is mistaken when he says that in the Nowell Codex there is only a vertical bounding line marking the left-hand margin of the text, and that "there is no corresponding boundary for the text in the right-hand margin." *Nowell Codex*, p. 16. Right and left margins can frequently be seen, even in the FSS, on folios in the first scribe's part. The writing space between his margins is usually about 10 cm. The second scribe's right margins are more difficult to see, even in the MS, and the scribe is rarely bound by them. The writing space between his margins is about 11.5 cm.

Plate 11. Fol. 129r, the first page of the *Beowulf* MS.

HÞÆT ÞE GARDE

na ingear dagum. þeod cyninga
þrym ge frunon huða æþelingas elle
fremedon. oft scyld scefing sceaþe
þreatum moneʒū mæʒþum meodo setl
ofteah egsode eorl syððan ærest wear
fea sceaft funden he þæs frofre geba
weox under wolcnum weorð myndum þah
oð þ him æghwylc þara ymb sitten dra
ofer hron rade hyran scolde ʒomban
ʒyldan þ wæs god cyning. ðæm eafera wæs
æfter cenned ʒeong in ʒeardum þone god
sende folce tofrofre fyren ðearfe on
ʒeat þ hie ær drugon aldor ... ase. lange
hwile him þæs lif frea wuldres wealdend
worold are for ʒeaf. beowulf wæs bren
blæd wide sprang scyldes eafera scede
landum in. Swa sceal ... ... ʒeda
ʒe wyrcean fromum feoh giftū ... fæder ...

can, however, be proved that Malone's explanation is wrong. First, Malone argues from the assumption, reasonable in itself, that the fifth, sixth, and seventh gatherings were natural, four-sheet quires composed, respectively, of fols. 123–130, 132–139, and 140–147A(131). Thus, by this traditional description of the gatherings, fols. 129 and 130, the first two folios of *Beowulf,* were part of the last gathering of *Alexander's Letter.* But the second stage of Malone's argument, and his proof that his description is right, is unacceptable. According to Malone, "Cotton's bookbinder seems to have found the outside sheet . . . of the seventh gathering [that is, fols. 140–147A(131)] loose and folded the wrong way: that is, in such a way that fol. [147A(131)] made the first two pages, fol. [140] the last two pages of the sheet. The binder took this sheet, so folded, for the outside one of the sixth gathering, which thus in his hands came to have five sheets or ten leaves, whereas the seventh gathering was reduced to three sheets or six leaves. In this way fol. [147A(131)] came to stand between fols. [130] and [132]" (*Nowell Codex,* p. 15). This theory explains how fol. 147A(131) came to stand between fols. 130 and 132, but it raises other, far more mysterious questions. Two of the most pressing are: how does one fold a sheet of parchment the wrong way, after it has been folded in another way for many hundreds of years? And, why would a professional bookbinder use the sheet as the outside sheet of what was already a natural quire, while ignoring the fact that the next gathering needed a sheet to make it a natural quire? So far, then, the only "proof" that *Beowulf* did not begin a separate codex depends on a whimsical bookbinder and an impossible fold.

Fortunately, there is no need to try to answer these questions, for there *is* proof that fol. 147A(131) was not misplaced until 1787, when Grímur Jónsson Thorkelin was making the second transcript of *Beowulf.* Thorkelin himself, or his hired copyist before him, was responsible for the misplacement, but that either of them folded the outside sheet of the seventh gathering the wrong way, making it the outside sheet of the sixth gathering, is unlikely in the extreme. Presumably, all that happened was that fol. 147A(131) came loose from the codex, and Thorkelin or his scribe put it back in the wrong place. In 1805, the error had a highly amusing effect on Sharon Turner's account of the poem between fols. 130 and 132, for the misplacement of fol. 147A(131) between them interposed Grendel's attack on Heorot at an unusually inauspicious time. Turner's ingenuous translation is the delightfully funny victim:

> The song of the poet said,
> He who knew
> The beginning of mankind
> From afar to narrate.   (fol. 130v)
>   "He took wilfully   (fol. 147A[131]r)
> By the nearest side
> The sleeping warrior.
> He slew the unheeding one
> With a club on the bones of his hair."[46]

But fol. 147A(131) had only been misplaced for eight years in 1805, for the Thorkelin transcripts show that the folio was not misplaced for the first transcript, but was for the second. The first transcript, known as A, attempts to reproduce the insular script of the MS, but does not attempt a facsimile in pagination. Scholars have overlooked the fact that A's procedure in this respect makes it clear that fol. 147A(131) was not out of order before 1787.

The virtue of A's procedure here is that, because his handwriting was tiny, each of his sheets contains much more than a single folio of the MS: in short, the order of the folios could not be subsequently rearranged in A, because A's pages do not correspond with the folios of the MS. In A, fol. 147A(131) is where it belongs, following fol. 146. It begins in the middle of line 1 of A (p. 25), and ends in the middle of line 4 (p. 26). Obviously, the text of fol. 147A(131) could not have been moved to this position after Thorkelin returned to Denmark, as has been supposed.[47]

---

46. *The History of the Manners, Landed Property, Government, Laws, Poetry, Literature, Religion, and Language, of the Anglo-Saxons,* p. 402. "With a club on the bones of his hair" is Turner's rendering of *bat banlocan* (742a)!

47. Förster says, "Die richtige Anordung dieses Blattes . . . gab zuerst der Isländer THORKELIN (1815), so dass TURNER in der 3. Auflage (1820) seiner Geschichte diesen Fehler verbessern konnte." *Die Beowulf-Handschrift,* p. 9n. But Turner would not have made the mistake in the first place if Thorkelin or his scribe had not misplaced fol. 147A(131). In 1817 J. J. Conybeare, while collating his interleaved copy of Thorkelin's edition with the MS, discovered the misplacement of this folio and noted on the blank leaf facing p. 9: *"reccan - finis fol: 130 / Cwœth - init fol 132. / Inseri videtur fol ex alio /loco q^d incip feng hrade & nume/ratur 131."* He wrote on the leaf facing

The same conclusion can be reached by looking at page 4 of A. The text of fol. 130 ends on line 2, and the text of fol. 132 begins on line 3. We may also conclude that the old foliation written on the vellum leaves of the MS was not made until after the A transcript, since fol. 147A(131) was not yet dislocated.

Thorkelin's transcript, known as B, shows that the folio had become misplaced by the time he copied the MS. Thorkelin copied the MS in 18th-century longhand, but he follows the pagination of the MS. By this procedure, he was able to rearrange the order of the folios, since his pages correspond to the folios of the MS. Moreover, two details in B show that fol. 147A(131) was out of place when the second transcript was made. Thorkelin, who otherwise never uses catchwords in B, has written the word *fyrst* at the bottom of his copy of fol. 132v (p. 6a). This is the first word of fol. 133r (p. 7a). The unique occurrence of a catchword here tells us that fol. 133 did not follow fol. 132 at the time: fol. 147A(131) must have been originally misplaced between these two folios, rather than between fols. 130 and 132. A second detail in B confirms this. Thorkelin numbered his transcript leaf by leaf, rather than page by page, so that his first leaf corresponds to fol. 129 of the MS, leaf 2 corresponds to fol. 130, and so on. The only exception occurs on the third leaf (fol. 132), which is numbered 3 on the recto, but 4 on the verso. The reason is now obvious. Thorkelin removed leaf 4 of his transcript, and placed it where it belonged, after leaf 18 (fol. 146). Unfortunately, he did not make the same correction in the MS, but for some reason merely moved the misplaced leaf back one folio. My guess is that Thorkelin was still in England when, in collation with A, he realized that a folio in his transcript was out of place. Then, in collation with the MS, he would have found the loose leaf, fol. 147A(131), at the point of the discrepancy between his transcript and A. Not knowing yet where the misplaced leaf belonged, he simply moved it back one folio, in order to continue his collation with the MS.

In any case, the Thorkelin transcripts prove that the misplacement of fol. 147A(131) has no bearing on the original construction of the

---

p. 61, *"Sweg. terminat paginam /male locatam."* Conybeare also noted the misplacement of fol. 189A(197) on the leaves facing pp. 197 and 231. Conybeare's copy of Thorkelin is now owned by Whitney F. Bolton, who has generously allowed me to borrow it.

gatherings. Malone's explanation for the misplacement, which he uses as proof that the first two folios of *Beowulf* belonged to the last gathering of *Alexander's Letter*, is definitely wrong, for the leaf was first misplaced *after* fol. 132. Since the misplacement of fol. 147A(131) dates from the B transcript in 1787, we must assume that the leaf came loose from the codex because the fold of the sheet to which it belonged broke. With Malone's argument gone, there is no longer any reason to believe that the first gathering of *Beowulf* was not comprised of ten leaves (fols. 129–139), or that *Beowulf* did indeed begin with a new gathering. The pattern of hair and flesh sides of this first gathering of the *Beowulf* codex indicates that it was originally arranged as a four-sheet quire, but that two half-sheets were then folded on, at even intervals, between the third and fourth sheets. For convenience of reference, the following diagram illustrates the construction of the gathering.

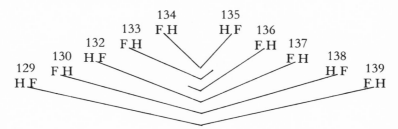

Before the two half-sheets (fols. 133 and 136) were folded on, the four-sheet quire was arranged following the normal insular practice, with the hair side on the outside of the quire, and within the quire with flesh facing flesh, and hair facing hair. Thus, the pattern was thrown off only where the half-sheets were inserted (so hair faces flesh between fols. 133 and 134, and between 136 and 137). Note that the MS foliation of the gathering shows by omission where fol. 147A(131) was formerly misplaced.

The probability that the *Beowulf* MS first existed as a distinct codex, unconnected with the prose texts of the Nowell Codex, should not be surprising. After all, it has nothing of significance in common with the prose texts that now precede it, despite Sisam's familiar characterization of the Nowell Codex as an English *Liber Monstrorum*. *Beowulf* may have been added to the prose codex in late Old English times because some Anglo-Saxon anthologist perceived a loose connection in the lore about monsters, yet it is sad to think that the same person did not also perceive how far apart *Beowulf* stands from the prose texts in all other respects. Its poetic style, its substantive subject matter, its Northern sources, its originality, and its overall aesthetic superiority, are all reasons for believing that *Beowulf* was not copied at the same time, or for the same collection, as the prose texts. It has more in common with the *Judith* fragment, which formerly was undoubtedly part of another codex, than it has with the *St. Christopher* fragment, *The Wonders of the East,* or *Alexander's Letter. Judith,* as we shall see, was almost certainly added to the codex in early modern times, and *Beowulf* may have been, too; but even if it was added in Old English times, there is no compelling evidence that it was done for any other purpose than to protect it from exposure. The real objection to the thesis that *Beowulf* was the fourth item in a decidedly eccentric *Liber Monstrorum* is the implication that 11th-century Anglo-Saxons had no sophisticated appreciation for an original epic written in their own tongue. At least our imaginary anthologist might have given *Beowulf* pride of place, for even the dullest anthologist would realize that Grendel outmonstered anything *The Wonders of the East* had to offer, much less *Alexander's Letter* or St. Christopher's curious pedigree.[48]

The fact that *Beowulf* was copied at a different time, and with a far different attitude on the part of the first scribe than he had when he copied the prose texts, is susceptible to paleographical and codicological proofs of varying weights. The first can be seen in the different styles of the capital letters in the respective parts of the Nowell Codex. If the scribe were truly copying continuously from the *St. Christopher* to *The Wonders of the East* to *Alexander's Letter,* and then on through *Beowulf,* the style of the capitals, all made by the same scribe, would pre-

---

48. "According to the *Old English Martyrology,*" Sisam points out, "'he had a dog's head, and his locks were extraordinarily long, and his eyes gleamed as bright as the morning star, and his teeth were as sharp as a boar's tusks.'" *Studies,* p. 66. But we do not know if St. Christopher was characterized as one of the Cenocephali in this text. Sisam argues that "the incipit of the same text which Wanley preserves from the burnt eleventh-century MS. Otho B x says: *se wǽs healfhundisces mancynnes*" (ibid.), but in fact Wanley nowhere says that these two versions were identical. Certainly the explicit that Wanley preserves from Cotton Otho B. x. (*Catalogus historico-criticus,* p. 191) is different from the ending in the Vitellius text.

sumably remain fairly constant. Significantly, the style of the capitals does remain constant through the prose texts, but it changes notably at the beginning of *Beowulf.* If one compares the line of capitals at the beginning of *Alexander's Letter* (fol. 104r1) with the line of capitals at the beginning of *Beowulf* (fol. 129r1), the difference will be immediately apparent. Aside from the most striking change, from uncial majuscule to capital majuscule,[49] the major difference is that the letters in the *Beowulf* line are drawn with more care, more evenness, more technical draftsmanship, than those in the line from *Alexander's Letter.* It is perhaps worth noting that the loops of three capitals from *Alexander's Letter* have been filled in with the paint used for the illuminations of *The Wonders of the East*—an *H* and a *C* (fol. 104r1 and 8) with orange, and an *O* (fol. 105v2) with red paint. Nothing of the sort occurs in *Beowulf,* despite the otherwise obvious effort to highlight the capitals. More important, the sharp distinction between the style of the capitals in all three of the prose texts and in *Beowulf* can be sustained. Most of the capitals in the prose texts are much smaller and thinner than the boldly drawn capitals in *Beowulf:* the *H*'s and *Ð*'s are usually made with particular care and skill (see, for example, those on fols. 129r1, 135v7, 141r15, 145r8, and 150r8). There are no capitals drawn with special care or skill in the prose texts. Another basic difference is that in *Beowulf* the capitals frequently occur in groups, while in the prose texts they ordinarily occur in isolation. A striking difference in letter-form can be seen by comparing the two kinds of capital *M* used in the prose texts with the entirely different capital *M* used in *Beowulf,* or by comparing the *U* used in *Alexander's Letter* with the corresponding *V* in *Beowulf.* The latter example, especially, reflects the general distinction between uncial and capital majuscule maintained between the two codices.[50]

But the most interesting and enlightening paleographical proof of the integrity of the *Beowulf* codex can be seen in the quantity and quality of the corrections in *Beowulf.* The poem was carefully proofread by

49. The only exception is uncial *H,* but the draftsmanship of this letter is far more accomplished in *Beowulf.*

50. The scribe's exemplar may be the influence responsible for the invariable use of a cursive capital *M* in *Alexander's Letter.* A full comparison of all the capitals in the Nowell Codex can easily be made with the aid of Malone's convenient table of occurrences (*Nowell Codex,* pp. 21–23).

both scribes, and about 180 intelligent corrections were made. By contrast, there is no evidence that the prose texts were proofread by the first scribe, and what few corrections there are tend to show that the scribe was utterly uninterested in the accuracy of his copy. The mass of corrections in *Beowulf* will be considered in detail in Part 3. In view of the first scribe's interest in *Beowulf,* as reflected in his large number of corrections, it is instructive at this point to characterize his marked lack of interest, amounting at times to outright negligence, in the prose texts.

The prose texts were very carelessly copied. They are marred by many scribal blunders, some of an egregious nature, which were left uncorrected despite the fact that the most cursory proofreading would have surely exposed them. In effect, there is no evidence that the scribe proofread his copy of the prose texts after it was made, with the possible exception of *Alexander's Letter.* Lengthy dittographs and omissions occur with almost ostentatious regularity. A few examples of the scribe's negligence on fol. 91(93), alone, of the *St. Christopher* fragment will suffice to show his attitude toward this text. He makes two dittographic errors on the verso. The first is insignificant: he wrote *liges* twice, once at the end of line 8, and again at the beginning of line 9 (the first has been mostly scraped off, whether by the scribe or a subsequent reader is impossible to tell). The second dittographic error is considerably more serious, for it involves rewriting nearly a line and a half of text, judging by the length of the erasure on lines 19 and 20. The traces suggest that the immediately following passage *(ond for þæs eges fyrhto he wæs swa abreged)* was the dittographic material erased. The length of the blunder needs to be stressed. A simple dittograph of a word, or even a few words, need not indicate a general lack of attention, but a long dittograph does, for each rewritten word increases the chances of the scribe's noticing his error. In this case the scribe began a new folio continuing the dittograph, and so there is no evidence that he ever did awaken to his error. Still another serious blunder occurs on the recto. Between lines 6 and 7 there is a contextual lacuna, where King Dagnus is proposing various tortures for St. Christopher. The gap creates an exceedingly unusual torture: *he het settan on his heafde þry weras,* "he ordered that three men be placed on his head." Fortunately, the Latin source restores the sense of the passage: *rex jussit . . . mitti in caput ejus cassidem igneam. Tunc dixerunt tres,* "the king ordered to be placed on his head *a fiery helmet. Then* the three (men) said." But the scribe could have made the restoration himself, if he reread his copy with the intention of correcting it.[51]

If possible, the scribe was even more heedless of his exemplar when he copied *The Wonders of the East.* The text is riddled with errors, nearly all of which have gone uncorrected. The two lonesome corrections (on fols. 101r5 and 102v11, the latter of which may not be a correction) hardly display the scribe's sense of duty. Elsewhere, on fol. 100(96)v2, he wrote *beabe* instead of *beame,* and though he noted his mistake, he underdotted the first *b* instead of the second, and even then failed to write in the correction. Some of the few "erasures" are more likely (one hopes) accidental abrasions: for example, on fol. 100(96)r6 the *st* of *stefne* is partially rubbed away, but *efne,* "even, likewise," makes no sense here. In addition to other errors there are three contextual lacunas on fol. 102r, which can be tentatively restored by reference to a variant version of *The Wonders of the East* in Cotton Tiberius B. v.[52] Obviously, a scribe who skips material on a previously illustrated page is easily found out: the honest men from *The Wonders of the East* who are said to live on the highest mountain between Media and Armenia are conspicuously situated instead on top of the text describing the bearded huntresses; similarly, most of the text that was supposed to accompany the picture of the bearded huntress on fol. 102v is on the recto, while the text that should flank the next illustration partly flanks, instead, the bearded huntress.[53]

---

51. The scribe may have skipped a line in his exemplar. The Old English for *cassidem igneam* and *tunc* may well have taken up an entire line. The usual translation for *tunc* in this text, for example on fol. 91(93)r12, is *þære ylcan tide. Helm* is the natural translation of *cassidem,* and *fyrsmeortendum* translates *ignitos* in Alfred's *Orosius.* Thus, a reasonable conjectural restoration for the skipped line would be *fyrsmeortende helm þære ylcan tide.* The error could have been caused by the similarity, in insular script, of *fyr-* and *þry.*

52. This is only a stopgap measure, since the Tiberius version differs markedly from the Vitellius text. The Latin source is also extant (see Rypins, *Three Texts,* pp. 101–107).

53. It might be noted in passing that two readers of *The Wonders of the East,* in Middle English times, wrote pseudoglosses above some words on fol. 99(95)v. That the codex was being read with some comprehension in Middle English times raises the possibility that *Beowulf,* too, was read, and could have inspired some Middle English poet. The possible continuity of Old English traditions in isolated areas has not been adequately explored.

Two stages of correction need to be considered in *Alexander's Letter.* The text has definitely been proofread, though not, evidently, by the scribe. The proofreader was a medieval spelling reformer, who went through *Alexander's Letter* rather fecklessly modernizing archaic spellings.[54] Presumably, then, this proofreader was not the scribe, since the words he alters are not errors. The possibility that the scribe himself was the spelling reformer cannot be ruled out, though it seems highly unlikely. On the one hand, the scribe may be responsible for the purely orthographical changes of *heofones* to *heofenes* on fol. 104r16; on the other hand, he is almost certainly not the alterer of *sægdon* to *sædon* on fol. 120r2, again reflecting later orthography, since in *Beowulf* he changes *sæde* to *sægde,* and in this case the form of the *g* identifies the correction as his (see fol. 130v19). Other erasures producing later orthographical forms can be seen in the changes of *heht* to *het* (fol. 118v2), *biwriton* to *biriton* (119r1), by someone for whom *w* before *r* was no longer pronounced or written, *burhg* to *burh* (119r9—cf. *sorhge* in *Beowulf,* fol. 184v18), and *usic* to *us* (108r5 and 19). The most systematic spelling reform, however, is the change of *mec* to *me* in nearly a dozen instances, by someone who apparently found *mec* annoyingly archaic (fols. 105r6, 118r2, 108v15, 16, and 17, 109r4 and v4, 5, and 7, 110r2, and 116v12). He apparently meant to make the same alteration on fol. 107r8, in the phrase *mec nænigre,* but erased the following *n* by mistake. If this explanation is right, even our spelling reformer worked mechanically.

The scribe made many errors in his copy of *Alexander's Letter,* and he left many of them uncorrected, but he himself also made many corrections. For example, he skipped an entire MS line between fols. 122 and 123, but he corrected his omission by ruling in an extra line at the bottom of fol. 122v. His errors by dittography can once again be used to characterize his general attitude toward the text he was copying. On fol. 108r16 about nine letters have been erased after the word *swa,* and the traces suggest that he had written *mid minne,* here, the same phrase that follows the erasure. On fol. 117r17 seven letters, by Rypins's count, have been erased before *ealne.* The error has been completely obliter-

54. Cf. the spelling reforms carried out by the "corrector" in the Junius MS, particularly in *Christ and Satan.* There is a good discussion in Robert Emmett Finnegan, ed., *Christ and Satan: A Critical Edition,* pp. 59–60.

ated except for the first letter, the abbreviation for *ond*. What happened, it seems, is that the scribe began a dittograph of the preceding phrase, *ond minne here,* but noted his error before recopying *here,* showing that his inattention was only a momentary lapse. He was not always so easily roused. On fol. 108v1–2 an entire line and part of the next of dittography had to be erased.[55] The lapse of attention is quite long. Another extensive dittograph that has not been noticed at all—or, at any rate, has not been erased—occurs on fol. 115r14–16, where the scribe has unknowingly written two times, *ond ic swiðe wundrade þa gesælignesse þære eorðan.* This long dittograph was no doubt induced by the coincidence that *ond ic* follows *eorðan* in the passage, and thus the scribe inadvertently recopied what came after the first *ond ic.* That such a lengthy dittograph was written at all shows that the scribe was inattentive; that it was never detected, and therefore never erased or crossed out, is a potent indication that the scribe never proofread *Alexander's Letter.*

The signs of extensive proofreading in the *Beowulf* codex, next to the lack of proofreading in the prose texts, provide persuasive, if implicit, testimony that the *Beowulf* codex was not always joined to the prose codex that now precedes it. As we shall see, the second scribe, in addition to proofreading his own copy, also proofread the part of *Beowulf* copied by the first scribe, for many corrections in this section of the poem are made in his hand.[56] Surely the second scribe would have proofread the prose texts as well if *Beowulf* at the time were merely the fourth item in an English *Liber Monstrorum.* As for the first scribe, the vast number of corrections in *Beowulf* and even the nature of the errors themselves show that he regarded *Beowulf* highly and made every effort to produce an accurate copy. The scribe's prevailing alertness is attested by the lack of any long dittographs of the type that are frequently found in the prose texts, and by the removal of all short dittographs in the course of later proofreading, if not while he was actually copying. His

55. A dittograph can be presumed here, for if the scribe had omitted material at this point he would have been able to rule an extra line at the bottom of the preceding folio, as he does for his omission between fols. 122 and 123.

56. See Tilman Westphalen, *Beowulf 3150–55: Textkritik und Editionsgeschichte.* This brilliant study contains an excellent discussion of the scribal corrections (pp. 99–108), in which Westphalen convincingly distinguishes the two scribes' corrections on paleographical grounds. He provides a summary outline on pp. 107–108.

written corrections and erasures show that he was generally very attentive, not only to the mechanical job of copying correctly, but also to the
more aesthetic aspects of grammar, syntax, sense, and even of meter and
alliteration. Moreover, differences in ink and in the sharpness of the
quill point show that the proofreading by both scribes was not done all
at once, but rather that both read the same copy more than once. When
combined with all the other evidence that *Beowulf* was initially a separate codex, the intelligent, conscientious proofreading of *Beowulf* alone,
by both scribes and in several stages, and the scribes' manifest efforts to
copy accurately in the first place, are the best confirmation of all that
Beowulf was a special poem in the early 11th century, and that it was
copied in our extant MS as a separate codex.

The first quire of this *Beowulf* codex has already been discussed in
detail and diagrammed. The remaining seven quires of *Beowulf*, the
seventh to the thirteenth of the Nowell Codex, are here described for
purposes of reference. The makeup of these gatherings is not controversial, and the arrangement of hair and flesh sides, with one explicable
exception, confirms the accounts of these gatherings given by Ker and
Malone. The twelfth and thirteenth, as mentioned earlier, are five-sheet
gatherings, with hair sides placed outward for all five sheets in both
gatherings (fols. 179–188 and 189A[197]–198). The rest of the gatherings are natural, four-sheet quires, with enough minor departures
from the normal insular sheet arrangement (that is, hair facing hair,
and flesh facing flesh) to make the identification of the quires, by conjugate pairs of folios, virtually certain. The tenth and eleventh quires
(fols. 163–170 and 171–178) have their sheets arranged identically,
with hair outside the gathering, so that flesh faces flesh between sheets
1 and 2; but the order is reversed with sheets 3 and 4, so that hair faces
hair between them, while hair faces flesh between sheets 2 and 3. The
unusual pattern clearly identifies the two quires, which is additionally
confirmed by the anomalous ruling for twenty-two lines per page in the
tenth quire. The ninth quire (fols. 155–162) follows the normal insular
practice without variation, while the eighth (fols. 147–154) has hair
outside the first two sheets, but then follows the normal practice. All of
the sheets in this account of the gatherings are comprised of conjugate
pairs of folios.

The only problem arises in the seventh quire (fols. 140–147A[131]):
sheets 1, 2, and 4 have conjugate pairs, but sheet 3 (fols. 142 and 145)

does not. But the evidence in this case does not suggest that the present, four-sheet quire was expanded from an original, three-sheet gathering. The arrangement of hair and flesh sides indicates that the quire was composed in the normal way, with hair on the outside for the first sheet, and with flesh facing flesh and hair facing hair inside. The pattern only breaks down on the sixth leaf, fol. 145, and for this reason I would suggest that the original leaf must have been replaced, and that the replacement leaf was folded on (perhaps inadvertently) with the hair side up, instead of the flesh side. It is very hard to distinguish hair from flesh on this leaf, anyway, for the vellum is of a finer quality than any other folio in the quire, and the hair dots appear on both sides of the thinned vellum. If the scribe was able to distinguish hair from flesh, he may still have placed the hair side up deliberately, because he had to draw a large capital on the recto, and ink generally looks better against a smooth, shiny hair side.

The following diagram illustrates the hair-flesh pattern of the sheets and highlights the thesis that fol. 145 was a replacement.

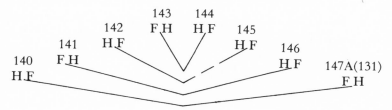

If the thesis is correct, the replacement of fol. 145 is a remarkable instance of responsible proofreading, for if the scribe merely made a mess of the page in the course of copying, he might have cut the page out, but he would not have to replace it. As Ker points out, "perfect quires, in the sense that no part of the text is missing, often contain an odd number of leaves, probably, as a rule, because the scribe made a mess of one of the leaves and excised it" (*Catalogue,* p. xxiv). Thus, if fol. 145 is a replacement, it indicates that the scribe noticed a major blunder on the original leaf, which could most easily, or most neatly, be corrected by replacing the entire leaf. A possible explanation can be deduced from the crowding of letters in line 6 of the recto, which holds more letters than any other line on the page, and from the runover of the text into line 7 at the end of the fitt. If the scribe had been writing normally, line 6 would contain thirty to thirty-one letters, instead of thirty-six; and if he followed his normal practice, *aldre gedigest* would have been written on a single line, and the fitt number X would have taken up another whole line.[57] The crowding and the overrun support the conjecture, therefore, that the scribe had to replace fol. 145 because he had skipped an entire line of text when he made his first copy. This of course is pure guesswork, but it would explain the one irregular leaf in the sheet arrangement of the seventh quire.

This collation of the sheets in the Nowell Codex confirms that the gatherings of the prose codex and the gatherings of the *Beowulf* codex are fundamentally different. The characteristic gathering of the prose codex was made up of three sheets, though two were expanded to natural quires by folding on extra leaves. The characteristic gathering of the *Beowulf* codex was a natural quire, though the first was expanded to a five-sheet gathering by folding on extra leaves. The last two gatherings of the *Beowulf* codex are uncharacteristic in several respects: they are five-sheet gatherings from the start, their sheets are all arranged so that hair side faces outward, and they are ruled for twenty-one lines to the page, instead of the normal twenty. The sheet arrangement, as the *Judith* quire shows, is an idiosyncrasy of the second scribe. The five-sheet gatherings and the additional rulings can both be used as circumstantial proof that fol. 198, the last folio of *Beowulf,* was formerly the last page of the codex. Scholars who know the MS, and particularly the physical state of fol. 198, will not doubt this, but enough confusion has been expressed in print to make a restatement of the facts highly desirable.

The second scribe's departure from the first scribe's format of using natural quires ruled for 20 lines to the page is easily explained. As Ker points out, "the variation from the normal number [of sheets in a quire] is usually explicable. If, for example, a scribe had matter for two and a half eight-leaf quires he would probably prefer to fit it into two ten-leaf quires" (*Catalogue,* p. xxiv). Ker's example, of course, fits the circumstances quite well. The second scribe had slightly more text left to copy than would easily fit in two five-sheet gatherings, as the extra rul-

---

57. Cf. fols. 134r, 138r, 141r, and 169v. The only other times the scribe runs the text over into the line of the fitt number are on fol. 142v (but here only four extra letters are involved, and there is no crowding in the previous line) and on fol. 151v.

ings indicate, but considerably less than would justify the use of three natural quires. The last two gatherings show that the scribe needed 840 lines (forty pages, each ruled for 21 lines) to finish copying *Beowulf.* If he had kept to the format established by the first scribe, three natural quires ruled for 20 lines to the page would provide him with 960 lines (forty-eight pages), which was much more than he needed. He would have had six blank pages left over at the end of the third quire, after he had finished copying *Beowulf.* This surplus would have been fine if he had something else to copy after *Beowulf* (*Judith,* for instance), and so the peculiar construction of the last two gatherings of *Beowulf* is reason enough to conclude that the last page of *Beowulf* was once the last page of a codex. *Judith,* whose only extant part is written on a natural quire ruled for 20 lines to the page, is a later, probably 16th-century, addition to the present, composite codex known as the Nowell Codex.

That the second scribe labored to squeeze the ending of *Beowulf* into two five-sheet gatherings is scarcely open to doubt, in view of the crowding of the text onto 198v. It is perfectly evident that the scribe had no more vellum available after the end of this page. His letters, which are normally well spaced, and formed with broad, bold strokes, are suddenly tightly packed together and considerably smaller. On fol. 172v, where he first begins to copy *Beowulf,* he fits between twenty-four and thirty-one letters on each line; now, on fol. 198v, he fits between thirty-four and forty-four letters per line. And the crowding of the letters is still not enough, for the scribe is also obliged to make use of abbreviations at a rate, and of a sort, unprecedented in the codex. For example, on lines 17–18 he writes -*dryħ wordū herḡ ferhðū freoḡ þoñ* as an abbreviated form of -*dryhten wordum herge ferhðum freoge þonne.* Even after all of the squeezing and clipping, -*geornost,* the last word of the poem, does not fit and spills over into a twenty-second line. Obviously, no crowding would have been necessary if a fresh quire ever followed the last gathering of *Beowulf* when the second scribe finished the poem.

The bad condition of fol. 198v can also be cited as evidence that it once served as an outside cover, as Holthausen was the first to observe.[58] The page suffered extraordinary damage in medieval times, and again in modern times from the fire and from the water used to put out the

58. In his edition, *Beowulf nebst dem Finnsburg-Bruchstück,* p. x.

fire. Zupitza had tersely noted in his FS transliteration that "almost all that is legible in this page [was] freshened up in a late hand" (p. 144); more recently, Westphalen has painstakingly vindicated the claim with his remarkable theory, based on a careful paleographical study, that the second scribe himself freshened up the page about ten years after he had originally copied it. As Westphalen realized, the page must have been exposed to unusual wear and tear to require later restoration.[59] Westphalen thus made the obvious deduction that the page must have been at one time the back cover of the MS. A discriminating, late medieval bookworm provides the culminating proof. He fortunately ate no words, but he did take a large meal, eating a tunnel from just above the *t* of *eahtodan* on fol. 198v16 back through all ten folios of the thirteenth gathering. Since the *Judith* quire contains no wormholes, the thirteenth gathering must have been exposed on the outside when the worm discovered *Beowulf.*

The *Judith* Fragment

Insufficient and inaccurate conceptions of the physical construction of the Nowell Codex, and of the *Judith* fragment's present position in the composite codex, have led to unwarranted conclusions about the original length of the poem. Almost certainly, *Judith* once was part of another codex entirely, and certainly it did not always follow *Beowulf.* Earlier scholars, because they ignored the physical state of the last gathering, and especially the last page of *Beowulf,* assumed that *Judith* always followed *Beowulf* in the codex.[60] Förster, for example, believed that *Beowulf* and *Judith* were once inseparable, and that when intervening gatherings fell out, *Judith* not only lost its beginning, but *Beowulf* may have lost its conclusion (p. 82). We now realize from fol. 198v that *Beo-*

59. The second scribe's extended interest in the *Beowulf* MS is impressive testimony of his interest in the poem itself. It is hard to believe that the same man who carefully watched over the physical condition of the MS had copied the poem carelessly and without comprehension ten years before. On the other hand, there is no good reason to doubt that the MS was used frequently after the poem was copied, and that the scribe, who stopped its physical deterioration, had a clear notion of the value of preserving it.

60. Rosemary Woolf takes the extreme view that *Judith* may have been copied as a fragment immediately after *Beowulf* ("The Lost Opening to the *Judith,*" p. 170).

wulf is complete, that the *Beowulf* and *Judith* MSS were always separable, and in fact were once separate, and that losses at the beginning of *Judith* had no effect on *Beowulf*. There is, however, no agreement yet on whether the *Judith* fragment is a late addition to the composite codex, or whether it was merely shifted from the beginning of the codex to the end, or even, as Ker suggests, from the end to the beginning, and then back to the end again.[61] Nor is there agreement on how much has been lost at the beginning of *Judith*. The extant fitt numbers have given the editors of *Judith* reason to believe that three entire gatherings, or about three-quarters of the poem, have been lost; yet aesthetic arguments strongly suggest that the poem is virtually complete. There is paleographical and codicological evidence that has not been brought forth that the *Judith* fragment, as a fragment, was indeed a late addition to the codex; more important, there is paleographical evidence that dismantles the only good case that *Judith* lost a major part of its original text.

One clear indication that *Judith* was formerly unassociated with the *Beowulf* codex is that the allotted writing space for the two MSS differs noticeably. What makes this especially valuable as evidence is that the number of lines per page in *Beowulf* varies in different quires from twenty lines, to twenty-one lines, to twenty-two lines, and yet the written space between the first and last rulings, regardless of the number of lines per page, is uniformly between 17 and 18 cm., usually about 17.5 cm. This shows that even when the scribes departed from the normal number of lines (twenty), they took care, for aesthetic reasons, to make the written space of all pages throughout the *Beowulf* codex a uniform size. In the case of the *Judith* fragment the written space between the first and last rulings is between 16 and 16.5 cm. The difference is distinct, and can hardly be fortuitous: *Judith* was not ruled to fit the same format as the *Beowulf* codex. The same marked discrepancy exists between the prose codex and the *Judith* fragment, which is reason enough to reject the idea that *Judith* was formerly bound at the beginning of the Nowell Codex. It seems quite safe to conclude, with Malone,

---

61. Ker recognized that "Judith was not always in its present position," but apparently it did not occur to him that it might be a late addition; he argues instead that, "since arts. 1–4 are inseparable, it must have come originally before art. 1 or have been shifted from the end to some other position before the worm got to work" on the last quire of *Beowulf* (*Catalogue*, p. 282).

that the monastic scriptorium that produced the prose codex and the *Beowulf* codex also produced a poem about *Judith*, which was combined with the former MSS "by Nowell or by some earlier owner . . . because the Judith fragment was obviously written by the scribe who wrote *Beowulf* 1940 [*sic*]–3182" (*Nowell Codex*, p. 17).

The precise manner in which the *Judith* fragment was added to the Nowell Codex in early modern times can even be reconstructed. We know that more than the extant quire still existed into the 16th century, for some early "Saxonist" copied the closing lines of *Judith*, in an awkward imitation of the insular script, on the bottom margin of fol. 206v. We know, too, that the original page from which the transcript was taken cannot have been lost accidentally, or we would have no transcript. The closing lines of the poem were deliberately removed, for reasons that will be speculated upon in a moment. At any rate, the extant quire was not simply tacked on at the end of *Beowulf*, as is usually assumed. Whoever added the *Judith* fragment to the Nowell Codex ripped off the outside sheet of the thirteenth gathering of *Beowulf*, and placed it as a protective covering on the outside of the *Judith* quire. In this way, the last page of *Beowulf*, fol. 198v, came for a time to be the last page of the Nowell Codex and was regarded as a flyleaf by Hutton and Wanley in 1703 and 1705. It still was the last page of the codex at the time of the Cotton fire in 1731, and consequently was burned more severely than the last page of *Judith*. Thus, there are two reasons, one medieval and one modern, for the extraordinary damage on fol. 198v. First it was an outside cover of the *Beowulf* codex, in Old English times, and as a result deteriorated enough to need to be freshened up by the scribe some time after he had originally copied the poem. In early modern times, it became the last page of the Nowell Codex, and so became the first page to face the Cotton fire.

With the notable exception of Westphalen, scholars have ignored the evident fire damage to fol. 198v. Even Westphalen, however, in his exhaustive study of the folio, does not address the problem of the fire damage directly, and it is briefly dismissed in a footnote. Still, Westphalen describes the folio as scorched, and correctly attributes the three great holes to burning, and to this extent his comments are far more accurate and revealing than any previous account (pp. 38–39, n. 52). Ker, for example, merely refers to "marks of exposure," while most other commentators vaguely allude to the "badly damaged" condition of the folio, but never mention the fire damage. On the other hand, Westphalen's fantastic explanation for the fire damage cannot be taken seriously. His suggestion that the codex popped open during the fire, burning and scorching fol. 198v, while the facing page, fol. 199r, somehow remained shielded from the tremendous heat, can be dismissed without ceremony. Fortunately, the codex remained tightly closed during the fire, so that the flames only destroyed the outer margins of the folios. If the codex had opened, Westphalen would have lost his subject. The flames also destroyed the back cover of the original binding and began to eat away at the last page of the codex, which, surprisingly enough, was fol. 198v at the time.

The proof that fol. 198, the last folio of *Beowulf*, followed fol. 206, the last folio of the *Judith* fragment, at the time of the fire is that some of the fire damage to fol. 198 has carried through to fol. 206. When the outside sheet of the thirteenth gathering was made the outside sheet of the *Judith* fragment, the binder lined up the top lines, so that the twenty lines of fol. 206 roughly correspond to the first twenty (of twenty-one) lines of fol. 198, and damage on line 17 of fol. 198v corresponds to damage on line 17 of fol. 206v of the *Judith* fragment, despite the discrepancy in the rulings. Specifically, there is a large hole, about 2 cm. in diameter, burned through fol. 198 between lines 16 and 18. When the Thorkelin transcripts were made, the hole was pretty much confined to line 17 (to judge from the Thorkelin readings), but bits of parchment subsequently crumbled away, until the hole extended to lines 16 and 18.[62] A glance at fol. 206v quickly reveals that fol. 198 followed it at the time of the fire. On line 17 of fol. 206v there is a corresponding hole burned through the parchment between *ealles* and *ðæs*. The fire had burned through fol. 198 and began to burn fol. 206 at the same point. There are other burn marks in the area of this second hole that further correspond with the primary hole on fol. 198: on fol. 206v16 there are burn marks on the *t* and the *a* of *beorhtan,* and just below the *t* there is a thin crack surrounded by scorched parchment, which shows through on 206r16, beneath the *e* of *scyne.* In addition, between lines 17 and 18 on the verso there are two tiny scorch marks that have not burned holes, but still have left marks on the recto (see Plates 6a and 6b). In view of

---

62. With the new binding, transparent paper was pasted over the hole on fol. 198 to prevent any further crumbling.

this evidence, there can be no question that the last page of *Beowulf* was misplaced at the end of the Nowell Codex at the time of the fire, and that the *Judith* fragment was bound in before it.

The outside sheet of the thirteenth gathering is comprised of fols. 189A(197) and 198. When the sheet was pulled from the thirteenth gathering to provide a cover for the *Judith* fragment, a tear was made in the parchment where the stitching held the sheet at the fold. If one looks in the lower right-hand corner of fol. 189A(197)v, one side of the tear can be seen; the other side can be seen in the lower left-hand corner of fol. 198r. The discovery that this sheet was placed around the *Judith* fragment in the original binding of Cotton Vitellius A. XV. opens the way to other, more important, discoveries. For instance, when fol. 198 became the last folio of the Nowell Codex, fol. 189A(197) became at the same time the last folio of the *Beowulf* codex. After the fire, when fol. 198 was put back in its proper place at the end of *Beowulf,* fol. 189A(197) remained out of place, as the folio number, 197, written on the vellum leaf, shows. We now know why fol. 189A(197) was the penultimate leaf in *Beowulf* when the MS foliation was written in the MS after the fire.[63] We also know why fol. 198 is in worse condition than we would expect from the normal wear and tear it suffered as an outside cover in Old English times. The knowledge of how, precisely, the *Judith* fragment was added to the Nowell Codex thus provides us with some useful information about the history of the *Beowulf* codex.[64]

Some useful conclusions can also be reached, somewhat more tentatively, about the history of the codex to which *Judith* formerly belonged. The addition of the *Judith* fragment to the Nowell Codex must now be

---

63. Förster (*Die Beowulf-Handschrift,* p. 23) and Dobbie (*Beowulf and Judith,* pp. xiv–xv) assumed that fol. 189A(197) was a single folded-on leaf, which came loose and was misplaced. Malone correctly describes fols. 189A(197) and 198 as the outside sheet of the thirteenth gathering, but then the only way he could explain the misplacement was by assuming that Cotton's bookbinder found the sheet loose, and decided to bind it alone at the end of the gathering (*Nowell Codex,* p. 16).

64. Remarkably, there is no evidence that fol. 189A(197) was out of place when the Thorkelin transcripts were made, yet we know that it was the penultimate leaf in *Beowulf* from the MS foliation, which was written afterward. The leaf was out of place, but Thorkelin and his scribe were still able to transcribe it where it belonged on the basis of the fitt number, XXXVII (v11).

assigned to early modern times, and before Cotton Vitellius A. XV. was bound in the early 17th century. Clearly, the use of the outside sheet of the thirteenth gathering as a protective covering for the *Judith* fragment is not the work of a medieval bookowner. We may reasonably assume that it is the work of a 16th-century collector of "Saxon remains," for whom the preservation of a biblical fragment, even from the Apocrypha, was more important than the textual continuity of a cryptic, but obviously secular, treatise like *Beowulf.* No doubt a scribe associated with this early collector copied out the closing lines of *Judith,* imitating the insular script, at the bottom of fol. 206v, before the extant quire from *Judith* was placed within the sheet taken from *Beowulf.* Malone reverses this proposed chronology, dating the early modern hand "*circa* 1600" (*Nowell Codex,* p. 12), yet dating the addition of the *Judith* fragment to the Nowell Codex "in Nowell's time or a bit earlier" (ibid., p. 119). But Malone did not know, of course, that the outside sheet from the thirteenth gathering was made a cover for the *Judith* fragment. He naturally assumed that the *Judith* fragment was merely tacked on at the end of *Beowulf.* Now, the manner in which the *Judith* fragment was added to the codex is persuasive evidence that the early modern hand that completes the poem for us should also be dated in Nowell's time, or a bit earlier. It is highly unlikely, at any rate, that whoever added the *Judith* fragment to the Nowell Codex would have bound more than the extant quire within the sheet from *Beowulf.*

It is possible, of course, as Ker, Malone, and Dobbie all argue, that the closing lines of *Judith* were once written on a single leaf, and that this single leaf was the last leaf of the codex to which *Judith* formerly belonged. It is much more probable, however, that *Judith* was followed by another text in its original codex. As Ker elsewhere admits (*Catalogue,* p. xxiv), single leaves are rarely placed outside of quires, where they might easily fall out. A single leaf at the end of a codex would be particularly vulnerable. Besides, the second scribe has shown us, in the last two gatherings of *Beowulf,* what he would have done if all he had

---

Plates 12a and 12b. Fols. 189A(197) and 198 constitute the outside sheet of the last gathering of the *Beowulf* MS; when this sheet was pulled from its gathering to furnish a cover for the *Judith* fragment, the sheet was torn where the lower stitching held it to the fold.

þonne his myne licað mæl. Iu þ gifede nepes
þ inwitnia ege mihton helpan æt hilde
þ io hond to for wrong seðe meca gehware
ne gewrace swenge þ ofer solde þon ne þa ytto
ece bær wæpen wundū hæard næs him
wihte ðe sel. Þa wæs þeod sceaða þridda
siðe frecne fyrn draca fæhða gemyndiz
ræsde on done rofan þa him rū agæald
hat ⁊ heaðo grim heals ealne ymbefeng
biteran banū he ge blod egod wearð sawul
driore swat yðū weoll.

                                              XXVII.

Ða ic æt þearfe þ wæs cyninges andlongne
eorl ellen cyðan cræft ⁊ cenðu swa him
gecynde wæs ne hedde he þæs heafolan ac
sio hand gebarn modiges mannes þær he
his mæges healp þ he þone nið gæst niodor
hwene sloh. Secg on searwū þ ðæt sweord ge
deaf fah ⁊ fæted þ ðæt fyr ongon sweðrian
syddan þazen sylf cyning gewold his
gewitte þwæll ræxe gebræd biter ⁊ beadu
scearp þ he on byrnan wæg for on wrat wedra

hæleþa...

...es þegnas
...ahta sū undei inp... ...olde sine su on
handa bær æled leoman ... on ofde siong
... on blijcme hpæt... holond ... sele
on þær de æni þne dæl sæzas geseton ...
þunan lif ne licgan lyt ænig meaun þ he ofo...
ut gefehedon dyne mæd mas onacan ...ur...
þinum or pæll clif let on þæ niman plod...
man ... þa hyrde ... þ þæs þund...
on þæn hladen æ hypæs unzun æþelinge b...
han hilde to hnones nægfe ·:· xliii

Him da ge zipedan zum leode ad on ...æn
un þæ licne helm behonzd hilde bordū
b...plitū byrnū spa he beæna þæs ... don da...
middes mæhne þeddei hæled hio þæ de hla...
læþne onzunnon þa on brinze bæl ryna...
mæst. pized peccan ... ...r astah spæiz...
of spicdole spozende ... ...e be þunda...
blond æt læz od þ hedæ ban hus zehioedi...
hæt on hneð ne hizū un... mod caine...
don mon dryh tnes ... ...n pylce zomon ...

to copy were a few extra lines at the end of *Judith*. The ending of *Beowulf* shows that he would not have used an extra leaf. Instead, he would have added extra rulings in his last quire, crowded his words together on the last pages and abbreviated freely. If one compares the last page of *Beowulf* with the last page of the *Judith* fragment, it will be evident that the scribe was going on to copy another text after *Judith*. Once this fact is recognized, it also becomes clear that the original *Judith* codex was deliberately dismembered in the 16th century. The closing lines of *Judith* were kept with the following quire or quires, but were copied in the bottom margin of fol. 206v. But if the original *Judith* codex was not dismembered until the 16th century, what happened to the lost opening of the poem, which according to current estimates, amounted to three full quires? The first page of the extant fragment is in good condition. There is no indication that it served as an outside cover after its opening was lost, which strongly suggests that it had material preceding it when it was removed from its original codex.

Because of the comparatively good condition of the surface of fol. 199, there is a good chance, at least, that the *Judith* fragment was removed from the middle of its original codex in early modern times, and that its beginning was lost to us in the same way and at the same time that its ending was lost. The obvious objection to this possibility is that there is no apparent reason why only the last quire of four would be removed. A fitting response to this objection is that there must not have been three additional quires of *Judith* to remove: the *Judith* fragment may well preserve a virtually complete text of the original poem. Presumably, more than a few lines were lost at the beginning, or they would have been copied at the beginning of fol. 199r, just as the closing lines were copied at the end of fol. 206v; but probably less than a complete folio was lost, or it could have been preserved with the extant quire. The theory that the *Judith* fragment is nearly complete is not new, of course, but it is decidedly controversial. In 1904, Albert S. Cook calmly observed, in the face of what have always seemed inarguable facts to the contrary, that "the poem seems virtually complete as it now stands," and he defended his view by pointing to the parallelism between lines 6b–7a and 344b–345a.[65] The envelope pattern clearly supports the idea

65. Ed., *Judith: An Old English Epic Fragment*, p. 21, n. 1. Cook's subtitle oddly contradicts his thesis.

that *Judith* has lost little of its beginning.[66] The great argument began when Förster, in his monograph, deduced the loss of exactly three quires on the basis of the Vulgate source, and with the corroboration of the extant fitt numbers.

An essentially paleographical approach to the argument is illuminating. It is helpful to begin with the historical context of the 16th century, which might well have left *Judith* a fragment. The neglect of the MS has rendered such speculation irrelevant, for all commentators on the *Judith* fragment have readily assumed that it was part of the Nowell Codex, as a fragment, from the start. Since we now know, from the ending, that at least part of the original *Judith* codex was dismembered in the 16th century, we must try to understand why it was added to the Nowell Codex in the way it was. First, one may presume that the *Judith* codex came into secular hands as a result of the dissolution of the monasteries, ordered by King Henry VIII in 1537. Since the five texts of the Nowell Codex are written in two hands, which are inseparably linked in *Beowulf* at line 1939b, it is certain that all five texts derive from the same scriptorium. The *Judith* codex must have been taken with the prose codex and the *Beowulf* codex (the last two of which may have been combined already) sometime after 1537, and all three codices must have been kept together by the same collector. Laurence Nowell, the earliest known owner, has written his name and the date, 1563, at the top of the first page of the present, composite codex. It would seem to follow that *Judith* was separated from its original codex, and made part of what is now called the Nowell Codex, some time between 1537 and 1563.

The historical setting provides a possible explanation for the dismemberment of the original *Judith* codex. The initial interest in Old English

---

66. In a convincing structural analysis, James F. Doubleday has shown that "the poem is divided into two major parts," which he goes on to say "are almost mathematically divided off." Beginning with the parallel passages pointed out by Cook, Doubleday goes on to argue that "the second passage in part one likewise parallels the next-to-last passage in part two, and so on, until two contrasting passages, Judith's triumph in the city and her speech urging her people to battle, are juxtaposed at the center of the poem." "The Principle of Contrast in *Judith*," p. 439. These aesthetic judgments are not trivial or evanescent. They thoroughly justify a revaluation of the reasons accepted by all current editors of *Judith* for viewing the extant fragment as no more than a quarter of the original poem.

texts during the Reformation in England was primarily polemical. As Eleanor N. Adams says in "The Beginnings of Old English Scholarship in the Sixteenth Century":

> In order to lay any foundation for their new institutions, the Reformers had to establish a precedent for their beliefs. Such precedent they sought in the liturgy and sermons of the "primitive church," and in the laws of their Anglo-Saxon forbears. Their first concern was to justify, by historical documents, their attitude towards the sacrament, the secular privileges of the clergy, and the use of the Scriptures in the vernacular.[67]

The Apocryphal Book of Judith participated in the polemics. The medieval Bible, Jerome's Vulgate, follows the Alexandrian canons, and thus includes the Apocrypha in the body of the Old Testament. The English Reformers, from Coverdale's first English Bible (1535) onward, followed the Hebrew canons, and so placed the Apocrypha at the end of the Old Testament. The Reformers had an Anglo-Saxon precedent for this placement in Ælfric's "On the Old and New Testament," for Ælfric discusses the Apocrypha and the Book of Judith at the end of the treatise.[68]

The polemics involving the Book of Judith may explain how the Old English poem *Judith* came to be a fragment in the 16th century. If we assume that *Judith* was originally included in a collection of biblical texts that followed the order of the Vulgate, or at least indicated that *Judith* was canonical, its removal from this collection between 1537 and 1563 is understandable. If he wanted to save all of the texts, a Reformer would be virtually obliged to remove *Judith* from a collection that adhered to the Vulgate order. The way the *Judith* fragment ends supports this conjecture, for it indicates that whatever followed *Judith* in

---

67. *Old English Scholarship in England from 1566–1800*, p. 11.

68. See S. J. Crawford, ed., *The Old English Version of the Heptateuch, Ælfric's Treatise on the Old and New Testament and His Preface to Genesis*, pp. 48–49. The title of the edition published by William L'Isle in 1623 reflects its polemical nature: *A Saxon Treatise Concerning the Old and New Testament. Written about the time of King Edgar (700 yeares agoe) by Ælfricus Abbas . . . whereby appeares what was the Canon of holy Scripture here then received, and that the Church of England had it so long agoe in her Mother-Tongue.*

the original collection was more important to the person who dismembered the codex than *Judith*. The early modern copy of the closing lines suggests, at any rate, that the ending of *Judith* was sacrificed so that the beginning of the succeeding text might be preserved intact. The only kind of text that would certainly take priority over *Judith* at this time would be a canonical biblical text. The same explanation can be applied to the lost opening of *Judith*, which, as we have seen, may have comprised less than a folio, containing perhaps a short proem along with the start of the poem proper. These lines, like the closing lines, would have been sacrificed in favor of the canonical biblical text that preceded *Judith* in the original codex.

The theory accounts for the state in which the *Judith* fragment has come down to us. As Ker says, "The *membra disiecta* have come into existence for various reasons and especially because one part of a manuscript seemed more important than another part or had a different sort of interest" (*Catalogue*, p. lxii). In this case, the texts on either side of *Judith* were of special interest, and if *Judith* was indeed expurgated, the beginning and closing lines that remained with the original codex would have to be scraped off by the expurgator to conceal the former existence of *Judith* at that point in the codex. There would be no point in removing the main body of the text, while retaining the fragmentary proof that *Judith* once came between the remaining texts. The deliberate destruction of Old English texts by early collectors is well documented in Ker's *Catalogue*. Ker points out that "a special kind of mutilation is found in some manuscripts belonging to Archbishop Parker. This consists in the deliberate removal by one means or another of the remaining portions of the imperfect texts. Thus in *21*, art. 1 was scrapped by pasting up two of the leaves and by erasing the part of the text which still remained visible after this had been done" (*Catalogue*, p. lxiii). He goes on to list many additional texts that were erased "either partially or completely" in early modern times. The erasure of the first thirty-eight lines of a fragmentary translation of the *Regularis concordia* at the beginning of the MS CCCC 201 "is probably due," Ker guesses, "to Parker's wish to contrive a tidy beginning" (ibid., p. 83). Perhaps the study of all of these erasures under ultraviolet light will reveal more complex motives behind the mutilation of Old English texts by early collectors. It is perhaps too much to hope that the beginning of *Judith* may some day reappear under ultraviolet light, but it is not unreasonable to suppose that it was lost by erasure.[69]

All of this may seem unduly speculative, but the original length of *Judith* is a matter of speculation that has led to widely divergent conclusions. The early modern transcript of the closing lines in the bottom margin of fol. 206v, and the manner in which the *Judith* fragment was added to the Nowell Codex, are demonstrable facts, both of which support the theory that *Judith* was taken from its original codex in early modern times. There is no obvious reason, under these circumstances, why three entire quires should have disappeared when the extant fragment was transferred from one codex to another. The alternative is that *Judith* was already a fragment when it was pulled from its original codex, but unless there is real evidence of this there is little point in accepting it. Here is the evidence: Förster reckoned that the poem must have lost a substantial part of its beginning, since the extant fragment preserved only parts of chapters 12, 13, 14, and 15 from the Vulgate Book of Judith; the scope of these losses (chapters 1 through 11), Förster argued, was confirmed by the extant fitt numbers, X, XI, and XII, which showed, he said, that well over eight fitts had been lost from the beginning.[70] There would seem to be little ground left for disagreement.

---

69. Who owned the codex before Nowell is still a mystery. In addition to the counterfeit insular script of the closing lines of *Judith,* the underlined proper names in *Beowulf* (for example, on fols. 138–140) suggest that the Nowell Codex may have formerly belonged to Parker; the underlinings, however, are in gray black lead, rather than the red traditionally assigned to Parker. John Bale died in 1563, and Nowell could have acquired the codex from what remained of the once vast collection of this zealous Reformer and tireless collector of MSS. It seems most likely, however, that Nowell acquired it through Sir William Cecil in 1563, when Nowell entered Cecil's household as tutor to his ward, the earl of Oxford. It is known from his correspondence with Parker that Cecil "kept artificers in his household for the purpose of 'improving' manuscripts." See May McKisack, *Medieval History in the Tudor Age,* p. 50 (and the letter cited on p. 35). For details of Nowell's life, see Robin Flower, "Laurence Nowell and the Discovery of England in Tudor Times"; and the introduction to Marckwardt's edition of the *Vocabularium Saxonicum,* pp. 1–19.

70. *Die Beowulf-Handschrift,* pp. 88–89; recently David Chamberlain, while acknowledging that much of the earlier chapters of the Vulgate Book of Judith was probably not versified in the lost part of the poem, still argues that "the poet could readily have created a poem of 1200 to 1300 lines that would have moved rapidly and

Förster appears to be dealing with facts, not speculation, and all editors of the poem have accepted his arguments as facts. Yet careful students of the poem, from Cook on, keep insisting that the poem is alive and whole.

Upon closer scrutiny, Förster's facts begin to evaporate. There is no need to argue at length that the Vulgate source does not really uphold the argument, for any objective comparison of *Judith* with the Book of Judith must conclude that the poet has deliberately neglected to rework some of his source material.[71] The way the poem ends shows beyond dispute that chapter 16 of the source was intentionally deleted. The extant poem shows that a great deal of chapters 12–15 was intentionally deleted, too. There is, then, adequate reason to believe that the substance of chapters 1–11 may never have been versified. Confirmation of this inference is easy to come by in the poem: part of chapter 10, at least, was not reworked in the lost part of the poem, for the famous *fleohnet* interpolation (lines 46–54) was inspired by the canopy mentioned in 10:19; the enlarged role in the poem of Holofernes as king of the Assyrians, as well as their general, and the deletion of the reference in 14:16 to King Nabuchodonosor, indicate that the poet never reworked Nabuchodonosor's story in chapter 1 or in 2:1–3;[72] the omission of Achior's

---

excitingly to the double climax we now have." "*Judith:* A Fragmentary and Political Poem," p. 145. It cannot be claimed, however, that the theory is supported by the source; Chamberlain relies almost exclusively on the mute testimony of the fitt numbers.

71. Still the best discussion of the relationship between the source and the poem is Cook's (*Judith*, pp. xii–xxiii).

72. As Cook observed (ibid., p. xvii), Nabuchodonosor "seems to be merged in Holofernes, who is accordingly both general and king." He is consistently given regal titles in the poem: *healdend ure, ðeoden, hlaford, eorla dryhten, winedryhten,* and so on. The poet doubtless realized that an Anglo-Saxon audience would find it hard to despise Holofernes the general, who is portrayed throughout the Apocryphal Book of Judith as a fanatically loyal retainer of his king. His actions stem from Nabuchodonosor's command in 2:5-6: "Go out against all the kingdoms of the west, and against them especially that despised my commandment. / Thy eye shall not spare any kingdom, and all the strong cities thou shalt bring under my yoke." *The Holy Bible, Translated from the Latin Vulgate . . . The Old Testament . . . Douay, A. D. 1609.* By making Holofernes king, the poet transformed him from a loyal retainer to an evil fiend.

vindication and conversion (13:27–31 and 14:6) from the preserved parts of the poem proves that the poet never told Achior's story from chapters 5 and 6. Without going further, it is hard to imagine how (or why) the poet would have expanded the residue of his source ten times over, before writing the extant "conclusion" that stands so well by itself. In view of the negative textual evidence it is unsafe, and quite misleading, to use the Vulgate even to corroborate the testimony of the fitt numbers. There is simply no justification for assuming that the poet reworked the first eleven chapters of his source.

The only evidence left that *Judith* lost much of its beginning are the extant fitt numbers, and they prove nothing, one way or the other, about the original length of the poem. Surely, they should not be ignored, as Cook did when he first proposed that the poem seemed virtually complete. Yet it is also wrong to assume that they necessarily show that over eight fitts have been lost. As Rosemary Woolf has shrewdly observed, only half of the numbered Old English poems (*Beowulf, Elene,* and *Christ and Satan*) are numbered separately; the rest (*Genesis, Exodus,* and *Daniel* from the Junius MS) are numbered seriatim (p. 170). The three poems from the Junius MS are numbered consecutively from I to LV; if *Daniel,* comprising fitts L–LV, had been separated from the MS, it would be possible to argue that forty-nine fitts had been lost from the beginning of the poem. This is precisely the argument that is used to gauge the losses at the beginning of *Judith,* but the possibility of seriatim numbering totally undermines the potency of the argument. The only weakness in Woolf's counterargument is that she ignored all of the paleographical and codicological evidence that *Judith* was a fragment when it was added to the Nowell Codex. As a result, her justification for the presence of the fitt numbers in the *Judith* fragment is unnecessarily lame, and badly weakens the efficacy of an otherwise sturdy theory.

Woolf had no idea that the *Judith* fragment was a late addition to the Nowell Codex. She was thus forced to conclude that the *Judith* fragment was copied *as a fragment,* and to maintain that the extant numbers derive from scribal inadvertence:

> Since the scribe of the Cotton Manuscript was presumably copying an incomplete text . . . they might mean that in an earlier manuscript *Judith*

had succeeded a poem that was numbered up to eight, and that this sequence had been continued in it. A scribe copying the poem, once its beginning was lost, would, of course, automatically repeat the numbers before him, without realizing that an adjustment was necessary. (p. 170)

The theory that *Judith* was numbered seriatim with other texts is not very persuasive, if it needs to rely so heavily on a groggy scribe, mechanically copying (from a fragmentary exemplar) the number X after transcribing only eighteen lines of text. The theory is more compelling once it is realized that the original *Judith* codex was dismembered in early modern times. It is easier to believe that *Judith* was numbered consecutively with other texts, rather than separately, once it is realized that the extant fitt numbers were not copied accidentally, and no doubt reliably reflect the original dimensions of the texts that once preceded the *Judith* fragment.

The argument over the original dimensions of *Judith* itself is really reduced to whether or not one believes that the poem was numbered separately or with other texts. Certainly the Vulgate source cannot be used to prove that very much has been lost at the beginning of the poem. One's view of the fitt numbers is, then, crucial. The argument can be settled by paleographical evidence that has never been brought forth before; the fitt numbers were written in the MS by someone other than the scribe. This fact can be definitely established by the distinct shape of the roman numeral X in the three extant fitt numbers. The scribe's X is well attested in the text of *Judith*, in the text of *Beowulf* (after line 1939b), and most notably in the thirty examples in the fitt numbers from *Beowulf* (**XXVIII–XLIII**). His X is consistently formed of three separate strokes: the main stroke is a heavy diagonal from upper left to lower right; usually the cross is made with two additional strokes—a heavy hook in the upper right of the main stroke, and a long, thin tail, extending well below the minim line at the lower left.[73] Sometimes the cross is made with a single stroke, but the style is unchanged, particu-

73. Cf. Malone's description of the letterforms (*Nowell Codex*, p. 20), and Westphalen's analysis (*Beowulf*, pp. 62–64, and n. 68–71). Curiously, neither considers the fitt numbers in *Judith*. A comparison with *x*'s in the text of *Judith* can be made with *feaxe*, 201v11, *feax*, 205v8, and *hupseax*, 206v4.

...anonan ophonn bozan senaslas ze
...de seypindon hlude gname gud pnæð
...nas sendon inhænd na ȝmanȝ hæled þscio
...ne land bueside ladū cynne scopon seym
...ode seciued þschlide ynelton un sopte sold
...nid lan medo þschuȝ mundū bnuȝdon scealcas
...sceadū sein mæled spynid æȝū ȝcoste sloȝon
...nnoste assnua onet mæȝas nid hyȝsnde
...panne ne spanedon þæs lisne polces hænne
...nice epicsna manna þe hie oþsn cuman
...snihton: XVII.
Spæda muȝo þȝnas onda monȝen tid elreon
...eldeoda ælle þnaȝe oð þ ohȝaron dæde
ȝname pænon dæs lisne polces hænod
...pænidas þ hū spynid ȝ spinȝ spnid lic copdon
...þsnas ebnusee hie yondū þ bæn yldestan eal
...don þsȝnū cydan codon ynelton cū bol
...pizan þ hū poulsclice þæn spel bodedon
...medo þsnuȝū monȝen collan ærolne æȝ
...plizan þais ædne ȝepnaȝn ylȝe þaȝehæled

larly with respect to the long, thin tail. This feature unequivocally distinguishes the scribe's X from the fitt numbers in *Judith*. The distinct paleographical style of the fitt numbers is most easily seen in the FS in number XII (204v11), but in the MS, number XI (202r12) presents the evidence equally well (number X is as faded in the MS as it appears to be in the FS). The manifest difference is in the cross-stroke, which does not descend below the minim line. On the contrary, it is made in a single stroke, starting *on the minim line,* and making a slanting *S*-like stroke across the main stroke.[74] Since someone other than the scribe wrote in the fitt numbers in *Judith*, it is apparent that the numbers did not exist in the scribe's exemplar.

It might still be argued that someone later decided to number the sections of *Judith* separately, but now the evidence favors the view that *Judith* was formerly part of a group of texts that were numbered seriatim. Presumably the fitt numbers were supplied by an overseer of the collection, or perhaps by another scribe who finished copying the codex to which *Judith* originally belonged. The discovery that the numbers in *Judith* are not the scribe's, and therefore have no immediate connection with the original length of the poem, accords well with the theory that *Judith* was expurgated in the 16th century from a collection of Old Testament texts. The Junius MS is a collection of poetic paraphrases from the Old Testament that was numbered seriatim. If *Judith* once belonged to a similar collection, and was numbered consecutively with other poetic paraphrases in the Vulgate order, its noncanonical status and the zeal of the Reformation explain why it was expurgated. From internal evidence Cook, and indeed most students of the poem, have felt that *Judith* seems nearly complete. The external evidence, once it is carefully weighed, supports them.

74. A comparison with the fitt numbers in *Beowulf* shows that the scribe did not use a special form of X for fitt numbers. The relevant fitt numbers in *Beowulf* are on fols. 173r5, 177r17, 179r13, 181r17, 183r8, 184v9, 187v11, 189A(197)v11, 189v17, 192v7, 193v7, 195v14, and 198r11; in *Judith* they are on fols. 199r18, 202r12, and 204v11.

Plate 13. Fol. 204v of the *Judith* fragment. Compare fitt number XII in line 11 with the second scribe's fitt numbers XXXVII and XLIII on Plates 12a and 12b.

Conclusion

The value of studying (and restudying) Cotton Vitellius A. xv. and the danger of neglecting it are well illustrated in the dispute over the original length of *Judith*. It is important to know about the construction of composite codices, which were assembled by enthusiastic antiquarians, like Nowell and Cotton, often enough after the original codices had been disassembled and otherwise transmogrified. It cannot be denied that Cotton Vitellius A. xv., as a composite codex, has been virtually ignored. The only full description of it, in German, is riddled with errors and contradictions, and yet by necessity is still regarded as definitive. The codex has not even been given, officially, an accurate foliation, though no fewer than six separate attempts were made to do so. The utter confusion over the multiple foliations is symptomatic of the general neglect of the codex, and emphasizes how difficult it presently is for scholars to communicate with one another about it: thus Förster uses one foliation under the impression that he was using another; Malone uses a different foliation in his FS of the Nowell Codex; and the two editions of Zupitza's FS of *Beowulf* use a third foliation. The same three works give three different accounts of the original gatherings, and yet the gatherings are the primary clues into the history, and prehistory, of the texts themselves. The modern construction of the Cotton and Nowell codices preserved the texts for us, but obscured the way they were originally assembled as Anglo-Saxon books.

The foregoing investigation into the original construction of the MSS in Cotton Vitellius A. xv. has as its main purpose a clearer understanding of the history and construction of the *Beowulf* MS. The curious neglect of the *Beowulf* MS is directly attributable to the ancient prejudice of Old English scholars that *Beowulf* was originally composed in the 7th or 8th century. In this way, the value of the early 11th-century MS of *Beowulf* was vitiated before it was ever studied. Without this underlying prejudice the *Beowulf* MS would have been carefully studied and restudied long ago, and long ago it would have been recognized that it held a hoard of paleographical and codicological mysteries that sharply distinguished it from the other texts in the Nowell Codex. For the most part, *Beowulf* scholars, even editors, have contented themselves with Zupitza's transcription of the MS, and with the good FSS of the MS that have been available since Zupitza. But there is more to the *Beowulf* MS than the text that shows up, with varying degrees of accuracy, in the very best reproductions. A collation of the leaves, to begin with, raises the exciting possibility that the *Beowulf* MS was originally copied as a separate book, and that only later did it become the fourth item in a prose anthology. At any rate, the 11th-century MS may well preserve an 11th-century poem, and the way is now open to study the body of evidence that it does.

3

∼∼∼∼∼∼∼∼∼∼∼∼∼∼∼∼∼∼∼∼∼∼∼∼∼∼∼∼∼∼∼

The *Beowulf* Codex and the
Making of the Poem

It now makes sense to study the *Beowulf* MS separately. The good possibility that *Beowulf* was composed in the early 11th century and the evidence that the poem in the unique MS was copied as a separate codex at about the same time fully justify a new investigation of the extant MS. The MS is certainly a copy, for the scribal errors are, for the most part, manifestly copying errors: but the transmission of *Beowulf* may have only been from the poet's wax tablets to the extant MS. The present study assumes that the MS we have inherited is extremely close to the archetype. Indeed, if both the poem and the extant MS were done after 1016, there is no other alternative. Paleographical evidence amply supports the thesis. Both scribes have carefully proofread their copies and have made many corrections. The second scribe has even proofread the first scribe's work. Evidence from the gatherings, and the corroborative evidence from the fitt numbers, indicate that the poem was revised in the course of being copied. The indications are that two distinct poems were combined for the first time in our extant MS, and that many years after the MS was copied, the second scribe was still working with it. He restored a damaged text on the last page, and he made a palimpsest of fol. 179 for a revised text; he also deleted, presumably as part of this revision, three lines from fol. 180v. These statements may well be incredible to those scholars who believe in a long transmission of the poem, but their biases have led them to ignore the paleographical and codicological reasons for making the statements. There is nothing incredible about correcting and revising the MS of a contemporary poem.

[171]

The Authority of the *Beowulf* Manuscript

The authority of Old English poetical MSS, in general, is the subject of an influential essay by Sisam, which has been reprinted several times,[1] and is frequently quoted approvingly by conjectural critics. Sisam's arguments do not inspire confidence in the authority of the poetic MSS, and it is necessary to consider the validity of his arguments before granting the *Beowulf* MS extraordinary authority. Sisam complains that if textual conservatism "has a basis in reason, it implies that the extant manuscripts of Old English poetry represent the original compositions with a high degree of accuracy. Yet there seems to be no modern work which attempts to establish a thesis so fundamental." The attitude, he feels, "that 'an accurate scribe did not as a rule depart from the *wording* of his original except as a result of oversight' is begging the question, unless the editor goes on to inquire whether the scribes with whom he is concerned were accurate in this sense, and whether, since the assumed date of composition, the transmission of the text has been entirely in the hands of scribes who aimed at copying what was before them."[2] Applied to *Beowulf,* these strictures would seem to leave the conservative critic at an impasse. Without the original, the degree of scribal accuracy is relatively unprovable. The case is not so desperate, however, if the poem was composed and the extant MS was copied after 1016, for then the transmission of the text might well have been entirely in the hands of the two scribes of our only MS. Even without the original, the scribes' corrections show conclusively that, while both scribes made some errors, as is to be expected in such a long work, both aimed at copying what was before them.

But Sisam's thesis, that the quality of scribal transmission was generally bad, can be confronted directly, for the type of evidence he adduces does not prove his thesis. To prove that scribal transmission was exceptionally faulty, we need poems that are preserved in both early

1. It first appeared as "Notes on Old English Poetry: The Authority of Old English Poetical Manuscripts," in 1946; it is Chapter 2 of Sisam's *Studies in the History of Old English Literature;* and it was reprinted again in Martin Stevens and Jerome Mandel, eds., *Old English Literature: Twenty-two Analytical Essays,* pp. 36–51.

2. Sisam (*Studies,* p. 30) is responding to R. W. Chambers's preface to his edition of *Beowulf,* which Sisam calls a "persuasive manifesto of the school which makes the defence or conservation of the MS. readings its ruling principle." Ibid., note.

and late copies. The quality of scribal transmission can be accurately traced only in poems preserved in multiple copies, and as Dobbie says, "that little progress has been made in this direction by students of most Anglo-Saxon poetry . . . is to be attributed entirely to the lack of sufficient materials, especially to the small number of the MS sources."[3] Indeed, the only Old English poems whose transmissions can be studied at all are *Cædmon's Hymn* and *Bede's Death Song*. Sisam would include the *Leiden Riddle* and the runic inscriptions on the Ruthwell Cross, but this recourse is reaching into the dark. Riddles were certainly transmitted memorially, and the minor variants do not prove scribal corruption.[4] He is quite right when he says that a comparison between the Cross runes and the *Dream of the Rood* (lines 38–64) "could not favour the hypothesis of accurate transmission," but even he admits that "it would be unsafe to make much of the detailed variants where the conditions of recording are so abnormal" (*Studies*, pp. 34–35). Certainly the artisan who cut the runes for the Ruthwell Cross cannot be compared to a scribe, nor can it be argued that he omitted great blocks of the original poem by oversight. For all that can be said from the available evidence, the *Dream of the Rood* was accurately transmitted from the original poem, which is now lost; the runic inscriptions on the Ruthwell Cross made no attempt to transmit the original poem accurately, for the artist's medium prohibited it.

The transmissions of *Cædmon's Hymn* and *Bede's Death Song* can be, and have been documented. To quote Dobbie again, "In Cædmon's Hymn and Bede's Death Song, which provide a striking contrast to the usual paucity of MS materials for Anglo-Saxon poetical texts, we find an unusually suitable opportunity for this method of study" (*Manuscripts*, p. 3). Surprisingly, Sisam rejects both as unsuitable evidence, even though the transmissions of these two poems are, in fact, the *only* evidence there is of scribal transmission from which to draw conclusions. There are seventeen MSS of *Cædmon's Hymn*, four in the Northum-

---

3. See Dobbie, *Manuscripts*, pp. 2–3.

4. It is likely that the Leiden Riddle was transmitted memorially by its scribe, who wrote it on the leftover parchment at the end of his copy of the Latin riddles of Symphosius and Aldhelm. Obviously, the inclusion of the Anglo-Saxon riddle, a creative translation of Aldhelm's "Lorica" riddle, was not planned out in advance, but was merely added by a scribe who hated to waste parchment. See Dobbie, *Anglo-Saxon Minor Poems*, pp. cviii–cx.

brian dialect, and the rest in West Saxon. The MSS range in date from the 8th century to the 15th.[5] Sisam's analysis is brief and may be fruitfully quoted in full:

> The exceptional character of Cædmon's *Hymn* is marked by the many copies in which it appears. If manuscripts later than the tenth century are excluded, the reproduction of the original words is good, with five variants, four minor and one major, of which only the last, *eorðan (bearnum)* for *aelda,* can be traced back to the ninth century. But it is a very short piece of miraculous origin, and it has been preserved as a quotation in historical prose texts, either the Latin of Bede's *History* or the late-ninth-century English translation from it. Here the conditions of transmission are abnormal, and again it is unsafe to rely on the evidence. (*Studies,* p. 35)

This dismissal of the Cædmon evidence is a bit misleading. It would probably be more accurate to say that the many copies of Bede's *History,* rather than the exceptional character of *Cædmon's Hymn,* provided the wealth of evidence in this case. Sisam's short characterization of the variants suggests more scribal corruption than there is in the transmission from the 8th century to the late 10th century. The length of the poem would not insure its accurate transmission: when it was embedded in a Latin text, its brevity might well have caused confusion and led to errors; when it appeared in the Alfredian translation, it would be hard for a scribe, copying mechanically, to distinguish it from the prose text, and this difficulty equally might have led to errors. The conditions of transmission, then, were difficult, and the general accuracy of the transmission in Anglo-Saxon times is commendable.

The accuracy of the transmission can be illustrated by comparing the earliest Northumbrian version (8th century) with the best West Saxon version (10th century). It may seem unfair to take the best 10th-century MS as a test for the accuracy of scribal transmission, but the point is to show that a late copy can accurately preserve a very early poem, despite modernization of forms. There is no point in taking a late, unique MS, as editors of *Beowulf* generally do, and assuming from the start that it does not accurately preserve its precedential texts. Aside from dialectal

---

5. See Dobbie, *Anglo-Saxon Minor Poems,* pp. xciv–c.

transliteration, the only significant difference between the 10th-century West Saxon MS (Tanner 10), and the early 8th-century Northumbrian MS (Kk. v. 16), known as the "Moore MS," is the *aelda* versus *eorðan* variant:

MS Kk. v. 16	MS Tanner 10	
Nu scylun hergan	Nu sculon herigean	
hefaenricaes uard,	heofonrices weard,	
metudæs maecti	meotodes meahte	
end his modgidanc,	and his modgeþanc,	
uerc uuldurfadur,	weorc wuldorfæder,	
sue he uundra gihuaes,	swa he wundra gehwæs,	3
eci dryctin,	ece drihten,	
or astelidæ.	or onstealde.	
He aerist scop	He ærest sceop	
aelda barnum	*eorðan* bearnum	
heben til hrofe,	heofon to hrofe,	
haleg scepen;	halig scyppend;	6
tha middungeard	þa middangeard	
moncynnæs uard,	moncynnes weard,	
eci dryctin,	ece drihten,	
æfter tiadæ	æfter teode	
firum foldu,	firum foldan,	
frea allmectig.	frea ælmihtig.	9

There is simply no evidence here of scribal corruption as the result of a long transmission from 8th-century Northumbrian to 10th-century West Saxon. Even *eorðan* cannot be used to show scribal corruption, for the word is good in the context, and is surely not a corruption of *ælda*. Moreover, as Dobbie says, "we cannot be absolutely sure whether Cædmon's original text had *ælda* or *eorðu* in l. 5" (*Manuscripts,* p. 47). Most scholars believe that *ælda* is original, but a strong case can be made for *eorðu*. The phrase *ælda barnum* may well have crept into the text at a very early stage because of the prestige of Bede's Latin translation, *filius hominum*. It seems most likely that this stock Latin phrase, which Bede may well have used to render the highly individualistic phrase *eorðu barnum*,[6] would lead to the natural English trans-

6. Dobbie points out that "*eorðu barnum* (or *eorðan bearnum*) is, so far as I know, unexampled elsewhere" (*Manuscripts,* p. 48), though he curiously cites the uniqueness of the phrase as evidence that Cædmon must not have used it.

lation, *ælda barnum*. The alternative is that Cædmon extemporane-
ously created an Old English phrase that corresponded to a Latin cliché.

The evidence of accurate scribal transmission of *Bede's Death Song*
in Anglo-Saxon times is not open to any of the doubts or difficulties that
might be raised by the *ælda/eorðu* variants in *Cædmon's Hymn*. There
are no fewer than twenty-nine copies of *Bede's Death Song,* ranging
from the 9th century to the 16th, included in the Latin text of *Epistola
Cuthberti de obitu Bedae* MSS. There are three copies from Anglo-Saxon
times, ranging from the 9th to the 11th century. They show how good
scribal transmission could really be, even when the transmission became
complicated by moving into other dialects. Sisam was evidently unaware
of a 10th-century non-Northumbrian MS when he dismissed *Bede's
Death Song* as unsuitable for comparison, despite its rich MS history.
He says in a footnote: "I omit *Bede's Death Song:* the Northumbrian
text is preserved in Continental MSS. from the ninth century onwards;
but, for comparison, there is only a very late West Saxon text, equally
uniform, preserved in MSS. from the twelfth century onwards. Its four
variants from the Northumbrian text have no claim to authority" (*Studies,* p. 35, n. 2). The 10th-century non-Northumbrian text had not yet
come to light in 1937 when Dobbie described the MSS of *Bede's Death
Song,* but N. R. Ker provided an edition in 1939 in "The Hague Manuscript of the Epistola Cuthberti de Obitu Bedæ with Bede's Song."

Sisam's oversight deprived him of an important comparison, for the
Hague MS underwent a complicated transmission that partly bridged
the formerly sharp cleavage between the continental version and the
insular version of the *Epistola Cuthberti.* Dobbie's later account of the
twenty-nine MSS of *Bede's Death Song* in the *Anglo-Saxon Minor
Poems* (p. ci) will help illustrate the significance of the Hague version.
Before the discovery of the Hague MS there was uniformity:

Eleven of these manuscripts, all in continental libraries, give the text of
the song in the Northumbrian dialect; seventeen manuscripts, all in
libraries of the British Isles, present a West Saxon version of the song
which differs in some respects from the Northumbrian version. The clas-
sification by dialects of the Anglo-Saxon texts of the song is borne out
also by the evidence of the Latin texts of the *Epistola Cuthberti.* All of
the eleven manuscripts which contain the song in the Northumbrian
dialect present a single recension of the Latin text, which may for con-

venience be called the Continental Version. All of the seventeen West Saxon texts of the song are found in a recension of the Latin text which differs in many significant details from the Continental Version, and which may be called the Insular Version.

But the Hague MS did not fall in line with these two distinct transmissions. As Dobbie says, "Its Latin text of the *Epistola Cuthberti* agrees in the main with the text of the Continental Version, but . . . there are a number of places in which it follows the readings of the Insular Version" (*Anglo-Saxon Minor Poems,* pp. civ–cv).

A comparison of the earliest Northumbrian text, the 9th-century MS 254, with the 10th-century non-Northumbrian Hague MS reveals the accuracy of the transmission of *Bede's Death Song,* despite the markedly divergent MS tradition of the Hague text:

9th-C. Northumbrian MS 254	10th-C. non-Northumbrian Hague MS
Fore thaem neidfaerae	Fore ðaem nedfere
naenig uuiurthit	nenig wiorðeð
thoncsnotturra,	ðon*o*snottorra
than him tharf sie	ðon him ðearf *r*iae
to ymbhycgannae	to ymbhycgenne
aer his hiniongae	aer his hinionge
huaet his gastae	hwet his gastę
godaes aeththa yflaes	godes oððe yfles
aefter deothdaege	*e*ster deaðdege
doemid uueorthae.	doemed wiorðe.

There are three minor scribal slips in the Hague MS which are italicized above. In line 2a the scribe wrote *o* for *c* (or closed the right side of the *c*) in *ðoncsnottorra,* no doubt influenced by the several other *o*'s in the word. In 2b he wrote *riae* for *siae:* if his exemplar was in caroline script he could have confused caroline *s* for *r,* as Ker suggests, though in an insular exemplar, low insular *s* could be confused for caroline *r,* as Brotanek argues.[7] The reading *ester* for *efter* would seem to favor Ker's suggestion, but since all of the later Northumbrian MSS read *aester,* the mistake may have been in the Hague scribe's exemplar. The transmis-

7. Rudolf Brotanek, "Nachlese zu den HSS. der *Epistola Cuthberti* und des *Sterbespruches Bedas,*" p. 164.

sion of the same error over many centuries is an indication of scribal accuracy in transmission.

If Ker is right, his explanation for the paleographical slips in the Hague text adds another stage to an already long and complicated transmission, from 8th-century Northumbria, southward, where at some point a new recension of the Latin text was made combining the Northumbrian and West Saxon recensions. The Anglo-Saxon text of the song went through the customary modernization of forms reflected in orthographical (for example, *wynn* for *uu,* and *ð* for *th*), and phonological changes (for example the breaking of *a* to *ea* in *ðearf*), presumably all before its transmission on the Continent. Thus, despite the long and complicated transmission, the text of *Bede's Death Song* was not corrupted by scribes. As far as we know, the earliest Northumbrian MS and the Hague MS, which are virtually identical aside from modernization in a different dialect, represent the original composition with a very high degree of accuracy. If we count the only other MS surviving from Anglo-Saxon times, the 11th-century Northumbrian Bamberg MS, the conclusion will be the same. Indeed, Dobbie has argued that "the Bamberg text of the Epistola is in some respects a more accurate transcript of the common prototype," and that "except for the form *thae* in l. 1, the text of Bede's Death Song in this MS does not exhibit any significant variation from the [9th-century] St. Gall text" (*Manuscripts,* p. 55). So the transmission in Anglo-Saxon times of *Cædmon's Hymn* and *Bede's Death Song,* which Sisam ignores in his study of the authority of Old English poetical MSS, establishes the fact that Anglo-Saxon scribes could be very accurate, that they did undoubtedly aim "at copying what was before them" (Sisam, *Studies,* p. 30).

While he neglects the only adequate evidence of scribal transmission of Old English poems, Sisam assembles for comparison some questionable evidence that not unexpectedly shows striking variants. Sisam says, "Nearly all the poetical texts depend on a single manuscript; but the contents of three out of the four great codices show a very small overlap" (ibid., p. 31). In fact, he takes only two comparisons from the Exeter, Vercelli, and Junius codices, and neither comparison is convincing. In both cases the overlapping occurs in two distinct poems, or rather, in two distinct reworkings of common source material. His first comparison is between "Soul and Body I" and "Soul and Body II" respectively from the Vercelli and Exeter books. The main differences in these two poems are not caused by scribal corruption, but by deliberate revision of a common source by different poets. A fair idea of the intentional nonconformity between the two poems can be seen in Dobbie's discussion of "Soul and Body II," in his edition of the Exeter Book.[8] The same is true of Sisam's second comparison, between the parallel sections in *Daniel* and *Azarias,* from the Junius MS. and the Exeter Book respectively. They are different poems, and as such they are not relevant in a study of the accuracy or inaccuracy of scribal transmission.[9]

The accuracy of scribal transmission is more of a factor in Sisam's last comparison, but there is still reason to doubt the validity of the evidence, as Sisam himself seems to acknowledge. "Two manuscripts," he says, "are available for lines 30–94 of *Solomon and Saturn,* MS. CCCC 422 of the second half of the tenth century and a fragment in the margin of CCCC 41 which may be a century later" (*Studies,* p. 32). Ordinarily, Sisam omits such late testimony as the second of these MSS, and it is unclear why he chooses to depend upon it for a major comparison here. As he admits in his note, "it is disadvantageous to use such a late copy, because the great bulk of the poetry is contained in MSS. of the second half of the tenth century . . . and new factors affecting transmission may arise in MSS. written much after that time. I have excluded the poems contained in the Chronicle partly for this reason, partly because they are all late compositions transmitted in an unusual way" (ibid., pp. 32–33, n. 1). The CCCC 41 MS may have been copied after the Norman Conquest. According to Robert Menner, "the ugly insular handwriting shows the effects of points and sharp corners learned from the post-Conquest style of Caroline minuscules, and may be dated at

---

8. Dobbie realized, of course, that the main differences were not caused by scribal corruption. He says, for example, "The Exeter Book version is shorter than the version in the Vercelli Book, omitting the fragmentary address of the blessed soul to the body, 11. 127–166 of the Vercelli Book text." G. P. Krapp and E. V. K. Dobbie, eds., *The Exeter Book,* p. lii; cf. G. P. Krapp, ed., *The Vercelli Book,* pp. xxxviii–xxxix.

9. As Krapp says, "A comparison of the Prayer of Azariah in AZARIAS with the corresponding passage in DANIEL will show so many dissimilarities of word forms and of word order, so many variations in phrasing, that we can hardly assume that the text of DANIEL at this place was mechanically copied from AZARIAS in the ordinary sense in which Anglo-Saxon scribes copied from their sources. We must assume two separate versions with a considerable amount of variation, both for the Prayer of Azariah and for the Song of the Three Children." Krapp and Dobbie, *The Exeter Book,* p. xxxiv; cf. Krapp, *The Junius Manuscript,* p. xxxiii.

the end of the eleventh or beginning of the twelfth century."[10] And it was certainly transmitted in an unusual way, having been copied as a fragment in the margin. Thus, by Sisam's own criteria the *Solomon and Saturn* material should not have been used as a test for the accuracy of scribal transmission in Anglo-Saxon times. If it is counted at all, it carries little weight, and may not tell us anything about the quality of scribal transmission before the Conquest.

After using these three comparisons, each in its own way invalid, to undermine the authority of the poetical MSS, and after dismissing the Cædmon and Bede material, Sisam moves on to the *Beowulf* MS. His procedure has provided no foundation for presuming a badly flawed copy of the original poem, and his pointed attack on the authority of the *Beowulf* MS ought to be considered in this light. He correctly anticipates the proper objection to his procedure when he says, "A defender of the manuscript readings might well say that the evidence so far adduced is not ample or varied enough, and might argue that the scribes were well trained, and that they knew more about Old English usage, thought, and tradition than a modern critic can" (*Studies,* pp. 36–37). He does not meet the first part of this objection at all. The second part would seem to be undisputable, but he says, "I doubt if this holds good for the earlier poetry," and cites as evidence the following textual cruces from *Beowulf:*

> In *Beowulf,* recent editors agree that the first scribe writes *gara (cyn)* 461 clearly and boldly for *Wedera (cyn),* without sense or alliteration, with no likeness in script or sound, or anything in the surrounding verses to mislead him; and the aberration is passed over in their commentaries. For *Cain* 1261 (misread as *cam*) he writes *camp* "battle." . . . At a critical point in the Finn episode (1127 ff.), he leaves us the meaningless "Hengest . . . wunode mid finnel unhlitme." Rather different is 1960 f.: "þonon geomor woc hæleðum to helpe," where, misled by a possible spelling or pronunciation of the initial diphthong, he has taken the proper name *Eomær* for the common adjective *geomor* "sad." . . . All these are proper names, which I have preferred because there can be little doubt about the true reading when a name is miswritten. (Ibid., p. 37)

10. *The Poetical Dialogues of Solomon and Saturn,* pp. 2–3. Ker, as Sisam indicates, places the script somewhat earlier; in his *Catalogue* (p. 45) he says without elaboration that the text is written "in one unusual angular hand of s. xi[1] or xi med." The question has not been settled.

A defender of the MS readings in these cases seems to be in trouble. But even if these were all undoubted errors, *Beowulf* is a long poem and the cruces cited above are widely distributed. The scribes have unquestionably made some mistakes in the course of copying this long poem, but as Sisam readily concedes at the start of his investigation, "single lapses are not necessarily inconsistent with a high general level of accuracy, and that is the quality to be discussed" (ibid., p. 31). Still, the thrust of Sisam's argument in the present case is that the modern critic easily recognizes four miswritten proper names, while the Anglo-Saxon scribe, who is supposed to know better, displays his ignorance. Unfortunately, the argument precludes learning anything about the poem that the scribe may have known, and that modern critics do not know. For this reason it is potentially useful to reverse the argument, beginning with the assumption that the scribe has *not* miswritten four proper names.

There is almost certainly some form of corruption in lines 1128–1129 of the Finnsburh episode, but the name Finn was not, strictly speaking, miswritten. Rather, it was combined with another word element, but strange combinations and divisions of words are characteristic of Old English MSS and are not in themselves regarded as scribal corruption in any meaningful sense of the term. An apt example occurs at the beginning of this episode at line 1070a, where the scribe wrote *infres wœle*[11] for what the editions print as *in Freswœle*. Similarly, editors know perfectly well that the corruption is not in the name Finn, but in whatever is joined to it at the end. They have solved the problem quite conservatively.[12] For MS *wunode mid finnel un hlitme* most of them read, *wunode mid Finne / [ea]l unhlitme*.[13] And since *mid* often takes the accusative in *Beowulf*, the scribe's error may have been only the omission of an *a* in the word *eal: wunode mid Finn / e[a]l unhlitme*. In either case there is no good evidence here that the scribe did not know that Hengest stayed with a man named Finn.

11. The MS actually reads *infr es wœle* (fol. 153r16), but the gap between *infr-* and *-es* is from an erasure the scribe made to correct a copying error. The scribe intended to write *infres wœle,* but in either case the combination and division of the words illustrate the point equally well.

12. For a full discussion in an unusually conservative edition, see Donald K. Fry, ed., *Finnsburh: Fragment and Episode,* pp. 20–23.

13. The meaning of *unhlitme* is obscure, and many interpretations have been proposed. James Rosier has recently suggested "with lack of choice" in "The *Unhlitm* of Finn and Hengest."

There is no reason to assume that proper names are even involved in the other three cruces, *gara, camp,* and *geomor,* singled out by Sisam. Surely one ought to be suspicious of the emendation *Wedera* for MS *gara,* for as Sisam himself observes there is no phonological or paleographical likeness, and there is nothing in the surrounding verses, either, that might have misled the scribe. A more plausible emendation was proposed over a century ago by Benjamin Thorpe, and it is accepted by Whitney Bolton in his revision of Wrenn's edition of *Beowulf.* To supply the missing alliteration Thorpe read *wara* (genitive plural of *wær,* "treaty"); Bolton translates the phrase *wara cyn,* "sworn colleagues." Joseph F. Tuso has recently defended Thorpe's emendation from a different standpoint, arguing that "*wara* is the genitive plural of the neuter noun *war* ('seaweed, sand, shore'), and *wara-cyn* ('the shore people' or 'the folk of the sands') might well refer to the Wylfings, who most probably lived on the sandy Pomeranian coast of the southern Baltic."[14] A chief objection to *wara* is that it ignores paleography, for it is hard to imagine how the scribe could confuse insular *g* with *wynn.* Malone did not ignore paleography when in "Ecgtheow" he proposed the emendation [*Wul*]*gara,* which he conceived of as another name for the Wylfings. The reading is attractive in that it accounts for the omission of the first syllable by haplography (cf. *Wilfingum* in the on-verse), as well as for MS *gara;* it is unattractive in that it makes Ecgþeow a Wylfing, for which there is no evidence. There are other possibilities. For a start perhaps it needs to be noted that the passage *ða hine gara cyn / for herebrogan habban ne mihte* makes sense if *gara cyn,* "folk of the spears," is construed as a *kenning* for "spear troop" or *comitatus.* The passage may be translated, "then his spear troop might not protect him because of their fear of war." John R. Byers accounts for the missing alliteration by assuming that the scribe's exemplar read *ða hine* [*wine-*] *gara cyn,* and that *hine* caused the haplographic error.[15] A simpler explanation would be that the scribe copied *hine* for *wine: ða wine gara cyn / for herebrogan habban ne mihte,* "then the spear troop might not protect their friend because of their fear of war." One last possibility can be mentioned in passing. The scribe may have miscopied *gara,* a word with high frequency in *Beowulf,* for the apparently rare synonym

14. "*Beowulf* 461b and Thorpe's *wara,*" p. 261.
15. "A Possible Emendation of *Beowulf* 461b."

wigara,[16] an error induced by haplography from *wi-* in the on-verse. Certainly, no matter how one solves the crux, there is no longer any justification for accepting Sisam's premise that *gara* is a nonsensical corruption of the proper name, *Wedera.*

Though the Bible is a source that a modern critic can know as well as an Anglo-Saxon scribe can, the modern critic need not assume that *camp,* at line 1261, is a corruption of the proper name, Cain. The word *camp* means "battle," as Sisam says, but in a transferred sense it means "strife, struggle, contention." An example of this usage is given in the Toller Supplement, from Gregory's *Dialogues:* "Se camp *(certamen)* in þæs mannes breoste" (p. 116). The passage in *Beowulf* surely alludes, at least elliptically, to the first murder, but there is no more need to mention Cain's name in this connection than Abel's.

> Grendles modor,
> ides aglæcwif,   yrmþe gemunde,
> se þe wæteregesan   wunian scolde,
> cealde streamas,   siþðan camp wearð
> to ecgbanan   angan breþer,
> fæderenmæge;   he þa fag gewat,
> morþre gemearcod   mandream fleon,
> westen warode.   þanon woc fela
> geosceaftgasta;   wæs þæra Grendel sum
> (1258–1266)

The passage may be translated: "Grendel's dam, the female monster, was mindful of sorrow, she who was obliged to inhabit the dreadful waters, the frigid streams, from the time when strife arose [*siþðan camp wearð*] as a sword slayer to an only brother, a paternal kinsman; then she went stained, marked by the murder, fled human joys, and inhabited the wilderness. From thence arose many fated spirits: Grendel was one of them." Klaeber points out in his note to line 1260 that "*se þe,* instead of *seo þe,* [is] applied to Grendel's mother just as in 1497, or *he,* instead of *heo,* in 1392, 1394." Hence the antecedent for *he* in line 1263 is not *camp,* "strife," and there is no need to supply an antecedent by emending the text. The antecedent may well be *Grendles*

16. See Bosworth-Toller under *wi-gar* and *wig-gar* (pp. 1220 and 1221). In *Beowulf,* compare *wig-freca* (1212, 2496) and *wig-fruma* (664, 2261).

modor, as lines 1392 and 1394 attest, or perhaps the first "sword slayer to an only brother," whom the Anglo-Saxons knew to be Cain.

Sisam's last supposed case of a miswritten proper name is at line 1960, where *geomor,* "sad, mournful," is presumed to be a mistake for *Eomær.* The Mercian royal genealogies include four generations of kings, Wærmund, Offa, Angengiot, and Eomær, who provide the impetus for this emendation.[17] It is difficult to see what advantages come with it, aside from alliteration. So far as we know, this Eomær never transcended the itemization of his name in the Mercian pedigree, and yet the emendation forces us to acknowledge him as *hæleðum to helpe, Heminges mæg,*[18] and *nefa Garmundes* (1961–1962). In the Mercian genealogies he is not the nephew, nor even the grandson of Wærmund, but the great-grandson: if the genealogies are to be used as a basis for emendation here, it would make more sense to emend *geomor* to *Angengiot,* and for that matter, to emend *Garmundes* to *Wærmundes.* And if *nefa* is understood in its general sense as "offspring," there is no reason why it should apply to Eomær and not Offa. The Mercian genealogies say nothing about Eomær (or any one else) being *Heminges mæg,* while the *Beowulf* poet has already called Offa this at line 1944. The main point of the digression is to praise Offa for putting a stop to his queen's murderous ways (1944 ff.), *hæleðum to helpe,* "as a help to his men." In short, the editorial intrusion of Eomær provides good alliteration but a bad anticlimax. The passage makes excellent sense without emendation:

> þonon geomor woc
> hæleðum to helpe,   Heminges mæg,
> nefa Garmundes,   niða cræftig.
> (1960–1962)

"Then mournful he [Offa] arose as a help to his men, the kinsman of Hemming and offspring of Garmund, powerful over [the queen's] hostile acts." Moreover, *þonon geomor woc* alliterates with the on-verse, *eðel sinne,* if, following Malone's suggestion, it is read as *þon ongeomor woc,* "then, exceedingly sad, he arose."[19] The form *þon,* "then," though

17. For a brief discussion of the Mercian genealogy, and its supposed relation to *Beowulf,* see Chambers's *Beowulf,* pp. 195–198.

18. Klaeber needlessly alters MS *heminges* to *Hem[m]inges.*

attested, is rare, while *þonon* is extremely common. A conservative emendation would be *þonon* [*on*]*geomor woc,* and the error could be explained either as a haplograph or as the scribe's attempt to correct what he perceived as a dittograph (*-onon on-*).

In the four cases cited by Sisam, unwarranted mistrust in the overall accuracy and integrity of the scribe along with unwarranted confidence in modern conjecture encourages radical emendations on a large scale. The premise itself, that all four cases represent bungled proper names, is pure conjecture, and yet Sisam presents it as if it were a fact: "All these are proper names, which I have preferred because there can be little doubt about the true reading when a name is miswritten" (*Studies,* p. 37). From a conservative view only one proper name, Finn, is involved, and it is not miswritten, though it is confusingly combined with another word element, as frequently happens in Old English MSS. The danger of conjectural criticism is that its ready disregard for MS forms inhibits thinking and rethinking about annoying MS readings by replacing the problems with easy, usually innocuous, alternatives. For instance, there is nothing objectionable or unusual in the conjectural reading *Wedera cyn* at line 461, and no one could have objected to it had it appeared in the MS at this point. It is too bad that *wedera* bears such little resemblance to the unusual MS reading *gara,* for [*We*]de*ra* is plainly a bad conjectural emendation. As we have seen, the lack of alliteration is the only convincing reason for deserting the otherwise acceptable MS reading, *ða hine gara cyn / for herebrogan   habban ne mihte,* "then his spear troop might not protect him because of their fear of war." Even this criterion for emendation can be legitimately questioned on conservative grounds, for there is evidence in the *Beowulf* MS that the poet did not always intend to use alliteration, nor even to adhere invariably to the normal on-verse/off-verse pattern of the traditional Old English poetic line.

Alliteration is probably the most obvious feature of Old English poetry, but the fact that *Beowulf* is an alliterative poem does not mean that the poet could not create, in all deliberation, an occasional line without alliteration. The intentional omission of it from time to time in a very long poem like *Beowulf* might better be viewed, in at least some cases, as intelligent variation rather than scribal corruption. The advantage of conservatism in this regard is that it enlarges the field of possibilities within a text, which a conjectural approach, by procedure, narrows. For conjectural criticism tends to be normative, while great poetry, even interesting poetry, seldom is. Quite properly, a conjectural emendation stands little chance of acceptance if it is in any way unexpected or extraordinary: it must always justify its validity by reference to ordinary rhythm, ordinary meter, ordinary syntax, ordinary sense, ordinariness. It is the declared foe of the unexpected and the extraordinary, the juices of poetry. Hence the conjectural critic of a poem like *Beowulf,* which emerged from an observable tradition, but which is still a unique poem in a unique MS, is perhaps at times more like a heady scribe in his conceptions than the poet. The critic and the scribe would be inclined to provide alliteration in a line from an alliterative poem, on the assumption that a variation was necessarily an error. Surely no scribe would consciously delete alliteration from an alliterative poem, and it does not make sense to assume that an inattentive scribe could inadvertently insert a meaningful word in the context that does not alliterate in place of a meaningful word from his exemplar that does alliterate. Yet this is the implication in such standard emendations as *mund* for *hand* in MS *þæt he for handgripe minum scolde* (965) or *lind* for *hild* in MS *beloren leofum æt þam hildplegan* (1073).

The refusal of modern editors to admit the possibility of nonalliterating lines in *Beowulf* frequently obliges them to make conjectural "restorations" of needlessly presumed lacunas. The price of editorial alliteration can be high. In line 586b the conjectural "restoration" of the word *fela* to supply alliteration in the stave leads inevitably to a comical effect. In context, Beowulf is giving his version of the Breca episode, to correct Hunferð's uncomplimentary rendition, and he feels obliged to remark by the way, *no ic þæs gylpe,* "I never brag about that." The sense, the syntax (*gylpan* takes a genitive object), and the meter are unassailable.[20] But for the sake of the alliteration editors interpolate, at Beowulf's expense: *no ic þæs [fela] gylpe,* "I never brag *much* about

---

20. W. P. Lehmann remarks that "this half-line is metrically adequate as the manuscript transmits it, and would accord with Beowulf's style. It has been emended, however, usually with *fela,* because it lacks alliteration. Yet the lengthened half-line seems less in agreement with the hero's manner of speaking than does that of the manuscript." Unfortunately, Lehmann is not attempting to avoid an emendation: "If we maintain the manuscript reading, we must either assume that a line or more has been omitted, or that the scribe miswrote 586a, possibly the adjective." See "On Posited Omissions in the *Beowulf,*" p. 224.

that." Another costly interpolation to provide missing alliteration occurs in lines 389–390. Hroðgar instructs his messenger, Wulfgar, to welcome Beowulf and his men to the court. The MS reading (fol. 138v8–11) makes excellent sense when punctuated in the following way:

> "Gesage him eac wordum   þæt hie sint wilcuman
> Deniga leodum."   Word inne abead:
> "Eow het secgan   sigedrihten min . . ."
>   (cf. Klaeber, 388–391)

"'Say to them in your speech, moreover, that they are welcome among the people of the Danes.' He announced the speech within: 'My lord orders me to tell you . . .'" Because there is no alliteration in the second line of this passage, editors invent a great lacuna of two half-lines between *leodum* and *word.* Klaeber, for instance, interpolates *þa to dura eode,* "then he went to the door," to alliterate with the on-verse, and *widcuð hæleð,* "the famous warrior," to alliterate with the off-verse. It seems obvious that both of these passages are marred by editorial alliteration. They ought to be printed without alliteration, the way they appear in the MS.

It is true that textual conservatism runs the risk of conserving scribal blunders as the poet's intended readings. The risk is greatly lessened, however, in a contemporary MS proofread and corrected by the scribes themselves. In such a MS we have evidence of scribal attentiveness and even a sense of the immanency of the exemplar, upon which the corrections are based. There is indeed a scrap of positive evidence in the *Beowulf* MS that some of the nonalliterating lines in the poem derive from the scribe's exemplar. Whether or not the scribe's exemplar was authoritative remains to be seen. At this point the scribe needs to be defended. For line 1981 (fol. 173v3–4) the scribe first wrote *geond þæt reced   Hæreðes dohtor,* a line without alliteration. After proofreading, the same scribe wrote *side* above the line, for insertion between *þæt* and *reced.* In other words, the scribe noted an error in his copy and corrected the line to read *geond þæt side reced   Hæreðes dohtor.* His correction makes perfect sense in the context, and is metrically sound, but the line still does not alliterate. It seems safe to conclude, therefore, that the line was not meant to alliterate. Yet even with this proof of scribal attentiveness the line has been subjected to the most bewildering forms of conjectural emendation. Klaeber emends the scribe's correction *side* to *heal,* an extremely audacious change. Von Schaubert omits the correction entirely, an equally audacious procedure, and then brings *hwearf* down from the preceding verse for *h*-alliteration with *Hæreðes.* Wrenn combines the bold conjectural readings of Klaeber and von Schaubert. They all ignore the correction, yet surely it is based on the scribe's exemplar. The alternative, at least, would seem to be that the scribe, after he finished copying, went back and spoiled his work by inserting spurious words between the lines.

The exemplar is doubtless the source of some variations on the alliterative norm in *Beowulf,* as well. One must remember that Old English spelling does not always precisely reflect Old English phonology. Thus in line 1 of *Beowulf* the velar stop [g] in *gar-* alliterates with the palatal semivowel [j] in *gear-* because both words begin with the graph *g.* Occasionally the difference between phonology and orthography causes some inconsistencies that cannot easily be blamed on the scribes of the extant MS. As M. F. Vaughan shows in "A Reconsideration of 'Unferð,'" this inconsistency is most likely to crop up in words beginning with the graph *h,* which was phonologically lost or significantly reduced in many linguistic environments. An unambiguous example of the wavering phonological status of *h* occurs in the adverb *hraþe,* "quickly." In lines 1576 and 1937, as well as elsewhere, *hraþe* alliterates with *h* (*hilderince, ac he hraþe wolde,* and *handgewriþene; hraþe seoþðan wæs*). But in line 724 it is spelled *raþe* and alliterates with *r (recedes muþan.   Raþe æfter þon).* Moreover, in line 1390 it is spelled with *h,* yet still alliterates with *r: Aris, rices weard, uton hraþe feran* (cf. line 1975, *Hraðe wæs gerymed, swa se rica bebead*). As Vaughan points out, the loss of initial, prevocalic *h* would similarly account for the vocalic alliteration of *handlean* (line 1541), *hondlean* (2094), *hondslyht* (2929, 2972), and *Hunferð* (499, 1165, 1488), which editors needlessly emend to *h*-less forms. While occasional spellings might well be charged to the scribes, these cases show "occasional alliteration" based on phonology. And such anomalies are far more likely to stem from the poet than the scribes, for a scribe's "blunder" would require him not only to disregard the poet's use of vocalic alliteration, but also to provide a synonymous, and virtually homonymous, "correction." In this light perhaps we ought to regard the MS crux *geomor,* in *eðel sinne;—þonon geomor woc* (1960), as another instance of phonetic alliteration, since the initial semivocalic phone [j] followed by the diphthong -*eo* would alliterate phonetically with vowels.[21] The poet of a contemporary MS, more than his scribes, can plausibly be charged with "blunders" involving phonetic alliteration.

Other possible alliterative variations, and even variations in the basic on-verse/off-verse structure of the lines, should be carefully reconsidered in *Beowulf*, in view of the probable 11th-century provenance of the poem. Early editors would not have been so ready to emend the MS text had they thought that the poem was so late. While we do know a great deal about Old English metrical practice now, the hypermetric lines show us that poets were willing to violate standard meter in ways we are not yet capable of explaining adequately. A possible variation that has not been sufficiently investigated is the use of single half-lines, or of three consecutive half-lines, rather than the traditional two. The only scholar who has clearly acknowledged this usage is Alan Bliss, who warns us that "in Old English poetry as a whole short lines are much more frequent than editors have been accustomed to allow."[22] An instance in *Beowulf* may well occur at lines 402–404, where Klaeber interpolates *heaþorinc eode* as line 403b. The passage makes excellent sense without the interpolation, which is merely an appositive for a preceding phrase, and the three half-lines alliterate and provide a fresh and effective variation:

Snyredon ætsomne: þa secg wisode
under Heorotes hrof,   heard under helm,   þæt he on heoðe gestod.

"They hastened together: the man, brave in helmet, led them under Heorot's roof, so that he stood in the hall."[23] Perhaps the theory of

21. Edith Rickert first argued for phonetic alliteration on *geomor* in "The Old English Offa Saga," p. 54. Sisam seems to acknowledge this argument when he says that the scribe was "misled by a possible spelling or pronunciation of the initial diphthong." *Studies*, p. 37.

22. "Single Half-Lines in Old English Poetry," p. 443. An undoubted example of a single half-line that is used alone on purpose occurs in the refrain of *Wulf and Eadwacer* from the *Exeter Book*.

23. Klaeber emends *heoðe* to *heo[r]ðe*, but there is no need for the emendation, in view of *helheoðo dreorig*, "mournful hell hall," in *Christ and Satan* (line 699). Most editors do not emend the word.

alliterative variation and of the use of three half-lines should be applied
as well to the hypermetric verses in lines 1163–1168. As Bliss notices,
line 1166a, *æt fotum sæt frean Scyldinga,* is not hypermetrical at all,
but a combination of two normal half-lines (cf. *þe æt fotum
sæt   frean Scyldinga* at line 500). If the entire hypermetric passage
is rearranged into normal half-lines some interesting and theoretically
tenable variations emerge:

> gan under gyldnum,   beage þær þa godan
> twegen sæton,   suhtergefæderan.   þa gyt wæs hiera sib
> ætgædere æghwylc,   oðrum trywe.   Swylce þær Hunferþ þyle
> æt fotum sæt   frean Scyldinga;
> gehwylc hiora   his ferhþe treowde,
> þæt he hæfde mod micel,   þeah þe he his magum
> nære arfæst   æt ecga gelacum.   Spræc ða ides Scyldinga:

"[Wealhþeow] went forth under gold trappings, with a necklace to the
place where the two brave ones sat, nephew and uncle. Still their kin-
ship endured, each together true to the other. Likewise Hunferð the
þyle sat there at the foot of the lord of the Scyldings; every one of them
trusted his spirit, that he had great courage, though he was not merciful
to his kinsmen at swordplay. The lady of the Scyldings spoke then."
The alliterative patterns here are:

> a a : x a
> x a : a x : x a
> a a : a x : a x
> a x : a x
> a a : x x
> a a : x a
> x a : a x : a x

In the first and sixth lines the alliteration of the off-verses is on the
fourth stress, rather than the third, but in both cases the alliterative
variation introduces lines of three verses, rather than two. The envelope
pattern is consonant with common rhetorical method in the poem. In
the fifth line there is no alliteration in the off-verse unless the pronoun
is stressed (cf. *and mín hláford, Maldon* line 224b), producing a verse
type D_4. While some stringent metrists might be unhappy with this

arrangement of lines 1163–1168, it should be remembered that they are otherwise hypermetrical. It seems that it would be far easier for an Anglo-Saxon reader of the MS to fall into the meter described above than it would be for him to grasp the hypermetrical or unmetrical arrangement given in modern editions.

We stand to learn much by trusting in the overall accuracy of the scribes of the *Beowulf* MS, but the question remains whether our trust is warranted. Sisam concludes his attack on the authority of Old English MSS in general with an argument that, if valid, would certainly undermine, if not destroy, the reliability of the *Beowulf* MS. He says:

> As a last resort, it might be argued in defence of the poetical manuscripts that their authority is confirmed because they have passed the scrutiny of Anglo-Saxon readers, who knew things unknown to us. In fact there is hardly a trace of intelligent scrutiny. It is a curious feature of the great poetical codices that no early reader seems to have noticed the most glaring errors left by the scribe. (*Studies*, p. 38)

In the following sections evidence is presented that will effectively refute this claim. The extensive proofreading done by both scribes, and the nature of their corrections, are proof that the *Beowulf* MS was subjected to intelligent scrutiny. The *Beowulf* MS contains scores of erasures and scores of written corrections. In view of this evidence it is impossible to believe that the scribes overlooked about three hundred blunders, the degree of inaccuracy that current editorial emendations and interpolations would have us accept. The *Beowulf* MS has indeed passed the scrutiny of Anglo-Saxon readers, and they certainly knew things unknown to us.

The Proofreading of the Scribes

There have been few efforts to assess the relative accuracy of the two *Beowulf* scribes, because their general inaccuracy is usually presumed.[24]

24. This presumption is, for example, the sine qua non of S. O. Andrew's interesting chapter "Scribal Error and Its Sources," in *Postscript on Beowulf*, pp. 133–152.

The primary reason for the neglect of this subject is, of course, that the two latest scribes in a transmission of the text over several centuries could present only a tiny slice of the vast material that would have to be weighed for a just appraisal. One's interest in these two scribes, however, should be greatly enhanced as the length of transmission is shortened. If *Beowulf* was written in the early 11th century, these two scribes become very important characters indeed. But no matter when the poem was created, the fact remains that the scribal errors in the extant copy have never been objectively investigated. All previous investigations are based on editorial emendations, which are often persuasive, but never are and never can be purely objective. There are errors that editors have objectively discovered, but their corrections are necessarily subjective; and there are many defensible readings in the MS that editors have subjectively perceived as errors. In short, "proof" of scribal error based solely on editorial emendations is circular, and leads to predictable results. The scribes' erasures and written corrections of their own perceived errors not only isolate real errors, but highlight the kinds of mistakes to which each scribe was susceptible. The greatest value of this evidence, however, is that it proves that the scribes carefully proofread their copy, and effectively discredits the extremely high percentage of error reflected in editorial emendations.

The pitfalls of relying on conjectural emendations of often conjectural errors, rather than on scribal corrections of undoubted errors, are well illustrated in Eduard Prokosch's "Two Types of Scribal Errors in the *Beowulf* MS." On the basis of emendations, many of which are unneeded, Prokosch claimed that "in an overwhelming number of instances the errors of the first part are phonetic, those of the second part, mechanical"; and he reached the remarkable conclusion that the first scribe wrote therefore from dictation (pp. 196–197), while the second scribe copied "laboriously" from a MS (p. 204). His proof is so flexible that, if one did not question the validity of the emendations, it would be equally possible to show that the second scribe wrote from dictation too. Prokosch himself admits that the first twenty-one examples of the second scribe's "mechanical" errors could easily be reconciled with dictation (pp. 204–206), and this is nearly half of the evidence. Much of the remaining evidence is even more open to phonetic explanations than are the twenty-one ambiguous examples, and for that matter, than are most of the examples of the first scribe's "phonetic" errors.

Certainly *bi werede* could be misheard for *biwenede, fela ða* for *se laða, wræce* for *wræte, fergendra* for *wergendra, for speof* for *forsweop,* and *hwæðre* for *hræðre*. Prokosch asserts that it is "difficult or impossible" to give phonetic reasons for the omission of endings, but in fact phonetic explanations do very well here: *helm*[*um*] (syncopation or apocope): *hilderinc*[*a*] and *rond*[*e*] (unstressed vowel confused with plosive stop); *fyrena* for *fyra* (excrescent nasal on the part of the reciter); and *sweordū* for *sweorda* (leveling). The proper names, beginning with *geomor* for *Eomer* (initial diphthong), are easily explained as phonetic errors. And the remaining "symptoms of mechanical copying" are for the most part better explained as phonetic errors: *sec* and *ec-* are occasional phonetic spellings for *secg* and *ecg; mæges* for *mægenes* (twice) shows the omission of a medial nasal, Prokosch's first example of a phonetic error in his discussion of the first scribe; surely *reðes ond hattres* could be misheard for *oreðes ond attres, nis* could be misheard for *næs, wundum* for *wundrum, wat* for *þæt, let* for *leg*. The putative dichotomy between the two types of scribal errors in the *Beowulf* MS, or their causes, does not in fact exist.

The scribes' own corrections of their work, on the other hand, show that they were both copying from exemplars, for the corrections are mostly of common mechanical errors like dittography and haplography. Phonetic errors and the occasional phonetic spellings in both parts of the MS might well have been caused by simple transcription, since it is likely that both scribes read aloud. Silent reading is an early modern phenomenon. If anything, the first scribe seems to have been more susceptible to mechanical errors than the second scribe. At any rate, the extensive proofreading by both scribes unequivocally displays their real interest in *Beowulf*: there can be no doubt that both scribes made determined efforts to present reliable copies. The first scribe's integrity regarding *Beowulf* is manifest in his alertness to incipient error; and this vigilance contrasts with his equally manifest lack of interest in the prose texts of the Nowell Codex, which he also copied but did not even bother to proofread. This marked difference in attitude also implies that the *Beowulf* MS was copied by the first scribe as a separate codex, originally unrelated to the prose codex. But the second scribe's interest in *Beowulf* is even more remarkable than the first scribe's. The second scribe too is clearminded and quick to notice his mechanical mistakes, but there are also signs that he continued to read the text, and to restore damaged parts of it, long after he finished copying the poem. Moreover, he read the first scribe's work with a critical eye, as numerous corrections by him in the first part of the MS testify. On the other hand, there are no signs that he read the prose texts, and his failure to do so further suggests that the *Beowulf* MS was added to the prose codex at a later stage.

The proofreading of these two scribes of *Beowulf* has only recently gained the attention of scholars. But that the scribes themselves made the extraordinarily large number of written corrections in the MS was firmly established by Westphalen, in his absorbing paleographical and textual study, *Beowulf 3150–55: Textkritik und Editionsgeschichte* (esp. pp. 107–108). On paleographical grounds he determined that the first scribe made no fewer than twenty-six corrections by superscript (that is, interlinearly, above the error or lacuna), and ten additional corrections and completions within the lines. Differences in ink and in the shape of the quill tip show that the first scribe's proofreading was done at various times. The second scribe makes twelve corrections by superscript in his part of the text, and thirteen additional corrections and completions within the lines in the course of making his copy. On the basis of the identity of the handwriting along with a dissimilarity in the quill tip, Westphalen posits the use of a "*'Korrektur' feder*" (p. 100), for some additional corrections by the second scribe, and accordingly assigns six superscripts and six corrections within the lines to later proofreading. He also reveals that eleven superscripts and three corrections within the lines in the first scribe's part of the MS were made by the second scribe, though he overlooks the enormous importance of this observation for showing the second scribe's unusual interest in the accuracy of the entire transcription. In all, Westphalen localizes eighty-eight written corrections in the seventy folios of the *Beowulf* MS: fifty-one in the first scribe's part, up to line 1939, and thirty-seven in the second scribe's part, from line 1939 to the end.

Yet these figures, impressive as they are, represent only about half of the evidence of scribal corrections and proofreading, for they do not include erasures. Westphalen deliberately neglected this part of the evidence, for he was concerned with identifying the script of the correctors. He did realize, however, that there were many erasures, and that they normally derived from the scribes themselves (p. 99, n. 111). It could scarcely be maintained that the written corrections were made exclusively by the scribes while someone else did the erasing. In most cases, in fact, erasures can be assigned to the scribe who made them, and so they need to be included in an evaluation of the scribal corrections. There are over ninety erasures. Together with the written corrections, then, we have about 180 positive examples of intelligent scrutiny on the part of the scribes on seventy MS folios. Naturally, erasures and written corrections are sometimes combined, and this overlapping inflates the figures, but the sheer bulk of the erasures and written corrections is testimony to the integrity of the scribes and the reliability of their final copy. The pervasive correction of the MS by the scribes has never been studied, and of course has never been used by any editor to support the authority of the transmitted text. It is highly suspicious that all of the "glaring errors" perceived by modern editors were not corrected by these Anglo-Saxon correctors whose proofreading seems to have been quite thorough.

In the following pages, written corrections and erasures are considered together. While discussing only representative cases of the scribal proofreading, I have nonetheless tried to present a full picture of the nature and extent of the corrections. Most of the evidence is straightforward and fairly well documented in Zupitza's notes. I have, however, independently restudied all of the evidence of scribal proofreading, and I was often able to correct and augment Zupitza's account with aids unavailable to him when he studied the MS between 1880 and 1882. The value of the simplest aid of all, the modern incandescent light bulb, cannot be overestimated. Today it allows the reader of the MS to see the script, even when it is faded, damaged, or covered by the 1845 binding frames, more clearly and uniformly than Zupitza was able to see it. The reader today who does not use this aid will experience the same kind of problems that Zupitza records in his notes: "*metodes?* I thought I saw all those letters pretty distinctly (except the two first strokes of *m*) on the tenth of September 1880, but on no other day. On the 12th of Sept., 1882, I thought I was able to read [*w*]*igendes // egesan*" (p. 144). I first studied all erasures in ordinary daylight (a marvelously protean light in London), then under a high-intensity incandescent or "daylight" lamp, and finally under ultraviolet light. I also tried infrared light, but found it of no special use. Low-level fiber-optic light, which rakes over the surface of the parchment, highlighting imperfections and pebbling, only occasionally helped to identify a deleted reading, and then only when the light was turned up to its full intensity and held directly over the erasure. In most of these cases, however, I achieved the same result with the daylight lamp. Ultraviolet light was most helpful of all when problems arose: in a significant number of cases deleted readings stood out clearly. My reason for determining deleted readings was, of course, to clarify the kind of error to which the scribe in question was particularly susceptible.

THE FIRST SCRIBE

The written corrections and erasures in the first scribe's part of the MS show that the first scribe carefully proofread his work. But they also show that he was generally very attentive not only to the mechanical job of copying correctly, but also to the more comprehensive aspects of grammar, syntax, sense, and even of meter and alliteration. Some corrections show that the scribe cared enough about the accuracy of his copy to note even the minutest errors and correct them. For example, on fol. 130v19 the scribe corrects *sæde* to *sægde* by squeezing a *g* in between the *æ* and *d*.[25] The correction is not, strictly speaking, necessary, since the two spellings are phonetically the same in Late Old English: one must assume then that the correction was made purely for the sake of orthographical conservatism. On the next folio (132r15), the scribe erased a false (and misleading) ligature between the *i* and the *n*

---

25. As Robert D. Stevick has rightly observed, "corrections in the manuscript—additions or changes after further text has been copied—often affect the spacing between consecutive morphs." By studying abnormal spacing features, he discovered a number of fairly certain corrections, which had never been noticed before. Thus on fol. 165r12, the unusually small space between *-drihten* and *selfne* suggested to him that the *n* in *drihten* was added later, a conclusion virtually confirmed by the makeshift ligature between the *e* and *n*. Stevick also infers from the spacing that *g* was added later to *hremig* on fol. 171r8–9. It might be added that although the word occurs in the first scribe's part of the MS, the correction was made by the second scribe, as the distinctive paleographical form of the *g* clearly shows. The second scribe regularly closes the loop on *g* with a hair stroke, while the loop is always left open by the first scribe. In this case the second scribe corrected a spelling variant of the first scribe (cf. *famig/fami*, lines 1909 and 218), not an error. As these two cases illustrate, further study of spacing features in the *Beowulf* MS may well add appreciably to the vast evidence of scribal proofreading of the poem. See Stevick, ed., *Beowulf: An Edition with Manuscript Spacing Notation and Graphotactic Analyses*, pp. xxiii–xxv.

of *caines,* perhaps to avoid confusion between *cames* and *caines.*[26] Minims are often falsely ligatured in insular script (*wundmi* is the most notable example), and the scribe usually makes no effort to disconnect them, for ordinarily no ambiguity results. The correction here, then, is extraordinary, and reveals not only attention to detail, but more important to the sense of the passage. A similar type of correction can be seen on fol. 136v6, where the scribe has altered *fæft* to *fæst* by scraping away the cross-stroke of the *f.* Since insular *f* and *s* are drawn identically, except for the cross-stroke, the error would be hard to notice, and the fact that the scribe has made the correction at all once again shows commendable care for even rather fine details. There are many other corrections of this nature in the first scribe's section of the MS.[27]

The other written corrections and erasures in his section break down into three basic categories: the removal of dittographic material; the restoration of material that was inadvertently omitted or was about to be omitted; and the conversion of legitimate, but contextually incorrect words to the contextually proper words. These three categories provide the most compelling evidence that the scribe was generally attentive to his work while he was copying, and that he later subjected his work to

26. Klaeber mentions in his note to this line that, "according to Irish belief, Cham inherited the curse of Cain and became the progenitor of monsters." *Beowulf,* p. 132. Presumably the scribe noted the possible ambiguity and erased the ligature.

27. For example *m* is corrected to *n* in *bunden* (first *n*) on fol. 158r19, and in *an* on fol. 146v5; metathesis *(cn/nc)* is corrected in *wlonc,* fol. 137r14; occasional spellings are corrected on fol. 135v11 *(ec-/ecg-),* fol. 158v17 *(-un/-en),* and fol. 160v12 *(-en/-an);* an apparent homoeographic error (*wynn* for crossed thorn, the abbreviation of *þæt*) is rectified on fol. 170r19; a point is erased after *mapðum* on fol. 158v14, a cross-stroke on the *d* of *sceaden* is erased on fol. 172v3, and an extra *l* in *sceal* is erased on fol. 170v11. A number of minor dittographs are also corrected by erasure: *gry(r)re* on fol. 158r16-17; *finda(a)n* on fol. 160v2; *eaxlge(a)steallan* on fol. 167v5-6, and probably *st(t)eapa* on fol. 157v3; cf. the "dittophone" *weor(ð)þan* on fol. 167r22. Omitted letters are restored by the scribe in *sidne* (fol. 139v13), *eft* (fol. 143v15), *gehwylcre* (fol. 147v1), *beado* (fol. 154r11), *gesellum* (fol. 162v11), *wearp* (fol. 163v12), *togeanes* (fol. 164r1), *heapo* (fol. 166v6), *geweox* (fol. 167v3), *breost* (fol. 167v10), *fehð* (fol. 168v3), and *gyrn* (fol. 168v21). These examples alone are enough to show that the scribe subjected *Beowulf* to much more careful scrutiny than he did the preceding three prose texts, and they also show later proofreading, since most of the superscripts have been made with a very sharp quill tip, different from the one used to write the text.

careful proofreading. The last category shows special care and intelligence in proofreading, for in order to notice that a meaningful word was incorrect the scribe would presumably have to have checked the context of the passage in which the mistake occurred. Some of these cases are so equivocal that the mistake could have been allowed to stand without seriously impairing the meaning. In such cases it is clear the poem has also been examined with great care. The other two categories also provide valuable evidence of the scribe's attentiveness, for the corrections often show at exactly what point the scribe realized that he was making an error. In most instances, the scribe's lapse of attention was fleeting, and the errors themselves thus help illustrate his clearmindedness while copying.

The removal of dittographic material may be indicative either of later proofreading or of the recognition of an error in the course of committing it. Sometimes it is impossible to tell whether or not the dittograph was noticed immediately, and then it is best merely to assume that the mistake was picked up in proofreading. Instances of dittographs presumably noted and corrected after proofreading are frequent. On fol. 135v15, however, a dittographic *hlaford* has not been erased, but rather crossed out, apparently in the same ink used to copy the text on the folio. In this case it seems that the scribe crossed out the dittograph right after he made it, intending to erase it when he proofread. Usually there are no such clues as these. On fol. 169v11 an extra *to,* still fairly visible in ordinary light, was erased between *æþeling* and *to.* On fol. 141r20 it appears from the very meager traces that a second *man* was erased between *man* and *æfre.* Ultraviolet light showed nothing whatever, but there is no trace of an erased descender below the lower minim line, eliminating the other obvious dittograph, *æfre.* A dittographic *ende* was probably erased at the beginning of line 2 on fol. 168v. As Zupitza says, "*Stæf* cannot well have originally stood at the beginning of this line, but there is nothing in [Thorkelin] AB, between *ende* and *stæf;* perhaps a word *(ende??)* erased before *stæf?*" On fol. 161v13 *ge* between *ge* and *nearwod* is erased, and on fol. 149r20 *moste* is erased between *moste* and *selfes* (here Zupitza conjectured that *selfes* had been erased, but *moste* shows up clearly under ultraviolet). The scribe could have erased these dittographs anytime after the text was copied.

It is not always impossible to tell when a dittograph was noticed. For example, on fol. 146v3 the scribe started to write *sona* a second time, no doubt coaxed toward the dittograph by the combination of the letters, *on a-*, following *sona* in his exemplar. However, we can be sure that he noted his error as soon as he had drawn the *s*, for he has erased the top of the *s*, and used the bottom for the left side of the *o* in *on*. If he had completed the dittograph, there would have been a space between the erased *s* and the *o*, and less of a gap between the *n* of *on* and the *a* of *arn*. The fact that he made the erasure when he did proves that he was quite attentive in his copying at the time of the (imminent) mistake. Another clear example of a dittograph corrected while the scribe was in the process of making it can be found on fol. 154r12–13. Ultraviolet light confirms Zupitza's claim that the words *on bæl* (at the end of line 12) and the word *gearu* (at the beginning of line 13) were erased. The scribe was probably led into the dittograph when his eye skipped from the *wæs* preceding *eþgesyne* to the *wæs* preceding *on bæl gearu* at the start of the same line. But it must be emphasized that although the erasure is not written on, the error was only a temporary lapse of attention. The scribe realized his error after writing *gearu*, or he would have gone on to recopy *æt þæm ade wæs*, as well. A correction of this nature obviously shows that the scribe was, despite his error, attentive enough to his work, and anxious enough to present an accurate copy, to stop copying repetitiously. The examples given earlier from the prose texts showed that he was not usually so attentive when copying those texts. Moreover, he did not even bother to correct all of the dittographs in them, even when, as in the cases cited above, it can be ascertained that he recognized he was recopying material and stopped.

One's confidence in the scribe's work on *Beowulf* also grows by examining the places where the scribe started to omit material, but caught his error and corrected it. A scribe who did not care much about the text he was copying would be sorely tempted to let the omission go, and to continue copying even though he had created a contextual lacuna. An example of this type of carelessness was seen in the *St. Christopher* fragment. There is no comparable evidence of deliberate irresponsibility in the *Beowulf* MS. On the contrary, the evidence suggests that the first scribe was particularly careful not to commit this error. He starts to omit the word *bote* on fol. 133r20: he first wrote *to*, but noted his omission before going on to *banum*, for he was able to convert *to* to *bote* simply by writing a *b* over the *t,* and adding *te.*[28] There are several cases in which the scribe was about to omit considerably more than a few letters. For fol. 147A(131)r6, Zupitza comments: "after *ræste* an erasure of some five letters, of which the first seems to have been *h,* the second was possibly *a.*" Under ultraviolet light, however, the erased material distinctly emerges as *he on.* In all probability the scribe's eye moved down a line in the exemplar after he had copied *ræste.* The same words, *he on,* now properly end line 7. We know that the scribe was immediately aware of his oversight though, for the next word he copies is *ræhte;* if he hadn't noticed his error at once he would have written *feng,* and an entire MS line would have been lost from the text.[29]

There are other less spectacular losses that would have been sustained had the scribe not been alert in the course of making his copy, or had he not proofread his work carefully afterward. A particularly meticulous correction can be seen on fol. 156v13, where the scribe has inserted the word *he* as a superscript between *þeoden* and *under.* The correction is not absolutely essential either to the sense or to the syntax, and the omission does not affect the alliteration or the meter. It is a good

28. Similarly, on fol. 134r9 the scribe first omitted *en* from *healfdenes,* but he noted the omission before proceeding to the next word, so that he was able to change the *s* to *n* by a bit of erasing and overwriting, and to add the *es* where it belonged. At the bottom of the same page, line 19, the scribe started to write *þerf* instead of *þearf,* but noted the mistake as soon as he wrote *r* or he would not have been able to change it to an *a* and write *rf* after it.

29. A more complicated example, but one not open to proof since ultraviolet light was of no use, apparently occurs on fol. 147r14. Zupitza felt that the erasure in this line might have removed a dittographic *feorh,* but the remaining ink traces immediately after *feorh* and before *ealgian* do not support his guess. With the daylight lamp, *ie* seem to be the letters after *feorh,* and *ht* the letters before *ealgian.* If so, the scribe started to skip a line in his exemplar, copying *hie meaht-* from line 15, and using the *h* in *feorh* as the first step in his mistake. After writing *meaht-* he realized what he was doing and resumed copying correctly. If he had not noted his mistake, lines 796–797 would have been collapsed in one line, reading *wolde freadrihtnes feorhie meahton swa.* Alliteration and meter would have been retained, but not a vestige of sense. A similar disaster was averted on fol. 152r14, where the *b* in *beowulf* was corrected from an original *f* (according to Zupitza, an original *w*). The scribe started to copy *feoh,* immediately below *beo-* in line 15, but caught his error before finishing the word. His alertness prevented him from producing a contextual lacuna, a line without alliteration, and a passage claiming that Beowulf had reason to be ashamed of the costly gifts Hroðgar gave him (*no,* "not at all," would have been omitted).

example of responsible proofreading. A far more significant omission is restored, again by superscript, on fol. 168r3. The scribe first wrote *snyttrum,* but later corrected the reading by adding *un-* above the line to read *unsnyttrum.* It was a crucial correction, involving as it does the difference between "wisdom" and "folly." In a case like this, the scribe was probably reading the text, not just mechanically proofreading. It should not be necessary to make such an obvious point were it not for the ubiquitous assumption that the scribes were ignorant of the meaning of what they were copying.

There is an extremely interesting erasure on fol. 140v19. It seems from the FS and from the MS under ordinary light that an *f* and one or two additional letters, the last of which had an ascender, were deleted here. These outward appearances suggest that the scribe's eye moved down a line in his exemplar, and that he consequently began to copy *fah* from line 20. Under ultraviolet light, however, the first letter appeared almost certainly to be caroline *s,* the second letter probably an *œ,* and the third an *l.* The *œ* could have been an *e* that came to look like an *œ* through smudging (perhaps the ink was still wet when the erasure was made); but the amount of space between the *s* and the *l* favors *œ.* The erasure raises some fascinating questions. There is no simple answer as to how the error came about. If the questionable vowel was an *e,* one may conjecture that the scribe unintentionally started to write *medosele,* instead of *medoheal* (both of which mean "meadhall"), by the power of suggestion: he had just written *beorsele* (line 17) and he was about to write *drihtsele* (lines 19–20). Or perhaps he started to copy dittographically from *-sele* in line 17, or to omit the material preceding *-sele* in line 20. In all of these cases, which start from the assumption that the vowel was an *e,* the scribe caught his mistake after writing only *sel-,* and one can conclude with certainty that the scribe's lapse was momentary. If, however, the questionable vowel was an *œ,* the word he first wrote was *sœl,* which also is synonymous with *heal* and *sele,* but in this case there is no obvious explanation for the scribe's error. The word *medoheal* may have been corrupted phonetically to *medosœl,* but this explanation means that the scribe knew the word *sœl,* a word for "hall" that only appears in poetry. If this was his mistake, it implies that the scribe should be credited with more knowledge of the poetry he was copying than he usually is. But whether he wrote *medosœl,* or started to write *medosele,* the erasure is testimony to the scribe's desire to copy accurately, for in either case the scribe deleted a perfectly good reading. The only conceivable reason why he should have gone to this trouble is that the perfectly good reading was not the reading of his exemplar. In the corrections of this kind the scribe dramatically demonstrates that his copy is, or attempts to be, trustworthy.

The remainder of the corrections of the first scribe to be considered fall roughly into this same category. They all convert meaningful, but incorrectly copied words into the right words, presumably the words of the scribe's exemplar, since there would be no reason to make the corrections otherwise. This category does not count false starts, immediately corrected by the scribe. Two examples of false starts occur in line 12 of fol. 169r: instead of *r* in *geswearc* the scribe first drew an ascender, but he erased it; and he first wrote *dryt* instead of *dryht*, but again he corrected the error at once. Another example occurs on fol. 134r5 where he changed *wenan* to *wendan;* both are real words, but *wendan* is the correct one in the context. The spacing informs us that the scribe realized his error before proceeding to the next word. The scribe is to be commended for picking up these errors and correcting them, particularly the last, for it shows that he was clearheaded in the course of copying, and was not content to leave an error even when faced with a recognizable word. A lazy scribe would be inclined to move on, hoping the error would go undetected.

The corrections that properly belong in the third category are of a different kind entirely. They are most impressive because they were made in all probability as a result of unusually careful proofreading. They all involve real words that sometimes even make sense in the context, but are nonetheless noted as errors by the scribe and corrected. Together they tend to prove better than anything else that the scribe was paying attention to sense and syntax, to grammar, and even to alliteration while he was proofreading for mechanical errors. Hence these corrections should most effectively dispel the false notion that the *Beowulf* MS was not subjected to intelligent scrutiny after it was copied.

On fol. 129r10, the letter erased between *hron* and *rade,* which shows up clearly under ultraviolet light, is an *e.* The correction of *hrone* to *hron* shows that the scribe was attentive to the meaning, for a form with final *e* following the preposition *ofer* would not in itself have signaled an error. Thus he must have realized that *hron-* was here part of the poetic compound *hronrade* and accordingly that the inflection belonged at the end of the compound. Presumably the exemplar had *hron,* too, but it is not likely that the scribe would have made the erasure unless he was certain of the meaning of the phrase. On fol. 135v15 the word *hige* was altered from the original word *hine,* "him," by writing a *g* over the *n.* A masculine accusative singular form here is entirely proper, and *hine* even makes some sense if it is taken in apposition to *hlaford.* The error would seem to be hard to detect, and then hard for the scribe to acknowledge. The correction to *hige,* an exclusively poetic term, suggests that the scribe was paying close attention to the sense of the text. Two corrections on fol. 138r17 and 18 lead to the same conclusion. The scribe must have been following the sense and the syntax to change *þis* to *his* and *holdre* to *holdne,* for both corrections involve the emendation of recognizable words. So too on fol. 138v20 the scribe alters the word *heaðorof,* "brave in battle," to *heaðoreaf,* "war-dress." Here the error implies that the scribe was at home with the language of heroic verse, for the erroneous *heaðorof* is an exclusively poetic term, while *heaðoreaf,* the correction, is a *hapax legomenon.*

An analogous case occurs on fol. 139r5. There the form *wæs,* instead of the expected imperative form *wes,* appears followed by a small erasure of about one letter. The interchange of *æ* and *e* is characteristic of the spelling of the poem, but *wes* is invariably the form elsewhere. The spelling *wæs,* therefore, is not technically incorrect, but it is still decidedly unusual. The erasure, when viewed under ultraviolet light, explains why *wæs* and not *wes* appears here. The *s* has been written over the descender of an original *r,* and the second stroke of the *r* and an *e* have been deleted. In other words the scribe, anticipating the next word, *þu,* wrote the second person singular past *indicative* (or *subjunctive*) of the verb "to be," *wære,* instead of the imperative, *wes.* Apparently the scribe made the error thinking he was correcting an error in his exemplar. When he realized that his "correction" was not right, he changed the form back to the imperative but did not change the vowel, nor was there any compelling reason to do so. Obviously the scribe would have no reason to change *wære þu* to *wæs þu* unless he fully comprehended the sense of the passage. A curious parallel to this interesting correction occurs on the next page, fol. 139v2. Under ultraviolet light it is fairly certain that a *t* was erased after *sceal,* and *scealt* is the second person singular present indicative of *sculan.* If the scribe was following the sense of the poem, he might have momentarily thought that Beowulf was again directly addressing Hroðgar, as he does earlier with *wæs þu,* at the beginning of this same speech. In fact, the scribe may have begun to write the enclitic form, *scealtu* (that is, *scealt þu*). In any event, the correction indicates that the scribe ultimately understood the meaning.

The correction of *him* to *his* on fol. 147A(131)r15 is particularly minute, and shows the scribe's desire to preserve the reading of his exemplar, despite the slight change in meaning caused by the error. Thus *ne wæs him drohtoð þær,* "the way was not there for him," might well have been kept in place of the corrected reading, *ne wæs his drohtoð þær,* "his way was not there." On fol. 149r6 he alters *fyrene* to *fyrena* by means of a superscript *a,* thus changing "crime" or "wickedness" from accusative singular to plural, or perhaps only correcting a leveled spelling. There was even less need to change *æt sæce* to *æt sæcce* on fol. 165v3. The phrases are synonymous, and *sæce/sæcce* can be in fact orthographical variants of the same feminine (*jo*-stem) noun, *sæc(c).* The reason for the alteration was probably to distinguish the poetic word *sæcc* from the common word *sacu,* both of which could appear as *æt sæce,* "at strife," in the dative singular. The fact that the scribe made the alteration suggests that he recognized the distinction.

In a significant number of additional cases, an Old English word that does not make any sense in the context has been altered to the right word. Many of these contextually incorrect words are so similar in appearance to the contextually correct words that it is highly unlikely that the scribe would recognize the error if he were merely proofreading mechanically. It seems, rather, that he was reading his copy with comprehension and noticed from the faulty sense that he must have made a mistake. Thus on fol. 148v16 either *cuðne* or *cuðre* was corrected to *cuðe* by erasure. All three are possible inflected forms of the adjective *cuð,* "well-known." In this and the following examples, the scribe's understanding the sense of the passage would certainly help identify an error more readily than would simple proofreading. And in any case a lazy scribe would not be inclined to correct a legitimate grammatical form, nor even to notice that the legitimate form he had miscopied differed so slightly from the form in his exemplar. The large number of corrections of this sort is a fairly sure sign that the scribe was reading and understanding the text he had copied.

On fol. 154v17 the scribe corrects *gewitiað* to *bewitiað* by erasure and superscript. On fol. 155v9 he changes *hunferþe* to *hunferþ* by erasure. Zupitza says "a letter seems to have been erased after this word," and ultraviolet light reveals that the letter was an *e*. The correction indicates that the scribe understood the sense and the syntax of the passage. He is obviously attentive, besides, to alliteration, as his correction of *wide* to *side* on fol. 157r5 shows. The words are synonyms, and there would be no reason for the scribe to make the change if he did not realize that the alliteration had been marred by the error. Other indications of his overall care can be seen in the alteration of *þone*, "that," to *þonne*, "then," on fol. 158r19; in the change of *geseah*, "beheld," to *gesæt*, "sat," by superscript on fol. 161v2; of *mæg*, "kinsman," to *mæl*, "time," by superscript on fol 163v13; of *werede*, "defended," to *wenede*, "entertained," by erasure of the *r* descender on fol. 169v18; of *wac*, "weak," to *wat*, "knew," by adding the top of a *t* to the *c* on fol. 170r5; and of *stefne* to *stefna*, a change in inflection or a correction of a leveled spelling, by superscript *a* on fol. 171v17. All of these corrections strongly suggest that the scribe was reading the text, and recognized an error through the lost sense. All of these mistakes were incorrect Old English words or word forms that bore a close resemblance to the correct words or word forms, and the fact that the scribe uncovered the errors is a tribute to his intelligence and reliability.

THE SECOND SCRIBE

The second scribe played a far larger role than the first in the transmission of the text of *Beowulf*. There are compelling reasons to believe that he read the poem repeatedly over many years and that his prolonged interest in it included restoration of damaged sections as well as corrections. His ordinary corrections can be categorized in the same way as the first scribe's: the removal of dittographic material; the restoration of omitted material; and the conversion of meaningful, but incorrect words, to the proper words in the context. As with the first scribe, there is also a smattering of miscellaneous corrections, some of which overlap with the main categories. Since the corrections by both scribes range from the erasure of a ligature or an extraneous minim to the restitution of a major passage that was about to be omitted, a high degree of confidence in the authority of the preserved MS is warranted. Certainly, the extent of the corrections throughout the MS undermines the rationale for making conjectural emendations in the first place. I shall begin an analysis of the second scribe's proofreading by considering some corrections that have been persistently ignored by modern editors, who have resorted to emending the scribe's corrections.

Emendations of words the scribe actually corrected show a lack of respect for the scribe, though in fairness to the emenders, it must be said that the readings in question present extraordinary problems. One problem has already been discussed in another context: the lack of alliteration in line 1981 forced Klaeber in his edition, for example, to change *side* (the scribe's correction) to *heal*. Basic respect for the scribe, rather than mechanical application of the alliterative rule, suggests that occasional nonalliterating lines were deliberate variations from the rule. Many other nonalliterating lines in *Beowulf*, all of which have been emended solely to supply alliteration, support this conclusion. There is less at stake in the editors' disregard of another correction on fol. 186v21, where, according to Zupitza, "a letter [was] erased between *l* and *a* in *glaw:* that it was *e* is not quite certain." In fact, this case may not even be an erasure, for everything after *gl-* is blurred, and the word may have been accidentally smudged right after it was written. The uncertainty is reflected in the Thorkelin transcripts: A reads *glaw,* while B reads *gleap.* It is remarkable that, while editors accept Zupitza's statement that *gleaw* was deliberately changed to *glaw,* not one editor prints *glaw.* For instance, Klaeber emends *(un)glaw* to *unslaw,* "not blunt, sharp," while the Wrenn-Bolton edition prints *ungleaw,* and wrenches out the dubious translation, "very sharp, very keen" (note, pp. 280–281). These examples are representative treatments of the problem: in the first case, the scribe supposedly changes *ea* to *a,* but mindlessly lets the critical error, *g* for *s,* stand uncorrected; in the second, he mindlessly changes a correct reading. Both explanations presuppose that, in going to the trouble of making an erasure, the scribe blundered.

To some extent it does not really matter here whether the scribe wrote *-gleaw* and accidentally smudged it, or consciously changed the spelling to *-glaw.* The two are variant spellings of the same word, glossed by Bosworth-Toller as "clear-sighted, wise, skillful, sagacious, prudent, good."[30] With the *un-* prefix the word would most probably

---

30. Cf. the variants *gleawnes/glauwnes* in Bosworth-Toller (p. 480).

mean "unwise, unskillful, imprudent," and the like. What seems most important here is the editors' scorn for the scribe, and their prejudgment of the meaning of the passage. Beowulf has just entered the dragon's barrow wielding a sword:

> Sweord ær gebræd,
> god guðcyning,   gomele lafe,
> ecgum ungl(e)aw.
> (2562–2564)

The assumption that *ungl(e)aw* modifies *sweord . . . gomele lafe* is by no means self-evident. The immediate antecedent, *gomele lafe,* is feminine accusative singular, while *ungl(e)aw* is either masculine or neuter, and either nominative or accusative singular. If the word modifies the subject, *god guðcyning,* a direct translation of the passage would be, "The good war king, unskillful (or imprudent) with swords, had already drawn his sword, the ancient heirloom." Editors have naturally resisted this literal translation of *ungl(e)aw,* for it is uncomplimentary to Beowulf; nonetheless the words "unskillful" and "imprudent" accurately foreshadow the outcome of Beowulf's fight with the dragon:

> Nægling forbærst,
> geswac æt sæcce   sweord Biowulfes
> gomol ond grægmæl.   Him þæt gifeðe ne wæs,
> þæt him irenna   ecge mihton
> helpan æt hilde;   wæs sio hond to strong,
> se ðe meca gehwane   mine gefræge
> swenge ofersohte.
> (2680–2686)

"Nægling broke apart, Beowulf's sword, ancient and gray colored, failed in battle. That was not granted to him, that the edges of swords might help him in warfare; his hand was too strong, which overtaxed with its blow each sword, as I have heard."[31] In view of these lines there

31. When Beowulf lies dead, the poet reiterates the theme:
> sweorde ne meahte
> on ðam aglæcean   ænige þinga
> wunde gewyrcean. (2904–2906)
"With his sword he could make no wound at all on that monster."

is no reason to doubt that the poet wrote, and the scribe faithfully copied, that Beowulf was *ecgum ungleaw,* "unskillful with swords." The
only doubt is whether *unglaw* came about through accidental smudging
or careful proofreading.

In order to appreciate the scribe's intelligence, and understand his
efforts to perfect his transcript, we must no longer reject the scribe's
corrections as blunders in themselves. Indeed, the corrections and the
mistakes they rectify need to be examined with more care. For example,
Zupitza inadequately characterizes a complicated correction on fol.
176v20 by saying, *"hladan* altered from *blædan."* There is no attempt
to understand how the scribe came to write the nonsense word *blædan,*
when his exemplar read *hladan.* There are two alterations here—*b* to
h, and *æ* to *a*—and they should be kept separate. The *b* was a simple
mechanical error, a dittograph induced by the initial *b* in the preceding
word, *bel,* and may have been corrected to *h* immediately. In any event
the scribe meant to write *hlædan,* which may be a legitimate variant of
hladan in the scribe's or the poet's speech or spelling. In *Beowulf* the
same variants are recorded for the past participle (*hladen,* 1897, 3134,
but -*hlæden,* 868). Thus, the change of *æ* to *a* may be nothing more
than a spelling normalization; but no matter what it is, it shows the
scribe attending to minor details. If the scribe were ignorant, careless,
and lazy, *blædan* would still be the reading of the MS—and it might not
have been emended to *hladan* by modern editors.

Scribal ineptitude is always assumed in order to explain the correction of *hæðnū* to *hænū* (by erasure) on fol. 173v5. As in the case of
ungleaw/unglaw, editors either keep the uncorrected reading *hæðnum,*
or emend the correction (usually to *hæleðum*). Once again, the implication in either case is that the scribe blundered while trying to make
a correction. Chambers's defense of the uncorrected reading *hæðnum*
includes a rare explanation for such supposedly irrational behavior on
the part of the scribe:

> *Hæ(ð)num* may be a proper name signifying the Geatas, or some tribe
> associated with them. So Bugge, who interprets "dwellers of the heath"
> (of Jutland) in accordance with his theory of the Geatas being Jutes. But
> the evidence of any name corresponding to *Hæ(ð)nas* in Jutland is not
> satisfactory. The *Hæ(ð)nas* would rather be identical with the O. N.
> *Hei(ð)nir,* the dwellers in *Heiðmǫrk,* Hedemarken, in central Scandi-

navia. Warriors from this district might well have been in the service of Hygelac; or the poet may be using loosely a familiar epic name. (p. 97n)

Unfortunately, *hæðnum* would have meant "to the heathens" to any Anglo-Saxon unfamiliar with this hypothetical epic name, and this confusion, Chambers says, explains the scribe's mistake: "The last transcriber of *Beowulf*, not understanding the name, and taking it for the adj. 'heathen,' may then (as Bugge supposes) have deleted the *ð*, not liking to apply such an epithet as 'heathen' to Hygelac's men."[32] The explanation will never do. It is interesting, though, that the explanation depends entirely on the assumption that the scribe understood what he was copying and was following its sense from the beginning of the poem, even though he had only been copying for about forty-five lines. This assumption does not accord well with the overall rationale for emendations, which needs to maintain mechanical transcription and ignorance or indifference to the meaning. But there is a more serious problem: if the scribe did not understand the putative tribal name, it cannot be cogently argued that he deleted the *ð* and arrived at a legitimate variant (cf. O. N. *Heinir, Heiðnir*) by sheer coincidence.

Those editors who emend the corrected form *hænum* have a more logical argument. They believe that the scribe did not finish his correction, that he intended to write in a correction after erasing the *ð*. This explanation is quite possible, though the usual emendation, *hæleðum,* is a bad guess. If the scribe had wanted to make this correction he could have inserted *le* as a superscript between *æ* and *ð*, and *nū* could have been easily converted to *um*. He certainly would not have erased the *ð*, and he probably would have erased the *n*. A better emendation, assuming the correction was left unfinished, would be *(Hygd) liðwæge bær/heanum to handa,* "Hygd carried the cup by hand to those of inferior rank."[33] The poet has made a special point of contrasting Hygd's humility with the arrogance of Offa's queen. The MS spelling *hænum* for *heanum* can be defended as a late Old English occasional spelling showing smoothing of the diphthong *ea* (cf. *-Ræmas,* line 519). Thus the scribe may have knowingly departed from the usual conservative

---

32. See Chambers's edition (p. 97n).
33. Toller Supplement (p. 523), *hean,* 1b: "*of inferior rank:*—Heanra cempa *miles ordinarius.*"

spelling simply to avoid further erasing, just as the first scribe used the unusual spelling *wæs* for the imperative *wes* when he corrected *wære* on fol. 139r5. Once again, there is no reason to assume that the scribe blundered when he made his correction. The fact that he noticed that *hæðnum,* a word that can work in the context, was wrong is striking testimony of careful proofreading.

An especially vexing corrected reading on fol. 172v8, which is always emended in the same way, will help illustrate the range of difficulties that sometimes attend these MS cruces. The scribe is supposed to have written *on hoh nod,* and to have altered the reading to *on hohsnod* by inserting a caroline *s* between the *h* and the *n* afterward. The problem is that *on hohsnod* is lexically obscure, a unique form with no clear pedigree. It helps that a verb was needed in the context: the *-od* ending readily suggested a class 2 weak verb, **onhohsnian,* though its meaning remained obscure, and a past participle was syntactically unworkable. The Bosworth-Toller dictionary lists this hypothetical verb, and glosses it on the basis of the general context, "(?) *to abominate, detest"* (p. 754). This solution, of course, was all admitted guesswork, to fill a lexical void. A believable etymology was needed, and well supplied by the suggestion of a denominative verb, from *hoh-sinu,* "hamstring," with the transferred meaning, "to restrain, weaken."[34] This etymological argument is more persuasive guesswork, but it still ignores a central problem: even if the etymology is accepted, a first preterit, not a past participle, is needed to complete the sense of the passage. Accordingly, all editors emend the corrected form *onhohsnod* to *onhohsnod[e].* Yet this procedure only obscures the problem, rather than solving it. The need for an emendation vitiates the explanation of the word. Whatever the word means, an emendation is insupportable here, for the scribe's correction shows that his attention was directed to an error, and one must assume that he corrected it. Beginning with the reasonably confident assumption that the word was right after the correction, *-snod* must be a strong preterit. Class 6 verbs have an ablaut with *o* in the first preterit, and *a* in the infinitive. There is no strong verb *snadan* recorded, but there is a weak verb *snædan,* "to slice," which apparently derives from *snað,* the first preterit of the strong verb *sniðan,* "to cut." In view of its apparent etymology, the original (or variant) form of the weak verb was

34. Dobbie provides a convenient review of opinion in *Beowulf and Judith,* p. 217.

snadan.[35] Analogy would then account for the strong preterit, *snod*. In short, the corrected MS reading could be a solecism, like the naive preterit "brang" from "bring." This solution is not inconsonant with an educated Anglo-Saxon, though, for in late Old English times such solecisms were in the process of transforming the weak and strong classes of all English verbs. If -*snod* is so understood as an analogical preterit, the verbal compound *onhohsnod* makes excellent sense in the context. The word element *hoh* is not necessarily the substantive "heel," and instead may be related to the adjectives *hohful*, "mindful, careful, anxious, troubled," and *hohmod*, "having an anxious mind, anxious" (Bosworth-Toller, p. 549). The verbal compound *onhohsnadan* can be literally translated, "to cut in anxiety," a meaning that fits the passage in question very well: "Indeed that [the behavior of Offa's queen] cut in anxiety the kinsman of Hemming." The natural preterit was *onhohsnæde* (or -*snade*), but an analogous preterit, *onhohsnod*, would have been a natural creation, paralleled elsewhere in *Beowulf* (*scepede/scod*, lines 1514 and 1887). And the scribe's correction strongly suggests that the scribe understood *onhohsnod*.

These seemingly intractable MS cruces can indeed be solved without resorting to emendation only by relying implicitly on the basic intelligence of the scribe. And it is imperative to trust a MS reading, no matter how extraordinary that reading might be, if it has actually been corrected by the scribe. Editorial emendations of these cruces may seem to be more sound, but this false security is an illusion created by appealing to readings more familiar to us, and by destroying, without any positive evidence, the scribe's credibility. There is considerable positive evidence that the scribe is trustworthy. Many minor corrections have been made by him throughout his section of the MS, and these corrections alone attest to both careful copying and intelligent proofreading.[36] The point can be further demonstrated by grouping corrections in main categories. As with the first scribe, the removal of dittographs reveals much about

35. Cf. *OED*, *snode*, "app. repr. OE *snad*, unrecorded variant of *snæd* . . . related to *sniðan*."

36. See, for example, fol. 174r5, -*dungum/dingum*; fol. 175v2, *sweorð/sweord*; fol. 179r9, *fac/fah*; fol. 187v2, *aglægcean/aglæcean*, and fol. 192v18, *aglægean/aglæcean*; fol. 190r18, *bil/bill*; fol. 190v4, *gemete/gemette*; fol. 193r6, *hetwære/hetware*; fol. 193r10, -*milts/-smilts*; and fol. 193v20, *ongenðio/ongenðiow*.

the attentiveness of the second scribe both while he was copying and again while he was proofreading. The second scribe did not make many dittographic errors, and those he did make he corrected later by erasure. On fol. 176v19 he erased a dittographic *bronde.* On fol. 181r14 ultra-violet light confirms Zupitza's guess that *leod* was erased (presumably an original *ū* was lost in the fire damage at the end of the line). On the verso, line 7, the scribe wrote *gege,* but immediately corrected the second *ge* to *tr,* or he would not have been able to complete the word *getruwode* correctly.[37] Another minor dittograph was averted on fol. 182v16, where the scribe started to write *he* twice. After writing the second *h,* however, he noted his error, erased the long first stroke, and then used the second stroke of the *h* for the first stroke of *y* in *yldra.* Here it is plain how quickly the scribe rectified his mistake. There are only two other certain dittographs in the second scribe's work. On fol. 189A(197)v19 a second *his* is erased at the end of the line, and on fol. 198r9 a second *hyrde* in the middle of the line. There are other possible cases,[38] but even admit-ting these, the second scribe was not as prone as the first to making dittographic mistakes, and none of his dittographs exceeds a single word.

The second scribe was more prone than the first to omit letters, and sometimes words; but, as was also true of the first scribe, he regularly noted his error in the act of making it. For instance, on fol. 176v14 he started to skip *un-* and write *hyre,* but he was aware of his oversight as soon as he had drawn the *h,* which he erased. On fol. 177v13, he started to skip *-ld-* in *scyldunga,* but noticed his mistake soon enough to convert the first three minims of *un* to *ld,* and complete the word correctly. A comparable correction is made on fol. 183r17; the scribe started to omit

37. Zupitza mistakenly says that the *u* (he means the *r*) was altered "it seems, from the beginning of *e.*" Malone confines the dittograph to the *g* (*Nowell Codex,* p. 88), but the bottom of the original dittographic *e* is quite clear beneath the *r.*

38. Zupitza is perhaps right in suggesting that dittographic *manigr (a)* was erased on fol. 176r6, though the "perpendicular stroke" preceding this proposed reading is hard to account for (cf. Malone, *Nowell Codex,* p. 80). Malone is probably right in his ingenious deduction, based on Thorkelin A and B, of an erased dittograph on fol. 182r3: "At the end of line 3, AB have *ge* and a blank space (A) or a dot (B); one may conjecture that the illegible letter was *b,* perhaps imperfectly erased to correct a case of dittography." Ibid., p. 89. A dittographic *to* may have been erased between *hilde* and *to* on fol. 198r11.

the *r* in *wyrme,* but made his correction by writing the *r* over the first two minims of the *m* he had drawn. A correction is made in a similar way on fol. 187r13. He began to write *hefde,* instead of *hæfde,* but the spacing tells us that he corrected the error, by using the *e* as the *a*-loop in the *æ* ligature, before writing the *f,* which is properly ligatured to the corrected *æ.* On fol. 194v15, he was supposed to write *efnde,* but wrote *es-*; to correct his error he wrote an insular *f* over the high caroline *s.* Still another omission noted at once can be seen on fol. 184r8, where the scribe started to write *ungefelice,* but stopped after making the *f* and finished copying *ungedefelice* correctly. Apparently the *f* was erased at once, even though the erasure was not written on, for it would have been difficult to erase the *f* and not damage the *d.*

Sometimes, however, the scribe did not notice that he had omitted a letter or letters at least until after he had completed copying the line in which the mistake occurs, and possibly not until he proofread later. Corrections of this nature are regularly made by superscript insertions, since there would be no room within the line for corrections once the entire line had been copied. An example of an error that, judging by the difference in the quill tip and ink, was noted in proofreading can be seen on fol. 184v16, where the scribe altered *heaðoric* to *heaðorinc.* Another example occurs on fol. 192v7, where *ewitlif* is corrected to *edwitlif* with another pen and ink. On fol. 187r3 the scribe omitted the *r* of *searwum,* but inserted it by superscript very soon after, to judge from the likeness in pen point and ink. The same may be said of the correction of *fæðe* to *fæhðe* on 193v9, and of *mæð* to *mægð* on 195r2. On fol. 196v19 *-gum* had to be inserted above the line after *stren-.* The source of this omission can probably be found in the word *gebæded,* which follows it. The scribe may have confused *strenge* with *strengū.* Because of the lack of spacing between the words, *ge* could be construed with either *strenge* or *gebæded,* and *strenge,* dative singular, rather than plural, is a perfectly good reading here. The fact that the scribe picked up this well-camouflaged omission is excellent testimony to his care for an accurate text. The scribe omitted a few entire words, too, that he also later inserted by superscript. On fol. 186r3 he first wrote, by haplography, *ac ðær,* instead of *ac ic ðær.* He may have thought at first that he was correcting a dittograph in his exemplar, but then realized that he had made a mistake. On fol. 188v13 he omitted *dæg* between *se* and *cuman,* but corrected the oversight, perhaps helped by the lack of meaning and alliteration his error produced. There is an unparalleled marginal insertion of an omitted word on fol. 189A(197)r4. The word *sceal,* flanked by dots, appears in the margin; the place in the text where the insertion belongs is redundantly marked by an *ð* above the line, a colon between *urum* and *sweord,* and a comma beneath the colon.[39] The margin was resorted to here because the *g*-loop from line 3, and the abbreviation for *m* and the high caroline *s* in line 4, did not leave room between lines 3 and 4 for the customary interlinear correction. The usual interlinear correction is made on fol. 193r11, where the scribe inserts *ne wene,* omitted in the course of copying.

All of the omissions discussed so far range from a single letter to two small words. The second scribe was on the verge of skipping a much more significant portion of the text on fol. 192v16. Ultraviolet light confirms Zupitza's impression that *bennū* was erased between *wæl* and *reste.*[40] The scribe wrote *bennum se-* (though possibly without completing the *e*-loop) before he caught his error; the strangely shaped *r* in *reste* is written over *se-* (that is, over a low insular *s* and the main stroke of the *e;* cf. *seoc* in line 18). If the scribe had not been alert, a contextual lacuna would have resulted from the middle of line 2902a to the middle of line 2904a.

The last group of corrections to be considered from the second scribe's part of the MS consists of meaningful words (but wrong for the context) subsequently altered to the correct words. This type of correction, as has already been stressed, is particularly indicative of scribal attentiveness, not only to simple copying, but also to the sense of what he was copying. Some of the corrections are extremely minute, and the errors would have been hard to find were the scribe not meticulously looking for mistakes. He changes the possible oblique-case noun *sine* ("sight"), to the correct word *sinne* ("his"), on fol. 180v8; the string of minims would make the error difficult to find. On fol. 187r14 he corrected *wearð* ("became, hap-

39. In the MS, but not in the FS, there are faint traces preceding *.sceal.* of a letter that Zupitza identified as another *ð* ("which, however, is almost entirely gone"). Perhaps, instead, we have here the "old insular device of *ħ* in the margin answering *ð* in the text," used to mark locations for marginal insertions (Ker, *Catalogue,* p. xxxvi). Two examples of this device can be seen in Ker's edition of *The Pastoral Care* (MS Hatton 20, fols. 63r and 82v).

40. What looks like a point in the FS in the center of the lacuna is actually a hole in the vellum, no doubt caused by the erasing.

pened") to *weard* ("guardian, keeper") by erasing the cross-stroke. He changes *þoñ* (*þonne*, "then") to *þone* ("that") on fol. 189v16, and before he went on to the next word, as the spacing tells us. On fol. 196v6 he has altered *þurh* ("through") to *burh* ("fortified place") by erasing the descender of the *þ*. There are several minor changes in inflection. Thus on fol. 185v2 *an* ("alone") is changed by superscript to the weak declension *ana,* a change reflecting a particularly subtle difference in the meter. Within the line on fol. 189r19 *dogorgerime* is altered to *dogorgerimes,* or from dative to genitive, a change showing careful attention to sense and syntax. The same is true of the change of *maðma* to *maðmum,* genitive plural to dative plural, on fol. 194v3. The spacing shows that the scribe made this correction before proceeding to the next word.

A more significant correction occurs on fol. 182v19, where *forgolden* was altered to *forhealden* by adding *h* above the line and by altering *go* to *ea.* It is worth noting that *forgolden* is not a copying error and that it makes good sense in the context. The word *forgyldan* is frequently used in *Beowulf* in the sense of ironic recompense:[41] in this sense the passage could have been translated, "the sons of Ohtere *repaid* the protector of the Scylfings" (for banishing them). *Forhealden,* "rebelled against," also fits the context, and presumably was the word in the scribe's exemplar, a word he somehow confused in his mind with *forgolden.* The mistake looks like one a clever scribe might make by anticipating the sense. Surely a lazy, unintelligent scribe would have let an error like this stand.[42] A similar case occurs on fol. 184r19, where *hrore* is altered to *hroðre* by means of a superscript *ð*. An inattentive scribe

41. See lines 114, 1541, 1577, 1584, 2094, 2305, 2843, and 2968.

42. According to Andrew, "there is one kind of corruption which our text has escaped, viz. that which is imported by a too clever scribe who thinks that he knows what his author ought to have written and 'mends his book' accordingly. Our two scribes were immune from this weakness; they were conscientious, if unintelligent, copyists who set down what they saw or thought they saw in their book (perhaps itself a copy) without worrying about sense or metre." *Postscript,* p. 145. One could easily argue that the second scribe's cleverness (and comprehension of the text) led to the corruption, *forgolden,* and his desire for a strictly accurate transcript led to the correction, *forhealden.* It might be noted in passing that Andrew's conception of how the scribes worked does not attempt to explain the different spellings in the two parts of the MS; and that his astonishing implication that the scribes' exemplar was *not* a copy would mean that the MS was contemporary with the poem, if they copied what was before them.

could have understood *to hrore* as "too strongly," but instead this scribe corrected the reading to *hroðre*, "joy, benefit." He was clearly following the sense of the text on fol. 189A(197)r13 when he inadvertently wrote *fyrwyrmum* instead of *fyrwylmum*. The error could have been induced by dittography (from *yr* in *fyr*), but it was more plausibly caused by the context of the dragon episode (*fyrwyrm*, "firedrake"). In either case, the correction shows that the scribe noted an error, despite its being an acceptable word in the general context. The same alertness was needed for his correction of *hogode*, "he thought, resolved" (or *forhogode*, "scorned") to *horde*, "hoard, treasure," by erasing the *g* and writing *r* over *o* on fol. 190r21. Only careful proofreading and an implicit trust in his exemplar would lead the scribe to make this correction. On fol. 192v6, he has changed *dæl* ("share, portion") to *dæd* ("deed, action") by deleting the *l* with dots and adding a *d*. *Dæl* could easily be defended in the context. All of these corrections show how careful the scribe was to preserve the readings of his exemplar. He was not mechanically copying a text he did not understand. On the contrary, the combined evidence suggests that he was absorbed in the poem. The bulk of corrections clearly shows that he was neither ignorant nor lazy, that he read the entire poem, that he understood what he read, and that he strove for an accurate transcript.

It cannot be argued that the scribes, by careful transcription in the first place and by diligent proofreading afterward, succeeded in transmitting a flawless copy of their exemplars. But it cannot be argued either that they made and overlooked hundreds of blunders; yet all current editions of *Beowulf* imply this rate of error, for they all contain hundreds of editorial emendations. The scribes' removal of dittographs can give a rough idea of the degree of thoroughness in their proofreading. There is only one dittograph in all the seventy folios that was not erased.[43] In the first scribe's section, the word *hilde* at the bottom of fol. 151r20 is repeated as the first word at the top of fol. 151v. It is even

---

43. Anyone might have erased these dittographs, of course, and, as we shall see, someone other than the scribes altered four fitt numbers by erasure, most likely in early modern times. But the erasure of dittographs implies careful reading of the text, and no one was reading the text carefully (if at all) after the Old English period until modern times. It is quite safe to assume that one or the other of the scribes, who undoubtedly made the written corrections, made the erasures, too.

possible because of its unobtrusive location that this dittograph was noted by one or both of the scribes, yet harmlessly left as a catchword. An erasure at the end or the beginning of the folio might well have been more unsightly than the error itself. But even if *hilde* was overlooked by both scribes, the change of page helps excuse the oversight, and it is, after all, their only oversight of this kind. The scribes' accuracy in picking up omissions cannot be demonstrated so conclusively, for omissions whether real or imagined are equally invisible. However, the cause of an omission is ordinarily homoeography, a mechanical error like dittography, whereby the scribe's eye skips from one word to another because of some similarity. One can infer from their respective interpolations that von Schaubert believed the scribes overlooked forty-one omitted words, while Klaeber believed they overlooked fifty. Sisam would increase the number considerably. Yet we have seen how frequently the scribes have restored letters and words they omitted or started to omit. There is no compelling reason to assume their copying and proofreading in this respect were appreciably less efficient than they were in removing dittographs.

At the same time it should be acknowledged that dittographs can be removed at any time without an exemplar, while omissions are most likely to be restored only with an exemplar. It should also be admitted that the later proofreading was perhaps not a word-for-word collation with the exemplar, for Anglo-Saxon scribes may not have used the rigorous methods of modern proofreading, and Anglo-Saxon readers may not have been troubled by minor, obvious mistakes. Perhaps the scribes picked up any omissions they overlooked while copying (and they noticed many while copying) simply by rereading the *Beowulf* MS, and referring to the exemplar whenever an ostensible problem arose.[44] This procedure is fallible enough, compared to modern attempts at total precision in proofreading, but it is not altogether unreliable when used by an intelligent, interested, and tutored reader, who makes a number of readings. It is obvious from their corrections that the scribes were well-qualified proofreaders of *Beowulf,* and that the proofreading was done

---

44. Perhaps an exemplar was read to a scribe while he checked his copy for errors. Under this method of proofreading, a scribe would be likely to overlook minor errors like the confusion or metathesis of letters, or the ambiguity of sloppy ligatures, but unlikely to overlook major omissions.

in several stages. Under these circumstances, it is improbable that major blunders, like contextual lacunas of any length, would have been continually overlooked. The kinds of mistakes that could be missed again and again are trivial mechanical ones: the failure to make the sign of abbreviation, or to cross an *eth;* an extraneous minim here and there; the omission of a letter or two; confusion between similar insular letters, like *c* and *t, r* and *n, a* and *u,* low *s* and *f,* and the like; false ligatures and spuriously combined letters in general. Errors like these could easily remain invisible, especially to someone who knew the text well.

There can be no doubt that the second scribe came to know the text very well indeed. As already mentioned, he played a larger role in the transmission of *Beowulf* than the first scribe. There is proof that he read it repeatedly over many years, perhaps decades, watching over the physical condition of the MS, and repairing damages as they occurred. A good instance can be seen on fol. 192v2. Something (perhaps dampness that had penetrated the vellum) caused the ink to bleed in many readings in the upper third of the page. Between the first two lines, above the erasure in line 2, the scribe has written the words *eowrū cynne·*. Under ultraviolet light the same words, *eowrū cynne,* emerge with startling clarity in the area of the erasure, which shows that the superscript constitutes a restoration, not a correction. One must assume that the original words deteriorated in time, and that the erasure and restoration were made considerably later than the original transcript. The same holds true for the scribe's extensive restoration of the last page. When the poem still was a separate codex, its outside covers, fols. 129r and 198v, were subject to wear and tear. The damage to the bottom right-hand corner of the first page was no doubt caused by early readers gripping the MS by the corner.[45] The damage to the last page was pervasive. The even fading of the text on this page suggests that it may have been subjected to direct and prolonged exposure to sunlight. In any event, Zupitza noted that nearly all of the text had to be freshened up by a late hand (p. 144), and Westphalen has shown in a convincing paleographical argument that the restorer was the second scribe, who after ten years or so had slightly modified his script in quite predictable ways.

---

45. The vellum has worn thin in this area, and the shine-through from the verso makes the FS somewhat misleading. It is worth noting that ultraviolet light partly confirms Grein's conjectural restoration (see Klaeber, *Beowulf,* p. 1n) [*geong g*]*uma,* for the lacuna on line 18: the first two letters are *ge-*.

The Palimpsest and the New Text of Folio 179

The scribe also worked on fol. 179, lines 2207–2252, long after he had originally copied the text. Zupitza noted at the start of his transcription of this most badly damaged folio: "All that is distinct in the FS. in fol. 179 has been freshened up by a later hand in the MS." In the 1960s Westphalen made the stunning discovery that the folio is in fact a palimpsest, and he once again identified the script as the second scribe's, but written about twenty years later than the original. The ordinary purpose of a palimpsest is, of course, to eradicate an old text in order to provide parchment for a new one. Believing as he did that *Beowulf* was an 8th-century poem imperfectly preserved in a late 10th- or early 11th-century MS, Westphalen was unable to realize the full significance of his discovery: he naturally concluded that the original text on fol. 179 must have been accidentally erased, and that the second scribe made a rather feeble effort to restore the original text. In other words, Westphalen was forced to subordinate his discovery to Zupitza's thesis that the folio had been freshened up by a later hand. There is conclusive evidence, however, that the palimpsest was made for the usual reason, to provide parchment for a new text. The text on fol. 179 is a late *revision,* not a restoration.

Westphalen is probably right that it was mainly the "ungewöhnliche Schriftbild" in general, not any peculiarities in the script, that led Zupitza to assert that all that was legible on fol. 179 had been freshened up by a later hand (Westphalen, p. 41). It is sure, at any rate, that Zupitza never justified his claim on the basis of any dissimilarity in the script. With fol. 179 Zupitza was faced with the sudden appearance of a folio that had been obviously damaged after copying, where clear and distinct letters and fragments randomly stood out sharply in the middle of weak traces and effective gaps, and where parts of lines appeared to have been deliberately effaced while the vellum was wet. He reasonably enough deduced that something had happened to the original text, and that the fragmentary text that remained must have been freshened up by a restorer. Unfortunately, Zupitza never explained his theory. We have only the listing in his notes to the transcript of fol. 179 of sixteen separate cases of letters that he claimed had been inaccurately freshened up. He asserted in these notes, moreover, that the original letters were clearly discernible beneath the mistakes of the restorer. It will be helpful to quote these notes here, since they constitute Zupitza's only explicit justification for assigning the text of fol. 179 to a later hand:

r2: *wintru* is owing to the later hand, the *u* standing in the place of an original *a* (cf. the FS.)

r4: *o* in *ón* written by the later hand instead of an original *a*, which is still pretty distinct

r6: *stearne* is owing to the later hand, *r* standing on an original *þ*

r14: *weoldum* the later hand instead of *wealdum,* the *a* being still recognisable

r18: *fleah* first hand [that is, not *fleoh,* as the MS reads]

r18: *weall* . . . but *w* stands on an original *f,* which is still recognisable

r19: *mwatide,* no doubt, the second hand [but no suggestions for what is beneath]

v2: *fœs* freshened up, but *s* seems to stand on an original *r*

v8: *si* the later hand, but *i* seems to stand on an original *e*

v10: *rihde* the later hand, but *wende* the first

v14: *innon* the later hand, but *o* stands on an original *a*

v16: *fec* later hand, but originally *fea*

v17: *mœstan* later hand, but I think I see an original *o* under the *œ*; *a* also seems to stand on another vowel (*u* or *o*?)

v19: *reorh bealc* later hand, but the first *r* stands on an original *f,* and *c* on an original *o*

v20: *þana* later hand, no doubt; nor do I see any sign of the third letter having originally been *r*

These notes and Zupitza's failure to explain any details of his theory almost inevitably led to the widespread confusion among textual scholars that Westphalen meticulously traces.

Zupitza never hinted at why the original script had all but disappeared, yet surely this stage must be accounted for first, before an overall restoration can be entertained, much less accepted. Since most editors, notably Klaeber and von Schaubert, have mainly depended on Zupitza's FS, rather than on the MS, Zupitza's theory was accepted uncritically by them, giving it a factual status it had not earned. At the same time, no scholar who checked the MS itself was able to corroborate, in every instance, what Zupitza claimed was the original reading beneath the restorer's mistakes. Essentially, the confusion that evolved centered around the sixteen putative errors, and scholars, as Westphalen has shown in embarrassing detail, frequently forgot that Zupitza maintained that *all* of the distinct script, not just the mistakes, had been freshened up. But in fairness, Zupitza must be blamed for the confusion. One often has to guess just what readings Zupitza regarded as "distinct." For example, in line 5 of the recto, Zupitza transcribes *hlæwe*. The reading is hardly distinct, in either the FS or the MS, and most other scholars have seen either *hæþe* or *hope* (the *l* of Zupitza's *hlæwe* is especially unlikely). All that is truly distinct here is part of the *h*, yet Zupitza notes, "very little of *hlæwe* freshened up; the *h* indistinct, *læwe* pretty certain." The implication is that the *h* was not freshened up, but that at least part of *læwe* was. Yet anyone looking at the MS would have to conclude that (if anything) part of the *h* had been freshened up, but nothing after it. Indeed, it seems likely that "indistinct" is a printer's error for "*is* distinct." The notes highlighting the restorer's errors contribute to the confusion, for Zupitza repeatedly asserts that the words in which they occur were written by the later hand, which can (and did) leave the impression that other distinct words had not been freshened up by the later hand.

The state of the uncertainty over Zupitza's theory before Westphalen's work appeared is reflected in Malone's rather surprising decision not to take a definite stand of his own, either for or against the theory, in his own FS. He says:

> This leaf is in bad condition not only at the top and side edges but also on many parts of the surface recto. Indeed, Z[upitza] states categorically that "all that is distinct" in his facsimile of the folio "has been freshened up by a later hand in the MS," and he distinguishes between original readings and changed ones made by this later hand. Others, especially Sedgefield, have disputed Z's accuracy here, finding no evidence in the MS that letters were touched up, though recognizing that this folio, like many others in the codex, shows altered readings. In the following, such alterations are duly signalized, as they are for the other folios, but the reader will be left to judge for himself how much touching up (if any) there has been, apart from changes in the text. (*Nowell Codex*, p. 83)

Obviously, a reader is in no position to make such a judgment on the basis of a FS. Malone's misunderstanding of the theory can be seen, as Westphalen notices (p. 52), in the comment that Zupitza distinguished between "original readings and changed ones." In fact, Zupitza only distinguished between partially or wholly freshened up readings (that is, all that is distinct, whether or not they were restored accurately) and the weak traces of original readings that were not freshened up at all. As Westphalen also observes, it is clear that Malone, despite his seeming impartiality, rejected Zupitza's claim that all that was distinct was in a later hand, for he uses examples from fol. 179 to illustrate some of the scribe's letterforms.

Westphalen's revolution harmonized Zupitza's theory that the folio had been freshened up by a later hand with the opposing theory that the handwriting was the second scribe's. He showed that the second scribe wrote the text on fol. 179, but much later than when he originally copied the other folios. And unlike Zupitza, Westphalen did not neglect to explain why the original script needed to be restored at a later time, for he explained the bad condition of the vellum surface as a palimpsest. In short, Westphalen was the first scholar to address the paleographical issue and the bad condition of the vellum as a single problem. The original text, Westphalen argued, had been deliberately eradicated by scraping, rubbing, and washing down the vellum. The damage to both sides of fol. 179, Westphalen reasoned, clearly distinguishes it from the accidental damage, by exposure, to the last page of *Beowulf* (fol. 198v).[46] The surface of both sides of fol. 179 is napped, which seems to have been caused by scouring the folio with a liquid solution to prepare a palimpsest. Westphalen's description is remarkably corroborated by the sheet collation: fols. 179 and 188 form the outside sheet of the twelfth gathering, yet it is clear that fol. 188 was not subjected to the same treatment that spoiled the text on fol. 179. It follows that fol. 179 was

---

46. Wolfgang Keller had suggested that, if the part of the MS containing the dragon episode once existed separately, there would be a reason for the bad condition of fols. 179r (the first page) and 198v (the last). His explanation ignored, however, the bad condition of fol. 179v. Review of M. Förster, *Die Beowulf-Handschrift*. Wrenn accepted the thesis, still ignoring fol. 179v, and further suggested that the discoloration on these pages "seems to have been caused by the application of some chemical in the attempt to improve their legibility." Wrenn, *Beowulf*, rev. Bolton, p. 12. There is no justification for this claim. The Thorkelin transcripts show that the text was in as bad shape in 1787 as it is today, and no one would have been treating the MS with chemicals before Thorkelin's time. Westphalen's elucidative analysis of these theories is excellent (*Beowulf*. pp. 28–42).

washed down after it had been stitched into the gathering.[47] After a close
look at the vellum of fol. 179, particularly in comparison with its conjugate leaf, fol. 188, one would have to agree with Westphalen that the
folio is indeed a palimpsest.

Westphalen's comparison of the script on fol. 179 with the script on
the other folios copied by the second scribe is exhaustive, and his conclusions are compelling. There can be little doubt that the script on the
palimpsest is still the second scribe's, but with a few notable developments that can be quite reasonably attributed to the scribe's maturity.[48]
If Westphalen's calculations are right, the second scribe was still involving himself with *Beowulf* and the *Beowulf* MS up to twenty years after
he had originally copied it. The question is, What was he doing on fol.
179 of *Beowulf* so many years later?

Westphalen's brilliant investigation of fol. 179 is, by itself, as Malone
has said of the book as a whole, "a landmark in the textual criticism of
the poem."[49] The one shortcoming in the investigation, and one that
Westphalen was ready to admit, was his hypothesis to explain the reason for the palimpsest, and hence the reason why the second scribe was
obliged to "freshen up" the original text in the first place. Naturally
enough, Westphalen could not conceive of a situation in which a palimpsest of a folio from *Beowulf* could have been authorized. He believed
that the MS is a late copy of an early poem: as he says, "Die Urform ist
uns für immer verloren" (p. 17). And if the palimpsest of fol. 179 were
made for the usual reason, the present text on fol. 179 might very well
be an *Urform*. In the face of this apparent impossibility, Westphalen
suggested that the palimpsest was begun by a parsimonious scribe from

47. The alternative is that the original fol. 179 was cut from the gathering and
replaced with the present defective leaf. But this is highly unlikely, first, because the
scribe would not want to dismember the outside sheet of a gathering, and second,
because there would be no reason for the defective text.

48. The development of the *a* form is the most convincing of all: it has gone from
a sharp quadrangular form to a rounded triangular form, resembling a modern cursive
a. Its variants are either rounded or pointed at the top. The incipient development of
this new letterform can occasionally be observed on other folios (when the left side of
the quadrangular *a* is shorter than usual, for example), but the rate of occurrence on
other folios is minimal. See Westphalen's important paleographical study of all the
letterforms on fol. 179 (*Beowulf*, pp. 58–69).

49. Review of Tilman Westphalen, p. 186.

the monastic establishment that owned the *Beowulf* MS. He needed parchment,[50] and *Beowulf* seemed expendable. Fortunately, West-phalen goes on, the mistake was discovered before all of the writing on fol. 179 had been obliterated (and before other folios were similarly spoiled), and the second scribe undertook the task of restoring his earlier work. He did the best he could, but was hampered by the extent of the damage, and by the extent of his own ignorance, inattention, and lazi-ness (pp. 96 ff.).

The explanation for the palimpsest, and so for the need to "freshen up" the text on fol. 179, is almost too chilling to contemplate. West-phalen himself was not committed to it, and admits rather apologeti-cally, "All dies klingt reichlich hypothetisch und mehr nach einem Roman denn nach der nüchternen Untersuchung eines Kodex" (p. 96). Westphalen was only committed to what he had so impressively shown to be true: that fol. 179 is a palimpsest, and that the new script was the second scribe's at a later stage of development. It can now be shown, however, that Westphalen did not in fact prove Zupitza's theory that fol. 179 had been freshened up by a later hand, and that he should have abandoned Zupitza's theory as soon as he realized that the folio was a palimpsest. For something far more important than Zupitza's theory was now before him. Without recognizing it, Westphalen had proved that *Beowulf* was revised on fol. 179 ten to twenty years after the extant MS was copied.

Before considering the new text it is necessary to show why Zupitza's theory, and Westphalen's refinement of it, can and must be rejected. In the first place, if the scribe were merely freshening up traces of his orig-inal script that he was still able to make out, the characteristics of his later handwriting would not be so clear. The unconscious features of his later script would be controlled by the earlier script he was tracing over. There would be no unruly *e* heads, for instance, because there would be no traces of them from the original text. The rounded, triangular

---

50. But parchment was not so hard to come by in England. N. Denholm-Young points out that "the lack of . . . palimpsests in England is perhaps in part due to the prevalence of sheep-breeding, so that there was never any real shortage of writing-material." *Handwriting in England and Wales*, p. 58. Cf. Ker's *Catalogue*, p. lxii.

Plates 14a and 14b. Fol. 179, recto and verso, of the *Beowulf* MS is a palimp-sest. The frontispiece reproduces the recto in color.

weardode . . . hord on hand[e]
lange heold tela . . . þæt þu þa
hrod cyning eald eþel . . . oððe
on organ dropen . . . dracan
sede on hea . . . hord be þeot
fran bæorh se . . . seg uncuþ li
eldū uncuð þah on innan giong . . .
nat . . . hæðnū . . .
hond . . . rince . . .
syððan . . . þ d . . . lacerde
ryne . . . þrores eardode þæt si
d . . . folc biorn . . . þær
bolge þær. xxxii

Nealles . . . weoldū wyrm hordia
ne cræft sylfes willū gede lū . . . ne
reawd ac þon þria nedlan . . .
. . . hæleða bearna hine spue . . .
fleoh . . . hra . . . dæg innc . . .
seg syn sig sona irparde þ
dū gyst . . . bur g hodhwe
se pin

se þær beȝeat sinc eaþe
þam þæs spilena feola inða wynd
ge ferwna spa hy on ȝeardum
ȝumena naþþylc wynmen lafe
ian cynnes þanc hycȝende þærȝe
me diope mad mas ealle lie dead
nam eþan mælu ⁊ ian daȝun
a duȝuðe sed ⁊ lengeſt hpaer
ȝeo mon wihde þær yldan
lycel þæt long ȝeferwna brucan
bioþh eal' ȝeawo puwode on ponȝe
ydu naah niþe benæſre neapo
ptu wæſt þær on innon heþ wyl
ferwna hrinȝa hynde hand yndne
þætcan ȝoldeſ fæt onda epað
hpæ nu hæleð ne mæſcun wyla
hpæt hit an onde ȝode beȝeaton
ud dad fon nam pwonþ bitle eprſcne
ynrna ȝel ⁊ylene liuda minna þanu
is ofȝraf ȝ ſapon fele dream

form of the *a* would not appear, at least not with such convincing regularity, for there would only be traces of the pointed quadrangular *a* to
trace over. The careless stagger of the later duct would disappear under
the influence of the earlier, more uniform and precise writing. It is precisely the freedom and fluidity of the later script that make it possible
to recognize what is different about it in comparison to the scribe's earlier work. The freshening-up theory is obliged to maintain that the
scribe worked without an exemplar, or the scribe would have been able
to restore the entire text. But if the scribe had to move laboriously from
letter to letter, trying to decipher indistinct traces, he can hardly have
written with the freedom and fluidity Westphalen rightly ascribes to his
mature script.

The freshening-up theory also depends very heavily on the scribe's
carelessness, laziness, and inattention. Surely these cannot be factors
here. The scribe's only task was to try to restore a damaged folio, not
copy an entire codex. Yet according to Zupitza's readings (which Westphalen accepts) the scribe inaccurately restored no fewer than sixteen
letters, which are supposed to be still clearly visible beneath the mistakes. The percentage of error—nearly one blunder every two and one
half lines—is staggering, particularly if the correct readings are still distinct today, one thousand years after the scribe made his meaningless
blunders. The scribe's ignorance of his own language is no less remarkable. On the recto, lines 12–13, he is supposed to have freshened up
þæt he gebolge wæs, rather than *þæt he gebolgen wæs,* equivalent to
writing today "that he was enrage" instead of "that he was enraged."
On the verso, line 16, he is supposed to have mistakenly freshened up
fea worda cwæð, a common expression meaning "he spoke few words,"
to *fec (-)orda cwæð.* The *w* in *worda,* Zupitza tells us, was not freshened up. Today in the MS (or even in the FSS), the traces of the *n* in
gebolgen, the *a* in *fea,* and the *w* in *worda,* are all quite distinct, and
they must have been at least as clear a thousand years ago. The best
explanation for these traces, and others like them, is that the ink of the
new text sometimes failed to adhere properly to the palimpsest. A likely
reason for this is that the palimpsest was used too soon after its preparation, so that in its damp state it was unable to retain the ink
uniformly.[51]

---

51. Denholm-Young notes that parchment could be cleaned "without pumice stone
with a preparation of cheese, milk, or flour." *Handwriting,* p. 58, n. 5.

Excluding for the moment the first line and a half of the verso, and the large gaps on the recto in lines 5, 8–12, and 18–21, which together present a markedly different appearance, this explanation would account for the general appearance of the text, both recto and verso. On the recto the ink is diluted, and often blurry. In line 2, for instance, the first half of the line is in a strong, deep brown, but from -*tig* on, the ink becomes a faded rusty brown. The fault lies in the condition of the vellum when it was written on, not in the ink. A damp palimpsest fits the circumstances. On the verso the ink is generally much darker, and is seldom diluted or blurry. The difference in appearance is no doubt attributable to the difference in texture and absorbency between a hair and a flesh side. On the verso the ink seems to have flaked off frequently, leaving faded traces of the original ink behind. Sometimes an entire word was affected, as in *fæt* v2; sometimes part of a word, as in *ær* in *seðær* v9; sometimes an entire letter, as the *w* in *worda* v16; and sometimes only part of a letter, as the *a* (that consequently looks like a *c*) in *fea* v16. Once this kind of damage to the text on the verso is recognized, most of the scribe's myopic blunders are cleared up. The so-called *c* in *fea* can be used as an illustration. It is not a *c* at all, but a partly damaged *a*. There is no other *c* like it on the folio. An especially appropriate comparison can be made with *fæc* v11, which provides an authentic *ec* ligature. Then, to see what happened to the *a* in *fea,* it is helpful to compare the *ea* ligature in *gearo* v12, for the right side of the *a* furnishes a striking parallel. If the ink of the off-stroke had failed to hold to the vellum, it would appear that the scribe had falsely freshened up *gea-* to *gec-*. Many of the scribe's supposed blunders on the verso are nothing more than *trompe l'œil* of this kind, which have established themselves as MS readings.

There is a legitimate doubt, then, that the scribe falsely freshened up some letters. A new transcript of the folio will show that there is no reason to believe that any letters were falsely freshened up, and this is the only evidence Zupitza explicitly gives that the folio was freshened up at all. A close examination of the gaps in the first line and a half of the verso, and in lines 5, 8–12, and 18–21 of the recto, will show that the palimpsest was not just partly freshened up. These gaps were definitely made by rubbing off parts of the text *after the palimpsest was written on.* The FSS give a very inaccurate impression of the gaps on the recto. They suggest that the writing in the gaps has simply faded away, and the overall appearance of the ink on the recto reinforces this false impression. Actually, the gaps were heavily rubbed while the vellum was damp, leaving them uniquely discolored and napped. Once again, a likely reason for the damage is that the palimpsest was written upon too soon after it was prepared, while it was still damp. As a result, the ink in these areas may have blotted or run together, and if the scribe then tried to erase the mess, the combination of fresh ink and damp vellum would account for the gray discoloration and the napping that characterize these gaps. Under ultraviolet light the gray discoloration of the gaps is sharply accentuated, which suggests that it derives from ink that has permeated the vellum. If the gaps were made when the general palimpsest was prepared, there would be no reason for them to stand out under ultraviolet light.

But there is clearer proof that the gaps were made after the new text had been written on the palimpsest. The gap in line 5 between *hea* and *hord* can be used as an example. The heaviest rubbing is confined to the upper and lower extremities of minims, so that part of an ascender has not been rubbed off in the middle of the gap, and clear traces of a descender are visible toward the end of the gap. Zupitza and Westphalen argue that the ascender was partially freshened up, but this is an untenable argument: no matter what the letter originally was, the scribe would know that he could safely freshen it up at least as far as the lower minim line. The question is settled by the fact that the gray discoloration of the gap has left a filmy residue over the dark brown *a* in *hea-*. Obviously, *hea-* must have been written before the rubbing that follows it. Hence the palimpsest at one time contained a full text, but some of the new text, for whatever reason, was subsequently erased a second time. Thus, the text on the palimpsest was not partially freshened up, but partially obliterated after the new copy was finished.

The great lacuna between *sc(ea)pen* r21 and *sceapen* v1, as well as the gap on v2, are of extraordinary interest. The gap after *sc(ea)pen* on the recto is not accurately represented in the FSS. It is part of a large, interconnected erasure, typically discolored, which winds its way back through lines 20, between *gyst-* and *br(o)g(a)*, 19, between *syn-* and *-sig,* and 18, between *fleoh* and *þea-,* and even includes in its snakelike progress the *ea* in *sc(ea)pen*. It does not include the gap at the beginning of r21, which is not discolored. On the other hand, the FSS are quite accurate in representing the appearance of the gaps in the first line and a half of the verso, even including the gray discoloration. Here the rubbing has not napped the vellum, as it has on the recto, though it has made the vellum extremely thin (what looks like a point before *sceapen* v1 in the FS is in fact a tiny hole). Some of the erased letters in line 1 are still quite distinct, despite the rubbing and the discoloration, and some can be identified with confidence. This alone shows that the erasing must have been done after the new text was copied on the palimpsest, for there is no conceivable reason why some of these letters would not have been freshened up with the rest of the page. Moreover, the ink in some of the traces is still strong enough to identify as that used throughout the verso. The general appearance of the gaps on the verso thus substantiates the view that the palimpsest at one time contained a full text, part of which was later deliberately effaced.

The writing that can be recovered with relative certainty from line 1 of the verso is: *roga s . . . (fyren) sceapen.* The second stroke of the *r* in *roga* is clear and distinct, even in the FS; the first stroke, the descender, is faint and partly covered by the paper frame, but the letter as a whole seems clear enough. The *o*, like many of the *o*'s on the folio, is angular (cf., for example, *ongan* r4, *folc* r12, *on* v4), though not as angular as the FS suggests. The bottom is faint, but all sides close. The shape of the *g* is slightly distorted by the discoloration, but clear traces of the large descending loop unequivocally identify the letter in the FS as well as in the MS. In the MS the *g* loop is emphasized by the pattern of the discolored erasure. In the MS the top-stroke of the *g* is also easy to see, though part of it coincides with a torn edge of vellum. The next letter, *a,* is exceptionally clear both in the FS and in the MS. It is the scribe's later, rounded *a,* very much like the one in *mwatide* r19. After a space of 5 mm. there is a low insular *s.* For the next 30 mm. no letters can be identified with any certainty from the many traces of ink (the darkest of which, above *se* v2, is mainly a shadow in the FS, from a deep wrinkle in the vellum). Then, directly above the high *e* head in *fœr* v2, there is an *f:* the top of the vertical descender and the top-stroke are clear, and there is a trace of the cross-stroke at the minim line. All that remains of the next letter is a single minim, yet it leans leftward, which suggests that it is the first stroke of *y.* There is no trace, however, of the hairline (the second stroke of *y*) nor of the dot. The next letter is surely an *r,* with both descender and minim stroke intact. The remaining discolored ink mass is the *en* ligature, which is clearer in the MS than in the FS: the high *e* head is faint, but recognizable, and the bottom of the *e* hooks in to meet the first minim of the *n*, all of which is quite distinct. As mentioned before, the point preceding *sceapen* is actually a hole in the parchment.

The reason this text was deliberately erased from the palimpsest is that it is a dittograph from lines 20–21 of the recto: *br(o)g(a) stod hwæðre / . . . sc(ea)pen.* A dittograph, in this case, is not by any means useless, for the lost word before *sc(ea)pen* on the recto can be restored as *fyren,* and the conjectural *o* and *a* in *br(o)g(a),* and the *ea* in *sc(ea)pen* are confirmed. The measurements between *broga* and *sceapen* corroborate these conclusions. The gap between *-roga* and *sceapen* on the verso is 57 mm. The gap between *broga* and *sceapen* on the recto cannot be so precisely measured, because it splits between lines 20 and 21, but a conservative estimate can be made. From the end of the traces of the *a* in *broga* to the end of the vellum in line 20 measures 39 mm.; and from the start of line 21 to *sceapen* measures exactly 20 mm. Thus the measurement of the gap between *broga* and *sceapen* on the recto is 59 mm., compared to the 57 mm. between *-roga* and *sceapen* on the verso. Moreover, there are 20 mm. from the beginning of *fyren* to *sceapen* on the verso, which corresponds exactly to the 20-mm. gap before *sceapen* on the recto, line 21. The ink traces are extremely faint, and the vellum badly napped, in this area on the recto, and there is a danger of seeing here what one is looking for. But the one piece of dark ink at the beginning of the gap looks like the top of an *f,* which is followed by a faint diagonal (the first stroke of *y*), and then by a short descender (the first stroke of *r*), the extremity of which survives as a point. Certainly the meager vestiges of the original writing in this gap do not disprove *fyren,* while they suggest it to anyone admittedly looking for *fyren.*

Possibly *sceapen* was left on the verso as a catchword, to indicate that, despite the appearances, nothing had been lost from the text between the two *sceapen*'s. The apparent problem with this explanation is that it would mean that nothing had been lost from the text after *sceapen* on the recto. It would mean that everything after *sceapen* on the recto had been deliberately deleted, and that despite the physical gaps in the MS from line r21 to line v2, there is no *contextual* loss to the text. The text itself supports the theory, for *hwæðre fyren-sceapen* is an on-verse, and *se fær begeat* is an off-verse, and the line as a whole is metrically and alliteratively sound. Nor is the syntax (adverb, object, subject, verb) unusual: in fact, it is exactly paralleled in *ða hie se fær begeat,* "when disaster befell them" (line 1068). Thus, *hwæðre fyren-sceapen   se fær begeat* may be translated, "yet disaster befell that crime," or "sought out that wicked deed," or the like. If there is no textual lacuna between *sceapen* on the recto and *se fær* on the verso, the material that was erased before *se fær* in line 2v must have been identical with whatever followed *sceapen* on the recto. In other words, the erased text in line 2 continued the dittograph begun in line 1 of the verso. Whatever this may have been was permanently deleted from the text, and the scribe, to show that nothing had really been lost, left *sceapen* as the catchword.

The huge dittograph may not have been a mistake, however. As the investigation of his corrections and erasures shows, the scribe was not prone to making dittographic errors, and none of his other repetitions exceeds a single word in length. It is hard to believe that the scribe made such a gross blunder here, when all he had to copy was a single folio. And there is no need to assume that a mistake has been made, for the problem can be explained in terms of the damage that occurred to the new text on the recto, after it was written on the damp palimpsest. The revised text of fol. 179 was shorter, by about two lines, than the original text it replaced. The scribe began copying the new text on the recto, but by the time he had finished it was evident that parts of the text (on lines 5, 8–12, and 18–21) would have to be erased and rewritten, because of the unsatisfactory way in which the ink had adhered to the damp vellum. This explains why parts of the text were erased in these areas after the new text was written on the palimpsest. And since the scribe had about two extra lines on the verso, he recopied in the first line and a half some of the damaged text from the recto. A restoration of the damages on the recto was never carried out, of course, but apparently was in progress when the scribe later erased the dittographic material on the verso. The hypothesis is complicated, and not susceptible to proof, but the evidence itself is dreadfully complicated, and it needs to be accounted for in some believable way.

Because the bulk of this evidence has not been available before, and because it materially affects one's view of the text on fol. 179, a new transcript of the folio is necessary. The transcriptions, which sometimes differ from Zupitza's, are based on a painstaking analysis of the folio under high-intensity light, an invention Zupitza could not have used. The value of a strong and stable light source should not be underestimated: it produces stable ink traces, while natural light, even direct sunlight, produces disturbingly variable traces, as even Zupitza acknowledged. High-intensity light undoubtedly gives us the best view of the text available to the naked eye. Ultraviolet light, with the exception of one reading, did not enhance this view, but it is quite possible that other technological means now available will. For instance, qualified scholars must be urged to try, using up-to-date techniques and equipment, infrared photography as well as electronic photography and digital image processing.[52] These methods are very likely to enhance the ink traces and firmly establish some currently disputable readings. Until these methods have been tried it is undesirable to pretend we have an established text for this folio. High-intensity light alone undermines the "received text" established by Zupitza a century ago. With variable lighting, what Zupitza saw, or thought he saw, in the MS was certainly affected by his belief that the original text had been freshened up, often inaccurately, by a later hand. While his transcript of the folio is basically accurate, his theory, particularly with regard to the supposed errors of the later hand, caused him to misrepresent the MS in some places. Along with the following transcriptions, Zupitza's readings will be discussed where they are felt to be wrong. To avoid confusion, purely conjectural restorations are not made in the transcript, and doubtful readings are placed within parentheses. The Thorkelin readings—at the end of the lines on the recto, and at the beginning of the lines on the verso—are separated by open parentheses to facilitate reference to the FS or the MS.

r1: *beowulfe brœde rice on hand ge (hwearf.* Except for *brœde,* which Zupitza transcribes as *brade,* the FS is good. The high *e* head is very faded, and covered by the transparent paper strip that holds the folio to the paper frame, but it is still visible in the MS under strong light. Both Thorkelin transcripts read *brœde,* from a time when the reading was not obscured by the transparent paper strip. The *e* tongue

---

52. For recent discussions of the value of these methods in the study of palimpsests, see *Applied Infrared Photography;* and John F. Benton, Alan R. Gillespie, and James M. Soha, "Digital Image-Processing Applied to the Photography of Manuscripts: With Examples Drawn from the Pincus MS of Arnald of Villanova."

of the *œ* has not faded, and Malone mistook the distorted remnants of this original *œ* as a unique example of an "oc" type of *a* (*Nowell Codex*, p. 84); but the same argument could be made for the *œ* distorted by fading in *wœs* r13. No special explanation is needed for the fading of the *e* head, in view of the similar fading in *rice on*, and throughout the folio in general. The spelling *brœde* (for *brade*) is the first of many linguistic or orthographic anomalies on this folio. Together they reflect the incipient breakdown of the Late West Saxon literary dialect, in the intrusion of late (seemingly Northern) dialectisms. In other words, the language (or the spellings), as well as the handwriting, is later on fol. 179 than it is elsewhere in the MS.

r2: *hege heold tela fiftig wintru wa(es ða.* Zupitza says that the *u* in *wintru* is "standing in the place of an original *a,*" and he may be right. All that is certain is that the scribe finally intended the letter to be a *u*, which is another late linguistic anomaly on the folio. As Malone says, "The *u* of *wintru* 2 is an alteration of *a* and reflects the speech of someone in whose dialect *fiftig* did not take the partitive construction" (*Nowell Codex*, p. 84). The form *wintru* is an analogical (neuter) plural, and there is no need for a specific genitive inflection. Uninflected *winter* is common. The ink is a strong, dark brown for the first half of the line, but from *-tig* it becomes a diluted, rusty brown.

r3: *frod cyning eald eþel weard oðða(et.* As Zupitza says, the "*w* in *weard* looks very much like *þ*," but it is not a *þ* (*pace* Malone, *Nowell Codex*, p. 84), as a comparison with the scribe's other *þ*'s will show. From *eald* on the ink becomes diluted.

r4: *ón ongan deorcū nihtū draca (rics[i]an.* There is no trace of an original *a* beneath the *o* in *ón*. The word is apparently a very early example of the linguistic and orthographic transition from *an* to *on*. The ink begins to fade in *deorcū*, and is decidedly diluted in *nihtū draca*.[53]

---

53. Malone is well worth quoting for the Thorkelin reading at the end of the line: "A ends the line with *rics an* (his *s* is on an erasure); B first wrote *ric an* and the *s* that Thorkelin, years later, inserted after *c* was probably got from A; it seems likely that the MS had *ricsian*, with a second *i* so faded that A and B saw only a blank space there; the word is now gone." *Nowell Codex*, p. 84. In view of the evidence from the Thorkelin transcripts it would be wrong to charge the *Beowulf* scribe with a blunder here.

r5: *seðe on hea(um hæþe) hord be weot(ode.* This is the first line in which part of the new text was rubbed off afterward, leaving the vellum napped and discolored between *hea-* and *hord.* As mentioned earlier, the rubbing left a light gray film over the dark brown ink of the *a* in *hea-,* and has also seemed to affect the strength of the ink of the *h* in *hord* at the other side of the gap. The FS is misleading in that it does not show the roughness and the discoloration of the vellum in the gap, nor the grayish film on the *a* of *hea-,* which proves that the rubbing was done after the new text had been copied. Under high-intensity light, the erased letters, *-um hæþe,* seem certain. As in the first four lines, the ink on the right side of the page is considerably more faded, or diluted, than on the left side.

r6: *stan beorh stearne stig under la(eg.* The FS is accurate. The first stroke of the *r* in *stearne* is particularly dark, with a slight gloss to it; the second stroke is dark only at the top, making it look as though an insular *s* was written over an original *r.* This *r* is remarkably like the *r* of *fær* v2, which Zupitza says is "*fæs* freshened up, but *s* seems to stand on an original *r.*" In both cases the off-stroke of the *r* has faded, probably because the scribe was applying less pressure to his pen as he finished the letter. Both *r*'s have unusually long descenders.[54]

r7: *eldū uncuð þær on innan giong· nið(a.* The FS is fairly accurate, except that it does not show the bleeding of the ink beneath *-cuð,* which may be a mild indication of the kind of bleeding that necessitated the deliberate removal of readings in the gaps. The faintness of the *i* in *nið-* at the end of the line, moreover, is caused by the transparent strip that holds the folio to the paper frame, rather than by fading. The ink is somewhat diluted in *-dū* and *-iong,* but on the whole the strength of the ink throughout the line is unusually uniform (dark brown, with a slight gloss). There is a ligature between the two *n*'s of *innan,* and beneath the last stroke of the first *n* there is an erased descender; together, they suggest that the scribe wrote an insular *s* or *f,* but immediately corrected his mistake. In the FS, the erased descender appears to

---

54. Malone is right that, contrary to what Zupitza says, there is no sign of an original *þ* beneath the *r,* and that "we must emend to get a reading that makes sense." *Nowell Codex,* p. 84. A possible reading is *stanbeorh stear[c]ne,* "stark" or "severe rocky cliff," rather than *steapne,* "steep." The first minim of the *n* has almost a *c*-like bow, and the scribe may have inadvertently made an *n* from the first stroke of his *c.*

float between r7 and r8, but in the MS it seems clearly to come from beneath the first *n* of *innan,* r7.

r8: *nathwylc (se þe ne)h gefeng hœðnū ho(rde.* The FS is good for showing the extant traces. Everything between *nat-* and *hœðnū* was rubbed off, but not as much heavy rubbing was done over *-hwylc* and *gefeng,* and both can be read in the MS with relative certainty. Sedgefield in his edition, and more recently Westphalen (p. 45), construed the erased descender from r7 as an ascender in r8, and read *geþrang* instead of *gefeng.* A glance at the FS will show that there is not enough room for *geþrang.* The rubbing in this line, as in r5, stays for the most part within the confines of minim strokes, so that the ascenders of the *h* and *l* of *hwylce,* the point over the *y,* the ascender of the *h* preceding *gefeng,* and the three descenders in *gefeng* are all clearly visible.

r9: *hond (ge:r::::m:::) since fa$\overset{h}{c}$ ne (he þ.* The ink is very dark, almost black, in *hond* and *sin-,* after which it becomes diluted, and is especially weak in *ne.* The discoloration caused by rubbing off the text in the gap has left a gray film, which can be clearly seen in the MS in any light, on the *s* of *since.* Again, this proves that the rubbing was done after the new text was written onto the palimpsest. A letter (perhaps *h*) seems to have been erased after *fa$\overset{h}{c}$.* In this line and throughout my transcription a colon represents an illegible letter.

r10: *syððan (:::::) þ(eah) ð(: le::)slœpende (be.* The FS is fairly reliable. The ink is very dark, again almost black, at the beginning of the line, and also for the letters *þ* and *ð* and the ascender after *ð,* in the gap. The rubbing was done around the *ð* and beneath the ascender of the *l* in *le::* (Zupitza suggests that this word is *he,* but there are more ink traces after the ascender than a minim and an *e*). The *þ,* however, was written *over* the rubbed and discolored vellum; presumably the scribe tested the vellum's ability to receive new writing after the rubbed area had thoroughly dried. The vertical stroke (not mentioned by Zupitza) immediately before the *s* of *slœpende* appears to be a high caroline *s.*

r11: *syre(d hrœde) þeofes crœfte þ si(e.* The FS is generally clear; the ink is diluted except in a few places where the vellum is napped, and has absorbed the ink (the *r* in *syre-, es* in *þeofes*). The restored reading, *hrœde* ("quickly"), can be read with confidence, though the usual restoration is *wurde*. The spellings *hrœde* (instead of *hrœðe, hraðe*) and *sie* (instead of *sio*) are unique to fol. 179, and thus are part of the evidence that the text on this folio constitutes a more advanced stage of the Late West Saxon literary dialect.[55]

r12: *ðiod (onfand) bufolc beorn(a) ꝥ hege.* The FS is quite reliable, aside from failing to show the abrasions on the vellum between *ð-* and *-folc.* The readings *-iod* and *bu-* are faint but distinct in the MS. Between them, the usual restoration, *onfand,* is highly probable. *Bufolc* (cf. *bifylc*), "neighboring people, region," is another linguistic anomaly on the folio. The *a* in *beorn(a)* may be *ū* (that is, *um*) instead.

r13: *bolgen wœs. XXXII.* The FS is accurate. The *n* in *bolgen* is faded, but still quite distinct in the MS and the FS. The faint marks between *wœs* and the fitt number are shine-through from the verso, but the condition of the vellum here suggests that the original text (before the palimpsest was made) may have extended beyond *wœs,* and perhaps up to a few millimeters of the fitt number.

r14: *Nealles (nœs) ge weoldū wyrmhorda(n).* A critical new reading in my transcript is *nœs* for Zupitza's *mid.* The *n* is distinct. What Zupitza mistook for the third minim of an *m* is the *a*-bow of an ash, which also is distinct, and may be fruitfully compared with the ash in *wœs* immediately above it in r13. What Zupitza took for an *i* is the main bar of the digraph: the *a*-loop to the left is triangular, and the *e*-loop to the right is large and unruly, like many of the *e*-heads on the folio. A millimeter to the right of this *e*-head (which Zupitza mistook for the tail of a *d*) there is a high caroline *s,* faintly visible even in the FS. In the MS, some rusty brown ink traces are still intact on the *s,* especially at the top and at the slight jag at the base of the curve (upper minim line).[56] As Malone says, there is no indication that the *o* in *ge-weoldum* is written over an original *a;* the spelling may be viewed as

---

55. Sisam makes the relevant point that dialect begins to intrude more often into the standard Late West Saxon literary dialect as the 11th century advances (*Studies,* p. 153).

56. Zupitza's very doubtful reading, *mid,* which all editors accept, left the principal clause without a verb; this in turn obliged the editors to emend MS *wyrmhorda crœft,* which was almost certainly *wyrmhordan crœft* before the edge of the MS crumbled, to *wyrmhord abrœc.* Surely a sounder procedure would have been to emend or reject the reading *mid.*

the common Northern confusion between *ea* and *eo*. The large capital
N at the beginning of r14–15 is very dark, though, as the FS shows,
some of the ink has flaked off. The FS also shows that the vellum
beneath the capital is very rough, and the shape of the roughened area
suggests that the *N* may have replaced a different capital (perhaps *H*
or *W*) from the original text. A minim overlooked by Zupitza at the end
of the line is presumably part of an original *n*.

r15: *cræft sylfes willū seðe hī sare (ge.* The FS is good; the ink in
sa- is very faded, while in *-re* it is very dark.

r16: *sceod acfor þrea nedlan þ(e::) nat.* The FS is fairly trustworthy. The lack of rulings on the palimpsest is most evident in the FS
by the way *sceod* is out of alignment with the words that follow it.
Whatever came after the thorn *(egn, eow, eof?)* was not rubbed off
deliberately, for the vellum is neither discolored nor abraded. Apparently the ink failed to adhere to an improperly prepared surface (after
the *a* in *þrea*, the ink becomes increasingly diluted and blurred).

r17: *hwylces hæleða bearna hete sweng(eas.* The FS is good.
Zupitza says, "*hwylces* not freshened up," but it seems rather that it
has been rubbed off, napping but not discoloring the vellum. On the
other hand, *-arna hete* is faint and blurred, but the parchment is not
napped.

r18: *fleoh (::::) þea(rfa) 7ðær inne weal(l.* Zupitza says that
the *o* in *fleoh* stands on an original *a,* but there is no trace of this *a.*
The spelling of the MS, as Malone suggests (*Nowell Codex,* p. 85),
should be seen with *geweoldum* r14 as an example of the Northern
orthographical confusion between *ea* and *eo*. The same explanation
may account for *weall* (instead of first preterit *weoll*), at the end of the
line (from *weallan,* "to boil"?). The reading *weall* is confirmed by both
Thorkelin transcripts, though it is usually emended to *fealh,* on
Zupitza's claim that *f* was falsely freshened up to *wynn*. Indeed, the
wynn may have been written over an original *f,* for the *wynn* is a bit
distorted (though less so in the MS than it appears in the FS); but since
there is no change in ink there is no justification for Zupitza's claim. If
anything, it should be viewed as a correction. The gap begins the ser-
pentine erasure that ends at the end of r21. The reading *þearfa* is relatively sure in its entirety.

r19: *secg syn(by)sig sona mwatide ꝥ (::::).* The long, discolored
erasure that begins in r18 between *fleoh* and *þearfa* cuts through the

line between *syn* and *-sig,* though *by-* still seems faintly legible. The
MS *mwatide* is clearly a case of a false ligature (for one thing, *mw-* is
an impossible combination).[57]

r20: *ðā gyst(e :::re) broga stod hwœ(ðre).* The interconnected
rubbing that began in r18 continues on this line between *gyst-* and
broga. The *-e* and the *-re* in this gap are faintly readable in the MS,
though not in the FS. The *o* and *a* in *broga* are faintly visible, and they
are confirmed by the dittograph on v1. At the end of the line, *-ðre,* with
part of the *e* head chipped off from the fire damage, is very light, but
distinct.

The readings by collation from r21–v1, as explained above in detail,
are: *(fyren) sceapen.* Since the corresponding gaps after *sceapen* on r21
and v2 were both made deliberately, it was suggested above that the
former readings here were also dittographic, but were permanently
deleted from the text, presumably as part of the revision of the folio.
Otherwise, the text on the verso is in much better shape than it is on the
recto. Aside from the first line and a half, the scribe has not had to
eradicate large areas of the text, as he did for the damaged readings on
the recto. There are still many problematic readings on the verso, however, which are mainly caused by the failure of the ink to adhere to the
vellum in some places. The distortions this occasionally produced in the
letterforms seemed to support Zupitza's freshening-up theory, but not
on closer analysis.

v2: [deleted readings] *se fœr begeat sinc fœt(:).* The FS is not reliable here, and the perils of depending on it can be illustrated. Just above
the damaged *r* in *fœr* there are in the FS what appear to be some letters
written in a modern hand. Indeed, Malone says in his FS edition, "Over
the *s* [*sic*] in a much later hand I read *fœr* (?)" (*Nowell Codex,* p. 85).
As Westphalen has pointed out (p. 109), what Malone read as an early
modern restoration in his FS is a smudge in the MS. Malone and Zupitza
both read *fœs* for MS *fœr,* and in fact, as Zupitza says, "*s* seems to stand
on an original *r.*" What makes the *r* look like an *s* is that the off-stroke

---

57. Read (with Thorkelin B) *in wa-tide,* but translate, "in time of misery" (cf.
Bosworth-Toller, *gewin-tid,* "time of distress"). There are several *wea-* compounds
in *Beowulf,* and the spelling *wa-* can be seen as part of the incipient abandonment of
Late West Saxon spellings, and the intrusion of dialectisms, on this folio. Bosworth-
Toller records *wa-med* for *wea-met,* "anger," in Laʒamon.

has failed to adhere to the vellum (cf. *stearne* r6), though traces of it are visible. The descender is unusually long because it is ligatured to the unusually high *e* tongue preceding it. But it is shorter than the descender of the insular *f* at the beginning of the word, which shows that it should not be mistaken for an insular *s*. The damage to the off-stroke of this *r* is paralleled by the damage to -*inc fœt* at the end of the line. Again, the ink has not held uniformly to the vellum. The letters -*inc* are far more distinct in the MS than they are in the FS. There are traces of a letter lost after *fœt* at the end of the line.

v3: (:::::) *þœr wœsswylcra fela inðā eorð.* The FS is more reliable here. The illegible word at the beginning of the line failed to hold to the vellum.

v4: *::se) œr ge streona swa hy on gearda.* The reading at the beginning of the line, before the parenthesis, is based on Thorkelin B. The rest of the line is accurately represented by the FS, though it should be noted that the damage to the *œ* in *œr* is comparable to the damage to the *r* in *fœr* v2, but without leaving behind an ambiguous letterform.

v5: *gū) gumena nathwylc eormen lafe.* The FS is reliable.

v6: *œþ)elan cynnes þanc hycgende þœrge.* Good FS (note the loss of ink where the top of the *e* connects with the first stroke in -*ge;* many of the *e* heads and tongues are similarly damaged on this page).

v7: *hy)dde · deore maðmas ealle hie deað.* Good FS (again, note the head of the first *e* in *deore,* and the heads of both *e*'s in *ealle*).

v8: *fo)r nam œrran mœlū · 7sian ðagen.* The *r* in *fornam* is partly covered by the paper frame, and is less distinct in the FS than in the MS. Zupitza says that the *i* in *si* "seems to stand on an original *e*," but there is no evidence of this whatever.[58]

v9: *leo)da duguðe seðœr lengest hwearf.* The surface of the vellum between *seð*- and *lengest* is napped, but -*œr* is certain.

v10: *we)ard wine geomor rende þœs yldan.* The ink on the line is

---

58. Malone concurs: "Of this *e* I see nothing." *Nowell Codex,* p. 86. Elsewhere he has implicitly defended *si* on limited evidence of a tendency for a closed long *e* to raise to *i.* "If *ē* actually became *ȳ* (*ī, īe*) in the mouths of some OE speakers, one would expect corresponding spellings to turn up . . . in other words as well." "Old English [*Ge*]*hȳdan* 'Heed,'" p. 47. The reading might also be defended as a subjunctive of the verb "to be" (cf. *sy, sie*). Then, *ond si an ða gen leoda duguðe* could be translated, "and there may be one" or "if there be one of the troop of people still." In either case *si* is one of the many unique (non–Late West Saxon) spellings on the folio.

generally dark brown (almost black), except for *wine,* which is faded light brown. Here the ink has failed to hold to the vellum. It has also failed to hold on the loop (top and bottom) of the first *e* in *rende,* making the word look like *rihde* (cf. the *en* of *fyrena* v20). Thus Zupitza says, "*rihde* the later hand, but *wende* the first" There is no trace of an original *wynn* under the *r,* and a true *h* would have a longer ascender, which would not curve, as this remnant of an *e*-head does. The *r* in *rende* is presumably a scribal dittograph from the preceding word, *geomor,* and an emendation to *wende* seems necessary. There is, however, no need, and no justification, for the editorial emendation of *yldan* to *ylcan.* If emendations were made for all awkwardly made letters, we would have another poem entirely.

v11: *ꝥ h)e lytel fœc long gestreona brucan.* The FS is good, and there are no controversies over the transcript. The awkward *o* in *long* or the *u* in *brucan* might be noted in passing, as an additional caveat against changing the *d* in *yldan* for the sake of an easier reading.

v12: *m)oste beorh eall gearo wunode on wonge.* The FS is accurate. The second *l* in *eall* has not adhered well, and the totally faded parts may be fruitfully compared with the faded parts of the first *e* in *rende* v10. Here, the lost ink does not make the *l* look like a different letter. In *wunode,* it seems that the scribe started to write *wuode,* but caught himself in time to change the *o* to *n,* and to finish the word correctly.

v13: *wœ)ter yðū neah niwe benœsse nearo.* The FS is reliable.

v14: *c)rœftū fœst þœr on innan bœr eorl.* Zupitza is mistaken when he says, "*innon* the later hand, but *o* stands on an original *a.*" The MS reads *innan:* the ink, as has so frequently happened on the page, has simply failed to hold to the vellum on the off-stroke of the *a.* It is impossible to believe that a restorer could have mistaken this letter for an *o;* the off-stroke of the *a* is even clearer in the MS than it is in the FS.

v15: *g)estreona hringa hyrde hard fyrdne.* As Zupitza says, the first letter of the last word in this line could be *wynn* or *f;* in the FS it looks a bit more like *wynn,* but in the MS the *f*-tongue seems certain. The advantage of *f* is that *hardfyrdne,* as Bosworth-Toller first glossed it, means "hard to carry, weighty," and is excellent in the immediate context. The unbroken *a* (instead of *heard*) is another Northern dialectal feature on the folio. The disadvantage of *wynn* is that it requires editors to change *hard* to *hord,* and *wyrdne* to *wyrðne.*

v16: *d)œl fœttan goldes fea worda cwœð . heald.* The readings have already been discussed. Failure of the ink to hold in a few places has metamorphosed *fea worda* to *fec- -orda,* but the traces of the original ink can still be seen, even in the FS. The damage to the ash in *cwœð* may be compared to the damage to *a* in *fea.*

v17: *þ)u nu hruse nu hœleð ne mœstan eorla.* The FS is somewhat misleading, in that *nu hruse* is noticeably faded in the MS, and *-ruse* seems to have been rubbed lightly with pumice, perhaps because the ink ran or bled. From the looks of it, the scribe first wrote *mastun,* as Malone suggests (*Nowell Codex,* p. 86), but then changed the spelling to *mœstan* by adding an *e* loop to the *a,* and by closing the top of the *u* with a tilde-like stroke.[59]

v18: *œhte hwœt hyt œr onðe gode begeaton.* Part of *a* is covered, but all of *œ* is distinct at the beginning of the line. The hair stroke of the *y* has not held to the vellum. The scribe started to write another letter (perhaps the *eth*) after *o* in *onðe,* but then wrote the *n* over the mistake (the bottom of the *n* closes in the MS more distinctly than it does in the FS).

v19: *guð deað for nam . feorh beal(e) frecne.* Zupitza reads *reorh bealc* for *feorh beale,* and says that "the first *r* stands on an original *f,* and *c* on an original *o.*" The *f* looks like an *r* because the scribe began a dittograph of *nam,* immediately preceding. He got as far as *na-* before realizing his error, and then, without erasing, he wrote *f* over *n,* and *eo* over *a,* using the right side of the *a* as the ligature. A comparison of the descenders of the *f* and *r* in *feorh* will show that the scribe was not confused.[60] The second *e* in *beale* is unusually small, but part of the middle stroke (not the tongue) is still faintly visible, even in the FS. The form in the nominative singular is a late analogical spelling.

v20: *fyrena gehwylcne . leoda minra þanœ.* The last letter in the line is not an *a,* but an *œ,* with the small loop all but gone, but with the faint tongue distinct in the FS, and more distinct in the MS (cf. the second

---

59. Editors assume that *mœstan* is a blunder for *moston,* but *mœstan,* "greatest," may be an adjective modifying *œhte.* The form *mastun* is a late Northern spelling of the adjective, which the scribe evidently decided to give in the standard Late West Saxon form.

60. The scribe probably refrained from erasing this, and other false starts on the page, because he knew from his erasure in the first line and a half that the damp vellum could not be erased without making a mess.

e in *sele* v21).[61] The loss of ink on the ash is similar to the losses on the *h* and *wynn* of *gehwylcne*, earlier in the same line.

v21: *ðeþis ofgeafgesawon . sele dream (as)*. The FS is good, even in showing the traces of letters after *dream-*, which Zupitza does not mention. Malone says, "At the end of line 21 are traces of letters but they cannot be read; the usual restoration *ic* is plausible enough" (*Nowell Codex*, p. 87). Under ultraviolet light, the first letter seems to be an *a* (perhaps an *e*), and the second an uncial *s*.

There can be little doubt that the folio is a palimpsest, and that the handwriting on it is later than the script that appears on the rest of the *Beowulf* folios. The spelling is also later, for forms like *bræde, wintru, on, hræde, sie, bufolc, geweoldum, fleoh, weall, watide, si, hardfyrdne, mastun* (changed to *mæstan*) and *beale*, all testify to the breakdown of the standard Late West Saxon literary dialect, in non–West Saxon areas, as the 11th century advanced. Perhaps the unique mixture of forms on this one folio will lead to some valid conclusions about the provenance of the poem. At any rate, a new edition of the text on the palimpsest is desperately needed, but must await further attempts, by modern technological methods, to decipher all of the extant ink traces. A conservative edition will strive to retain all of the readings that are clear in the MS, and will try to make sense of the text by emending conjectural restorations (for which there is little or no MS support), Thorkelin readings, and then doubtful MS readings. Scholars need to begin to study the revised text on folio 179.

Beowulf in the Making

When viewed in isolation, the palimpsest and the new text on fol. 179 perhaps remain incredible phenomena. An 11th-century revision of the

---

61. Unfortunately, *þanœ* (like *þana*) makes no sense, and an emendation is still unavoidable. The missing alliteration in line 2251, however, can be supplied simply by emending *n* to *m*, and reading *þanœ/ðe* (v20–21) as *þa mœðe*, "portion, measure"; the half-line, *þa mœðe þis ofgeaf*, can be translated, "then this [that is, *guðdeað*, 'death by war'] left behind this portion." The lacking minim (*n* for *m*) is not a serious error, and could have been induced by the scribe mistaking the right side of the *a* in *þa* for the first minim of *m*. What Zupitza took for an *a* rather than an *œ* in *þanœ* is the quadrangular form still used by the scribe on fol. 179 in the digraph *œ*, but never elsewhere on the folio for a single, unligatured *a*.

... heð bæan ...
... san ... hædit gold ...
... quam ... nebid hit pihte ...

... þe dod rcæada þuw hund pintra .
... ld on hpusam hond æhnaru eucñ
... etg oddæt hyne an abealch mon
... mode man dryhtne bæn . fæted
... pucdo pæpe bad hlapond sinn
... hond nagod on bopsi beaza
... bone getidad fea sceaptu mñ
... sceapode . ripa þyn n zepbyuc
... man side . þase þynm on poc prolt
... zenpad . froneda æhcðsi rtane .
... heont oupand frondes rot
... hero pond gestop . dyman cuzea
... nucan heapde neah . spa meg unpæte
... ade gedigan pean ippine sid sede pal
... des hyldo gehralch hond pean
... te glopne lecðu gruide poldu
... man emdan pone þelu onsp
... te sane getedde . hæt þhpole mo

poem has been unthinkable until now, and the MS itself has been considered relatively unimportant, because the original poem and the extant MS are supposed to be centuries apart. Yet the mere existence of a palimpsest in the middle of *Beowulf* is, at the very least, circumstantial proof that the poem was revised, and consequently that at least one folio of the poem, containing lines 2207–2252, is contemporary with the MS. The new text, from all aspects, leads to the same conclusion: the handwriting is the scribe's, but much later in development; the language is essentially the same, but shows, proportionately, many more orthographical idiosyncrasies, attesting to the later breakdown of the standard literary dialect; and the text is apparently shorter than the one it replaced. Thus, all of the evidence on the folio would seem to lead inexorably to the conclusion that it is a revision. Assuredly, this evidence cannot be used to support the traditional view that the MS as a whole is a late copy, many stages removed from the 8th-century archetype. It must hold a critical place in all theories describing the transmission of the poem.

The signs of revision on fol. 179 receive repeated support elsewhere in the MS. To begin with, it is not the only folio in the *Beowulf* MS from which the original text has been deliberately deleted. The first three lines of text on fol. 180v have been carefully rubbed off with the aid of some liquid solution, which has left the vellum napped and discolored. Moreover, the rubbing was done only over the script, not over the vellum generally, which shows that the text was purposely removed, not damaged accidentally. The FS gives a very inadequate and inaccurate impression of all of this,[62] and yet neither Zupitza nor Malone describes the appearance of the MS here. It is not surprising, then, that no modern editor draws attention to the extraordinary condition of the text. It is surprising, though, that both Thorkelin and his scribe treated the first

---

62. In the FS the condition of the facing page, fol. 181r, looks quite similar to the first three lines of fol. 180v, but not in the MS. Fols. 181 and 186 constitute the third sheet of the twelfth gathering, a sheet that was badly prepared before it was written on: there is still a whitish caking on both sides of this entire sheet, and in places the ink has not held well to the vellum surface. The contrasting appearances in the FS and the MS are a pertinent warning of the dangers of relying totally on FSS.

Plate 15. The first three lines of fol. 180v were deliberately deleted.

three lines of fol. 180v as a deliberate deletion. Thorkelin A leaves three corresponding lines blank in his copy, without making any effort to record what was still legible, even when he proofread. Thorkelin A knew no Old English at all, and his testimony in this respect is totally objective, unimpaired by any prejudices about the authority of the MS.

Thorkelin himself records what he can make out of these three lines in his transcript (B), but he leaves no doubt whatever that he regarded them as intentionally deleted. In the first place, he highlights the lines in his transcript by setting them off between long rows of dots, in the following manner:

> . . . .
>
> . . . hege . . . . . . sceall bearn
> . . . rusan þær he hæðen gold waráð
> wintrum frod ne byð him wihte . .
>
> . . . .

Then, he explicitly says in the margin: *"hic lacu/na trium/ linearum si/ve 15 versu/um incidit/ qui in au/tographo/ defuisse/ videntur/ et enim mem/brana, ex/ qua hoc apo/graphum/ desumtum/ hic vacua/ est."*[63] It is possible, even likely, that the palimpsest on fol. 179 and the deleted lines on fol. 180v1–3 are part of the same incipient revision. In any case, there can be no doubt that the first three lines of fol. 180v were deliberately expurgated by someone, and editors need to consider this before automatically restoring them to the text. There are indications that the received text of this deletion may be spurious in other ways, as well.

In fact, Zupitza's transcript of these erased lines is strangely less reliable than Thorkelin's. Zupitza's desire to provide a semiedited text (including conjectural restorations) along with his transcript has here affected the accuracy of his transcript. His readings need to be reviewed:

---

63. "Here a lacuna occurs of three lines, or 15 verses, which seem to be missing in the autograph, for indeed the vellum, from which the partial transcription is derived, is void here." Malone, *The Thorkelin Transcripts*, p. 104a. Malone should have drawn attention to this note in his FS of the Thorkelin transcripts, and both he and Zupitza should have described the physical state of the text on fol. 180v1–3 in their respective FSS of *Beowulf*.

[swiðe ondræ]da[ð] he gesecean sceall [ho]r[d]
[on] hrusan þær he hæðen gold warað
wintrum frod ne byð him wihte ðy sel.

Zupitza improved on Thorkelin's transcript by providing *secean,* which, as he says is "pretty certain," and *ðy sel,* which are "tolerably distinct." But thereafter Thorkelin has the advantage. In line 2 of Zupitza, there is a trivial oversight; *on* is a reasonable conjectural restoration, but the *h* in *hrusan* is equally conjectural (and equally reasonable). In the first line, however, subjective editing has taken precedence over the job of objective transcription. The conjectural restoration [*swiðe ondræ*]*da*[*ð*] is not securely based: of the unbracketed letters *da,* only *a* is visible; the so-called *d,* which Zupitza says is "not perfect," is a shadowy remain that could be almost any letter. Wishful thinking also accounts for the bracketed letter [*ð*] following the *a.* Zupitza says that this "may have been *ð* as well as *n*"; but the letter is almost unquestionably an *n,* which is distorted in the FS by a tear in the vellum. In short, Zupitza's conjectural restoration, [*swiðe ondræ*]*da*[*ð*], ought to be abandoned, in favor of a restoration ending with MS -*an.*

Similarly, Zupitza's reading, [*ho*]*r*[*d*], at the end of the line should be viewed as an emendation, not a conjectural restoration. The rejection of Thorkelin's reading *bearn,* though textually justified, is totally unjustified from a paleographical standpoint. To begin with, one must assume that the edge of the vellum was still intact, and that the reading seemed obvious to Thorkelin when he made his transcript. Surely he had more of the word to study than had Zupitza.[64] If the reading were as doubtful in the 18th century as it is now, Thorkelin would have skipped over it, just as he skips *secean* and *ðy sel* in the same passage. And while it may be admitted that Thorkelin is not always entirely trustworthy as a copyist, there is no evidence elsewhere in his transcript that would account for his mistaking *hord* for *bearn* here. Indeed, such evidence (if it existed) would utterly destroy the value of his transcript.

64. We know, for example, that some vellum was lost along the top of the word after the transcripts were made. Thorkelin A and B both copy *nah* with confidence from the other side (the first word on the recto), but now the top of *nah* is chipped away.

Thorkelin's unreliability is of a different nature. He often miswrites one vowel for another,[65] and here he may have mistaken the common word *bearn,* "son" (which he had already transcribed over thirty times, and which was readily understandable to an Icelander), for the rarer poetic word *beorn,* "man." The mutilation of the text would explain and excuse the mistake in this case. All of the letters in the disputed word have been distorted by the rubbing and discoloration, and by the crumbled edge of the vellum, but *beorn* (or Thorkelin's *bearn,* for that matter) can still be defended, while *hord* cannot. The ascender of the first letter is now gone, but the bottom closes, eliminating *h.* The closed bottom is clearer in the MS than in the FS, and clearer still under ultraviolet light. The space between this letter and the relatively certain *r* is more than is needed for an *o,* and the rather involved ink traces (resembling a modern *w*) support a digraph like *eo* (or *ea*), but not a simple *o.* A single minim stroke after the *r* is all that remains of Thorkelin's *n,* but there is no inward curve to it that would support Zupitza's *d.* One can only surmise that Zupitza favored *hord* over *bearn* on textual, rather than paleographical grounds. The word *beorn,* on the other hand, does not disregard the evidence Thorkelin must have had when he copied down *bearn;* and *beorn* is both textually and paleographically acceptable.

The effect on the text is that *beorn* must be the subject (in variation with *he*), rather than the object, as *hord* was construed.

> ...]an.   He gesecean sceall
> beorn [on h]rusan,   þær he hæðen gold
> waráð wintrum frod;   ne byð him wihte ðy sel.
> (cf. Klaeber, 2275–2277)

"A man will search in the earth where he [the dragon], old in winters, guards the heathen gold; he [the man] will be nothing the better for it." The change in referent for the personal pronoun in line 2276 will present no difficulty for anyone familiar with this practice in *Beowulf* (a notorious example occurs in lines 168–169). The apparent meaning of the passage may explain why it was deleted: it was replaced, and expanded, by the revised text on the palimpsest.

---

65. See Malone's lists of such errors in *The Thorkelin Transcripts,* pp. 27 ff.

Because the vellum itself is lost between *hyne foldbuend* (2274b) and *-an* (2275a), it is impossible to be certain about the contextual and syntactical relationships originally made clear in the lacuna. The *-an* following the lacuna leaves a great deal of room for speculation: it might be the vestiges of a preterit (such as *hran, ongan, wan, can*), it might be an adverb *(ongean, þonan),* a conjunction *(siððan),* a noun (in phrases such as *for sincgifan, for sinfrean, on sefan,* and the like), or any infinitive. The possibilities for conjecture are innumerable. Speculation on the lost text from a lost piece of vellum is frustrating, and perhaps ultimately futile. Yet the current conjectural restoration, [*swiðe ondræ*]-*da*[*ð*], has been part of the received text for nearly a century, even though the unbracketed *d* is a guess and the last two letters are almost certainly *-an,* not *-að.* And it is not speculation that everything on fol. 180v1–3 from *-an* to *ðy sel* was deliberately deleted by someone. The reason for the deletion may be as permanently lost as the piece of vellum from the upper left corner of the page; but the apparent substance of the deleted text suggests that it was associated with the palimpsest and the revised text of fol. 179.

It should be easier to accept the concept that the palimpsest on fol. 179 represents a revision once it is realized that a related text was deliberately erased on the next folio. It cannot be denied, at any rate, that both folios provide striking evidence that can be legitimately interpreted as revisions. Aside from the bias that *Beowulf* is a 7th- or 8th-century poem preserved in a late 10th- or early 11th-century MS, the chief impediment to accepting this interpretation is no doubt the apparent lack of a believable motive for the revisions. Even if one grants the possibility that the poem is contemporary with the MS, the need for a total revision of one particular folio, deep in the MS and deep in the poem, is hard to imagine. The particular position of fol. 179, both in the MS and in the poem, can, however, account for this need. Textually and codicologically, the folio marks off significant boundaries: in the poem, it marks the beginning of the dragon episode, a totally new development in the poem; in the MS, it is the first leaf of two five-sheet gatherings, which do not adhere to the physical format used in the rest of the *Beowulf* MS. From these facts it can be argued that *Beowulf,* as we now have it, is an amalgamation of two originally distinct poems, which first came together in the MS that has come down to us. If the dragon episode was already copied when two stories about Beowulf were fused into one, there would be an explanation for the change in format, and, more important, for the palimpsest. The original text of fol. 179 was eventually erased and replaced to mend the contextual leap that would naturally exist at this contextually artificial juncture.

Surprisingly, there is considerable paleographical and codicological support for this hypothesis. Before considering this evidence, it is well to keep in mind that the theory has been repeatedly urged by scholars on textual grounds. These arguments are systematically rejected by other scholars almost as soon as they are made, and it is safe to say that the theory is generally repudiated by Beowulfians as a group. Those who have argued for multiple authorship of the poem are characterized as "dissectors,"[66] usually with some justification. The idea first surfaced as the so-called *Liedertheorie,* which held that the poem consists of many originally separate lays, loosely slapped together by carefree interpolators or enterprising scribes. Expressed in this way, the theory amounts to what most readers have rightly dismissed as an impotent assault on the artistic integrity of the poem. The essential unity of *Beowulf* is not in question here. Whether one poet, or two, or more, composed two or more poems, and then conceived of a collaboration, is perhaps not even important, for whatever the "inner history" of its constituent parts may have been, *Beowulf* as it has come down to us is now unquestionably unified. Accordingly, the present argument stresses artistic fusion rather than critical dissection. It maintains only that the paleographical and codicological evidence suggest that *Beowulf* was created in more than one stage in the course of the 11th century, and that our extant MS preserves the most exciting stages of its creation.

Karl Müllenhoff, who in 1869, in "Die innere Geschichte des Beovulfs,"[67] presented the first extensive explanation of the poem's inner history, broke the story into four main parts, each of which, he believed, derived from a different author:

1. Beowulf's fight with Grendel (lines 194–836);
2. His fight with Grendel's dam (837–1628);

---

66. See Klaeber, *Beowulf,* pp. cii ff.; and Chambers, *Beowulf: An Introduction,* pp. 112–120. The most elaborate attempt to delineate the "inner history" of the poem is by Walter A. Berendsohn, *Zur Vorgeschichte des 'Beowulf.'*

67. Müllenhoff's essay is reprinted as Chapter 3 of his *Beovulf: Untersuchungen über das angelsächsische Epos und die älteste Geschichte der germanischen Seevölker.*

3. Beowulf's homecoming (1629–2199);
4. His fight with the dragon, and his death (2200–3183).

Müllenhoff believed that the fight with Grendel and the fight with the dragon were originally two distinct lays that eventually came together in *Beowulf,* after a third poet added the fight with Grendel's dam, and a fourth added Beowulf's homecoming. But one does not have to believe in the *Liedertheorie,* or even in multiple authorship, to see that a single poet in the 11th century could have composed the epic from diverse sources, in several stages, in much the same way as Müllenhoff imagines. Certainly, Müllenhoff has not distorted the basic structure of the poem. Indeed, Klaeber, who argues persuasively for single authorship (pp. cii–cvii), describes the structure of the poem in essentially the same way, as the following outline, using Klaeber's headings (pp. ix–xii), will illustrate.

    I. Beowulf the young hero
      1. The fight with Grendel (lines 1–1250)
      2. The fight with Grendel's mother (1251–1887)
      3. Beowulf's homecoming and report to Hygelac (1888–2199)
    II. Beowulf's death
      The fight with the dragon (2200–3182)

Klaeber emphasizes the unity of the first three episodes, and disagrees with Müllenhoff over where, precisely, one episode ends and another begins, but the four-part episodic structure of the poem is not challenged. It might be argued, from Müllenhoff's view, that the first three episodes form a unit because successive poets deliberately unified them; the fourth episode stands apart, even in Klaeber's scheme, because as an older lay it was not written as a continuation, but was artificially appended. In fact, Klaeber's view of the structure helps illustrate Müllenhoff's theory of how the poem grew, by accretion, into an epic. But one 11th-century poet could account for the creative process, as well.

Most readers of the poem, from Tolkien on,[68] are probably impressed most by the three-part *thematic* structure, based on Beowulf's three great fights. The structural role of Beowulf's homecoming, because it is not a heroic event in Beowulf's life, tends to be forgotten. Yet the transition is structurally essential, and it ought to be seen as a transition,

---

68. J. R. R. Tolkien, "*Beowulf:* The Monsters and the Critics."

rather than as material integral to Klaeber's Part I, "Beowulf the young hero," but not to Part II, "Beowulf's death." While the three great fights of Beowulf's life must remain prominent, the structural link between the early fights in Denmark and the last fight in Geatland should be highlighted, to stress its crucial function. Without it, the dragon episode could be seen only as an awkward accretion, thematically but not structurally related to the rest of the poem. Beowulf's homecoming furnishes an adequate transition, when Beowulf, back in Geatland, tells Hygelac what he had accomplished in Denmark. The transition then swiftly moves from Danish to Geatish affairs, and prepares for Beowulf's kingship (lines 2166b–2206).

While the transitional text known as Beowulf's homecoming firmly unites two disparate phases in Beowulf's career, it also raises some legitimate questions about the original dimensions of the poem, and provides tenable reasons for believing in composite authorship. The problem is that Beowulf's account of his exploits in Denmark is not in complete accord, at least not on the face of it, with earlier parts of the poem. The discrepancies are, of course, overplayed by those who believe in multiple authorship, and underplayed by those who believe in single authorship. But the fact that there are, indeed, discrepancies means that the case for multiple, or composite, authorship is not entirely a subjective judgment. Composite authorship might better be seen as a pleasant alternative to Klaeber's view, for example, that, "in explanation of some discrepancies and blemishes of structure and execution it may also be urged that very possibly the author had no complete plan of the poem in his head when he embarked upon his work" (p. cvi). A late collaboration that attempted to weld together two slightly different versions of the same story would explain the minor variants in question without the need to depend on authorial ineptitude.

The textual case for composite authorship has been best marshaled by Levin Schücking.[69] In *Beowulfs Rückkehr,* Schücking made an objective, and exhaustive, stylistic investigation of the particular usage in Beowulf's homecoming of formulas, nominal compounds, metrics, syntax, and moods and tenses. Most of the results, as Schücking was the first to admit, are not compelling for anyone believing in single author-

69. *Beowulfs Rückkehr: Eine kritische Studie.*

ship,[70] yet they do provide some support for the belief in multiple, or composite, authorship. For instance, Schücking uncovers some syntactical usages in Beowulf's homecoming that are unique in the poem: the conjunction *þy-læs,* "lest" (1918b, *þæt ne* elsewhere); *ac* used as an interrogative particle (1990b, used pervasively as the conjunction "but"); the placement of the adverb *ða,* "then" (2192b); the only certain case of *forþam,* rather than *forþan* or *forþon,* as the conjunction "because, since" (1957b). Unique syntactical transitions are made in the phrases *Ic sceal forð sprecan* (2069b) and *To lang ys to reccenne* (2093a). Chambers has objected that this "is natural when we realize that we have here the longest speech in the whole poem, which obviously calls for such apologies for prolixity" (p. 119); but Chambers's objection merely puts the unique phrases in their broad context, which as he implies is equally unique in the poem.

While it may be admitted that Schücking does not prove separate authorship of Beowulf's homecoming, one ought not to lose sight of the issues that led him to make the argument in the first place. Even Chambers was ready to admit Schücking's premises. As he says, "Schücking starts from the fact, upon which we are all agreed, that the poem falls into two main divisions: the story of how Beowulf at Heorot slew Grendel and Grendel's mother, and the story of the dragon, which fifty years later he slew at his home. These are connected by the section which tells how Beowulf returned from Heorot to his own home and was honorably received by his king, Hygelac." Chambers goes on to say that, "as Schücking rightly urges, instances *are* forthcoming of two O. E. poems having been clumsily connected into one [*Genesis,* for example]. Therefore, whilst no one would now urge that *Beowulf* is put together out of two older lays, *merely* because it can so easily be divided into two sections, this fact does suggest that a case exists for examination" (pp. 117–

---

70. And Chambers disputes them from this bias in his *Beowulf: An Introduction* (pp. 117–120). He concludes, "To me, the fact that so careful and elaborate a study of the story of *Beowulf's Return* fails to betray any satisfactory evidence of separate authorship, is a confirmation of the verdict of 'not proven' against the 'dividers.' But there can be no doubt that Schücking's method, his attempt to prove differences in treatment, grammar, and style, is the right one." Ibid., p. 120. As we shall see, paleographical and codicological evidence adds an entirely new dimension to the argument.

118). But these concessions insufficiently account for the purpose of Schücking's investigations, and thus unfairly minimize the validity of his results. As Schücking makes clear in his second chapter, "Der Ausgangspunkt der folgenden Untersuchung" (*Beowulfs Rückkehr,* pp. 9–15), it is the textual contradictions in Beowulf's homecoming, more than the gulf between the fights in Denmark and the fight in Geatland, that oblige one to scrutinize even minor syntactical idiosyncrasies of the type mentioned above. They corroborate the more obvious textual evidence of composite authorship. Schücking is usually characterized as a dissector or divider of *Beowulf.* Actually, his conclusions stress the ultimate unity of the poem, and the creative ingenuity of an Anglo-Saxon poet who (in an eminently medieval way) drew on the work of other poets to create a new poem of epic proportions (ibid., pp. 73–74).

The same body of evidence has been interpreted quite differently by Francis P. Magoun, Jr.[71] His conclusions stress the ultimate disunity of the poem, for he views the three distinct parts of *Beowulf* (Beowulf's youthful exploits in Denmark, Beowulf's homecoming, and Beowulf's death in Geatland) as three distinct folk poems, brought together through the industry of "an anthologizing scribe." In short, Magoun's theory resuscitates the old *Liedertheorie,* in the light of current conceptions of oral performance. Magoun refers to the three separate parts as *Béowulf A, Béowulf A',* and *Béowulf B.* From his folkloric standpoint, the question of the ultimate unity of the poem is irrelevant, and this frees him to emphasize textual discrepancies in the three parts as natural variants. As he says in *"Béowulf A': A Folk-Variant"* (p. 100):

> Rather than assume the existence of an incredibly careless singer or irresponsible lettered poet it would seem more natural to assume the insertion by an anthologizing scribe of a variant (*A'*) which, though giving a far shorter version of the *fabula* in question, included what seemed to him like a lot of curious and interesting features not in *A* and that he made his insertion for just that reason. Such a solution allows one to have a higher opinion of the work of both *A* and *A'* and relieves a critic of feeling obliged to try to convert inconsistencies into artistic triumphs.

71. In *"Béowulf A': A Folk Variant"*; and *"Béowulf B: a Folk-Poem on Béowulf's Death."*

If one is looking for inconsistencies, as Magoun is, it is easy to find them, though many of the ones he cites are more imagined than real. Most can be explained, if not as artistic triumphs, then as natural shifts in emphasis or pleasing variations in detail.[72]

Still, there are some inconsistencies between *A* and *A'* that are hard to ignore or gloss over: Hroðgar's sons, Hreðric and Hroðmund, figure rather prominently in *A* (lines 1169–1231), yet in *A'* Beowulf does not mention them by name and tells Hygelac all about the impending marriage of Ingeld the Heaðobard and Freawaru, Hroðgar's daughter, who is not even mentioned in *A* (see 2020–2069); in *A'* Grendel seems less savage and primitive than in *A*, for Beowulf tells Hygelac that Grendel carried some kind of gaming bag (*glof*, 2085), in which to stow his victims. These variants, alone, provide a case for Magoun. The variants he urges between *A* and *B* are perhaps less persuasive than these, but since all scholars agree that there is a rift between Beowulf's youthful exploits in Denmark and his death in Geatland, there is no need to hunt out specific variants. Whether or not they were composed by one person, the stories are different, and are presented differently enough to sustain Magoun's belief in an *A* singer and a *B* singer. In "*Béowulf B:* a Folk-Poem on Béowulf's Death," Magoun summarizes the entire theory in the following way (pp. 129–130):

What we actually have are two stories about the Gautish hero Béowulf. The first is about a youthful adventure with a couple of trolls at the Scielding court . . . in Denmark and is told twice, once at some length by a narrator (*Béowulf A* . . .), once much more briefly (cp. 11. 1999–2176) by Béowulf himself to his uncle Hyʒelác, king of the Gauts (*Béowulf A'*). *Béowulf A'* ends up with a somewhat curious miscellany of remarks (11. 2177–99) that seem only to casually concern what precedes or follows. The second Béowulf story starting at line 2200 tells of Béowulf's death at the hands [*sic*] of a sort of flying dragon and begins in an almost

---

72. See, especially, A. G. Brodeur, "*Beowulf:* One Poem or Three?"; Sherman Kuhn, "*Beowulf* and the Life of Beowulf: A Study in Epic Structure"; and Walter Scheps, "The Sequential Nature of Beowulf's Three Fights." For a recent and finely detailed structural analysis, see John D. Niles, "Ring Composition and the Structure of *Beowulf.*"

jolting fashion, considering that some odd sixty-five years separate this part of Béowulf's life history from what precedes.

While the evidence is malleable, there can be no doubt that there are textual and structural grounds for these arguments in favor of multiple authorship of the poem. The problem with Magoun's folkloric explanation of the evidence is that it does not sufficiently confront the unquestionably literary activity of the "anthologizing scribe[s]" who supposedly fused three oral performances into one literary (recorded) epic. It is here that Magoun's and Schücking's theories merge. From his own point of view Magoun may have been a dissector or divider of the poem, since he was primarily interested in the oral performances, the prehistory of the transmitted text. But what must ultimately be of primary interest is the transmitted text itself. Even if one accepts Magoun's outline of the prehistory of the epic, with its three independent oral sources, the person whom Magoun labels an "anthologizing scribe" must have been a lettered poet, who unified his diverse sources. Magoun himself unconsciously says as much: "The question of just where A' begins and ends, similarly to what extent the original ending of A may be involved, is presumably unanswerable short of the discovery of more manuscript material, for my postulated anthologizer had presumably to some extent mastered the technique of oral singing and hence was able to compose authentically in his own words neatly soldered joints. Presumably part of the original ending of A was sacrificed, . . . likewise no doubt the original beginning of A'."[73] In short, to round off his theory, Magoun is forced to create a lettered poet who had mastered the techniques of oral performers, who saw a great design in three narratives, and who had the talent to reshape them, using what he needed and discarding what he did not, into a unified epic. Regardless of his antecedents, this person is the *Beowulf* poet.

The textual arguments for composite or multiple authorship of *Beowulf* are decisively reinforced by paleographical and codicological evidence that has been totally ignored. It can hardly be fortuitous that all of this evidence falls within the broadest limits, as first defined by Müllenhoff, of Beowulf's homecoming (that is, lines 1629–2199). Moreover, the clearest and most significant evidence falls within the narrower lim-

---

73. "*Béowulf A'*: A Folk Variant," pp. 100–101.

its of Beowulf's homecoming as defined, for instance, by Klaeber (lines 1888–2199). Nor, in retrospect, is it likely to be a coincidence that the second scribe copied the part of Beowulf's homecoming that holds all of the textual discrepancies (from line 1939 on). Indeed, the two scribes' work precisely parallels the textual case for composite or multiple authorship. As shown in "The *Beowulf* Codex" in Part 2, the *Beowulf* MS comprises the sixth through the thirteenth gatherings of the Nowell Codex. The first scribe alone copied all of Beowulf's youthful exploits in Denmark on the sixth through the tenth gatherings, and on the first fourteen lines of the eleventh gathering (fol. 171r, to line 1887); the second scribe alone copied all of the section on Beowulf's death, which conventionally begins with the last six lines of the eleventh gathering[74] (fol. 178v, from line 2200), and of course includes the twelfth and thirteenth gatherings; the two scribes collaborated on Beowulf's homecoming, the eleventh gathering, lines 1888–2199. It is therefore possible that Beowulf's homecoming was first composed to join together two different *Beowulf* MSS, and that the extant MS preserves the actual collaboration.

The exceptional nature of the eleventh gathering as the essential link between two otherwise disparate paleographical and codicological units is well illustrated by considering the MS minus the eleventh gathering. Without this gathering, paleographers would have every reason to conclude that the two gatherings preserving Beowulf's fight with the dragon had been copied many years before the five preserving Beowulf's youthful exploits in Denmark. The archaic script of the second scribe, in which insular letterforms like the low *s* still effectively compete with the high caroline *s,* would suggest that the second scribe's work was somewhat older than the first scribe's, in which the caroline influence is more advanced. It would seem most probable as well that the two

---

74. A case can be made for starting the dragon episode at line 2207, with the palimpsest, the first page of the twelfth gathering. The last few lines of the eleventh gathering (lines 2200–2207a) do not lead inexorably to the kingship of Beowulf, the first line of the twelfth gathering. On the contrary, they seem to be leading elsewhere: "Again it came about in later days, in the crash of battle, after Hygelac lay dead, and battle swords became the slayer of Heardred under his shield covering, when fierce warriors, the Battle-Scilfings, sought him out among his victorious people, with force assailed the nephew of Hereric, after." The transition to Beowulf's rule is decidedly abrupt, even with a full stop after *nefan Hererices.* The former independent existence of the dragon episode might account for this.

Beowulf MSS derived from different scriptoria, for while the first scribe regularly uses gatherings of four sheets, ruled for twenty lines to the page,[75] and generally arranged so that hair faces hair and flesh faces flesh, the second scribe uses gatherings of five sheets, ruled for twenty-one lines to the page, and invariably arranged with the hair side facing out. In short, without the eleventh gathering, scholars would have reasonably concluded that two unrelated *Beowulf* stories had been preserved in two unrelated MSS, attesting to a lively *Beowulf* tradition throughout the country in late Anglo-Saxon times. Linguistic peculiarities of the two poems (for example, unbroken *a* in the first, or the *io* forms in the second) would tend to confirm this deduction, by suggesting that the two distinct Beowulf stories must have derived from different dialect areas. Surely, it would have been a reckless guess, attacked from all sides, to say that the first scribe's MS and the second scribe's MS were parts of the same MS, or that the two stories were part of the same poem.

So the eleventh gathering, containing Beowulf's homecoming, is paleographically and codicologically as well as textually transitional. The second scribe takes over the copying on the second leaf (fol. 172v4). Naturally, the gathering was made up in the first scribe's manner: it is a four-sheet quire, ruled for twenty lines of text to the page; the first two sheets are arranged with flesh facing flesh, the second two with hair facing hair. Between these paired sheets, hair faces flesh. One assumes that the first scribe fully intended to finish copying the gathering, if not the entire poem. Because the handwriting of the two scribes is so ill matched, it is clear that they did not plan beforehand a place for the second scribe to take over the copying. If they had, the change of hands could have been obscured by the first scribe stopping at the end of fol. 172r. There is compelling codicological evidence that the first scribe suddenly halted where he did, and the second took over, because at that point a collaboration had been devised to join two originally distinct MSS, and two originally distinct poems.

It is virtually certain, at any rate, that the second scribe copied the eleventh gathering—Beowulf's homecoming—after he had already cop-

---

75. The first gathering of the poem is comprised of four full sheets, and two half-sheets (or leaves) folded on between the third and fourth sheets. The only anomalously ruled gathering by the first scribe is the tenth, which is fully discussed below.

ied the twelfth and thirteenth gatherings. Obviously, one cannot afford to ignore such an amazing parallel to the independent structural and textual arguments that the homecoming episode was written after the dragon episode, as a transitional link between two formerly unrelated *Beowulf* narratives. The evidence that the second scribe copied the eleventh gathering last is that he had to squeeze in four extra lines of text, in disregard of the original rulings, on fols. 174v–176r. This compression would not have been necessary if the scribe knew he had at least two extra gatherings of unused vellum ahead of him. The squeezing in of twenty-one lines of text, at this early stage, on four successive folios ruled for twenty lines of text can only mean that the scribe did not have vellum available after the eleventh gathering. Certainly, if he had more vellum beyond the eleventh gathering, he could have easily fit in the text of four extra lines by adding a few extra letters per line, in the course of copying the eleventh, twelfth, and thirteenth gatherings. Unless he was compelled to fit the extra material into the eleventh gathering, it is far too early in the copying for the scribe to be worrying about running out of vellum. If he really had over twenty empty folios left on which to copy, the scribe's desperate recourse of ignoring the rulings of the eleventh gathering is inexplicable. The twelfth and thirteenth gatherings must have been copied already.

In view of the importance of this conclusion, it will be helpful to demonstrate that the four extra lines could not have been added inadvertently. It might seem, for instance, that one sheet of the eleventh gathering could have been unintentionally ruled for twenty-one lines, rather than twenty. This simple solution, however, cannot apply here. Sheets are only ruled on one side, since the indentations made by the awl simultaneously provide identical rulings on the reverse side. Hence it is patently impossible for a sheet to be ruled for twenty lines on the hair side, but for twenty-one lines on the flesh side. Since fol. 174v–176r do not (and cannot) constitute a single sheet, the extra lines of text cannot be accounted for through any kind of oversight. The third sheet of the gathering consists of fols. 173 and 176, while the innermost sheet consists of fols. 174 and 175. By virtue of the method of ruling both sides of a sheet simultaneously, the third sheet cannot have been ruled by mistake for twenty lines on fol. 173, recto and verso, and fol. 176v, but for twenty-one lines on fol. 176r; similarly, the fourth sheet cannot

...ræ ne to setle gong. hpile þ
...se dohtor hnod gapes cynlum
...nde ealu pæge beah þære ypen pape
...sicchde. nan nan hynde þæhpno
...ed pine hæledu sealde sio gehæten
...pinz gold hnodth gladu runa. ypodan.
...ad þær geponden pine scyldinza þu
...hynde þhæt pæd talad þ he middy
...se pæl pæhda dæl ræcca gesecte op
...dan hypæn. æptæn læod hpyne lyde
...te bongan buged þeah seo bnyd duge
...g þær þon op þyncan dædæn hæado
...aydna þhegna zehpam þana læda
...onne he mid pæmnan on plett gæd.
...hphte bæyin dæna duguda bipsthede.
...on hum gladiad gomelpa lape hæyid
...hbyninz mæl heada bayina zesthbon
...sthgthi lnedha pæspnu pealdan mosom
...ddæt hip pon læddan to dam lind
...plezan spæse zesidas ond hyra sylp
...na pronli þon cpid æt bæyne sede beah

have been ruled for twenty lines on fol. 174r, but for twenty-one lines on fol. 174v, and fol. 175 recto and verso. The extra lines of text on these four folios are not there by accident.

A closer look at these pages reveals how they came to have twenty-one lines of text, despite the fact that they were originally ruled, with the rest of the eleventh gathering, for twenty lines. First, it must be said that the extra line on fols. 174v–176r was not simply ruled in at the bottom of each page.[76] A measurement of 174r (twenty lines) and 174v (twenty-one lines) from the first ruled line to the last shows that both pages have the same writing space (175 mm.). Since the eleventh gathering was already ruled for twenty lines throughout, it is surprising that the scribe was able to achieve a uniform written space while still using the first and last lines of the original rulings. The MS shows that the scribe achieved this result by deliberately ignoring the original rulings, and by spacing the lines of text so that he would progressively pick up enough room for an extra line of text. The FS of fol. 174v is clear enough to illustrate the method, for it faintly shows the original rulings.[77] Starting at line 3, the scribe begins lifting the line of text away from the ruling, until, at line 17, an entire line of text has been added, and the rulings can once more coincide with the lines of text. For this reason if one counts the rulings on fol. 174v there are twenty, but if one counts the lines of text there are twenty-one. This extremely difficult way of

76. This was done once in the Nowell Codex, on fol. 122v, in *Alexander's Letter.* The scribe probably skipped a line, either at the end of fol. 122v or at the beginning of fol. 123r. It is certain that this extra ruling was added by the scribe after he had copied the text on fol. 122r, because the indentation shows through clearly on the recto, and yet the scribe failed to use the line on the recto. It should be noted in passing that the second scribe did not create twenty-one lines from twenty rulings on fols. 174v–176r to make his text in the eleventh gathering consistent with the text in the twelfth and thirteenth gatherings: he follows the twenty-line rulings on fols. 172v–174r and on fols. 176v–178v.

77. Oddly enough, Malone's FS, using the same photograph as Zupitza's, does not show the rulings very clearly at all. In the MS, the original rulings are most easily seen on fols. 174v and 176r.

Plate 16. Fol. 174v. In order to fit more text on the page than the first scribe's writing grid allowed, the second scribe omitted the fitt number, ignored the right margin, and wrote 21 lines of text within the space of the 20 rulings.

including the extra material emphasizes that the scribe was compelled to fit it all in within the eleventh gathering.

There are other sure signs of his need to fit more text in than the gathering was designed to hold. On fol. 174v, the same page on which the scribe began squeezing in an extra line of text in disregard of the rulings, he omitted fitt number XXX for lack of space. It is not surprising that he did not squander the line he had so laboriously gained on a fitt number, and that he drew the large capital *O* outside the area of the text. He garnered a good deal more space throughout the gathering by ignoring the first scribe's margins, or bounding lines, which permitted him only about 10 cm. of text per line. The second scribe added between 1 and 2 cm. of additional space per line by ignoring one or both of the first scribe's margins. Again, fol. 174v provides a good example, because of the clarity of the rulings: the right bounding line can be easily seen in the FS in line 10, between *hryre* and *lytle*. By ignoring the margin on this one page, the scribe added outside the margin over sixty characters, the equivalent of at least two whole lines, to his text. The scribe normally ignored the right margin, as in this example, though a few times he disregarded the left bounding line too. We can even see in the FS the point at which the scribe knew that the rest of his text would fit into the gathering without further violating the bounds of the first scribe's grid. By fol. 176v he stopped squeezing in an extra line of text in disregard of the first scribe's rulings; on the next page, fol. 177r, after ignoring the first scribe's left margin for the first eighteen lines, he used the first scribe's margin for the last two, and thereafter generally adhered to the 10-cm. boundaries until the last page of the gathering (fol. 178v). The scribe undeniably went to great lengths to fit a certain amount of text within the transitional eleventh gathering. And the only conceivable reason he would be compelled to do so would be that the following gatherings had already been copied.

Thus a clear pattern emerges from all of the extraordinary paleographical and codicological data associated with the second scribe. He has not only corrected errors, and restored damage caused by age and use. His part of the MS provides compelling codicological evidence that he copied a new episode, designed to fuse Beowulf's Danish and Geatish exploits into a unified epic. Apparently, many years later, he was still working toward a better fusion of the parts, on the revised text of fol. 179. But there is also some evidence that the first scribe took part in the last revisions of the poem. The indications are that the text of what is now the tenth gathering was subjected to major revisions after the scribe stopped copying the eleventh gathering. Since the tenth gathering (fols. 163–170) contains that part of the text that Müllenhoff would include in Beowulf's homecoming (lines 1629 ff.), there is at least a case to examine. And if the second scribe was copying an entirely new text in the eleventh gathering, it should not be surprising that the text immediately preceding it might need some revision, too, to accommodate the new direction of the narrative. Together, the rulings of the tenth gathering, and the fitt numbers after line 1629, make a solid case in favor of such a revision.

The first scribe, as we have seen, ruled all of his gatherings, except the tenth, for twenty lines of text to the page.[78] His absolute uniformity in this respect, not only in *Beowulf,* but in the prose texts as well, makes the twenty-two-line rulings of the tenth gathering somewhat suspicious. The only obvious explanations are that the scribe had more material to copy in the gathering than he originally had planned for it, which is consonant with revision, or that the gathering was ruled anomalously by mistake. The latter can be safely eliminated. The gathering was intentionally ruled for twenty-two lines, as a measurement of the written space, from the first ruling to the last, makes clear. If two extra pricks had been inadvertently made through the sheets when the rulings were prepared, the written space would be approximately 20 mm. longer than the written space of pages having only twenty lines per page. In fact, the written space for the twenty-two-line folios is the same as it is for the twenty-line folios (c. 175 mm.). Thus it is certain that the rulings were not expanded from twenty to twenty-two lines. On the

---

78. All apparent exceptions have nothing to do with the original rulings. The extra ruling on fol. 122 is explained in note 76, Part 3. The other exceptions are not in the number of rulings themselves, but in the number of rulings used. The recto of fol. 95(97) has only seventeen lines of text on a page ruled for twenty lines because that was all that was needed to finish the *St. Christopher* legend; similarly, fol. 103v has only nineteen lines of text, the number needed to finish *The Wonders of the East,* and fol. 128v has only seven, to finish *Alexander's Letter.* Fol. 108v in *Alexander's Letter* has nineteen lines, because the entire first line (and part of the second) was erased. Finally, the first page of *Beowulf* (fol. 129r) has only nineteen lines of text, for the first line of capitals occupies the space between the first two rulings. In short, the first scribe was absolutely consistent in his ruling, until the tenth gathering.

contrary, it shows that the scribe took care from the beginning that an anomalously ruled gathering would not look remarkably different from the rest of his gatherings, by keeping the writing space identical, despite the extra rulings.

It is not extraordinary in itself, of course, that the scribe ruled his gathering commensurate with the amount of text he had to copy. What is extraordinary is that, for some reason, he had to restrict the extra rulings to the tenth gathering. In short, it is hard to explain why he made the tenth gathering with twenty-two lines per page, and the eleventh with twenty lines, instead of ruling both for twenty-one lines. The only apparent reason is that the scribe had to copy more material onto the tenth gathering than had been originally planned for it, and curiously could not spread the extra material over two gatherings. Once again, this kind of restriction implies revision in the circumscribed area. It is precisely the same kind of restriction that impelled the second scribe to fit in four extra lines of text on the eleventh gathering. The first scribe, after ceasing work on the eleventh gathering, must have gone back and copied a revised text on the tenth.

The revised text, it seems, was either considerably shorter or somewhat longer than the original text. At first glance, it would appear that the revised text was longer, since it required a gathering ruled for 22 lines per page, while the original text only needed 20 lines per page. In other words, the revised text was about 32 lines longer than the original text. But these appearances are probably deceiving. Evidence from the fitt numbers indicates that the poem was shortened, which could mean that a gathering ruled for 22 lines replaced two original quires ruled for the customary 20 lines. In this case the revision is quite radical, for it means that about 288 lines (the difference between two quires ruled for 20 lines and one quire ruled for 22) were deleted from the poem. However, it is unrealistic to conceive of a major revision as simple addition or subtraction of lines. In all probability, parts of the text were deleted, while other parts were expanded. There is evidence from the fitt numbers that an entire fitt was deleted from the poem, but aside from this, the precise nature and scope of the apparent revision of the text of the tenth gathering remain a mystery.

The fitt numbers indicate that the twenty-fourth fitt of the original text was deleted in its entirety. Accordingly, they independently corroborate the conclusions reached on the basis of the anomalous rulings. All of the fitt numbers in *Beowulf* preceding line 1629 in the tenth gathering, from I to XXIII, are in perfect order, and have not been tampered with in any way. But beginning with the second number of the anomalously ruled tenth gathering, and continuing through the eleventh gathering to number XXXI, all of the fitt numbers either have been altered or were never written in the first place. Since the reasons for these curious difficulties in the simple act of consecutive numbering have never been sought, no special significance has ever been attached to them. It has not even been recognized that the alterations of the fitt numbers were not made by either of the scribes.[79]

The alterer was, it seems, an early modern reader of the codex, for the changes had already been made in time for the Thorkelin transcripts. On fol. 164r the scribe correctly wrote XXIII for the first fitt of the tenth gathering. However, on fol. 166r he mistakenly wrote XXV for the next fitt, instead of XXIIII, and thereafter he and the second scribe held to the new, erroneous sequence. The alterer made an abortive effort to correct the sequence, but in the process obscured the first scribe's real error, and left the false impression that the second scribe had made a series of errors. In all, five numbers were altered: of the first scribe's numbers, XXV was changed to XXIIII by writing two of the four I's over the V;[80] XXVI, XXVII, and XXVIII on fols. 168r, 169v, and 171r were changed to XXV,[81] XXVI and XXVII, simply by erasing the last I of each number; similarly, the second scribe's number

79. Malone says, "The fit number [XXIIII] is obviously corrected in another hand, presumably the second scribe's" (*Nowell Codex,* p. 71), and Westphalen concurs (*Beowulf,* p. 108, n. 140).

80. The first two I's are joined at the bottom, because of the original V they attempt to obscure.

81. There is an inkblot covering everything after XX- (fol. 168r9), but it seems to be the same ink used to draw the four I's of the preceding fitt number. As Malone says, "Only the *xx* of the fit number is easy to read, because of the great blot (modern) over the rest of it. But [Thorkelin] AB have *xxv,* in A followed by a point, and I think I can make out both *v* and point. In all likelihood the scribe wrote *vi* (rather than *v*), later corrected by rubbing out the *i,* but the blot keeps us from finding signs of erasure." *Nowell Codex,* p. 73. Under high-intensity light the V is certain, and what Malone takes for a point could just as well be faint signs of the original I, erased. Perhaps the alterer, after erasing the I, started to touch up the V when his pen ran.

XXVIIII was changed to XXVIII by erasing the last I. Only the first alteration, XXIIII, can be judged from a paleographical viewpoint, but it is easy to see in the stiff, childlike counterfeiting of the I's that neither of the two scribes made them. Yet even if the I's had been drawn more skillfully, it would still be hard to assign these changes to either of the scribes. The first scribe had no conceivable opportunity to correct one of the second scribe's numbers, while it is highly unlikely that the second scribe would correct four of the first scribe's numbers, and leave all but one of his own uncorrected. One may safely conclude that the five altered fitt numbers are later changes.

The untenable belief that these alterations were made by the second scribe has led to some unwarranted conclusions about the number of fitts in the poem. The second scribe wrote only two fitt numbers in the eleventh gathering: XXVIIII on fol. 173r, and XXXI on fol. 177r. He did not write XXX on fol. 174v for lack of space. After all, this is the first folio on which the scribe squeezed in an extra line of text in disregard of the rulings. He did, however, clearly mark the fitt by the large capital *O*. When the alterer changed XXVIIII to XXVIII by erasing the last I, he left the impression that the second scribe had failed to write in *two* fitt numbers, XXVIIII and XXX, and worse, that he had failed even to mark the beginning of one of the fitts with a capital letter.[82] Thus the alterer ingenuously shifted the first scribe's mistake over to the second scribe, for the illusion that two fitt numbers are missing here can be directly traced back to the first scribe's error of skipping number XXIIII, and writing XXV instead. The second scribe, who relied on the accuracy of the first scribe's number sequence, continued numbering the fitts where the first scribe left off. Hence the disarray in the fitt

---

82. Most editors authorize this false impression. Klaeber and von Schaubert, for instance, print in brackets the numbers XXVIIII and XXX at the beginning of line 2039. This procedure implies a major scribal corruption of the text where no corruption at all exists. The only justification there is for the notion that the unnumbered fitt [XXX] is in fact two fitts is its length—105 verses (lines 2039–2143); yet fitt VIII consists of 103 verses, XLI of 112, and XXXV of 142 verses.

Plate 17. Fol. 166r11. The first scribe's fitt number XXV was sloppily altered by a later hand to XXIIII.

semninga tosele comon pɲ ome pɲ
hpate ꝼeopeɽtyne geata gongan ᵹ
dɲyhten mid modiᵹ onᵹe monᵹe meod
ponᵹaꝼ tɲæd · Dacom inᵹan ealdoɽ
ᵹeᵹna dæd cene won dome ᵹe pu̇ɲ þ
hæle hilde deoɽ hɲoðᵹaɲ ᵹɲetan᷑
þaꝼ beꝼeaxe ouꝼlæt boꝛen ᵹꝛend lᷓ
heaꝼod þæɲ ᵹuman dɲuncon eᵹeꝼ lic ᵹ
eoplum ᵹþæꝛe ideꝼe mid plite ꝼeon᷑
lic peɲaꝼ onꝼaꝛon ·

                              xxaɲ
Beopulꝼ maþelode beaɽn ecᵹ þeope
hpæt þe þe þaꝼ ꝼælac sunu healꝼden
leodꝼcyldinᵹa luꝼtū bꝛohton tiɲeꝼ
to tacne þe þu heɲ tolocaꝼt · ic þ uu
ꝼoꝛte ealdɲe ᵹe diᵹde piᵹᵹe undeɲ
pæteɲeꝼ peoɽc ᵹeneꝼ de eaɲꝼoð lic
æt ꝛuhte pæꝼ ᵹud ᵹe tpæꝛed nymðe
mec ᵹod ꝼcylde · Ne meahte ic æt hil
de mid huntinᵹe puht ᵹe pyɲcan
þeah þ pæpen duᵹe · ac me ᵹe ude
ylda paldend þ ic on paᵹe ᵹeꝼeah pliᵹ

numbers of the tenth and eleventh gatherings, and the confusion over the actual number of fitts in the poem, can all be reduced to the first scribe's omission of XXIIII. If one ignores the later alterations, the fitts were numbered from I to XXIII, and then from XXV to XLIII, indicating that there are forty-three fitts in the poem, whereas in fact there are only forty-two.

Despite the hiatus between XXIII and XXV, the scribes' erroneous number sequence ought to be maintained, for it preserves an interesting, and possibly very significant, feature from the making of the text. The following table provides at a glance a full account of this sequence, noting the five spurious alterations in the margin.

Fitt	Folio	Verses	Fitt	Folio	Verses	Altered Numbers
I	130r	62	XXII	162v	84	
II	132v	74	XXIII	164r	94	
III	134r	69	[ ]	—	—	
IIII	135v	62	XXV	166r	89	[XXIIII]
V	137r	51	XXVI	168r	77	[XXV]
VI	138r	85	XXVII	169v	71	[XXVI]
VII	140r	43	XXVIII	171r	75	[XXVII]
VIII	141r	60	XXVIIII	173r	76	[XXVIII]
VIIII	142v	103	[XXX]	174v	105	
X	145r	48	XXXI	177r	77	
XI	146r	81	XXXII	179r	91	
XII	147r	46	XXXIII	181r	79	
XIII	148r	88	XXXIIII	183r	69	
XIIII	150r	66	XXXV	184v	142	
XV	151v	59	XXXVI	187v	92	
XVI	152v	75	XXXVII	189A(197)v	58	
XVII	154v	67	XXXVIII	189v	69	
XVIII	156r	59	[XXXVIIII]	191r	71	
XVIIII	157v	70	XL	192v	54	
XX	159r	62	XLI	193v	112	
XXI	160v	90	XLII	195v	79	
			XLIII	198r	46	

The table highlights the source of all apparent errors in the number sequence as the first scribe's omission of number XXIIII. All of the numbers following this omission are in proper sequence, if one ignores the alterer's abortive effort to correct the first scribe's oversight.[83]

The scribes' number sequence is, in any event, quite significant. No matter how one interprets the evidence, it effectively proves that the fitts of the poem had not been numbered before the extant MS, and this in turn is consonant with a contemporary MS. At the very least, the omission of XXIIII suggests that the first scribe was numbering the fitts of *Beowulf* for the first time, without the aid of numbers in his exemplar, and that he omitted a number by mistake. The second scribe did not have numbers in his exemplar, for his numbers follow the first scribe's erroneous sequence. The alternative—that their exemplars contained the same errors—should not be too tempting. We are sure that some of the fitt numbers in the Nowell Codex were drawn in after the texts had been copied. In *Beowulf,* the numbers up to fol. 168r were drawn by the first scribe with a much sharper quill than the one he used to copy the text. For the *Judith* fragment, we have seen that the numbers were put in later, by someone other than the scribe, presumably after the *Judith* codex was complete and all texts could be properly numbered seriatim. The evidence in the last two gatherings of the *Beowulf* MS likewise suggests that these numbers too were added later, after the entire text had been copied. It is obvious, though, that the second scribe intended to leave space for planned fitt numbers, for on fol. 183r he left an entire line free for a number. But it is equally clear that he did not have numbers in his exemplar, for in other cases he forgot to leave space for them. On fol. 189v he inadvertently began a new fitt without leaving space; part way through the first line of the new fitt he realized his oversight and improvised space by cutting off the name *Wihstanes* after writing only *wih-*. And on fol. 191r, he assumed he had left space for a number at the end of the fitt, but he must not have known at the time that the number would be XXXVIIII, the longest of all, too long he apparently decided for the space he had reserved for it: he left the space blank. Thus, all of the signs point to the conclusion that the fitts of the poem were first numbered in the extant MS.

83. The alterer no doubt stopped where he did because he did not want to write in number XXVIIII on fol. 174v (for lack of skill as well as lack of space), and then continue altering all the rest of the numbers throughout the poem. The second scribe's omission of number XXX on fol. 174v provided a well-camouflaged place to stop.

On the other hand, the first scribe's omission of XXIIII may really point to a far more significant conclusion. The numbering could have been initially thrown off if a revised text of the tenth gathering in part entailed the deletion of the original twenty-fourth fitt. The first scribe's numerical oversight is easily understood if one assumes that the revisions were made on the quires replaced by the tenth gathering. When the scribe copied the revised text, he mechanically copied as well the fitt numbers he had formerly written on his first copy. In this light, the fitt numbers remarkably corroborate the conclusion, arrived at on the basis of the anomalous rulings, that the tenth gathering comprises a late revision of the poem.

Conclusion

Quite obviously, this study of the *Beowulf* MS is not totally objective, for it is founded on the premise of a contemporary MS, and therefore actively seeks significance in paleographical and codicological evidence. It deliberately searches for any indications in the MS that *Beowulf* was not mechanically copied, after the prose texts that now precede it in the Nowell Codex, as the fourth item in a humdrum anthology. It concludes, through paleographical and codicological evidence, not only that the premise is warranted, but that the extant MS actually was the poet's (or poets') working copy. All previous investigations of the MS are equally subjective, and far less descriptive, because they are founded on the premise that the MS is a late, corrupt copy of an early poem. Accordingly, though there has never been any attempt to justify this premise, the possible significance of paleographical and codicological evidence is assiduously ignored. If the conclusions of the present study are not inevitable, however, the mass of MS data on which they are based provides for the first time relevant evidence to evaluate. Taken all together, the evidence sustains the view of a contemporary MS: it assuredly cannot support the traditional view that study of the MS, in the case of *Beowulf*, is not pertinent.

The traditional view of the MS is faced, for the first time, with paleographical and codicological data in direct conflict with it. The most probable construction of the original gatherings shows that the poem was probably copied as a separate codex. The capital lettering, particularly in the first line of *Beowulf*, sharply contrasts with the capital lettering in the prose texts; also on the first page of *Beowulf*, the rulings, the deterioration of the script in the lower right corner, and the partly obliterated inscription, *Vi*[*tellius*] *A. 15*, all indicate that *Beowulf* existed (and thus was copied) as a separate codex. Wanley, who expertly studied and described the composite codex before the fire destroyed the gatherings, refers to the *Beowulf* MS as a separate book. If it was a separate book, it was not mechanically copied with the prose texts. More specifically, the traditional view must now be reconciled with the thorough and repeated scribal proofreading of *Beowulf* alone, which suggests that the MS was copied separately, and then corrected with care and comprehension. The MS was also repaired by the second scribe as time and use damaged it. Finally, the traditional view must ponder the palimpsest and the revised text on fol. 179; the three deliberately deleted lines on fol. 180v; the four inserted lines in the eleventh gathering which flagrantly disregard the rulings; the anomalously ruled tenth gathering; and the ramifications of the skipped fitt number, XXIIII. Without ignoring all of this paleographical and codicological evidence, there is now an obligation, for those who would adhere to the traditional view, to prove that the *Beowulf* MS is *not* a contemporary MS of the poem.

For now, it seems more fruitful to pursue the possibility, which much of this paleographical and codicological evidence supports, that the *Beowulf* MS is an unfinished draft of the poem, and that it preserves for us the artistic fusion of two originally distinct *Beowulf* narratives. It is unlikely that a final draft would have provided such consistent evidence that *Beowulf* is a composite poem: structurally and orthographically (so perhaps linguistically) there are two distinct parts to the poem, excluding Beowulf's homecoming; paleographically and codicologically there are two distinct parts to the MS, excluding the transitional gathering containing Beowulf's homecoming; in the transitional gathering the orthographic (or linguistic), paleographic, and codicological differences all converge, and as they are fused, so too are the heroic events of Beowulf's life. Here the division in the poem and the division of labor between the two scribes are quite remarkably reconciled. A final draft would at least obscure the transition paleographically (aside from the change of hands) and codicologically, rather than highlight it, as the *Beowulf* MS does, in the tenth and eleventh gatherings, and in the palimpsest. The *Beowulf* MS appears to be an unfinished draft of a late collaboration because there is evidence of collaboration in precisely the part of the MS where all of the different transitions—structural, orthographical or linguistic, paleographical, and codicological—had to be made. Coincidence can be stretched to cover many contingencies, perhaps, but even it will snap when stretched too far. In the tenth gathering, the first scribe begins fitt XXVI (altered to XXV) with the word *Oðþæt,* in the middle of a sentence (line 1740); in the eleventh gathering, the second scribe begins fitt [XXX] with the same word, *Oððæt,* again in the middle of a sentence (line 2039). Elsewhere, neither scribe ever begins a sentence with *Oððæt,*[84] or a fitt in the middle of a sentence. This coincidence at least implies that the division between fitts in these two crucial gatherings was not carefully planned out in advance. If a collaboration was in progress, there were more exciting things to think about.

One final paleographical clue that *Beowulf* is a late fusion of two originally separate poems first accomplished, and therefore preserved, in the extant MS, may be deduced from the second scribe's proofreading of the first scribe's copy. This material has not been discussed with the rest of the scribal proofreading, because it seems fundamentally different from the rest of the proofreading. This additional evidence also reveals truly exceptional interest in the poem by a scribe who is usually supposed to have been largely ignorant of its meaning, and so inattentive, careless, and lazy in copying it. As we have seen from the scribe's proofreading of his own work, these suppositions are untenable. But, in his proofreading of the first scribe's work, already carefully proofread by the first scribe, he picks up some decidedly minute oversights. His superscript corrections are easy to identify, not only by the difference in hand, but by his characteristic use of a comma to mark the place of insertion: thus, on fol. 133r20 he corrects *beortre* to *beor^h,tre;* on fol.

---

84. Von Schaubert interprets *oððæt,* in these cases in an adverbial sense—"afterward"—rather than in the customary conjunctive sense, "until." Thus, in her text, *Oððæt,* begins new sentences as the new fitts begin. The fact that the word is used to begin new fitts suggests that von Schaubert is right.

Plate 18. The comma beneath the correction on fol. 142r13, in the first scribe's part of the MS, indicates that the correction was made by the second scribe.

beot ealird þe sumi beanstanes
gelæste· don þene ic to þe wyrsan
hingeñ deah þu heado razu ge hwær
dohte zwimme zude· zif þu wendl
deapst niht longne wyrst ne an b
beowulf maþelode becπn ecz þeower
hwæt þu worn fela wine min hunferð
beope druncen ymb brecan spræce
sæzdest from his siðe soð ic talize
þic mere strengo maran ahte eop
reþo on yþum donne ænig oþer man·
wit þ ge cwædon cniht wesende
beotedon wæron begen þazið oð geozoð
feore þæt on zarsecz utaldrum
ned don þ ge æfndon swa· hæfdon swurd
nacod þa wit onsund reon hæfdon on
handa wit unc wið hron fixas werian
þohton· no he wiht fram me flod yþ
feor fleotan mæhte hraþor on hol
me no ic fram him wolde· ða wit æt

142r13 *o* is corrected to $o^n_,$; *gan* to $gan^g_,$, on fol. 160v14, and *feh* to
$feh^{\eth}_,$, on fol. 168v3. These corrections reflect close attention to detail; the
last two emphasize as well the scribe's comprehension of the text, for
real linguistic forms that are wrong in the context are corrected. But
most of the second scribe's corrections in the first scribe's section of the
MS are not corrections at all: they are *emendations*. In many cases, the
second scribe changes perfectly acceptable linguistic (or orthographic)
forms to forms generally found in his own part of the MS. Together,
these changes support the view that *Beowulf* and the *Beowulf* MS are
one and the same, for the second scribe's emendations can be seen as the
first steps toward normalizing the orthography of the composite text.

On fol. 140v14, the second scribe emends *dol-scaðan* to *dol-sceaðan*.
The first scribe's spelling is certainly not an error: the word appears
with the *a* spelling frequently in his part of the text (554, 707, 712, 737,
766, 801, 1339, 1803, 1895), and the other spelling occurs, too, but only
in the genitive plural (4, 274). The second scribe's *e* represents a glide
that developed in some dialects after palatalization of *sc-*. The spelling
without the *e* is evidently a Mercian feature, for as Campbell points
out, "there is no trace of the development of a glide between *sc* and a
back vowel" in Mercian texts (*Old English Grammar*, p. 68). The
spelling with the *e*, on the other hand, cannot be localized, because it is
standard Late West Saxon, which at this late date was used as the literary dialect by Mercians as well as West Saxons. In a contemporary
MS it is very strange indeed that the two scribes followed such discrepant
orthographical traditions to copy the same poem. After all, it is impossible to believe that the scribes' exemplar followed two different orthographical traditions, too, which corresponded exactly with the parts of
the poem later copied by the two scribes of the extant MS. In short, if
one believes in a single exemplar, one or the other (or both) of the two
scribes radically altered its spellings in the course of copying his part of
the poem.

The implications here are worth exploring. A single exemplar must
have been uniformly written, either in a nonstandard, presumably Mercian orthography, or in the standard Late West Saxon orthography. In
the case of the former, the first scribe copied *-scaða* accurately, while
the second scribe transliterated *-scaða* into the Late West Saxon spelling
-sceaða, and even went so far as to start transliterating the first scribe's
work. The alternative is less believable: the exemplar was basically

written in the standard Late West Saxon orthography, but for some reason the first scribe transliterated his portion of the MS into a non-standard, local orthography. These deductions apply, of course, to other major discrepancies in spelling, as well, the most famous of which is the preponderance of *io* (over *eo*) spellings in the second scribe's part of the MS. And, assuming a single exemplar (no matter who is supposed to have done the transliterating), it is astonishing that the two scribes worked on the same poem with such different aims and methods. The argument that either transliterated, however, cannot be easily upheld. As many of the scribes' written corrections and erasures illustrate, both scribes attempted to copy what was before them: a dittograph is not made by someone who is transliterating rather than copying. Furthermore, though the spellings in the prose codex and in the *Judith* fragment are not appreciably different from the spellings in *Beowulf,* there are enough minor differences to suggest that both scribes faithfully copied the spellings of their exemplars. Hence a possible explanation for the orthographical differences between the first and second scribe in *Beowulf* is that their respective parts of the MS are based on two different exemplars.

The second scribe's emendations in the first scribe's text (like *scaða* to *sceaða*) make a good deal more sense once it is realized that they are not corrections, and that they are not based on the first scribe's exemplar. The second scribe did not need an exemplar to read the first scribe's copy, detect and correct a few minor mistakes, and normalize a few spellings in accordance with predominant spellings in his own copy. On fol. 132r14 he emends the occasional spelling *scyppen* to the standard form, *scyppend.*[85] On fol. 144r5 he changes *wealhþeo* to *wealhþeow;* as in the case of *-scaðan,* he only makes the change the first time the word occurs, letting it stand without the *w* thereafter (629, 664, 1162, 1215).[86] Zupitza believed that the change of *œngum* to the unsyncopated form, *œnigum,* on fol. 147r11 was made "in the same hand,"

---

85. The first scribe's form, *scyppen,* has been defended by Malone in "Notes on *Beowulf:* I." Von Schaubert prints *scyppen* in her edition.

86. Moreover, he spells the name without final *w* in his own part of the MS (2173); his emendation of the first scribe's form should perhaps still be seen as an attempt to regularize spellings throughout the MS, for at line 2961 (in his own section) he alters *ongenðio* to *ongenðiow.* It appears, then, that the second scribe ultimately wanted to return to the conservative spelling of the name element, *-þeow* (or *-þiow*).

but it was clearly made by the second scribe. A single minim is virtually impossible to identify with any real certitude on paleographical grounds; but since the first scribe only uses the spellings *œngum* (474, 1461) or *œnegum* (655, 842) for the dative, while the second scribe uses the form *œnigum* (2416) elsewhere, the emendation must have been made by him. A similar case occurs on fol. 158v15, where *on* has been altered to *in*. Here the *i* does look like the first scribe's, but once again the usage is more in keeping with the second scribe: the alteration occurs in the phrase *in Heorote,* which the first scribe invariably writes *on Heorote* (475, 497, 593, 1330, 1671). The second scribe's usage varies. He writes *on Hiorte* (2099) once, but elsewhere he writes *in Swiorice* (2383, 2495) and *in Hrefnesholt* (2935). The significance of the change is hard to imagine, but in any event it is an emendation, not a correction.

The second scribe makes another emendation on fol. 167v10, where he changes *ferþe* to *ferhþe*. He himself uses the first scribe's form as a variant spelling in *collenferð* (2787; versus *collenferhð* 1806) and *sar-igferð* (2447). The change was perhaps motivated by an erratic desire for a conservative spelling. Curiously, he emends a conservative form on fol. 169r19, by altering *dogor* to the analogical form *dogore*. The first scribe's original reading, *þy dogor,* is the correct dative-instrumental for nouns of the *-es -os* declension, and the first scribe uses the form elsewhere (1395). The second scribe apparently made the emendation to refine the meter, though *dogore* is the form he uses anyway (2573). Since the emendation transcends orthography, it supports the view that the two scribes worked with two different exemplars. On the other hand, orthographical variety is perhaps unusually significant in the second scribe's final emendation, of *hreþe* to *hraþe,* on fol. 171v20. The word appears frequently, with a variety of spellings, in the first scribe's part of the MS: *hraþe* (748), *hraðe* (224), *hrœþe* (1437), *raþe* (724, where it alliterates with *recedes*), and *hreþe* again (991). The word appears three times in the second scribe's section, twice in the eleventh gathering, and always spelled with *a* (1975, 2117, 2968). The revised text on the palimpsest contains the late, nonstandard spelling, *hrœde* (fol. 179r11). The word seems more familiar to poet and scribe in the first part of the MS than in the second. And if the eleventh gathering was in fact written after the twelfth and thirteenth, word frequency alone would suggest that *hraðe* became an active word in the second scribe's part of the MS in the transitional text of Beowulf's homecoming.

As we have seen, most of the second scribe's alterations in the first scribe's copy are emendations rather than corrections. As a whole, they show the scribe normalizing the spelling between the first and second parts of the poem. There is no reason to assume that the scribe made any of these emendations on the basis of the first scribe's exemplar. There is, however, one bit of evidence that strongly implies that the second scribe did not have an exemplar to refer to when he read and altered the first scribe's work. After the word *hafelan,* on fol. 160r17, there is a mark that Zupitza transcribed as a colon, but that in all likelihood is a mark for insertion, made by the second scribe. The spacing makes it clear that the mark was made after the text was copied, and the mark itself is what the second scribe ordinarily uses to signal the place where an insertion belongs.[87] As Malone says, "After *hafelan* 17 comes what I take for a mark of insertion, printed by Z[upitza] as a colon. It looks like the handiwork of the second scribe. . . . The first scribe here seems to have skipped a verb, which modern editors have to supply, since the correction was never made" (*Nowell Codex,* p. 68). The apparent significance of this has gone unnoticed. It is difficult to believe that the scribe would note the omission of a verb, mark the place, and then fail to write in the missing word,[88] if indeed he had the exemplar. We know he had an exemplar for his own part of the MS, but it now seems quite evident that it was not the same as the exemplar used by the first scribe.

Paleographically and codicologically, at least, all of the facts converge to support the theory that *Beowulf* is an 11th-century composite poem,

87. See, for example, his marks for insertion on fols. 186r3, 188v13, 189A(197)r4, 193r11, and 196v19.

88. The passage, as it stands in the MS, is not in need of an infinitive, as far as the sense is concerned, for *wille* alone is syntactically and contextually sufficient: thus, *ær he in wille hafelan* (1371–1372) means "before he would want his head within." Moreover, *willan* is frequently used with an infinitive understood from the context, and so it would be possible to translate the same phrase "before he will (put) his head within." Perhaps the second scribe refrained from making an interpolation here, because he came to realize that no interpolation was required. Lines 1371–1372 should be read as three half-lines:

> *aldre on ofre,   ær he in wille hafelan: nis þæt heoru stow!*

The enjambment of alliteration provided by the second half-line is effective.

and that the *Beowulf* MS is the archetype of the epic as we now have it. Students of the poem first need a new, truly conservative, edition before the poem can be easily, or even adequately, revaluated in the light of this theory. But it is not hard to imagine how Anglo-Saxon poems like *Beowulf* might have emerged during the reign of Cnut the Great, as an aesthetic aftermath of the Danish Conquest. On its most basic level, the subject matter is thoroughly Scandinavian, and the poem begins with a dedicatory salute to the founding of the king's royal Scylding dynasty. Surely Hroðgar, the dominant power in Scandinavia, who received exiles like Hunferð and Ecgþeow; who married a foreign queen—worried about the succession of her sons—and who was honored by heroes like Beowulf, could have been modeled on the latest Scylding king, Cnut the Great. The Anglo-Saxon poet who created the exploits of Beowulf in Denmark was content to suggest that even the mighty Scyldings, led by a wise and noble king, were not immune to irrational disaster. Cnut would not have been embarrassed by the implication that everything in this life is transitory, or that God rules the universe.

But the Anglo-Saxon poet who created the dragon episode was more poignant. He traces the actual disintegration of a dynasty, which culminates in the death of a glorious hero and implies the subsequent extinction of an entire race. This poet had for his model the fall of the house of Alfred, and the subsumption of his homeland and his race in the Danish empire. If he knew Anglo-Saxon history from the Chronicle, he might have remembered that fiery dragons first portended the Viking invasions of England (A.D. 793); at any rate, he would have known that many Anglo-Saxon thanes deserted their lords when the dragon ships came in the 11th-century Danish conquest. His mood is elegiac and, in the light of 11th-century events, unbearably sad. The poet himself is a "last survivor of a noble race," who was left an enormous legacy after the death of his lord. If the last poet of *Beowulf* was the second scribe, as the paleographical and codicological evidence encourages one to believe, he increased, and continued to polish, an Anglo-Saxon treasure during the reign of a Danish Scylding lord.

Works Cited

Adams, Eleanor. *Old English Scholarship in England from 1566–1800.* Yale Studies in English, no. 55. New Haven: Yale University Press, 1917.

Andrew, Samuel Ogden. *Postscript on Beowulf.* New York: Russell & Russell, 1948.

Applied Infrared Photography. Eastman Kodak Publication no. M-28. Rochester, N.Y.: Eastman Kodak Co., 1977.

Armborst, David. "Evidence for Phonetic Weakening in Inflectional Syllables in *Beowulf.*" *Leeds Studies in English,* n. s. 9 (1977): 1–18.

Benediktsson, Jakob, ed. *Arngrimi Jonae Opera Latine Conscripta.* Copenhagen: Ejnar Munksgaard, 1950.

Bennett, J. A. W. "Hickes's 'Thesaurus': A Study in Oxford Book-Production." *English Studies: Essays and Studies Collected for the English Association,* n. s. 1 (1948): 28–45.

Benton, John F.; Gillespie, Alan R.; and Soha, James M. "Digital Image-Processing Applied to the Photography of Manuscripts: With Examples Drawn from the Pincus MS of Arnald of Villanova." *Scriptorium: International Review of Manuscript Studies* 33 (1979): 40–55.

Berendsohn, Walter A. *Zur Vorgeschichte des 'Beowulf.'* Copenhagen: Levin & Munksgaard, 1935.

Bethurum, Dorothy, ed. *The Homilies of Wulfstan.* Oxford: The Clarendon Press, 1957.

Blake, Norman F. "The Dating of Old English Poetry." In *An English Miscellany Presented to W. S. Mackie,* edited by Brian S. Lee, pp. 14–27. New York: Oxford University Press, 1977.

Bliss, Alan J. *The Metre of 'Beowulf.'* Oxford: Basil Blackwell, 1963.

———. "Single Half-Lines in Old English Poetry." *Notes and Queries,* n. s. 18 (1971): 442–449.

BL Add. MS 24,932. *A Report from the Committee Appointed to View the Cottonian Library, &c. . . . Published by Order of the House of Commons.* London, 1732.

BL Add. MS 36,789. *Catalogue of the Cotton MSS. Circa 1635.*

BL Add. MSS 43,472, 43,473, and 44,875. Signatures of George Frederic Warner.

BL Cotton MS Vitellius A. XV. *Anglo-Saxon Versions and Poems: Flores Soliloquiorum S. Augustini, Nicodemi Evangelium, Etc., Beowulf, and Judith and Holofernes.*

BL Harley MS 6018. *Catalogus Librorum Manuscriptorum in Bibliotheca Roberti Cottoni, 1621.*

BL Harley MS 7055. *Papers of Humphrey Wanley.*

BL Royal MS 13 D. I*. *Psalterium.*

Bodleian MS Add. D. 82. Report to the House of Commons by Matthew Hutton, John Anstis, and Humfrey Wanley, on the State of the Cottonian Library, dated 22 June 1703. Prefixed to Speaker Robert Harley's copy of Thomas Smith's *Catalogus Librorum Manuscriptorum Bibliothecæ Cottonianæ.* Oxford: Sheldonian Theater, 1696.

Bodleian MS Junius 105. *Fragmentum historiæ Judith, descriptum ex Cottonianæ bibliothecæ MS^{to} codice, qui inscribitur* VITELLIVS. A. 15. *paginâ 199.*

Bodleian MS Selden supra 63. Laurence Nowell's *Vocabularium Saxonicum.*

Bosworth, Joseph, and Toller, T. Northcote. *An Anglo-Saxon Dictionary.* 1898. Reprint. London: Oxford University Press, 1973.

Brodeur, Arthur G. "*Beowulf:* One Poem or Three?" In *Medieval Literature and Folklore Studies: Essays in Honor of Francis Lee Utley,* edited by Jerome Mandel and Bruce A. Rosenberg, pp. 3–26. New Brunswick: Rutgers University Press, 1970.

Brook, George L. *English Dialects.* London: Andre Deutsch, 1963.

———. "The Textual and Linguistic Study of Old English." In *The Anglo-Saxons: Studies in Some Aspects of Their History and Culture, Presented to Bruce Dickins,* edited by Peter Clemoes, pp. 280–291. London: Bowes & Bowes, 1959.

Brotanek, Rudolf. "Nachlese zu den HSS. der *Epistola Cuthberti* und des *Sterbespruches Bedas.*" *Anglia: Zeitschrift für englische Philologie* 64 (1940): 159–190.

Byers, John R. "A Possible Emendation of *Beowulf* 461b." *Philological Quarterly* 46 (1967): 125–128.

Campbell, Alistair, ed. *The Chronicle of Æthelweard.* New York: Thomas Nelson & Sons, 1962.

———. *Old English Grammar.* Oxford: The Clarendon Press, 1959.

Campbell, Jackson J. "The Harley Glossary and 'Saxon Patois.'" *Philological Quarterly* 34 (1955): 71–74.

Chadwick, Hector M. *The Origin of the English Nation.* Cambridge: The University Press, 1924.

Chamberlain, David. "*Judith:* A Fragmentary and Political Poem." In *Anglo-Saxon Poetry: Essays in Appreciation for John C. McGalliard,* edited by Lewis E. Nicholson and Dolores Warwick Frese, pp. 135–159. South Bend: University of Notre Dame Press, 1975.

Chambers, Raymond W. *Beowulf: An Introduction to the Study of the Poem, With a Discussion of the Stories of Offa and Finn.* 1921. 3rd ed. with a supplement by C. L. Wrenn. Cambridge: The University Press, 1959.

Cook, Albert S., ed. *Judith: An Old English Epic Fragment.* Boston: D. C. Heath, 1904.

Coveney, Dorothy K. "The Ruling of the *Exeter Book.*" *Scriptorium* 12 (1959): 51–55.

Crawford, Samuel J., ed. *The Old English Version of the Heptateuch, Ælfric's Treatise on the Old and New Testament and His Preface to Genesis.* Early English Text Society, o. s., 160. London: Oxford University Press, 1922.

Daunt, Marjorie. "Old English Studies." *The Year's Work in English Studies* 9 (1928): 74–75.

DeCamp, David. "The Genesis of the Old English Dialects: A New Hypothesis." *Language* 34 (1958): 232–244. Reprinted in *Approaches to English Historical Linguistics,* edited by Roger Lass, pp. 355–368. New York: Holt, Rinehart & Winston, 1969.

Denholm-Young, N. *Handwriting in England and Wales.* Cardiff: University of Wales Press, 1954.

Dobbie, E. V. K., ed. *The Anglo-Saxon Minor Poems.* The Anglo-Saxon Poetic Records, vol. 6. 1942. Reprint. New York: Columbia University Press, 1968.

———, ed. *Beowulf and Judith.* The Anglo-Saxon Poetic Records, vol. 4. 1953. Reprint. New York: Columbia University Press, 1965.

———, ed. *The Manuscripts of Cædmon's Hymn and Bede's Death Song.* New York: Columbia University Press, 1937.

Doubleday, James F. "The Principle of Contrast in *Judith.*" *Neuphilologische Mitteilungen* 72 (1971): 436–441.

Esdaile, Arundell. *The British Museum: A Short History and Survey.* London: George Allen & Unwin, 1946.

Finnegan, Robert Emmett, ed. *Christ and Satan: A Critical Edition.* Waterloo, Ont.: Wilfrid Laurier University Press, 1977.

Flower, Robin. "Laurence Nowell and the Discovery of England in Tudor Times." *Proceedings of the British Academy* 21 (1935): 47–73.

Förster, Max. *Die Beowulf-Handschrift. Berichte über die Verhandlungen der Sächsischen Akademie der Wissenschaften zu Leipzig, Philologisch-historische Klasse* 71 (1919).

Fry, Donald K., ed. *Finnsburh: Fragment and Episode.* London: Methuen & Co., 1974.

Gneuss, Helmut. "The Origin of Standard Old English and Æthelwold's School at Winchester." *Anglo-Saxon England* 1 (1972): 63–83.

Graevius, Johannes Georgius. "Vita Francisci F. F. Junii." *Francisci Junii F. F. De Pictura Veterum Libri Tres.* Rotterdam, 1694.

Halliwell, James Orchard, ed. *The Autobiography and Correspondence of Sir Simonds d'Ewes,* vol. 2. London: Richard Bentley, 1845.

Hickes, George. *Linguarum Vett. Septentrionalium Thesaurus Grammatico-Criticus et Archaeologicus,* vol. 1. 1705. Reprinted in *English Linguistics, 1500–1800,* no. 247. Menston, Eng.: The Scolar Press, 1970.

Hill, G. F. *The Development of Arabic Numerals in Europe, Exhibited in Sixty-four Tables.* Oxford: The Clarendon Press, 1915.

———. "On the Early Use of Arabic Numerals in Europe." *Archaeologia* 62 (1910): 137–190.

Holmes, George. *The Later Middle Ages: 1272–1485.* New York: W. W. Norton, 1962.

Holthausen, Ferdinand, ed. *Beowulf nebst dem Finnsburg-Bruchstück.* vol. 2, *Einleitung, Glossar und Anmerkungen.* New York: G. E. Stechert, 1906.

The Holy Bible, Translated from the Latin Vulgate, Diligently Compared with the Hebrew, Greek, and Other Editions in Divers Languages. The Old Testament, first Published by the English College at Douay, A. D. 1609. Baltimore, Md.: John Murphy, 1914.

Hoops, Johannes. "Die Foliierung der *Beowulf*-Handschrift." *Englische Studien* 63 (1928): 1–11.

Jacobs, Nicholas. "Anglo-Danish Relations, Poetic Archaism and the Date of *Beowulf:* A Reconsideration of the Evidence." *Poetica* (Tokyo) 8 (1978): 23–43.

Jespersen, Otto. *Growth and Structure of the English Language.* 1905. 9th ed. 1948. Reprint. Oxford: Basil Blackwell, 1962.

Jones, Gwyn. *A History of the Vikings.* London: Oxford University Press, 1968.

Jones, Leslie Webber. "Pricking Manuscripts: The Instruments and Their Significance." *Speculum* 21 (1946): 389–403.

Junius, Franciscus, ed. *Quatuor D. N. Jesu Christi* EVANGELIORUM *versiones perantiquae duae, Gothica scil. et Anglo-Saxonica.* Dordrecht: Henricus & Johannes Essaei, 1665.

Keller, Wolfgang. *Angelsächsische Palaeographie: Die Schrift der Angelsach-*

sen mit besonderer Rücksicht auf die Denkmäler in der Volkssprache, vol.
1. Berlin: Mayer & Müller, 1906.

———. Review of Max Föster, *Die Beowulf-Handschrift. Beiblatt zur Anglia*
34 (1923): 4–5.

Ker, Neil R. *Catalogue of Manuscripts Containing Anglo-Saxon.* Oxford: The
Clarendon Press, 1957.

———. "The Hague Manuscript of the Epistola Cuthberti de Obitu Bedæ
with Bede's Song." *Medium Ævum* 8 (1939): 40–44.

———, ed. *The Pastoral Care.* Early English Manuscripts in Facsimile, vol.
6. Copenhagen: Rosenkilde & Bagger, 1956.

Keyser, Samuel Jay. "Old English Prosody." *College English* 30 (1969): 331–
356.

Klaeber, Frederick, ed. *Beowulf and the Fight at Finnsburg.* 3rd ed. with first
and second supplements. Boston: D. C. Heath, 1950.

Klingender, Francis. *Animals in Art and Thought to the End of the Middle
Ages.* Edited by Evelyn Antal and John Harthan. Cambridge, Mass.:
M. I. T. Press, 1971.

Krapp, George Philip, ed. *The Junius Manuscript.* The Anglo-Saxon Poetic
Records, vol. 1. 1931. Reprint. New York: Columbia University Press,
1969.

———, ed. *The Paris Psalter and the Meters of Boethius.* The Anglo-Saxon
Poetic Records, vol. 5. 1932. Reprint. New York: Columbia University
Press, 1961.

———, ed. *The Vercelli Book.* The Anglo-Saxon Poetic Records, vol. 2. 1932.
Reprint. New York: Columbia University Press, 1961.

Krapp, George Philip, and Dobbie, E. V. K., eds. *The Exeter Book.* The
Anglo-Saxon Poetic Records, vol. 3. 1936. Reprint. New York: Columbia
University Press, 1966.

Kuhn, Sherman M. "*Beowulf* and the Life of Beowulf: A Study in Epic Structure." In *Studies in Language, Literature, and Culture of the Middle Ages
and Later,* edited by E. Bagby Atwood and Archibald A. Hill, pp. 243–264.
Austin: University of Texas, 1969.

———. "The Sword of Healfdene." *Journal of English and Germanic Philology* 42 (1943): 82–95.

Larson, Laurence M. *Canute the Great.* New York: G. P. Putnam's Sons,
1912.

Lehmann, Winfred P. "On Posited Omissions in the *Beowulf.*" In *Studies in
Language, Literature, and Culture of the Middle Ages and Later,* edited by
E. Bagby Atwood and Archibald A. Hill, pp. 220–229. Austin: University
of Texas, 1969.

L'Isle, William. *A Saxon Treatise Concerning the Old and New Testament.*

Written about the time of King Edgar (700 yeares agoe) by Ælfricus Abbas ... whereby appeares what was the Canon of holy Scripture here then received, and that the Church of England had it so long agoe in her Mother-Tongue. London, 1623.

Loyn, H. R. *The Vikings in Britain.* London: B. T. Batsford, 1977.

Luick, Karl. *Historische Grammatik der englischen Sprache,* vol. 1, pt. 1. Stuttgart: Bernhard Tauchnitz, 1914–1921.

McKisack, May. *Medieval History in the Tudor Age.* Oxford: The Clarendon Press, 1971.

Madden, Frederic. *Cottonian MSS. Repairing and Binding Account.* A currently uncatalogued notebook in the departmental archives of the Department of Manuscripts, British Library.

Magoun, Francis P. "*Béowulf A':* A Folk Variant." *ARV: Tidskrift för Nordisk Folkminnesforskning* 25 (1958): 95–101.

———. "*Béowulf B:* a Folk-Poem on Béowulf's Death." In *Early English and Norse Studies: Presented to Hugh Smith in Honor of His Sixtieth Birthday,* edited by Arthur Brown and Peter Foote, pp. 127–140. London: Methuen & Co., 1963.

Malone, Kemp. "Ecgtheow." *Modern Language Quarterly* 1 (1940): 37–44.

———. "Notes on *Beowulf:* I." *Anglia: Zeitschrift für englische Philologie* 53 (1929): 335–336.

———, ed. *The Nowell Codex (British Museum Cotton Vitellius A. XV, Second MS).* Early English Manuscripts in Facsimile, 12. Copenhagen: Rosenkilde & Bagger, 1963.

———. "Old English [*Ge*]*hȳdan* 'Heed'." In *A Grammatical Miscellany Offered to Otto Jespersen on His 70th Birthday,* edited by N. Bøgholm, Aage Brusendorff, and C. A. Bodelsen, pp. 45–54. Copenhagen: Levin & Munksgaard, 1930.

———. Review of Tilman Westphalen, *Beowulf 3150–55: Textkritik und Editionsgeschichte. Speculum* 44 (1969): 182–186.

———. "Swerting." *Germanic Review* 14 (1939): 235–257.

———, ed. *The Thorkelin Transcripts of Beowulf.* Early English Manuscripts in Facsimile, vol. 1. Copenhagen: Rosenkilde & Bagger, 1951.

———. "When Did Middle English Begin?" In *Curme Volume of Linguistic Studies,* edited by James Taft Hatfield, Werner Leopold, and A. J. Friedrich Zieglschmid. *Language Monographs* 7 (1930): 110–117.

Marckwardt, Albert H., ed. *Laurence Nowell's Vocabularium Saxonicum.* Ann Arbor: University of Michigan Press, 1952.

———. "Verb Inflections in Late Old English." In *Philologica: The Malone Anniversary Studies,* edited by Thomas A. Kirby and H. B. Woolf, pp. 79–88. Baltimore: The Johns Hopkins Press, 1949.

Marquardt, Hertha. "Fürstenund Kriegerkenning im *Beowulf*." *Anglia: Zeitschrift für englische Philologie* 60 (1936): 390–395.

Menner, Robert J. "Anglian and Saxon Elements in Wulfstan's Vocabulary." *Modern Language Notes* 63 (1948): 1–10.

———, ed. *The Poetical Dialogues of Solomon and Saturn*. The MLA Monograph Series, no. 13. New York: The Modern Language Association, 1941.

———. "The Vocabulary of the Old English Poems on Judgment Day." *PMLA* 62 (1947): 583–597.

Müllenhoff, Karl. *Beovulf: Untersuchungen über das angelsächsische Epos und die älteste Geschichte der germanischen Seevölker*. Berlin: Weidmannsche Buchhandlung, 1889.

Needham, Geoffrey, I., ed. *Ælfric: Lives of Three English Saints*. London: Methuen & Co., 1966.

Niles, John D. "Ring Composition and the Structure of *Beowulf*." *PMLA* 94 (1979): 924–935.

Planta, Joseph. *A Catalogue of the Manuscripts in the Cottonian Library, Deposited in the British Museum. Printed by Command of His Majesty King George III*. London, 1802.

Prokosch, Eduard. "Two Types of Scribal Errors in the *Beowulf* MS." In *Studies in English Philology: A Miscellany in Honor of Frederick Klaeber*, edited by Kemp Malone and Martin B. Ruud, pp. 196–207. Minneapolis: University of Minnesota Press, 1929.

Quirk, Randolph, and Wrenn, C. L., eds. *An Old English Grammar*. 2d ed. London: Methuen & Co., 1957.

Ricci, Aldo. "The Chronology of Anglo-Saxon Poetry." *Review of English Studies* 5 (1929): 257–266.

Rickert, Edith. "The Old English Offa Saga." *Modern Philology* 2 (1904): 29–76.

Robertson, A. J., ed. *The Laws of the Kings of England from Edmund to Henry I*. Cambridge: The University Press, 1925.

Robinson, Fred C. Review of Wrenn-Bolton. *Speculum* 52 (1977): 188–192.

Rosier, James. "The *Unhlitm* of Finn and Hengest." *Review of English Studies,* n. s. 17 (1966): 171–174.

Rypins, Stanley, ed. *Three Old English Prose Texts in MS Cotton Vitellius A. XV*. Early English Text Society, o. s., 161. London: Oxford University Press, 1924.

Schabram, Hans. *Superbia: Studien zum altenglischen Wortschatz*. Vol. 1, *Die dialektale und zeitliche Verbreitung des Wortguts*. Munich: Wilhelm Fink, 1965.

Scheps, Walter. "The Sequential Nature of Beowulf's Three Fights." *Ren-*

dezvous: Idaho State University Journal of Arts and Letters 9 (1974–1975): 41–50.

Schlemilch, Willy. *Beiträge zur Sprache und Orthographie spätaltengl. Sprachdenkmäler der Übergangszeit (1000–1150)*. Studien zur englischen Philologie, no. 34. Halle: S. M. Niemeyer, 1914.

Schücking, Levin. "Die Beowulfdatierung: Eine Replik." *Beiträge zur Geschichte der deutschen Sprache und Literatur* 47 (1923): 293–311.

———. *Beowulfs Rückkehr: Eine kritische Studie*. Studien zur englischen Philologie, no. 21. Halle: S. M. Niemeyer, 1905.

———. "Wann entstand der Beowulf? Glossen, Zweifel, und Fragen." *Beiträge zur Geschichte der deutschen Sprache und Literatur* 42 (1917): 347–410.

Sedgefield, Walter J., ed. *Beowulf Edited with Introduction, Bibliography, Notes, Glossary, and Appendices*. 3rd ed. Manchester: University of Manchester Press, 1935.

Seward, Desmond. *The Hundred Years War: The English in France, 1337–1453*. New York: Atheneum, 1978.

Sievers, Eduard. *Altgermanische Metrik*. Halle: Max Niemeyer, 1893.

———. "Zur Rhythmik des germanischen Alliterationsverses: Erster Abschnitt, Die Metrik des Beowulf." *Beiträge zur Geschichte der deutschen Sprache und Literatur* 10 (1885): 209–314.

Sisam, Kenneth. "Canterbury, Lichfield, and the Vespasian Psalter." *Review of English Studies* 26 (1956): 113–131.

———. "Notes on Old English Poetry: The Authority of Old English Poetical Manuscripts." *Review of English Studies* 22 (1946): 257–268.

———. *Studies in the History of Old English Literature*. Oxford: The Clarendon Press, 1953.

Skeat, Walter W., ed. *The Lay of Havelok the Dane*. Early English Text Society, e. s. 4. 1868. 2d ed., revised by Kenneth Sisam, 1915. Reprint. Oxford: The Clarendon Press, 1956.

Smith, David Eugene, and Karpinski, Louis Charles. *The Hindu-Arabic Numerals*. Boston: Ginn & Co., 1911.

Smith, Thomas. *Catalogus Librorum Manuscriptorum Bibliothecæ Cottonianæ*. Oxford: Sheldonian Theater, 1696.

Stanley, Eric G. "Spellings of the *Waldend* Group." In *Studies in Language, Literature, and Culture of the Middle Ages and Later*, edited by E. Bagby Atwood and Archibald A. Hill, pp. 38–69. Austin: University of Texas, 1969.

Stenton, Frank. *Anglo-Saxon England*. 3rd ed. Oxford: The Clarendon Press, 1971.

———. "The Scandinavian Colonies in England and Normandy." *Transactions of the Royal Historical Society, London,* 4th ser. 27 (1945): 1–12.

Stevens, Martin, and Mandel, Jerome, eds. *Old English Literature: Twenty-two Analytical Essays.* Lincoln: University of Nebraska Press, 1968.

Stevick, Robert D., ed. *Beowulf: An Edition with Manuscript Spacing Notation and Graphotactic Analyses.* New York: Garland Publishing, 1975.

Sweet, Henry, ed. *The Oldest English Texts.* Early English Text Society, o. s. 83. London: N. Trübner & Co., 1885.

ten Brink, Bernhard. *Beowulf: Untersuchungen, Quellen und Forschungen zur Sprach- und Kulturgeschichte der germanischen Völker* 62 (1888).

Thomas, Percy G. "Notes on the Language of *Beowulf.*" *Modern Language Review* 1 (1906): 202–207.

Thorkelin, Grímur Jónsson, ed. *De Danorum Rebus Gestis Secul. III & IV. Poëma Danicum Dialecto Anglosaxonica.* Copenhagen, 1815.

Thwaites, Edward, ed. *Heptateuchus, Liber Job, et Evangelium Nicodemi; Anglo-Saxonice. Historiae Judith Fragmentum; Dano-Saxonice.* Oxford: Sheldonian Theater, 1698.

Timmer, Benno J., ed. *Judith.* London: Methuen & Co., 1952.

Tolkien, J. R. R. "*Beowulf:* The Monsters and the Critics." *Proceedings of the British Academy* 22 (1936): 245–295.

Toller, T. Northcote. *An Anglo-Saxon Dictionary, Supplement.* 1921. With revised and enlarged addenda by Alistair Campbell. Oxford: Oxford University Press, 1972.

Tupper, Frederick, Jr. "The Philological Legend of Cynewulf." *Publications of the Modern Language Association* 26 (1911): 235–279.

———, ed. *The Riddles of the Exeter Book.* Boston: Ginn & Co., 1910.

Turner, Sharon. *The History of the Manners, Landed Property, Government, Laws, Poetry, Literature, Religion, and Language, of the Anglo-Saxons,* vol. 4. London: Longman, Hurst, Rees, and Orme, 1805.

Tuso, Joseph F. "*Beowulf* 461b and Thorpe's *wara.*" *Modern Language Quarterly* 29 (1968):259–262.

Vaughan, M. F. "A Reconsideration of 'Unferð.'" *Neuphilologische Mitteilungen* 77 (1976): 32–48.

Vigfusson, Gudbrand, and Powell, F. York, eds. *Corpus Poeticum Boreale,* vol. 2. 1883. Reprint. New York: Russell & Russell, 1965.

Vleeskruyer, Rudolf, ed. *The Life of St. Chad: An Old English Homily.* Amsterdam: North-Holland Publishing Co., 1953.

von Schaubert, Else, ed. *Heyne-Schückings Beowulf.* Pt. 1, *Text.* 18th ed. Paderborn: Ferdinand Schöningh, 1963.

Wanley, Humfrey. *Antiquae Literaturae Septentrionalis Liber Alter, seu*

Humphredi Wanleii Librorum Vett. Septentrionalium, qui in Angliae Bibliothecis extant, nec non multorum Vett. Codd. Septentrionalium alibi extantium Catalogus Historico-Criticus, cum totius Thesauri Linguarum Septentrionalium sex Indicibus. 1705. Reprinted in *English Linguistics: 1500–1800,* no. 248. Menston, Eng.: The Scolar Press, 1970.

Weightman, Jane. *The Language and Dialect of the Later Old English Poetry.* Liverpool: University Press of Liverpool, 1907.

Westphalen, Tilman. *Beowulf 3150–55: Textkritik und Editionsgeschichte.* Munich: Wilhelm Fink, 1967.

Whitelock, Dorothy. *The Audience of Beowulf.* Oxford: The Clarendon Press, 1951.

————, ed. *English Historical Documents.* Vol. 1, *c. 500–1042.* London: Eyre & Spottiswoode, 1955.

————. "Wulfstan and the Laws of Cnut." *English Historical Review* 249 (1948): 433–452.

Whitelock, Dorothy; Douglas, David C.; and Tucker, Susie I., eds. *The Anglo-Saxon Chronicle: A Revised Translation.* New Brunswick: Rutgers University Press, 1961.

Willard, Rudolf, ed. *The Blickling Homilies.* Early English Manuscripts in Facsimile, 10. Copenhagen: Rosenkilde & Bagger, 1960.

Wilson, R. M. "The Provenance of the Vespasian Psalter Gloss: The Linguistic Evidence." In *The Anglo-Saxons: Studies in Some Aspects of Their History and Culture, Presented to Bruce Dickins,* edited by Peter Clemoes, pp. 292–310. London: Bowes & Bowes, 1959.

Woolf, Rosemary. "The Lost Opening to the *Judith.*" *Modern Language Review* 50 (1955): 168–172.

Wrenn, Charles L., ed. *Beowulf with the Finnesburg Fragment.* London: George G. Harrup, 1953.

————, ed. *Beowulf with the Finnesburg Fragment.* 3rd ed. Revised by Whitney F. Bolton. New York: St. Martin's Press, 1973.

————. "'Standard' Old English." *Transactions of the Philological Society, London* (1933): 65–88.

————. *A Study of Old English Literature.* New York: W. W. Norton, 1967.

————. "The Value of Spelling as Evidence." *Transactions of the Philological Society, London* (1943): 14–39.

Wright, C. E. *The Cultivation of Saga in Anglo-Saxon England.* London: Oliver & Boyd, 1939.

————. "The Elizabethan Society of Antiquaries and the Formation of the Cottonian Library." In *The English Library before 1700: Studies in Its History,* edited by Francis Wormald and C. E. Wright, pp. 176–212. London: The Athlone Press, 1958.

————. "Humfrey Wanley: Saxonist and Library-Keeper." *Proceedings of the British Academy* 46 (1960): 99–129.

Wyatt, Alfred J., ed. *Beowulf: Edited with Textual Foot-Notes, Index of Proper Names, and Alphabetical Glossary.* Cambridge: The University Press, 1894.

————, ed. *Beowulf, with the Finnsburg Fragment.* 2d ed. Revised by R. W. Chambers. Cambridge: The University Press, 1920.

Zupitza, Julius, ed. *Beowulf: Reproduced in Facsimile from the Unique Manuscript, British Museum MS. Cotton Vitellius A. xv, with a Transliteration and Notes.* 1882. 2d ed., containing a new reproduction of the manuscript, with an introductory note, by Norman Davis, 1959. Reprint. Early English Text Society, 245. London: Oxford University Press, 1967.

Index

[For clarity and ease of reference, distinct *indices rerum* are provided for the headings, *Beowulf, Beowulf* MS, BL MS Cotton Vitellius A. XV., Nowell Codex, and Southwick Codex.]